# TIBETANS IN INDIA:
## The Uprooted People And Their Cultural Transplantation

## Sociological Publication in Honour of Dr. K. Ishwaran

**ISBN: 81-85047-82-0**



---

### *Vol. XIV Issue Editor*

---

*Already Published*

Vol. I *Rural Development and Factional Politics* by K G. Gurmurthy
Issue Editor: **Anil Mahajan** ISBN: 81-85047-40-4

Vol II *Blood, Women and Territory* by P.K. Nayak
Issue Editor: **Mario D. Zamora** ISBN: 81-85047-43-X

Vol III *The Panchayat Tradition* by Mario D. Zamora
Issue Editor: **L.K. Mahapatra** ISBN: 81-85047-44-8

Vol IV *Agrarian Unrest in Karnataka* by D. Murahari Naik
Issue Editor: **K. Raghavendra Rao** ISBN: 81-85047-45-6

Vol V *Tribal Encounter With Industry* by A.R.N. Srivastava
Issue Editor: **Bhupinder Singh** ISBN: 81-85047-56-1

Vol VI *Development and Backwardness: Coexistence or Confrontation ?*
(A Study of Leather Workers of Karnataka ) by S. Parameswara
Issue Editor: **R. T. Jangam** ISBN: 81-85047-62-6

Vol VII *Sociology of an Industrial Complex* by C.A. Somashekhrappa
Issue Editor: **K. Chandrasekharaiah** ISBN: 81-85047-64-2

Vol IX *Devadasi Custom: Rural Flesh Markets and Social Structure* by K.C. Tarachand
Issue Editor. **K.G. Gurumurthy** ISBN: 81-85047-73-1

Vol X *Bhutan :* Ethnic Identity and National Dilemma 2nd rev. ed. by A. C. Sinha
Issue Editor: **K. Raghvendra Rao** ISBN: 81-85972-41-9

Vol XI *The Town and The Raj: Urbanisation in British India* by Anil G Mudbidri
Issue Editor: **K. Chandrasekhariah** ISBN: 81-85847-81-9

Vol. XII *Self Rule and Chanding Rural Leadership* by M.P. Jahagirdar
Issue Editor: **G. Prakash Reddy** ISBN: 81-85047-91-X

Vol XIII *Workers' Participation in Management* by Prem Misir
Issue Editor: **J. Michael Pool** ISBN: 81-85972-30-3

# TIBETANS IN INDIA:
## The Uprooted People And Their Cultural Transplantation

A.V. ARAKERI

RELIANCE PUBLISHING HOUSE
NEW DELHI

*The opinions expressed in this book are the author's own and not concerned with A.S.I. or the R.G.I.*

First Published 1998

ISBN: 81-85972-68-0



*Published by:*

Dr. S.K. Bhatia (Life member ILA, FEPI and INSA)
for **Reliance Publishing House**
3026/7H, Ranjit Nagar,
New Delhi-110008 Ph: 5737377 / 5722605. Fax 5772748

*Composed by:*

M/s Spectrum Marketing Pvt Ltd.,
305, Pragati Chambers,
Ranjit Nagar Commercial Complex,
New Delhi- 110008

*Printed at:* **Printline, New Delhi**

# General Editor's Note

The process of rehabilitation of refugees is known in anthropological and sociological literature as Cultural Transplantation. Such studies were started during 1940s with the study of Bikinis of Marshal Islands in the Pacific. It was found that unlike migration which is planned and voluntary, forced shifts of refugees, which is involuntary and sudden, pose altogether different problems to the administrators, refugees and also to the hosts who accept them. Therefore such situations need a detailed and indepth study of the society and culture of both the victims and hosts to facilitate a successful and smooth grafting.

The present book of Dr. A.V. Arakeri, is on the Tibetan refugees settled in South India. Before going into the problems and consequences of rehabilitation, the author provides the proper background by presenting data, on the land and culture of Tibet, problems faced by the refugees while they were on flight, in transit camps and finally in the rehabilitation settlements. He also gives in detail about the agencies involved and the type of help they render and also the role played by H.H. the Dalai Lama in making the processes of adjustment smooth.

Though the data for the book were collected during 1978-79 when the rehabilitation activities had reached stage and later during 1980s when readjustments and further planning was going on, the author says that he could not publish the same owing to with holding of permission by agencies concerned. The checking and rechecking of the data according to the suggestions made by these agencies, the author says, took away some more time before he finally sent it to press.

On behalf of the Editorial Advisory Board of SPIHOKI Dr. K.G. Gurumurthy has reviewed the manuscript for publication. He has also acted as the Issue Editor of the volume and has written the Issue Editor's Note. On behalf of the Advisory Board, I thank him and the author, for their active involvement in the promotion of the book series.

1.3.1997
Dharwad - 3

General Editor

# Issue Editor's Note

Human history is full of instances of movement of mass of people from one geographical region to another. They are both voluntary and forced. If immigrants come under the former category and the refugees come under the latter. Forced shifts take place owing to natural calamities such as floods, droughts, earthquakes, volcanic activities and famines and also due to man made calamities by political, racial and religious persecutions. Though all types of shifts bring separation and sufferings, those brought about by the forced shifts will be more painful. Those who migrate plan their shift well in advance, choosing their place of migration and more leisurely. Settling in an alien society takes lot of time and effort because one has to adjust to the physical and socio-cultural environment there. The necessary household articles are procured and contacts are established bit by bit and each object telling a story as to how it was acquired and what type of ties and relations it initiated. Some of these might be received as gifts and acquire emotional value. In other words a person who volunteers will have enough time to prepare himself mentally to adapt to new conditions.

On the other hand the involuntary and unexpected shifts are sudden and also painful. Among these, going as refugees is much more painful. Because the victims of natural calamities can return to their traditional home after the worst is over and can rebuild their life. If it is not possible they can atleast visit their place now and then, to satisfy their emotions. But this is not possible for the refugees and so the pain and sufferings brought about by man made calamities are harsher and deeper.

Right from the beginning of Man's history, there have been persecutions of one or the other groups and for one or the other reason. Among them, the instances of religious persecutions are many. The wars fought during the Medieval times in Europe, Arabia and in the Indian sub-continent stand out as good examples. During these wars thousands were either sent out of their land, away from their dear ones after confiscation of their property or killed them. The second main cause was the political ideology. Exodus of people at different points of time from communist countries serve as examples of political persecution.

Racial hatredness too has brought about movement of millions under Nazi and Palestenian rule. All these have brought untold misery to the millions of people in different places and at different times in human history,

Exodus of thousands of Tibetan refugees is a recent one in human history. Tibet, lying in the Himalayas at an altitude ranging from 6000 to 12,000 feet, was a theocracy and known for its version of Buddhism. Owing to its geographical location agriculture as a means of food supply was not able to support a big population. They adopted a number of strategies to maintain its population at lower level. Among them, adoption of a type of Buddhism which requires at least one son from each family, especially those who could not afford a family or fit into a polyandrous system, is required to go as monk to a monastry. Female infanticide and polyandry were prevalent. It is due to these reasons that they had a very low birth rate and were scantily populated. Tibet could not afford the luxury of a royal court and hence a religious king called the Dalai Lama, was adopted. He Was assisted in state administration at different levels, by lama and monk officials, since Tibet had no army, its relations with neighbours such as India, China and Mangolia were based on neutrality. Their religion prohibited any type of tampering of nature and hence no mining was undertaken to harness the natural resources. All theses, aspects of Tibetan life tempted land hungry China to move into the region.

Tibetans, who traditionally enjoined a good neighbourly relation with China, had least information about the latters intervention. With the sudden moving of troops, officials and party workers, there came a sudden and drastic change in the theocratic, slow moving, orthodox society of Tibet. When the news of Dalai Lamas flight to India was heard, his officials, monks, lamas and lay alike, started moving towards Indian border. Since it was a sudden exodus they could not bring their family members and all their belongings along with them. They did not come in one batch and from one place, but trickled at the check points along the Indian border with Tibet, as many of them had fled from where ever they were such as business, grazing and pilgrimage places.

That was the time India had a very strained diplomatic relation with China due to the border dispute. Initially the Indian government was reluctant to receive the refugees as it was thought that it might further worsen the relations with China. However, as the international pressure was mounted, India had to agree to give asylum to Dalai Lama and his followers.

On their arrival, the Dalai Lama was taken to a safe place and the others were housed in transit camps set-up along the international border. Later, owing to security reasons they were shifted further inside. Here, they were provided with food, medicine and other basic facilities which were made possible by both Indian government and the international aid agencies. When it was realised that the refugees are not going back soon, they were rehabilitated in colonies built in different Indian states and Karnataka is one among them. Mainly three agencies were involved in rehabilitating the Tibetan refugees Viz. the Indian government, the state government and the international aid agencies such as the CARE, Red Cross, UNHR and OXFOM.

It was planned to transplant the refugees as agriculturists. On the request of the central government, the government of Karnataka provided deforested land in three districts and the Mundgod colony under study is one of them. Much before the arrival of the refugees houses were constructed and the deforested land was cleared of stubs and also leveled utilising aid given by MYRDA and SWISS AID. The latter also provided the farm machinery and the required technical knowhow, Hospitals, schools and homes for the infirm and the aged were also constructed with the aid from such agencies as WHO, Red Cross and Government of India. A craft training centre was also established to train the refugees in Tibetan art and carpet weaving. A machine shop was also provided to repair tractors and other machinery. These facilities are also used for training and Tibetan youth in such works as welding, drilling and fabrication work.

The Tibetan settlement at Mundgod comprise eleven villages and among them two are mean exclusively for the lamas. While all the sects of Tibetan Buddhism have their monastaries and Geluk-pa, the monastry of the Dalai Lama and of these with larger following are comparatively bigger than others.

The administration of the Tibetan settlement is looked after by three agencies Viz. the representative of the Dalai Lama, the Rehabilitation officer of the State government and the officials from the Central government. The state officials are concerned with the safety of the refugees and all help that comes to the refugees from different agencies including those from abroad, is channalised through his office. Whatever is to be done within the Tibetan colony, is accomplished through the Representative of the Dalai Lama. The village is being administered according to the New constitution adopted by the Dalai Lama's Tibetan government in exile. Each village elect a leader. He and the heads of families living in the village are responsible for the administration of the village. All the village leaders meet under the chairmanship of the Representative of the Dalai Lama and, plan and implement programmes for the development of the colony.

The relief agencies have constructed a hospital with X-ray, laboratory and ward facilities. There is a secondary school exclusively meant for the Tibetan students, where the medium of instruction is English with a Central Board Syllabus. To acquaint the students with their culture values, separate teachers have been appointed to teach Tibetan language and culture. A lama teaches Tibetan religion and morals. In addition to curricular subjects the students are made to involve in extra-curricular and co-curricular activities such as sports, games, dance, music and so on.

The youth out of school, are provided with library and reading room, sports and other passtime and recreational facilities with the aid from YMCA. Inter-colony sports and cultural meets are regularly arranged to bring the Tibetan refugees together. These activities are intended to develop competitive and co-operative feeling among themselves.

Although much care was taken to plan and implement the rehabilitation programmes for the Tibetan refugees many problems still remain unattended. Firstly, the local weather was warm for the Tibetans who came from the Himalayan heights. As a result, initially they had developed skin and lung diseases. Though the houses were planned and built using durable construction material, they were not finding them comfortable since they were designed by engineers who did not know the Tibetan culture. Much of the dwelling space was not utilised for the purpose for which it was planned. Religion plays a major role in the life of the Tibetans and more so when they started living in exile. Traditionally they need a big room for their domestic alter and since no separate room was provided in the plan, the refugees converted the biggest room in the house for this purpose and kept it closed for most of the time in the day. Further, since not many houses were available, the refugees belong to one village or province in Tibet were grouped together and alloted with a house thinking they would be happy. But this created problems of adjustment among themselves. However, as refugees and without a house to live in, they had accepted the allotment. Later as and when required they went on extending the building maring the original structure and road plans.

The refugees also had to cope with the change in their food. In Tibet barley formed their staple food. Yak which provided milk and other products served as their pack animal. Here they are provided with cows and buffaloes. Rice, maze and wheat from their staple food. Instead of the yak butter, they use edible oil often the palm oil, as cooking medium. Mango, papaya, goa and other local variety of fruits, nuts and a variety of vegetables, are grown and consumed. It took sometime to the refugees to adopt to these food habits.

The Tibetans also faced problems in establishing social contact with the local population. They always viewed India as a holy land since it is associated with Buddha and Buddhism. There are many sacred placed associated with their religion in India. As such they had a very high regard towards India and Indian people. When the Tibetans were rehabilitated amidst the local population with land, electricity, farm machinary, the latter were not happy. They though that the government is giving all these facilities at their cost. Often they became jealous of them. Further, the Tibetans look different racially and speak a different language and belong to a different religion and culture. The two groups had very little in common and maintained distance. Hence, very few neighbourly and community level contacts were established between the two groups.

The Tibetans coming from different provinces in Tibet had very little in common among themselves. To effect interaction among them many cultural and sports activities were introduced. The social gathering for children and parents provided opportunities for interaction. Another means of interaction open to them was when they go out to sell woolen goods in neighbouring towns and cities. The new year celebration and the annual visit of the Dalai Lama to different Tibetan colonies also provided opportunities to visit different colonies and develop contact with other Tibetans. The places of pilgrimage such as

Dharmasala where the Dalai Lama resides and the Buddhist sacred centers in India are the other places where they congregate and know each other.

Dr. Arakeri identifies a few problems being faced by the Tibetan refugees and among them the psychological ones are worthy to be taken note of. The aged refugees believe that dying in holy Tibet bring them merit and as such they crave to go back which now is not possible. Moreover, the Tibetan method of disposal of the dead is not possible here and the old people who wish that type of disposal are disillusioned. Those who left their spouse behind in Tibet not only suffer from separation but also are in dilemma whether to remarry here since they do not know whether their spouse in Tibet are dead or alive. Dr. Arakeri also mentions a few remedial measures to minimise these stresses and strains.

Dr. Arakeri's book is a welcome addition to the anthropological literature. Infact this is the only study made so far on the Mundgod Tibetans in particular. This study is all the more important since a large number of lamas and old and infirm people live here in separate villages. Since this work is based on the data collected almost two decades earlier there is a need to update by restudy as lot of changes have taken place in the past twenty years. The author admits this lacuna and quite candidly expresses that his work would form the base line material for his forth coming books.

1.3.1997

Dharwad - 3

K. G. Gurumurthy

# Preface

Social Anthropology in India deals with the studies of castes, tribes, peasant societies, village and urban studies, arts and crafts, fairs and festivals etc. in various dimensions such as social, economic, political, religion and the change. The applied perspective of the anthropology has its active role in the administration and welfare of the people it studies. The anthropological study of a society is not only of scientific interest but also adds to the practical value and its utility in the implementation of developmental programmes and welfare. The programmes implemented for any society should be based on adequate and first hand knowledge of local customs, beliefs and practices, socio-cultural, economic and other aspects. This is achieved by the anthropologists through the study of a society at the micro level and in a holistic perspective. The anthropologists thus have also an important role as advisors in social planning and execution of policy programmes. Sometimes the programmes fail and misunderstandings arise and ill feelings are generated if the development programmes are initiated without the knowledge of the cultural background of the community especially the tradition bound societies. Thus the applied research by the anthropologists in an important field of anthropology in the study of basic concepts of the society and its application in the day to day life. This has become more imperative in the process of rehabilitation of refugees who hail from a different world of culture to facilitate them to adjust in the host society having a different culture. Anthropology, thus is an intellectual equipment of officers in all the levels of administrative services.

The problems of refugees be more special, complicated and interesting from the point of view of an anthropologist. The refugees have to adjust better to the cultural, economic and geographical factors in the new cultural set-up of the host society. The Tibetan refugees in India, who belong to a different world of culture, have to adjust to the local situation in their place of rehabilitation. The present study, an anthropological perspective deals with the understanding of the traditional culture and background of the Tibetan refugees, the process of this rehabilitation, stresses and strains their face in adjusting to the new environment.

The Tibet was a forbidden land and not many accounts are available on Tibetan culture except a few travellers and historians who were able to visit Tibet, wrote about Tibet and its people. This study is one of the first of its kind from the cultural anthropologist's view giving a full account of traditional Tibetan socio-cultural life and the process of rehabilitation and its adjustment in an alien land. This book aims at understanding the individual and group adjustment of the Tibetan refugees, the process of rehabilitation and introduction of cultural traits in the Tibetan refugees, the process of rehabilitation and introduction of cultural traits in the Tibetan society from the host culture through acculturation, assimilation, etc., to adjust in the new cultural set-up. The book also deals with the understanding of how the Tibetans try to attain normalcy and revive their traditions, customs and beliefs which were disturbed due to their refugee situation. It also deals with the survival of their cultural elements and religion in an alien land with the hope for the future. The extent of the success of the transplantation programme and the change in the value systems of the old and the young to adjust better to the new land is also assessed.

This book is based on the first hand data collected by the author among the Tibetans at Mundgod (Karnataka) and the opinions expressed are his own and nothing to do with the organisations where he is attached to. This book is utmost useful to the social researchers, planners, administrators, advisors to the government engaged in the refugee rehabilitation programmes and the scholars who are interested in Tibetan culture.

A.V. ARAKERI

# Acknowledgements

I am deeply indebted to the following people and institutions for their assistance in various ways:

Dr. K.G. Gurumurthy, Professor and Chairman, Department of Anthropology, Karnatak University, Dharwad, for his guidance, training and inspiration at all stages of my research work;

Shri S.D. Desai, Ex-Administrator, Tibetan Refugees Rehabilitation Scheme II, Hubli and his staff, Sri Kesang Yarphel, Representative of H.H. the Dalai Lama, and his office staff at Tattihalli, Mundgod, for their help and encouragement;

the village leaders, villagers, Lamas and youths of the Tibetan villages at the Mundgod Settlement for their cooperation while conducting field work;

the Vice-Principal and staff members of the Central School for Tibetans, Mundgod Settlement, Doctor and his staff of the Mundgod Tibetan Refugee Hospital, the managers and their staff of the Syndicate Bank and Kanara District Co-operative Credit Bank Ltd., Tattihalli, Secretary and his staff of the Tibetan Co-operative Society, Officials of the Agriculture, Revenue, Police, Health and Forest Departments, Government of Karnataka at the Tahsil headquarters, Mundgod and at Tibetan Refugee Rehabilitation Camp, Tattihalli, for their help while collecting the data;

the staff and students of Department of Anthropology, Karnatak University, Dharwad for their help and encouragement during my research work;

the Librarian and his staff, Karnatak University Library, Dharwad for providing me all the facilities and also getting me a few rare books on loan basis from other libraries;

the Ministry of Supply and Rehabilitation, Government of India, New Delhi for giving us the necessary permission to conduct fieldwork in Mundgod Settlement;

# CONTENTS

# List of Tables

Page

# List of Maps and Sketches

## Maps



## Sketches

# List of Photographs

# 1

# Introduction

Anthropology, the science of man, is the most comprehensive of the academic disciplines dealing with mankind both in its physical, and socio-cultural aspects. Anthropologists have always aimed at scientific study of man in the greater understanding of ourselves, and our society. Social Anthropology concerns understanding, and explaining the diversity of human behaviour by a comparative study of the social relationships and processes over a wide range of societies. Anthropology also deals with the problems of social reform. Therefore Anthropology has also its active role in the administration, and welfare of the people it studies.

The first intensive application of modern anthropological concepts, and techniques to administrative problems of governments was introduced by colonial administrators, and in United States of America by Mr. John Collier, Commissioner of the Bureau of Indian Affairs. Applied anthropology, aims at: (1) the knowledge, and understanding of human ecology, and environment, economic, and social organization, law, and government; (2) the development of qualities to fit men to live in the modern world, such as personal judgement and initiative, freedom from fear and superstition, sympathy and understanding from different points of view; (3) spiritual, and moral development, belief in ethical ideals, and the habit of acting upon them, with the duty to examine traditional standards of behaviour and to modify them to suit to new conditions (Metraux, 1953; 882).

A state document on native administration in East Africa shows how current anthroplogical studies can help to solve many problems of the natives. Barnett (1956:10) says that "the considerations by many involve not only early investigation but also continuous study of all the institutions of the native communities, in order that the action taken from time to time by the local governments should be based upon adequate knowledge of habits, and customs". Anthropology, as a science, in the past, was more interested in studying the dead man rather than the living one. Presently, this tendency has changed. Interest has increased in studying many more cultures which were not found by easy means, of many tribes in many more areas of the world.

The anthropologist's field of study is the society. He deals with the immaterial relations of claim, and obligation, right, and duty, superiority and subordination that exist among individuals. A few anthropologists who have given special attention to the study of social change, and its influences, describe their work by the adjective 'applied' (Mair, 1957; 10-11). Anthropology also has given a central place to the study of culture contact phenomena. It studies the groups living in primitive isolation, and the changing society. It advocated a study of the culture, and the process of cultural assimilation, and the human problems involved in it.

It is laudable for an anthropologist, says Evans Pritchard (1946: 94), to investigate practical problems possibly. If he does so he must realize that he is no longer acting within the anthropological field; he will be in the non-scientific field of administration. Sol Tax (loc. cit. Barnett, 1956:53-54) says, an anthropologist can become an administrator or the other way round. If the anthropologist or the so called administrator persues researches in terms of scientific problems then he is doing anthropological study. If he persues them in terms of social or practical problems then he is not doing anthropology. Leighton (1946:668) says, applied social sciences can well be the meeting place of both science and practice as in clinical research... . Moreover, social theories can be reduced to working hypotheses leading to predictions that are testable by observation of subsequent events. Through such a series of steps, science as well as the techniques of application can be advanced. Anthropologists can also help administrators as advisors, and consultants.

Firth says that anthropologist's knowledge can be best utilised not in prescribing policies but in calling attention to the possibly unforeseen implications of the policies proposed by governments (loc. cit. Mair, 1961:14). Anthropologists with their specific training in handling smaller groups can study, and deal with the problems of a village or a tribal community. They understand the problems not in terms of common factors applicable to the humanity in general but they can concentrate in terms of the culture and traditions of the particular community and within itself. In addition, the anthropologist has developed special techniques to explore, and record the manifestations of the life of the people of a particular group of community, and the rules and standards of which may differ from any other community in general.

To an administrator the application of political, social and economic problems, and policies as the existing problems in the society means not only the early investigation of these but also a continuous study of all the institutions of the native communities in order that the action taken from time to time by the local governments should be based upon adequate knoweldge of the native habits, and customs. So anthropology is an intellectual equipment of officers in all the levels of administrative services in at least some of the countries of the world.

In the course of their understanding of relation between environment, and man - the society and culture, anthropologists have studied the influence of geographical environment on man's culture. Men are found everywhere on the earth but they differ from one another in their mode of living, art, lite re, belief system, social institutions, food habits, customs, law and social control, values and outlook on life all of which can be termed in total as culture. Here we can quote Malinowski (1944: 36), who says ' culture is the integral whole consisting of implements and consumers' goods, of constitutional charters for the various social groupings, of human ideas and crafts, beliefs and customs'. Malinowski views culture in terms of vast apparatus; partly material, partly human and partly spiritual by which the man is able to cope up with the concrete specific problems that face him. He further understands culture as a means for new needs, and new imperatives imposed on human behaviour. So any change in these aspects will naturally interest an Anthropologist.

Firth (1951:27) understands culture as the "given way of life". Culture emphasizes the components of accumulated resources, immaterial as well as material, which the people inherit, employ, transmute, add to and transmit. As we have already discussed there is a close relation between the cultures and the social systems of a society. So anthropologists would like to study the influence of changed culture or a broken culture or the social system or even its worming.

There is a close relation between culture, and the social

system in a society. Radcliffe-Brown (1952:181), defines a social system as "the total structure of a society together with the totality of social usages in which that structure appears and on which it depends for its continued existence". To him social usages mean morals, law, etiquette, religion, government, education and every kind of social phenomenon which is a part of the complex mechanism by which social structure exists and persists (Ibid: 195). Thus Radcliffe-Brown specifies culture in terms of social relations existing in the total structure of a society. Kroeber and Kluckhonn (1952: 186) say, "culture is an interesting variable betweem human organism and environment". Culture, according to Radcliffe-Brown, Kroeber and Kluckhonn, is a process by which, in a given social group or social class, learned ways of thinking, feeling and acting are transmitted from person to person and from one generation to the other. This is however subjected to the environmental conditions.

Anthropologists also study how each and every individual's life and personality is moulded by the culture in which he is born or lives; through enculturation. Each and every individual is bound by the cultural patterns in which he lives by the process of socialization or enculturation. In this way an individual who is a product of his culture will not have any difficulty in making a comfortable living in it. He will have been taught to adapt to the socio-cultural environment through his participation in socio-cultural activities during the enculturation process. However, there is always a gradual and a slow cultural change going on due to such factors as evolution, diffusion, assimilation, acculturation etc. Cultural change may be from within or by the factors affecting from outside.

An applied anthropologist is also concerned with the change which takes place in the society he is interested. Evon Z. Vogt (1968:555) gives three general factors that can influence change in a given culture: Firstly any change in the ecological niche occupied by a society brings cultural change. Such a change may occur as a result of either: (a) natural environmental change or (b) the migration of a society from one ecological niche to another. New cultural adaptations are always required for survival in case of such shifts in ecological niche. Secondly, any contact between two societies with different cultural pattern influence change in both societies. The diffusion or borrowing of cultural elements that occur also brings culture change. Thirdly, any change occuring within a society also brings change.

Rogers (1969:3-5) refers change brought by three factors: Invention – the process by which new ideas are created or developed; Diffusion – the process by which new ideas are communicated through a given social system and Consequence – the change occuring within the system as a result of the adoption or rejection of the innovations. Rogers (Ibid:5) further gives two processes of change: (a) *immanent change*, when invention takes place within a given social system with little or no external influence being exerted; (b) *contact change*, which is of two types: (1) *selective change*, which occurs when outsiders unintentionally or spontaneously communicate a new idea to members of a social system, who in turn select these ideas they wish to adopt; and (2) *directed contact change*, caused by outsiders who on their own or as representatives of programmes of planned change, introduce new ideas in order to achieve definite goals. The culture which is the integral whole of the material world, the values and norms, the ideas, beliefs, practices and the customs are transmitted from one generation to the next by the process of enculturation and the new needs and imperatives are fulfilled by the means of culture, thus serving as an intervening variable between the organism and environment. The culture, and the environmental factors thus are both interrelated, and stand in relation to one another. The culture from one environmental or the ecological set up varies depending upon the needs and the means of that people. A change in the environment brings the change in the culture with adoption of new modifications or imperatives in the original culture form to satisfy the means of adjustment by the processes namely, evolution, diffusion, assimilation, acculturation, cultural integration, etc. Thus depending upon the type of changes in the environment, cultural change is brought with a gradual or a sudden effect.

Cultural change can also be explained in terms of acculturation.. The use of the term acculturation refers interchangeably to diffusion, assimilation, borrowing and others. Acculturation was first legitimized in 1936 by a committee of the American Social Science Research Council as follows: "those phenomena which result when groups of individuals having different cultures come into continuous first hand contact with subsequent changes in the original culture patterns of either or both groups" (*loc.cit.* Keesing and Keesing, 1971:352). Malinowski (1961:1) remarks that culture change may be induced by factors and forces spontaneously arising within the community, or it may take place through the contact of different cultures by independent invention or by diffusion. Fortes (1936:53) says "culture contact has to be regarded not as a transferance of elements from one culture to another but as a continuous process of interaction between groups of different cultures"

Acculturation is the process by which the exchange of cultural elements takes place on both the sides. The term, however, is sometimes replaced by assimilation. "Assimilation is that form of acculturation which results in groups of individuals wholly replacing the original culture by another" (Beals, 1959: 627-28).

With all these factors affecting a culture bringing in the factors of gradual or a slow process of cultural change, an individual either readily accepts the new cultural traits to balance the culture with the neighbouring one or himself to survive in his own ecological set-up. Here since the individual accepts them readily, he does not feel any type of stress or strain, But removing a portion of the group from its original world of culture and society will completely cut off its relations with the total culture from which it derived moral, social and spiritual inspirations, beliefs, practices and values. This results in the disruption of the morale of the group, and affects its normal working and force them to various stresses and strains. These people thus dislocated are called *uprooted people*. These uprooted people are not mentally, and physically prepared to face the new ecological set up, with a new culture at the place of the refuge, and face considerable strain. The resettlement of such uprooted people, in a different world of culture is known as *cultural transplantation*. This *cultural transplantation* results in the cultural factors to be assimilated between the two cultures – the host and the guest cultures. The ratio of the flow of cultural factors or the elements may vary depending on the nature of the cultures standing at an ecological set-up and the dominant culture is more apt to give its cultural elements to the recessive one and itself may accept less cultural factors in return from it. The migration of the people from one ecological niche to the other and transplanting them into another cultural set-up will bring many changes in their culture.

Now let us consider what is migration and what are its different types and how it is different from going as refugees.

Migration is defined by Eisenstadt (1954:1) as "physical transition of an individual or a group from one society to another. This transition usually involves abandoning of one social setting and entering another and different one". Another definition is given by Mangalam (1968:5), who says, migration is a "relatively permanent moving away of a collectivity called migrants from one geographical location to another preceeded by decision making on the part of the migrants – on the basis of hierarchically ordered set of values, or valued ends and resulting in changes in the interactional system of the migrants" (loc. cit, Jackson, 1969:13).

As there are different types of migrations there are several reasons for migration. Migration may be voluntary or non-voluntary. The former may take place owing to (1) ambition for better opportunities of job, (2) hope of better future for the children and mainly for better economic opportunities. Beijer (loc. cit., Jackson, 1969:14) says that migration involves a complete change and adjustment, readjustment of the community affiliations of an individual. In this way we can say a voluntary immigrant is one who chooses his future home. There are some factors like pulls from outside and pushes from within which makes him to leave his original set up. He will be the master of his decision and he will also have time to think about it. Hence he plans his departure and can dispose off his belongings and bid good-bye from his relatives and friends. Sometimes it is only a temporary shift, from one culture to another. Above all he will be mentally prepared to face all the strains he will encounter in his new cultural setting.

The other group of migrants are the non-voluntary migrants. They are the refugees or the displaced persons. The people thus dislocated are called uprooted people, since they have been pulled out from the soil or culture into which they were born. Under this class we can include people who are the victims of politics, religion, war or national catastrophe or we can also include the people disturbed by natural calamities who were temporarily or permanently removed and rehabilitated in some other setting. Added to these are the people affected of deforestation, construction of hydro-electric dams, etc., which also make people to leave their traditional homeland.

We can specify these dislocated people as displaced persons and refugees. The displaced persons will have more problems, losses, etc., which makes them different from the voluntary migraints. These displaced persons, for example, who are affected by the natural calamities, will have certainly lost their property, dearer and nearer ones and in most of the cases their traditional homeland also. Their rehabilitation, however, will be done in their own cultural context, and by their own people. The problems of the refugees on the other hand, will be still more special, complicated and interesting from the point of view of an anthropologist.

Following the usual national, and international legal norms the jurist's definition of an international refugee will have two main elements: (a) they are persons or categories of persons who have left the territory, the state of which they were nationals and (b) the events preceeding a person's becoming a refugee are connected with the relation between the state and also the nationals (Vernanant, 1953:4ff)(loc. cit. Saksena, 1961:2) In the similar lines Saksena (1961:3) defines a refugee as - "a person who would not like to migrate from his homeland but for reasons beyond his control, political, religious and economic, that might have rendered his life unbearable and unlivable". We have to note the following things about the refugees: (i) They did not leave their society and culture on their own like the immigrants, (ii) their place of origin and the practices of worship are disturbed and, (iii) their rehabilitation will be made in a different society and culture by receiving grants from different societies.

Sir John Hope Simpson (loc. cit. Saksena, 1961:2) described a refugee as one who "finds himself deprived of legal protection, and mutual support, the access to employment, and the measure of freedom of movement. The refugee is one who has left his country of regular residence as a result of political or the religious events in that country, is forced to take refuge in another country of origin without a danger to his life or liberty as a result of the direct consequences of the existing conditions there".

The involuntary or the forced migration dislocates social life, splits families and disorganizes community life of refugees. Refugee migrants are always anxious about the safety of their relatives in the motherland. Many separated families do not know the fate of other kins and this leads to psychological problems. Sometimes this may lead to serious repurcussions on their adjustment to the new culture and ecological setting.

Refugees, being a different group both culturally and socially are segregated from the host society for some time till they settle well socio-culturally and economically. Total acceptance of the refugees by the hosts is also very much essential in any rehabilitation programme. Sometimes refugees may be placed under restrictions not to go out of their settlement for earning, trading etc., so that they will not directly come in contact with the host society. This may be essential for internal security. The refugees, not being the citizens, are treated as aliens and asked to follow certain rules and regulations applicable to any other foreigner. This is because anti-national elements may take advantage of the situation, and create problems with regard to the security of the host country. Secondly the refugees may come in direct contact with the local population and create some problems to themselves as well as to others. Owing to scarcity of good food or earning opportunities inside the camp, the refugees may go out of the settlement and compete with the local people. Further their special status as refugees or foreigners may be misused by the local people or by themselves, for personal benefits. To avoid all these problems, the refugees may be asked to confine to a particular area. These restrictions, sometimes, may create psychological problems to the refugees.

Change in the climatic and ecological factors for the refugees owing to shift from their place of origin, may also bring problems in adjusting to the new climatic conditions, soil, water, food, and its quality and quantity, change in the quality of work, housing patterns and recreational facilities. This restricted life may lead to frustration and further loss of their original culture. This distrubance may also destroy many of their original beliefs and customs. Their life in another culture may also become inefficient, demanding, and less creative.

Applied anthropoligists, also suggest ways and means for the assimilation of people to solve their miseries. These remedies will not be universally applicable and depends upon the situation and people involved. Here we can take up Eisenstadt's indices of full absorption (1954:11-13). These are of three fold: (1) acculturation, i.e., the learning of new roles, norms and customs and the internalization of these new patterns of behaviour, (2) personal adjustment so that there will be few or no indices of personal dis-organization like delinquency, crime or mental illness and; (3) institutional dispersion i.e., immigrants are not concentrated in one sector of the economic, political, ecological or cultural spheres and hence cease to have a separate identity within the new social structure. Gordon (1964:7) gives the following basic sub-processes in the assimilation of a group. They are: (1) change in cultural patterns; (2) complete entry into the social structure through the primary group relations with the host society; (3) inter-marriage; (4) development of ethnicity with the host society; (5) a lack of discriminatory behaviour by the hosts to the new groups; and (6) lack of conflict with the host society. This results to the adaptation of the host society and its culture resulting in the evolving of a new culture. Still the cultural pluralism allows for the preserving of communal identities.

For a refugee to move from one social system to another means acquiring training to enter into new network of groups, and norms. In the long run adjustment implies loss of new group identity since they may become indistinguishable from their hosts. This is accomplished through a process of increasing conformity to the latter's norms and cultural patterns. The extent to which the group will in fact become invisible depends not only on members of the group but also on the extent to which the host society demands complete conformity or tolerates differential cultural patterning.

Ultimately, the adoption of the cultural patterning by the refugee society leads to its adjustment with the host society in the given cultural set-up. Entry of the refugee society into the economic systems, is often accompanied by considerable downward mobility. As refugees have little choice, they are forced to accept jobs at a lower status level, than those they have been accustomed to. This downward mobility produces frustration and tends to show up in the other aspects of the migration. Entry in the social system of the host society by refugee is also one of the important factors. This may take place by the working situation with members of the host society, which may be limited to the formal, instrumental relationship, and may provide little overlap with the more informal spheres. Other criteria of adjustment that may have been used are knowledge of the host society's language, and culture, social relationship, membership in host groups, satisfaction with the host society and identification with and conformity to the norms and patterns of the host country, weakening of the traditional group patterns, adoption of membership in the host society in the form of practices like clothing, food habits, recreation etc. The immigrant has to learn the local language to gain a livelihood. He also has to adopt to few cultural, economic and geographical factors in the given cultural set up of the host society.

The removal of a portion of a society from its original world of culture, and rehabilitating it amidst a different culture brings many stresses and strains to its people. This is the situation under which the Tibetan refugees are living in Mundgod and in other refugee camps in India. Tibetans who belong to different world of culture were forcibly sent out of their country. The action was more sudden in nature and the refugees were not prepared to face the drastic situation. This study aims at understanding the background of these Tibetan refugees, their rehabilitation, stresses and strains they face or faced as refugees in India particularly at the rehabilitation camp Mundgod.

## Refugees and Society

Man's story in large measure is the story of wanderings. Man migrated from one place to another in all the periods of time. Man is found to have been affected by the factors of pushes, and pulls at a certain region in which he lives forcing him to migrate from one place to another in search of better opportunities of life. When this movement becomes a forced one and a large scale one, it creates problems to the migrants as well as to their hosts. Moreover such a problem to a greater mass of human beings is viewed as an international problem and world bodies such as League of Nations and later United Nations Organization have done their best to solve the problem. The political history of the world has many such instances to its credit. Wars, racial and religious movements have left people who do not belong to the revolted group in danger. Here is a short history of such refugees and their rehabilitation.

## Refugees Expelled by Political Authorities

Between 1912 and 1923, Greece was continuously at war leading to many changes in the boundaries of Greece, Turkey, Bulgaria, and other adjoining states, resulting into the expulsion of 10,00,000 Greek population to flee to Greece. It also led to a compulsory transfer to Greece of the surviving 1,89,000 Greeks in Asia Minor and also a compulsory transfer of the 3,55,000 strong Turkish minority in Greek Macedonia to Turkey.

During World War II and afterwards, many peoples in Eastern and Central Europe such as Bulgarians, Romanians, Czechs, Slovaks, Ukrainians, Russians, White Russians, Germans, Poles, Hungarians and others, were thus exchanged. In 1946, Hungary and Czechoslovakia agreed on a voluntary exchange of their respective ethnic minorities involving the tranfer of 31,000 Magyurs to Hungary and of 33,000 Slovaks to erstwhile Czechoslovakia.

The refugees of politically motivated nature are occurring intermittently. The Russian revolution in October 1917, and the post revolutionary civil war resulted in the expulsion of 1,50,000 refugees, scattered throughout France, Germany, Poland and the Baltic states, parts of the Far East and the Balkan countries. More than a million Armenians fled from Turkish Asia Minor to Russia, the Middle East, the Balkan states and North and South America between 1915 and 1923. Following the Hungarian Revolution in 1956, about 2,03,000 Hungarians fled the country. Between 1945 and 1961 during the rule of communist regime a total of 3,70,000 political refugees from East Germany found asylum in West Germany.

When peoples Republic of China was established in 1949 some 2,00,000 Chinese remnants of Chiang Kaishek's army and civilians escaped to the island of Taiwan. In 1959, 76,000 Tibetans flight to India, Bhutan, Sikkim, Nepal and Macau as refugees.

Many became refugees owing to religious and racial intolerance. In the 1930s, as a result of anti-Jewish policies, in all 4,00,000 Jewish refugees, fled from Germany proper, Austria and Sudeten highlands. More than 50,000 Jewish refugees from Yemen were transported to Israel in 1949-50; 7,700 Jews of Aden fled to Israel; 1,23,000 Jewish refugees were lifted from Iraq to Israel in 1950-51. There are also many incidences of refugee movements caused by the partition of existing territorial entities. Nearly 1,05,00,000 German population were made to get away from Germany and were placed under Polish and Soviet administration. The 1,65,000 of ethnic Germans and 1,50,000 of Yugoslovian refugees were put in West and East Germany. The partition of the Indian sub-continent in 1947, resulted in the two way flight of 1,80,00,000 Hindus from Pakistan and Muslims from India.

In 1921 Fridtjof Nansen of Norway was appointed by the League of Nations as High Commissioner for Russian and Armenian refugees and he devised a so-called League of Nations passport (Nansen passport), a travel document recognized by 53 states. After his death in 1930 the protection of refugees was entrusted by the League to Nansen International Office for Refugees, established as an autonomous body in 1938. However, the efforts were fruitless owing to non-cooperation by various governments.

In 1932 a conference was called under the presidentship of Franklin D. Roosevelt, President of the United States of America, and formed an Inter-governmental Committee on Refugees (IGCR). Even these efforts became fruitless. In 1943, a conference of 44 nations was called and a committee called United Nations Relief and Rehabilitation Administration (UNRRA) was formed. In 1947 a new and nonpermanent specialized agency of the United Nations, the International Refugee Organization (IRO) was created. It worked upto 1952. While it was still housed in Europe, there were refugees to be rehabilitated. At the initiative of the United States a group of 16 nations met in Brussels in December, 1952 and set up the Inter-governmental Committee for European Migration (ICEM). By 1971 the number of sponsoring agencies reached to 31, and was successful to move 17,75,000 European refugees to resettlement countries. The Office of the United Nations High Commissioner for Refugees (UNHCR) was established to ensure the legal and political protection to refugees, and to promote permanent solutions to their problems.UNHCR is enabling the refugees to freely choose to return voluntarily to their country of origin, or to remain permanently in the country of first asylum or to settle in another country depending on the possibilities made available by governments. The United Nations General Assembly established two more relief agencies - the United Nations Relief and Works Agency for Palestine Refugees (UNRWA) and United Nations Korean Reconstruction Agency (UNKRA). There are also many non-governmental, and voluntary agencies working for the solution of refugees.

Besides, the relief activities, a number of researches have also been done to understand the problems the refugees and their rehabilitators face. Our study on the Tibetan refugees is one such attempt of fact finding. Anthropologists have already studied and helped successfully to rehabilitate uprooted people such as the

Bikinis of Pacific. The exiled native of Bikini in the Marshall Islands (Barnett, 1953:151-154) faced many difficulties in adjusting and settling well in their new place of rehabilitation. An emergency investigation of its causes and recommendations for its relief by an anthropologist took place in the early 1948. The study includes observations on the physiographic structure of the island, its water supply, its vegetations, and its food resources and their utilization. Thus a detailed investigation was conducted on the community organization, important personalities, work organization, patterns of land use, the use of resources of the island and their utilization, agricultural and livestock production, commercial activities and attitudes.

The study also included the historical survey of events. The attitudes of the Bikinis towards the local population, and vice-versa were also studied. Emphasis was given to the study of the economic set-up of the Bikinis in the island depending upon the type of land they have been provided with, the agricultural operations carried out – traditional or the modern ones, size of land allotted to the individual families, the utilization of their resources from their land, etc.

A study of Mungod Tibetans has been made by Palakshappa, an Indian Sociologist (1978). This study was made using schedules and interview techniques, with the help of both Indian and Tibetan investigators, presents both the insiders' and outsiders' views of the problem. Though this is a sociological study and lacks depth and details of the Tibetan society and culture, it has its own contribution to make for the understanding of the refugees, the stresses and strains faced by them, their rehabilitation, aspirations and so on.

In the light of these and other studies made on refugees, voluntary migrants, displaced persons etc. this study of the Tibetan refugees settled in Mundgod (Karnataka) is made.

## The Present Study

The broad aims of the present study are to understand: (i) the traditional cultural background of the Tibetans, (ii) the individual and group adjustment and (iii) the process of rehabilitation of Tibetan refugees, the problems involved in this and the introduction of cultural factors in the Tibetan society from the host culture through acculturation, the process of modification and adjustment. The uprooted people will have difficulties in adjusting to the new socio-cultural environment. Since this environmental adjustment brings many social, psychological and physical problems, the aim will be to understand the stress and strain the Tibetan refugees are facing in settling in the new eco-cultural environment and also in maintaining their traditional culture, customs practices and values, thus the overall effects on their socio-cultural and economic life. The Tibetans cannot adjust better to the new life as long as they are not received well by the local population. Further the Tibetans who look different racially and speak a different language may not freely mingle with the local population. In due course these situations may bring problems to the Tibetan as well as the local population. This type of situation is understood through studying the opinions and attitudes of the administrators, school teachers and the local population towards the refugees. Further the effect of the Indian culture on the refugees and the dynamics of social and cultural changes are studied. Thus the acculturation in terms of intensity of contacts with alien cultures, factors affecting cultural receptivity, instances of culture borrowing, the modifications of introduced elements in their socio-cultural trends are studied.

Under the present study an attempt is made to analyse how a group disturbed in its physical or socio-cultural setting gains its normalcy as early as possible, and through adjustments.

How an uprooted group tries to survive in its new home on some hope - faith or a leader, and this not only lessens the stress and strain but also unites the members to achieve their goal.

The rehabilitation personnel and programmes may be good, and effective but the temporary stay of the rehabilitated group makes the programme incomplete.

The success of any transplantation programme depends upon the acceptance of refugees and the host population.

The changes which occur in the refugee group brings conflict between the younger and older age groups, because the old want to retain the traditional order and the young want to be away from that.

The present study is confined to the Tibetan Refugee Rehabilitation Scheme No. II (TRRS II) settlement situated near Mundgod in Uttar Kannada district of Karnataka State. This settlement consists of nine Tibetan villages for lay people, two lama villages and an old and Infirm Peoples' Home.

The actual fieldwork to collect data needed, was conducted during 1976, 1977 and 1978. However several brief visits were made earlier and after this, to the Settlement and the TRRS.II office, to collect preliminary data. With these preliminary visits and the library consultation a household census schedule was prepared. During the first visit a house to house census was conducted using the household census schedule. Simultaneously general information about the Tibetans was collected when available and found essential. During the later visits a detailed study of the Tibetan society and culture was conducted with the help of depth interview schedule. Both the schedules were thoroughly pre-tested before use. The census schedule helped to get information on the family details such as members of the family, sex, age, marital status, education, religion, caste and class status, economic and political status, size of the family, places from which they came from Tibet, information regarding their stay in transit camps and so on. Suitable persons were also interviewed for general and particular information regarding their traditional culture, the problems, stresses and strains they were facing under the present situations. A suitable number of case studies were also conducted to get deeper perspective of the situations faced by the refugees.

During the field work the researcher lived in one of the Tibetan villages. At first the representative of H.H. the Dalai Lama in the settlement, introduced him to a few religious and socio-political leaders. After a few days the researcher was able to acquaint with the people and their settlement and began to visit other villages. The earlier reactions of the Tibetans towards the researcher were of suspicion. Gradually they changed, and later they were proud of him since he proposed to eat, and live with them and understand their society and culture. By the time the actual house to house census work was started he had the fullest cooperation from the Tibetans.

When the researcher visited Tibetan families to observe the religious ceremonies and festivals, he noted the significances of these through key informants. He followed the method of participant observation and also enquired into their problems and showed sympathy. This type of a more personal relation helped him to establish a good rapport with the Tibetans.

Apart from these surprise visits were also made by him to the families to note the actual situations and check the data.

For the depth interview informants were selected giving equal representation to age, sex, class and provincial groups. Adequate care was taken to select informants depending upon their knowledge and contacts with outsiders. The schedule had 14 sections namely, settlement, social organization, marriage and marriage practices, leadership, economic organization, material culture, education, religion, health and hygiene, food and food habits, dress and ornaments, leisure and recreation, interaction with local poeple and future. In an average, it took three or four sittings of six to eight hours each to interview an informant. Stress was also given to know the psychological, social and cultural problems the old people, lamas and the monks face in the new environment. The informants talked freely even though the information given by them was recorded and a few questions were asked to recollect their past. The Tibetans by now have also learnt Hindi and a few even know Kannada and can converse fluently in the new tongues. The difficulty in the beginning was only with those informants who knew only Tibetan. For sometime in the beginning the researcher took the help of an interpreter, a Tibetan, when he interviewed the older age sets. Within a few months he could himself learn Tibetan language and converse with the informant without the need of the interpreter. Extensive field notes were produced and this was essential since many things, especially the Tibetan language was new to the researcher. To know the earlier history and culture of Tibet descriptive material is also drawn from the earlier ethnographers, historians, tourists and other authors for which the books were even borrowed from distant places such as National Library, Calcutta, Banaras Hindu University, Varanasi, and so on. This was essential to know the traditional, social and cultural life of Tibetans in their homeland.

# 2

# Tibet Through The Ages

The Tibetans, according to a legendary among them trace their origin to a divine monkey - a protege of Avalokiteshwar (*Chen-Re-Zi*, the compassionate, the patron god of Tibet) and a mountain (Ogress). Out of their union, six children were born, who later, raised in number and formed six tribes. The offsprings gradually lost their tails and hairs on the body. It is a common belief among the Tibetans that unlike their descendents they have retained only the red face. It is also believed that in the beginning these groups were short of food supply and pitying them, God gave five kinds of grains which they soon learnt to sow, and grow their food thereby.

The first Tibetan King was Spu-rgyal. A stone inscription belonging to the eighth century refers to him as *O'lde-Spurgyal*. The early works belonging to the *Bon-po* period, have referred to him as *O'lde Gung-rgyal*. *Bon-po* religion was practised by the Pre-Buddhist Tibetans and the same is said to be similar to Taoism of China. Buddhism, which came to Tibet owing to its contact with China and India, soon displaced the Bon religion. Lama historians began to write accounts of the rise of Buddhist doctrine in Tibet in which the royal primogeniture is said to have been the son of an Indian King and related to the Buddha. It is said that the first Tibetan king Spu-rgyal was born with miraculous powers. As a child he was thrown afloat in a river and was later found by shepherds. After the rescue, people enthroned him (*Khri*) thinking that he was sent to the earth by God and supported on the napes of the neck (*Gnya*). He was, therefore named as *Gnya-Khri-btsan-po* (neck enthroned ruler). He was the first Tibetan king recorded in the traditional Buddhist geneologies.

The first seven Tibetan kings in the royal lineage, are called "the heavenly thrones". They are said to have been descended from the heaven by a celestial rope. After their death, it is believed that, they ascended back to the sky. The Tibetans attach a lot of importance to this link in establishing marital relationship. They consider the parental blood continues to flow upto the seventh generation in both the matrilineal and patrilineal descendents. It is believed that at the eighth generation the same breaks off and, therefore, one can then marry in his own clan.

After the Gnya-Khri-tsan-po, it is said, twenty seven or more kings ruled Tibet. These in turn are put into three groups: Heavenly, Earthly and Human. This geneology of Tibetan kings is generally regarded as a later elaboration of the lost tradition.

The King Nam-ri-San-tsan-po, who reigned Tibet for about fifty years, beginning from 570 A.D. unified and shaped it into a strong power. This king practised *Bon-po* religion. At that time the people were rude and were given to war plundering, and lived on the simplest food. They sacrificed sheep, dog, monkey, horse, ox, ass and even human beings to the deities. They had no knowledge of a script to write with. His son Son-tsan Gan-po, who ascended the throne in 620-650 A.D., sent his two great statesmen - Tho-mi Sam-bho-ta and Gar-don Tsan, to India to study the language systems in reading and writing. Tho-mi Sam-bho-ta studied characters and phonetics of the Indian languages and invented Tibetan alphabets with four vowels and thirty consonants. Son-tsan Gan-po got married to princess Bhrikutidevi, daughter of King Amsuvarman of Nepal, a devout Buddhist. She brought several Buddhist images to Tibet. The most important of them is that of Sakyamuni which is found in the second important temple of the city of Lhasa, and now called Ra-mo-che. Lama historians referred to this King as Chos-rgyal (Religious King). Another Chinese princess was given in matrimony to the King Khri-lde-gtsung-btsan. By this time many Buddhist monks who were forced out of Mongolia by the Arab forces, arrived in Central Tibet. The Central Tibet was then ridden with a Cholera epidemic, and it is said that the princess became a victim to it. The monks were blamed for this and they were later banished from Tibet.

By 747 A.D. Padmasambhava and Shantirakshita, the great Buddhist scholars of India, were invited to Tibet to teach the Indian School of Buddhism, known as Vajrayana, to the Tibetans. This is based on the philosophical system of the Madhyamika process, combined with the teachings of Tantrism. This, in course of time replaced the *Bon-po* religion completely. Later the *Bon-po* religion moved to the Eastern Tibet.

In 836 A.D. the King Glang Darma came to the throne. He

was an anti-Buddhist, and was, therefore killed by a Buddhist monk. Thus there was no focus for the feudal loyalty as no heir apparent was designated to the kingdom. This situation helped to lay the foundation for the birth of the local lords.

By that time there came up a kingdom in Western Tibet. Its king, La-bla-Ma, invited Atisha, an Indian scholar, to Tibet and this scholar formulated the Tibetan calendar based on the lunar system with sixty year cycles. He also founded a first reformed sect in Tibetan Buddhism.

During the thirteenth century, Tibet was divided among a number of local lords and religious leaders who ruled by right of succession. At that time Kublai Khan, the Mongolian emperor, was ruling the entire Tibet. Soon after his death, i.e. by the middle of fourteenth century, the local ruling myriads led to the rise of Phag-mo-gru myriarchs. Their leader the Byang-chub rgyal-mtshen, conquered Central Tibet ending the Mongol control. He established the system of local administration and replaced it with the *rdzong* or the district unit system. The adminisrators of the district were appointed by the Phag-mo-gru ruler, thereby forming a centralized authority; one based on personnel loyalty rather than outside military force.

Tsong-Kha-pa (1357 - 1419 A.D.), so named after his birth place, the district of Tsong-kha near the Koko Nor, was a monk of exceptional intellectual attainments. He started a reformistic movement and had many followers who aspired power, and wealth. Their aim was to end the divisions and rivalries prevalent among the Tibetan monastries. Many of the local rulers shifted their loyalty from Phag-mo-gru, belonging to Bka-brgyud-pa sect, to the reformed Dge-lugs-pa sect of Tsong-kha-pa.

The practice of maintaining a spiritual lineage of lamas through reincarnation, arose in the fourteenth century, when black hat Karma-pa, the Rang-byang rdo-rje (1284-1338) proclaimed that he would be reborn and his incarnation would be found to be Rol-pai rdo-rje. Taking the clue the other sects also began to adopt this practice and each soon had its various lineages of reborn lamas. The third in the lineage, Bsod-nams rgya-mtso (1543-88), was invited to Mongolia by Altan Khan of the Mongols. He was impressed by the lama and so bestowed on him the title of Dalai Lama in 1578 A.D. Dalai (*Talai*) is a Mongol word for ocean. The title signifies the vast and deep wisdom of the lama. The title was applied to the two earlier lamas in the lineage. The nephew of the Tson-kha-pa, the Dge-dun grub-pa, was regarded as the first Dalai Lama who was also the founder of the Tra-Shi Lun-Po monastery. The Tibetans do not address the Dalai Lama by that title but refer him as *Yid-bzhin Nor-bu* (wish granting jewel) or *Rgyul-ba Rin-po-che* (Great precious conqueror).

Other Tibetan lamas had their followers in Mongolia but they did not appear to have shown the proselytising energy of the new sect which in a very short time commanded the spiritual allegience of almost all the rival tribes of Mongolia. It laid the foundation for the supremacy of the Dalai Lama and the ultimate union of disunited Mongol tribes into a Mongol empire. So the Gelug-pa sect which commanded the loyalty of most of the Mongols, became the ruling power of Tibet. At the time of Sonam Gyatso, the third incarnation in the series among the Gelug-pas, the Dalai Lama had no temporal influence on Tibet. But the austerity, discipline and spiritual quality of lamas attracted the growing number of followers, including a few influential nobles. Thus through its lay supporters the new sect gradually become involved in the political contentions of the day, and was seen the principal rival of the dominant Karma-pas.

Nga-wang Lo-bzong Gyam-tsho, the Fifty Dalai Lama, is another epoch making figure in the history of the Tibet, and is called as "Great Fifth". His teacher Blo-bzong Chos-Kyi rgyal-mtshen (1567-1662), was considered a manifaestation of the Buddha. He was installed on the abbot's throne at Tra-Shi Lun-Po by the Dalai Lama and he became the First Panchen Lama. After that the successors were considered to be reincarnation of Blo-bzang Chos-Kyi rgyal-mtshen and they were discovered and confirmed in the way the rebirth of the Dalai Lama's is traced.

Ascendency of the Gelug-pa sects in Tibet which began with the defeat of the Tsang-pa kings by Gushri Khan and culminating in the patron-chaplain relationship between the Dalai and Panchen Lamas on one hand and the Chinese emperor on the other, was now complete with their superb organization. But at first the Dalai Lama's authority was under the protection of Gushri Khan, who assumed the title "king of Tibet", which he consequently transmitted to his descendents. Though Gushri Khan himself maintained most friendly, and respectful relations, to some extent, he was a check on the supremacy of his religious collegue, the Dalai Lama. After his death in 1655, his successors showed little interest in the administration of Tibet. They lived in upland hunting grounds, North of Lhasa, in their native Koko-Nor country. They appointed a regent to look after their interests at Lhasa.

The Fifth Dalai Lama was a man of great determination and force of character, he drew all powers into his own hands, including that of the appointment of the regent. As a result the Mongolians lost their control over Tibet, and made no effort to influence the Dalai Lama's government and the country. The conquests of the Geluk-pa went even farther than U and Tsang province to Mongolia. In Khamba and Ngari provinces all the more important monasteries were incorporated into the Geluk-pa sect. On account of the flourishing career of Dre-Pung, Se-Ra and Gan-Dan with their many affiliated institutions the Dalai incarnation moved his court in Lhasa from Dre-Pung to the Po-ta-la. Since then the Dalai Lama rose to prominence, especially in the nineteenth century and after, as the representative, not only of the Geluk-pa sect, but also of the whole of Tibet.

In 1659, Dayan Khan - the Mongolian King, once again helped the Fifth Dalai Lama to suppress a revolt in Tsang. Qosot Mongols from Koko-Nor had a rival in the person of Galdan, the king of Dzungars (1676-1697) who had founded a kingdom in Turkestan. The Regent Sangye Gyatso, as it happened, had made an ally of king Galden. Whilst Lhapsang Khan and Qosot king were allied with the emperor of China (Kang hsi) who had just been at war with the Dzungars. The young man whom this same regent has recognized as Sixth Dalai Lama, Tshangyang Gyatso (1683-1705), moved about with young women, and wrote love poems. Making this questionable behaviour as an excuse, Lhapsang Khan attacked Lhasa, and with the consent of Kang hsi, killed the regent, and kidnapped the Sixth Dalai Lama, who died soon afterwards on the way to China. The Tibetans appealed to the Dzungars, who invaded Tibet and defeated Lapsang Khan. China reacted at once. An army dispatched by Kang hsi entered Lhasa in 1720 A.D. The Seventh Dalai Lama, who was born at Litang, and recognized as incarnate, was enthroned at the Po-ta-la (Kesang Gyatso 1708-1747). The walls of Lhasa were pulled down, a Chinese garrison was installed at

Lhasa, and Khan, and their representatives were placed throughout the eastern Tibet and the Lhasa.

## Tibetans as refugees:

Tibet remained a poor country as before and was made up of a large, barren and treeless plateaus and secluded valleys. It is bound on the north by Chinese province of Sinkiang, on the South by Nepal, Bhutan and Sikkim, along with 800 miles of Indian territory, on the west by the Ladakh area of Kashmir; and on the east by China (Anand, 1969:401). In the second half of the seventeenth century Tibet was blessed with a remarkable Dalai Lama, Lobsong Gyatso. He was also known as the Great Fifth, it was he who united athe entire Tibet. The Dalai Lama was invited by the then Manchu Emperor of China, and he too treated Tibet as an independent sovereign country (Shakabpa, 1967: 113ff).

Ever since the Seventh Dalai Lama, the whole of Tibet was beset with political problems. Thus resulted in the fatal poisoning of the Dalai Lamas right from the seventh upto the twelfth. As Tibet lacked a strong leadership Chinese took command over Lhasa and installed two of their residents who were designated as Ambans, each strong with thousand troops. Though Tibet was under the complete control of Chinese troops the office of the Dalai Lama, was accepted by the Chinese and the Dalai Lama was considered to be the supreme ruler of Tibet. About the middle of the nineteenth century the political power of the Chinese declined and her weak government was hardly able to maintain a hold over Tibet. Tibetans now openly repudiated the China's authority over Tibet. When this was the situation the British India signed a treaty with China in 1890 delimiting the boundary between Sikkim and Tibet (Rubin, 1968: 112). In 1893 another Anglo-Chinese Convention was signed proposing to open Tibetan territory to British trade but the Tibetan government flatly rejected to recognize the Anglo-Chinese convention. Tibetans were very much irritated by the British interference regarding their territory and, therefore, did not accept any direct negotiations with the British. In 1894 when the Thirteenth Dalai Lama was eighteen years of age, the national parties at Lhasa set him on the throne. The Dalai Lama being powerful, and intelligent turned towards Russia to secure an ally against both China and Britain.

Rebuffed by the Tibetans, and apprehensive of Russian intentions, Britain decided to straighten out its relations with Tibet (Techman, 1938: 222). Lord Curzon wrote in his letter to the Secretary of the State for India, that "the Chinese suzerainty over Tibet is a constitutional fiction, a political affection which has only be maintained because of its convenience to both parties. He maintained that the Dalai Lama was the "defacto as well as de jure sovereign of the country" (Ram Gopal, 1964:12). Lord Curzon, the the Viceroy of India, seeing the Dalai Lama not negotiable with the British and China, and having no control over Tibet, sent a military expedition into Tibet, in 1903, under the command of colonel Francis Younghusband. Dalai Lama, therefore, fled to Mongolia. A treaty was signed between the British commander and the Government of Tibet (in the absence of Dalai Lama) to respect Anglo-Chinese convention of 1890 and to recognize the frontier between the Sikkim and Tibet as defined in Article I of the said convention. Certain trade rights were also demanded by British and the following treaty was laid down that:

(a) Without the previous consent of the British Government, no portion of Tibetan territory shall be ceded, sold, leased, mortgaged or otherwise given for occupation to any foreign power;

(b) No such power shall be permitted to intervene in Tibetan affairs;

(c) No representatives or agents of any foreign power shall be admitted into Tibet;

(d) No concessions for railways, road, telegraphs, minings or other rights, shall be granted to any foreign power, or to an individual subject of any foreign country. In case if such concessions are granted to any foreign power, equivalent concessions shall have to be granted to the British also;

(e) No Tibetan revenues, whether in kind or in cash, shall be pledged or assigned to any foreign power, or to the subjects of any foreign power.

It should be noted here that regarding the above treaty neither the Government of China nor her representatives in Lhasa uttered a single word of protest (Anand, 1969: 406). In the year 1906 and 1907 another agreement was signed between China and Britain regarding trade regulations through the Tibetan territory without consulting Tibet herself. Thus Tibet felt further humiliated and drifted more and more into the Chinese fold. This was later realized by the British. The convention signed between Russia and Britain in 1907, made Dalai Lama XIII more helpless. Welcoming an invitation from China he immediately left for China. After five years of continued absence the Dalai Lama returned to Lhasa in 1909. In 1910, once again the Dalai Lama had to flee over to India, because the Chinese troops attacked the city of Lhasa. The Government of China had promised the Dalai Lama that "They had no intention of altering the administration of Tibet, still less of converting it into a province of China" (Bell, 1924:112) But very soon the Chinese Amban took control of Lhasa and the Central administration. The British administrators in India felt that, for the safety and protection of Northern Frontier of India, the neighbouring country like Tibet should be independent and strong (Bell 1946: 98). But they could do nothing about it, because they were already tied down by the treaties of 1906 and 1907. It, therefore, decided to remain neutral in the struggle between China and Tibet and thus abandoned Tibet to the tender mercies of China (Anand 1969: 410), and China was able to claim suzerainty and also the sovereignty over Tibet.

By the end of 1911 because of the revolution started in China the Chinese rule over Tibet became weak, and the Chinese administrators left for home. The Tibetans thus declared independence and until the advent of communists in 1950 Tibet enjoyed all freedom and independence a country could enjoy.

In 1912 the President of the Republic of China once again proclaimed Tibet to be the province of China and also dispatched troops to Tibet. Tibetans, howedver, conceded China's right to station a representative in Lhasa but not to keep unlimited army in Tibet. Later a tripartite conference between China, Britain and Tibet took place to settle the status of Tibet. The meeting took place at Simla in October 1913. It was concluded to divide Tibet into two parts - outer and the inner Tibet. The Chinese suzerainty over the whole of Tibet should be recognized in return for the Chinese undertaking not to convert Tibet into a Chinese province. Outer Tibet was to be recognized as fully autonomous, and no

Chinese interference was to be permitted, and inner Tibet was to be administered both by the Governments of Tibet and China. The latter were to be allowed to maintain their own officials and administer their communities (Bell 1924: 154-155). China was dissatisfied and rejected to sign, thereupon the British and the Tibetans together declared the convention binding among themselves.

Tibet functioned in practice, as an independent country until 1951 and was able to defend its frontiers against Chinese on occasional fightings. But apparently logic or law did not mean much for China (Anand 1969:429). In February 1950 Tibet sent a mission to discuss things over with the Chinese communists in the neutral territory of Hong Kong. Later the talks were arranged to be conducted at Delhi. China was represented by her ambassadors in Delhi. The talks did not materialize. Finally the negotiations were shifted to Peking, and right at this time the Chinese army began to move into Tibet. On 24th October 1950, the Chinese announced that the Chinese liberation force had been ordered "to advance into Tibet to liberate three million Tibetans from imperialistic aggression" (International Commission of Jurists, 1959:94). The Government of Tibet which was by now the mouth piece of China declared that - "Tibet is an integral part of China, and the problem of Tibet is entirely a domestic problem of China. The Chinese People's Liberation Army must enter Tibet, liberate the Tibetan people, and defend the frontiers of China" (Ram Gopal 1964:32-33).

In a desperate appeal to the United Nations on 11th November 1950, the Dalai Lama's Government begged to the nations of the world to intercede on their behalf, and check the Chinese aggression. It expressed the view that if China wanted to press its claim over Tibetan opposition, there were other civilized methods available, methods not involving the use of force or coersion. Armed invasion by China through sheer physical force was said to be clearly a case of aggression (loc. cit. Anand 1969:431).

The case of Tibet was discussed in the United Nations Organization. The Soviet and the Chinese Nationalist delegates opposed discussion on the ground that Tibet was an integral part of China. The United States agreed to an adjournment because even the Government of India entertained a hope that the problem could be peacefully and honourably settled (loc.cit. Anand

1969:433). The case was, however, adjourned from the discussion.

In April 1951, a Tibetan delegation went to Peking to negotiate and concluded Sino-Tibetans agreement with China. On 23rd May 1951 Tibetans agreed to return to the big family of the motherland - the People's Republic of China. It guaranteed the continuance of the existing political system in Tibet, including the established status, functions and powers of the Dalai Lama and the Panchen Lama. It also conceded the internal autonomy to Tibet in the matters of custom and religion, and declared that the external relations of Tibet would be handled exclusively by the Peking Government. The Chinese could not keep up this Sino-Tibetan agreement and many changes were made in the status and powers of the Dalai Lama. Under the new set-up his officials took away most of his powers. The Chinese also prosecuted hundreds of religious leaders branding them as yellow brigands and red robbers, and many of them were killed. Many trade agreements were broken and every effort was made to stop the entry of the Indian, and the Nepalese traders (Yishi Wangel 1964:60-61).

In 1952 Tibet was divided into three administrative zones, the Central and the Western portions under the Dalai Lama, the Shigatse area under the Panchen Lama and the Eastern areas under the Chamdo Liberation Committee, headed by a Chinese General.

The People's Liberation Army and the communist party officials of China entered Tibet in the year 1953. They told the Tibetans that they have come to help them and lead Tibet into a new era of progress. They also assured them that they will go back as soon the Tibetans learn to stand on their own legs. Further, they set-up Imperial Resident (Amban) in Lhasa as their representative and posted about 200 soldiers as his escorts.

As a second move, in 1955 a large number of Chinese entered and called themselves as 'working personnel'. They began to set-up youth and other organizations. They also established a local branch of the Preparatory Committee for Tibetan Autonomy - the body which in due course replaced the erstwhile Tibetan government.

Chinese on their arrival began to give importance to the

sinonization of Tibetans at various levels. First to make the noble and high class Tibetans to realize the importance of the new democratic reforms, they made them to send their children to the new schools. Here the youngsters were made to develop interest towards mainland China. The Chinese communists also spent silver dollars liberally to win the active cooperation of the local administrators and passive acquiescence of the masses. Young were also paid with these silver coins to make them to attend the Chinese schools. The labourers, who built roads and bridges to facilitate the movement of Chinese military, were also paid in white coins. Side by side, Chinese also brought restriction on the movement of the Tibetans. By this act of the Chinese it was the people of the Khamba province who were the first to be affected. Therefore they began to resist the Chinese move right from the year 1954. But the widespread revolt took place throughout Tibet, only in 1959. By now the Chinese were helped by few Tibetans who were completely indoctrinated by Chinese ideas. The Chinese also took the help of criminals in their activities. When the signs of revolt were noticed the rich and the higher class Tibetans were picked up and put to public denunciation and beating and later imprisoned. Their land and livestock were confiscated and their long hairs were cut off. Women and children were left without any property for maintenance and ultimately their children were taken away to schools in mainland China and women to work in concentration camps. Prisoners were mostly made to work on road construction. The entire harvest for the year was taken away and an allowance of 28 pounds of barley per month was paid to each member of the family.

On the religious side the Dalai Lama was publicly denounced. Lamas and senior monks were insulted and imprisoned. The other monks were not given any food as long as they stayed in the monasteries and thus they were forced to come out. Monks were also forced to marry and lead a worldly life. Thus many monasteries were destroyed along with their sacred images and books. Many of the Tibetan religious teachers including many holy places were also destroyed.

The Tibetan refugees alleged that though the Tibetans did not share any cultural similarities with China, yet they had to face many Chinese intrusions in their way of life. In the past the Tibetans had struggled hard to preserve identity of their culture, institutions, religion, etc., which they have maintained ever since the 6th century; and that this valuable culture of Tibet which, according to them developed preserving its peculiar qualities and differences from rest of the world cultures was tremendously disturbed by China by flooding her own population and culture into Tibet. It is also alleged that they took away the male population of Tibet to mainland China as free labourers, that there were also attempts to destroy the Tibetans as a religious group and by this Chinese violated the law of human rights and that in addition to this many other violent activities like murder, torture, rape, deportation and destruction of the family in socio-economic and religious life took place. The Tibetan refugees alleged that in this way the sinonization took place at various levels of Tibetan culture.

The principles of Panchashila were reaffirmed in a joint statement by the prime ministers of India and China, in June 1954. The preamble reads that "The Government of the Republic of India and the Central People's Government of the Peoples' Republic of China being desirous of promoting trade, and cultural intercourse between the region of China and India and of facilitating pilgrimage and travel by the peoples of China and India, they resolved to enter into five principles : (1) Mutual respect for territorial integrity and sovereignty, (2) Non-aggression, (3) Non-interference in internal affairs, (4) Equality and mutual benefit, and (5) Peaceful coexistance" (Frank Morees 1959:126).

In 1956 the Dalai Lama and the Panchen Lama visited India. Dalai Lama revealed that he was unhappy with the situations in Tibet. With all assurances by the Chinese Prime Minister who was then present in India, Nehru persuaded Dalai Lama to return to Tibet. Dalai Lama also invited Panchen Lama to return to Tibet. Accordingly both of them returned to Tibet. Dalai Lama always had a suspicion on Panchen Lama that he may help the Chinese and thereby harm the cause of Tibet. This was in fact an old Chinese policy to extend its influence by creating a split between the two and support the lesser of the two (Dastur 1964:64) for their own political ends.

Marshall Chen Yi, a Deputy Prime Minister who was assigned the task of preparing Tibet for a regional autonomy within the Chinese People's Republic had on April 22, 1956 publicly stated that the transition of the nationalities of the country to socialism will be achieved separately and in different ways. He said further that - "both the Chinese Government and the Communist Party held the view that reforms in Tibet can only be carried out when the Tibetan leaders and people unanimously demanded them" (*loc.cit.* Dastur 1964:64).

In 1956 Preparatory Committee for the Autonomous Region of Tibet was formed by the Chinese rulers with the Dalai Lama as its Chairman and the Panchen Lama as its Vice-Chairman. However the ruling power was exercised by the Chinese. In the name of introducing the reforms the Chinese also interfered in all the matters including religion and administration. This led to a revolt in Tibet. By March 10, 1959, the people of the upper strata also joined the rebels. As a result, the Dalai Lama was put under duress and the seventeen point agreement was broken by the Chinese. 'China ordered her military, to crush the rebelion in order to protect the unification of Tibet and national unity and to relieve the people of the Tibetan religion from misery and suffering' (International Commission of Jurists, 1959:94). On March 28, 1959 State Council in Peking dissolved the Tibetan local government and the eighteen members of the Preparatory Committee were branded as traitors. Thus rapid socialization of Tibet carried out abruptly caused greater dissatisfaction and displeasure among the Tibetans.

On March 9, 1959 Dalai Lama received an invitation from the Commander at Lhasa to present himself at the Chinese barracks, without his ministers and his usual escort. This brought a kind of fear among Tibetans. On hearing this, the people of Lhasa of all classes and ranks flooded into the grounds of Norbu Lingka and many more outside the enclosure. Many Tibetan troops joined them under their commanders to defend their leader H.H. the Dalai Lama. For the safety of the Dalai Lama all the Tibetans urged him to leave Lhasa. On 17th March, 1959, the Chinese fired two shells into the grounds of Norbu Lingka, very close to the Dalai Lama's palace.

The high ranking officials and the spiritual leaders of Tibet thought that the continued stay of the Dalai Lama in Tibet was a danger to his life. Therefore as planned by the top leaders, the Dalai Lama escaped Tibet from his winter palace, Potala, to India, on the 17th March 1959 along with a few of his body guards. He was able to enter India only on March 31, 1959 near Tawang in Assam. The departure of Dalai Lama from Tibet made the Chinese still more angry and then followed many of their violent retaliations in which several military personnel and civilians alike were slaughtered. This ultimately lead to the fleeing of Tibetans both lay and the ecclesiastic, as refugees to India, on a large scale.

Tibetans, as Buddhists and as belonging to a single religious race, believe that their gods save them against all type of evils. Now, as refugees, they think that owing to their evil deeds and the working of the bad spirits, they lost their motherland and freedom. A few refugees think that it is only by doing good deeds that they can earn merit in life and thus once again please the gods and get their land back. However, other refugees feel that all this has happened because of their weakness. The Tibetan army of 8,500 rifles, 50 pieces of artillery, 250 mortars and 200 machine guns did not stand against the huge and powerful Chinese army. Now they think that, only way open to them is to make China realise her fault and compel her to vacate Tibet.

About the conditions prevailing in Tibet in the year 1959 H.H. the Dalai Lama (1962:221-223) himself says as follows: "Ten thousands of our people have been killed, not only in military actions, but individually and deliberately. They have been killed without trial on the suspicion of opposing communism, or of hoarding money or simply because of their position or for no reason at all. Mainly they were killed because they did not renounce their religion. They have not only been shot, but beaten to death, crucified, burnt alive, drowned, vivisected, starved, strangled, hanged, scalded and beheaded. They were killed in the public places and the fellow villagers, friends and neighbours were made to watch the terrible massacre. Many men and women have been slowly killed, and even children were forced to shoot their parents". He says further "the Chinese called the Lamas unproductive and lived on the money of the common people. Many lamas were tortured to death by harnessing them to ploughs, riding them like horses and many other methods too evil to mention. Chinese taunted them with religion, calling on them to perform miracles to save themselves from the pain. Many Tibetan men and women and the children were taken to unknown destinations in interior China to work as forced labourers and many have committed suicide in despair, and misery. Many villages were attacked by machine guns where a number of men, women and children were killed. Men and women were also sterilized. The Chinese have also destroyed hundreds of monasteries, either by physically wrecking them, or by killing the lamas and sending the monks to labour camps, ordering monks under pain of death to break off their vows of celibacy."

H.H. the Dalai Lama (Ibid:223-224) gave three main reasons for the Chinese attack on Tibet. First Tibet had a vast space with sparse population. Hence the Chinese intended to use Tibet as an extra space to live. Secondly, since the Tibetans had no desire for wordly riches they did not exploit the rich resources of the land. Though the Chinese declared that the development of Tibet was their motive, their main desire was the enrichment of their country at the cost of Tibet. Thirdly the Chinese intended to dominate Asia and the conquest of Tibet was a first step in this regard.

However the history of Tibet makes it clear that Tibet was an independent country. History also shows that the Tibetans took to arms many times against China and they had successfully pushed them back. Whenever the Chinese became strong they attacked Tibet, but Tibet had never been a part of China. Unfortunately Tibet remained isolated and so failed to impress the outside world about its independent existence.

At a critical time like this with the Communist China taking over complete administrative control of Tibet, what the Indian Government could do was to accept the Tibetans as refugees, on humanitarian grounds. The Executive Committee of the ruling Indian National Congress Party had put the following in support of the government's policy towards the Tibetans:

"The recent event in Tibet have evoked much concern and sympathy among large number of people in India. This is natural because of neighbourly relations and as many places in Tibet have from time immemorial have been a part of the religious and cultural consciousness of the Indian people. Any happening there which leads to the suffering of the people of Tibet is, therefore, a matter of sorrow for people in India. The Committee reaffirms the basic policy of India which is one of the friendly relations with all countries, non alignment with any military grouping ..no interference in the internal affairs of these countries .... The Committee is anxious that there should be friendly relations with China and earnestly hope that peaceful conditions will soon be established in Tibet ......" (loc.cit. Dastur 1964:64).

Consequently about 80,000 Tibetans came to India Nepal and Bhutan as refugees in 1959 and ever since the coming of refugees is continuing.

Tim McGirk (1994) reports the arrival of four young Buddhist nuns recently from Tibet who have just escaped to freedom after a seventeen-day terrifying trek across the Himalayas. He interviewed them at the Dalai Lama's headquarters at Dharmasala, the excerpts of which are as follows: "The nuns had two motives for braving the Himalayan trek: they wanted to practice their religion under the guidance of the Dalai Lama. The nuns also wanted to tell human rights groups about torture, the beatings and humiliations that they had suffered inside Chinese prisons." However, H.H. the Dalai Lama forsees a different picture as reported in his own words by Payal Singh(1993:9) that "I am certain that totalitarianism in China will go. There will be a more democratic atmosphere. Already more and more Chinese are showing sympathy and concern for the Tibetan nation, their culture and human rights, so if there is an opportunity for the Chinese to express their genuine feelings, I am sure this problem can be solved. I foresee a lot of changes - more freedom, greater human dignity.

When the Tibetan refugees started pouring into India after the arrival of H.H. the Dalai Lama to India in the year 1959, the Government of India appointed Mr. B.N. Nanda a senior officer of the External Affairs Ministry, on special duty, to look after them and report immediately about the arrangements to be made. First, temporary arrangements were made at Tezpur (Assam) for the stay of the refugees. Offers of assistance to refugees started pouring in from individuals and organizations both in India and abroad and these were being handled by the Central Tibetan Relief Committee, a non-official organization, led by Shri J.B. Kripalani, an Indian Socialist leader. To plan better rehabilitation projects, 21 leading social workers were brought into a committee with Mrs. Sucheta Kripalani, the General Secretary, Indian National Congress Party, at Tezpur, as its Chairman.

A committee of the non-official unit of the Central Committee for relief to Tibetan refugees, handed by Sri K.P. Agarwala, Chairman, Tezpur Municipality, was also formed. As the number of refugees swelled, immediate measures were taken to send them to Massourie (Assam), where huts were errected initially, for their stay. A well equipped hospital with nine wards, was also opened there to attend to the needs of the refugees. For all this, an amount of Rs.5.95 lakhs was provided by the Committee. Gradually the refugees were shifted to other areas and were provided with food and work. Their voluntary services were utilized in the construction of roads, schools, hospitals and the administration buildings which were used by Tibetans and they were paid for it. Initially Tibetan language schools were started in Darjeeling, Simla, Sikkim; to which the children from these refugee settlements were sent. The old (men and women) who could not bear the hardships of the transitory situation and could not work, were sent to Dalhousie where they were provided with accommodation in special camps, constructed by Government of India. Monks and lamas got shelter and food in Buxa, where a school of religious education to student monks, was also started by the Government of India. Dalai Lama also expressed his desire that young refugees should also get technical training in Indian institutes. Therefore such institutes were opened for Tibetans at Mount Abu by Indian Government.

H.H. the Dalai Lama expresses his feelings as reported by Payal Singh 1993:9) that "In fact for the last 35 years the government of India has been very helpful to the community, the Tibetan refugees here. It has helped not only with resettlement but with education too. Initially, all the expenses for the education of several thousand Tibetan Children were met by the government of India. When we became refugees, our main task was to ensure the preservation of Tibetan identity and culture and give a proper education to our younger generation. All this was achieved with the Indian government's help.

It was proposed that a batch of one thousand Tibetan students to be sent to other foreign countries like, Japan, Australia, Austria, Germany and the United States for technical trainings. Dalai Lama wished that after their arrival, these trained Tibetans may help other refugees. The World Veteran Federation and the All India Rehabilitation Centre, Bombay, helped the physically handicapped Tibetans by providing them free accommodation, food and the medical treatment.

Mr. Thubten Jigme Norbu, the brother of the Dalai Lama in his address to a Press Conference in West Germany, in August 1959, appealed to all nations of the free world to give a chance to Tibetan refugees to work and make a living in their countries. Further, he said, Tibetan Goverment in exile hoped that the young refugees could come to European countries to study and learn to work in modern enterprises. As a result, hundreds of refugees got scholarships and jobs in these countries.

According to the statistics of September 1976, a total of 36,319 Tibetans were settled in India, 3,000 in Bhutan and 4,500 in Nepal; bringing the total number of Tibetan refugees settled in the Indian sub-continent and the neighbouring kingdoms to 43,819. The remaining Tibetans have resettled themselves holding their own occupations like sweater business, carpet making, owning hotel, etc. These figures were released by Mr. W. Dorje, Director of the Council for Home Affairs of His Holiness the Dalai Lama. There are also about 1,850 Tibetans either settled or studying in Western countries. According to the information from the Information and Publicity Office of the Dalai Lama's, establishment in Dharamasala a total of 82, 546 Tibetans are in exile.

The 36,319 Tibetans rehabilitated in India are distributed in the following settlements: (1976):

| | |
|---|---|
| 1. Karnataka | i) Byalakoppe |
| | ii) Mundgod |
| | iii) Cauvery valley |
| | iv) Hunsur |
| | v) Kollegal |
| 2. Maharashtra | i) Bhandara |
| 3. Madhya Pradesh | i) Mainpet |
| 4. Orissa | i) Chandragiri |
| 5. Arunachal Pradesh | |
| | i) Tezu |
| | ii) Maiao |
| | iii) Bomdila |

| | |
|---|---|
| 6. Uttar Pradesh | i) Tondupling |
| | ii) Rajpur |
| | iii) Lingstang |
| | iv) Habarpur |
| 7. Himachal Pradesh | i) Dalhousie |
| | ii) Shimla |
| | iii) Tashijong |
| | iv) Bir |
| | v) Paonta |
| | vi) Sataon |
| | vii) Khumrao |
| 8. West Bengal | i) Darjeeling |
| | ii) Sonada |
| 9. Jammu and Kashmir | i) Ladakh-Leh. |

A few older people, labourers and also those who were in temporary settlements were awaiting resettlement till 1980. They were at Dharamsala, Darjeeling, Mandi, Kalimpong, Dehradun and Delhi camp. Several old people have been already rehabilitated at Kulu, Dalhousie and Mundgod. The Swiss Red Cross Society and later Swiss Aid to Tibetans, enabled to start sponsorships for old people who were over 60 years, at Rs. 30 per month. The amount was later increased to Rs. 50 per month. In 1971 600 elderly people aged above 50 years who were without families, and handicapped persons who were unable to work, were settled in Mundgod. United Nations High Commissioner for Refugees gave money to provide them housing facilities. Government of India paid Rs. 45 per month to them (1978). In addition the Catholic Relief Services, had made arrangements to give 13 Kg. of dry ration to each person per month. Provision was also made to supply them with milk powder and oil. This assistance from the Catholic Relief Services was stopped since 1978. This has caused some problems. However, the

Government of India is now studying several schemes to get a regular source for their maintenance. One among them is to give them a land grant of about 480 acres which coluld be cultivated by the Settlement Co-operative Society on their behalf, and their maintenance cost could be met out of it. Owing to scarcity of money needed for the purchase and reclamation of land the project is yet to be executed.

Many factors forced the Tibetans to flee from Tibet. Here are a few told by the informants:

1. Most of the Tibetans coming from the border districts of India, simply heard the news of attack of the Chinese army and fled to India.

2. A few families were directly attacked by the Chinese army since they were either officials or wealthy. Their property and even many members of their family were taken away.

3. The communist policies were not acceptable to the Tibetans since they tood away all their rights from social, ritual and economic life.

4. Many families were attacked during night with machine-guns killing most of them. So the remaining fled.

5. They feared that the Chinese might ask them to send their children to schools in China;

6. They had joined the Tibetan troops to fight against China and were lastly thrown out to India.

7. They were lamas in Tibet and Chinese removed them from the monastry and forced them to marry;

8. They had to attend day-to-day meetings conducted by the Chinese and had to answer many questions posed by Chinese at the point of bayonets.

9. The property of many of them was taken away and were forced to work as labourers in return to a very limited and bad food.

10. The people were forced to eat meat and flesh of the animals forbidden by the Tibetan custom.

11. A few Tibetans were also used by the Chinese to create rift between lords and serfs, children and parents, husbands and wives, etc., and even forced them to kill each other.

12. A few of those 'good medicine men', those who were proficient in some other fields like spirit controlling, etc. were caught, and killed by the Chinese to do away with the old system of beliefs.

13. A few of them were also forced to change their culture and social customs and to mingle with the Chinese men and women, sing and dance together with them and learn their habits and customs.

14. A few Tibetans had planned to fight against the Chinese, but they were caught and sentenced to death. Others knowing this fled away.

15. Many fled away because the monastry where there were monks or lamas was burnt along with the sacred idols and the books therein.

These are but a few reasons which led to their flight and there are many more reasons given in this connection. Most of them told that they feared another attack by the Chinese on their areas, and that they used to hear news of violence by the Chinese from the refugees coming from the interior parts of Tibet on their way towards the Indian borders. A few really have heartbreaking stories to tell as to how their spouses or children were taken away or killed by the Chinese or starved to death leading to their flight. The fear thus created made the Tibetans living in the border districts of India, to flee into India. Above all since their supreme head H.H. the Dalai Lama had fled to India, they too followed him. Their strong belief in their God and religious leader made them to think that they should stay wherever he stayed.

The arrival of Tibetan refugees in India thus began immediately after the entry of the Dalai Lama into India in the year 1959. Even today Tibetan refugees continue to arrive in India. A survey conducted among the Mundgod Tibetans shows that every year fresh refugees arrive in Mundgod Settlement. The table shows the year, of arrival of Mundgod Tibetan refugees in India.

It is observed that out of 1015 families in Mundgod settlement 531 (52.32%) migrated to India in the year 1959. This is followed by 207 (20.39%) families in 1960. Then onwards there is a constant entry of Tibetans every year. From 1969 onwards, as Table 1 shows, very few Tibetan refugees were able to end India. It is also found that 383 persons in the old and infirm peoples' home and 908 monks and lamas in the lama villages of Mundgod arrived in India during the year 1959 followed by 18 old and infirm persons, in 1960.

The Tibetan refugees in Mundgod Settlement belong to all the three provinces of Tibet. It is evident from Table 2 that 955 (94.10%) families come from U-Tsang Province, while 43 (4.23%) families come from Khamba Province and only 17 (1.67%) families come from Amdo Province. The U-Tsang Province being very close to Indian border the refugees from this province, especially those from the border districts, not only came in big number but also without much loss of life or property.

Even within the U-Tsang province the Chaprang district sent away more number [211 (20.79%) families] of refugees to India. This is followed by the Purong [135 (13.31%) families] and Ngarighar [126 (12.42%) families]. As a whole it is observed that the Mundgod Tibetans came to India from 62 districts/places of the U-Tsang province as shown in Table 2. Since the Amdo and Kham-ba provinces are nearer to the Chinese border and are also in the interior area of Tibet, many people could not come to India. Inspite of these 43 (4.238%) families in Mundgod camp came from Khamba province and 17 (1.67%) from the Amdo province.

These Tibetan refugees claimed to belong to all status groups; aristocrats, laymen, lamas, scholars, monks, government officials, merchants, soldiers, peasants, nomads and artisans. (42 (4.14%) families claim to belong to lord or the aristocratic group in Tibet and 973 (95.86%) families to commoner group. Among the commoners 607 (59.58%) families claimed to be peasants (*Shing-bã*); 320 (31.36%) nomads (*Drok-pa*); 26 (2.55%) traders (*tsong-bã*); 44 (4.31%) shepherds and peasants, *(Sama-drok-pã)*; 7 (0.78%)peasants and traders, one shepherd and trader and 10 (0.98%) families to other classes.

The Tibetan refugees faced many types of difficulties and

**Table 1: Chronological Order and Number of Tibetan Families of Mundgod Settlement Entering India**

| S.r No. | Year / Village No. | 1959 | 1960 | 1961 | 1962 | 1963 | 1964 | 1965 | 1966 | 1967 | 1968 | 1969 | 1970 | 1971 | 1972 | 1973 | 1974 | Before 1959 | Total | Total Population (1976) in the settlement | | |
|---|---|---|---|---|---|---|---|---|---|---|---|---|---|---|---|---|---|---|---|---|---|---|
| | | | | | | | | | | | | | | | | | | | | Males | Females | Total |
| 1. | I | 59 | 63 | 4 | - | - | 1 | 4 | 6 | - | 2 | 1 | - | - | - | - | - | - | 140 | 288 | 302 | 590 |
| 2. | II | 15 | 12 | - | 3 | 1 | - | 1 | 4 | 8 | 19 | 1 | - | - | 1 | - | - | 1 | 66 | 146 | 155 | 301 |
| 3. | III | 87 | 12 | 6 | 2 | 1 | 1 | 2 | 4 | 13 | 5 | 1 | - | - | - | - | 1 | 1 | 136 | 285 | 259 | 544 |
| 4. | IV | 101 | 20 | 5 | 2 | 4 | 2 | 26 | 28 | 17 | 2 | 1 | - | - | - | - | - | - | 208 | 426 | 437 | 863 |
| 5. | V | 32 | 13 | 2 | - | 1 | 3 | - | 1 | 3 | 3 | - | - | - | - | - | 1 | - | 59 | 161 | 139 | 300 |
| 6. | VI | 102 | 28 | 1 | - | 1 | - | - | - | - | - | - | - | - | - | - | - | - | 132 | 287 | 278 | 565 |
| 7. | VII | 83 | 23 | 13 | 9 | 9 | 2 | 1 | 2 | 5 | 2 | 5 | 1 | 1 | 1 | 4 | - | - | 161 | 320 | 311 | 631 |
| 8. | VIII | 28 | 29 | 3 | 11 | 4 | 1 | 1 | 1 | - | - | - | - | - | - | - | - | - | 78 | 167 | 170 | 337 |
| 9. | IX | 24 | 7 | - | 1 | 1 | - | - | - | 1 | - | 1 | - | - | - | - | - | - | 35 | 67 | 69 | 136 |
| | Total | 531 | 207 | 34 | 28 | 22 | 10 | 35 | 46 | 47 | 33 | 10 | 1 | 1 | 2 | 4 | 2 | 2 | 1015 | 2147 | 2120 | 4267 |
| | Percentage | 52.32 | 20.39 | 3.36 | 2.76 | 2.17 | 0.98 | 3.45 | 4.54 | 4.63 | 3.26 | 0.98 | 0.10 | 0.10 | 0.20 | 0.39 | 0.20 | 0.20 | 100.00 | | | |

**Table 2: Original Provinces and Places the Tibetan Families settled at Mundgod, belonged to.**

| Village Number | I | II | III | IV | V | VI | VII | VIII | IX | Total |
|---|---|---|---|---|---|---|---|---|---|---|
| **Province of Utsang: Place of their origin:** | | | | | | | | | | |
| Ngarighar | 2 | 4 | 1 | 13 | 1 | 16 | 60 | 27 | 2 | 126 |
| Ruthok | 6 | 7 | 3 | 12 | 1 | 3 | 14 | 8 | - | 53 |
| Lhasa | 10 | 4 | 16 | 2 | 8 | 6 | 10 | 3 | - | 59 |
| Chaprang | 27 | - | 1 | 76 | 18 | 34 | 11 | 25 | 19 | 211 |
| Pongrong | - | - | - | - | 1 | 1 | - | 1 | - | 3 |
| Nyanam | 1 | - | 2 | 1 | - | 1 | 1 | 3 | 2 | 11 |
| Surso | - | - | - | - | - | - | - | 1 | - | 1 |
| Zonga | - | - | 11 | - | 2 | 4 | 8 | 3 | 2 | 30 |
| Chala | - | - | 4 | 3 | - | - | - | 1 | - | 8 |
| Labharang | 1 | - | 1 | 1 | 2 | 5 | - | 1 | 1 | 12 |
| Gangze | - | - | - | - | - | - | - | 1 | - | 1 |
| Phari | - | 4 | 1 | 1 | 6 | 2 | 9 | 1 | 1 | 25 |
| Rungzung | - | - | - | 5 | - | 10 | - | - | 6 | 21 |
| Shegar | - | 3 | - | 2 | 3 | 1 | - | - | 1 | 10 |
| Shigatse | - | 1 | 3 | 1 | - | 1 | - | - | 1 | 7 |
| Purong | 72 | 17 | 9 | 28 | 2 | 3 | 4 | - | - | 135 |
| Shey | 1 | - | - | - | - | - | - | - | - | 1 |
| Worong | 6 | - | - | - | - | 1 | 1 | - | - | 8 |
| Mangal | 1 | - | - | - | - | - | - | - | - | 1 |
| Kyirong | 3 | 1 | 7 | - | 1 | 31 | 7 | - | - | 50 |
| Lethong | 1 | - | - | - | - | 1 | - | - | - | 2 |
| Shahi | 1 | - | 1 | - | - | - | - | - | - | 2 |
| Totali | 1 | - | - | - | - | - | - | - | - | 1 |

| Village Number | I | II | III | IV | V | VI | VII | VIII | IX | Total |
|---|---|---|---|---|---|---|---|---|---|---|
| Sakya | 1 | - | 2 | 4 | - | 1 | 3 | - | - | 11 |
| Gethong | 1 | - | 1 | 1 | - | - | - | - | - | 3 |
| Tsona | - | 5 | 18 | - | - | - | - | - | - | 23 |
| Namring | - | 3 | - | - | - | 1 | - | - | - | 4 |
| Ngalinghar | - | 3 | 1 | - | - | - | 3 | - | - | 7 |
| Gerung | - | 2 | - | - | - | - | - | - | - | 2 |
| Truchikang | - | 1 | - | - | - | - | 1 | - | - | 2 |
| Dawa | - | 4 | 4 | 30 | 1 | - | - | - | - | 39 |
| Tejen | - | 1 | - | - | - | - | - | - | - | 1 |
| Loseling | - | 1 | 1 | - | - | - | - | - | - | 2 |
| Lokha | - | - | 1 | 1 | 1 | - | 2 | - | - | 5 |
| Thargey | - | - | 1 | - | - | - | - | - | - | 1 |
| Kyitong |  | - | 3 | - | - | - | - | - | - | 3 |
| Changba | - | - | 1 | - | 2 | - | - | - | - | 3 |
| Njithok | - | - | 1 | - | - | - | - | - | - | 1 |
| Laghang | - | - | 1 | 2 | - | - | - | - | - | 3 |
| Hoga | - | - | 1 | - | 1 | - | - | - | - | 2 |
| Nakchuka | - | - | 1 | 4 | - | - | - | - | - | 5 |
| Rasur | - | - | 16 | 3 | - | - | 2 | - | - | 21 |
| Dhowa | - | - | 5 | 1 | - | 1 | 2 | - | - | 9 |
| Yamgtao | - | - | 3 | - | - | 3 | - | - | - | 6 |
| Pamda | - | - | 1 | - | - | - | - | - | - | 1 |
| Nyichu | - | - | - | - | 2 | - | - | - | - | 2 |
| Hunchy | - | - | - | 1 | - | - | - | - | - | 1 |
| Meta Kunga | - | - | - | 1 | - | - | - | - | - | 1 |
| Gartok | - | - | - | 2 | - | 1 | 2 | - | - | 5 |
| Chamdo | - | - | 1 | 1 | - | - | - | - | - | 2 |

| Village Number | I | II | III | IV | V | VI | VII | VIII | IX | Total |
|---|---|---|---|---|---|---|---|---|---|---|
| Tezeng | - | - | - | 2 | - | - | - | - | - | 2 |
| Kacha Theba | - | - | - | 1 | - | - | - | - | - | 1 |
| Horwa | - | - | - | 3 | - | - | - | - | - | 3 |
| Sera | - | - | - | 1 | - | - | - | - | - | 1 |
| Lokhachikap | - | - | - | - | - | 1 | - | - | - | 1 |
| Samgyer | - | - | - | - | - | - | 1 | - | - | 1 |
| Ngabhri | - | - | - | 1 | - | - | 1 | - | - | 2 |
| **Khamba or Dhothey (Province of Khamba)** | 4 | 5 | 7 | 2 | 6 | 3 | 13 | 3 | - | 43 |
| **Amdo or Dhomey (Province of Amdo)** | 1 | - | 5 | 3 | 1 | 1 | 6 | - | - | 17 |
| Total | 140 | 66 | 136 | 208 | 59 | 132 | 161 | 78 | 35 | 1015 |

problems in reaching India. First there were no proper roads and they had to pass through high mountains. Further there was always the danger of being attacked by the Chinese. Many of them managed to bring their entire families. Other families lost some or other members owing to capture or killings by the Chinese. Table 3 shows that out of the total of 1015 families at Mundgod, only 676 (66.54%) were able to come to India with all their family members, while 339(33.46%) lost some or other members in the flight. Their kin could not come to India because of several reasons such as: they were away from the family on trade on rearing the livestocks, a few were not told about the flight by the fleeing family members, children were taken away by the Chinese army and many members were taken away as forced labourers to mainland China. 287 (28.36%) families could not leave with all their family members to India and were left behind in Tibet. Among the families whose members were lost in the flight, 22 (2.15%) lost by death owing to the strains of the journey. 18 (1.78%) families were attacked and some of their members were taken away by the Chinese army. In case of 12 (1.17%) families their members were killed by the Chinese army.

A few refugees expressed that they were lucky in the sense they reached India safe and without encountering the Chinese army. These people were also able to bring their movable properties with them. They were first settled in Nepal, Bhutan, Sikkim and the Himalayan regions of India. They reared their cattle and were not interested in any other occupation. Situations like non-availability of the grass in the region, heavy snow fall, etc., forced them to sell away their livestocks for a very low price and live on that money. A few of them did not have any means to earn their livelihood and so they sold their gold and silver ornaments and clothes to feed themselves. About 70 (6.89%) families claim to have sold their belongings to buy food, 126 (12.42%) families sold their livestocks to the government of India at a fixed price, 34 (3.35%) families lost their livestocks owing to the deadly diseases, 16 (1.58%) kept the property for themselves, 690 (67.98%) families could not bring any property to India and 74 (7.29%) families told they owned no movable property in Tibet.

The Tibetans after crossing the Indian border were first settled in temporary camps. Here they were housed in tents, bamboo huts and buildings provided by the Central Relief Committee, New Delhi. They were later settled in transit camps in Simla, Ladakh, Gangtok, Dharmasala, Dalhousie, Pachamari, Pauri,

**Table 3: Fate of Tibetan Families who Fled to India**

| Sr.No. | Village Number | Incomplete Families* | | | | | Complete Families** | Grand Total |
|---|---|---|---|---|---|---|---|---|
| | | Left in Tibet | Died in Flight | Caught by Chinese Army | Killed by Chinese | Total | Reached safely | |
| 1. | I | 32 | 3 | 6 | 4 | 45 | 95 | 140 |
| 2. | II | 25 | - | - | 3 | 28 | 38 | 66 |
| 3. | III | 51 | 1 | 4 | 3 | 59 | 77 | 136 |
| 4. | IV | 37 | 3 | 2 | 2 | 44 | 164 | 208 |
| 5. | V | 26 | 4 | - | - | 30 | 29 | 59 |
| 6. | VI | 42 | 5 | 2 | - | 49 | 83 | 132 |
| 7. | VII | 55 | 4 | 2 | - | 61 | 100 | 161 |
| 8. | VIII | 14 | 2 | 2 | - | 18 | 60 | 78 |
| 9. | IX | 5 | - | - | - | 5 | 30 | 35 |
| | Total | 287 | 22 | 18 | 12 | 339 | 676 | 1015 |
| | Percentage | 28.36 | 2.15 | 1.78 | 1.17 | 33.46 | 66.54 | 100.00 |

* Families who lost their members during transit.

** Families who could reach India with all their members.

Bomdila, Mossourie, Dehradun, Kalimpong, Chamba, Biry, Delhi, Dushmati, Shiliguri, Naregenda, Trishaling, Jullundur, Chumurthy which are in the states of Himachal Pradesh, Uttar Pradesh, Punjab, Arunachal Pradesh, Assam, Madhya Pradesh, Sikkim, Rajasthan, Nagaland, etc. In these camps they were provided with free rations of food to start with and later with job opportunities to earn their livelihood. The Mundgod Tibetan refugees said they had a very critical time at the transit camps since there was scarcity of space and daily needs.

While in transit situation the Tibetans took up different occupations which were provided by the Indian Government. Others managed self employments, namely running hotels, sweater business, etc. Still others were able to earn a living using their skills, namely, painting, sculpturing, carpentry, weaving carpets, etc. Most of the Mundgod Tibetans, 658 families (64.84%), were employed as labourers in road construction at extrteme north of the Himalayan regions. They admitted that construction of roads in mountain regions was a tiresome and a dangerous job. Though they were not used to it, they were required to work with the help of the explosives to loosen the mountain rocks. In the course of this a few of them died. Owing to warm weather in the area, they could not live well and a few more died. Therefore, the Indian Government took immediate measures to shift them to places in high mountains in summers and brought them down to low lands during winter to protect them against extreme weather changes. A few worked as domestic servants, teachers, part-time employees in various government and non-government organisations in the close vicinity. Others worked as construction labourers and porters and helped transporting materials needed by the Indian army stationed at high altitudes. Still others got employment in the factories in different cities of India. Refugees who were unable to work due to old age or illness, were given free supply of rations of wheat, oil and milk powder. A few of them even had to depend on alms and begged for food and a few reported that they were kept under custody of the security personnel for internal scrutiny reasons of the country.

Refugees who entered India were first kept in protected camps to know their validity since it was possible that Chinese might have trained and sent them to endanger the security of India. During this observation period they were isolated from the other Tibetans and Indians for a period of eight months to one year and in a few cases they were kept for 3-4 years and their activities keenly observed.

The economic condition of the refugees at the transit camps was moderately better. Out of the 1015 families in the settlement 606 (59.71%) agreed that their family economy was sound enough to have good life in the transit camp. A few of them were able to save some amount of money for their future. But 205 (20.2%) families who had many dependants - children and disabled members were not able to lead even a comfortable living, and maintained themselves by borrowing from others 48 (4.73%), cutting their extra expenditures [134 (13.0%)] and even eating less and begging for food [23 (2.27%)]. On the other hand, 183 (18.20%) families told they got sufficient help to maintain themselves, 415 (40.90%) families had sufficient ration, 8 (0.79%) families had their own business and earned their food from it, 159 (15.7%) families had both the ration and salary and it was sufficient to manage their living.

Apart from these there were also some problems faced by the young and infant Tibetans in the transit situation. To provide shelter and schooling arrangements were made in Dharamsala, Dalhousie, Darjeeling, Pachamari and Simla. To get this, they were separated from their families and were kept in better equipped residential schools. Besides many foreign agencies, and donors sponsored schooling of a few Tibetans in a number of private schools in India and abroad.

The refugees who were stationed in the transit camps from 1959 to 1966, were later shifted to rehabilitation settlements in different states, namely, Karnataka, Himachal Pradesh, Punjab, Orissa and Maharashtra. In Karnataka, there are four such settlements: (1) Byalakoppe -I Tibetan Refugee Rehabilitation Scheme (TRR) (1960) (2) Mundgod - II TRR Scheme (1966); (3) Cauvery Valley - III TRR Scheme (1971); and (4) Kollegal - IV TRR Scheme (1974).

Mundgod area was selected for rehabilitation for many reasons, such as the area was sparingly populated, had plenty of available forest land and the area was less developed. The taluka statistics show that the cultivable area can still be increased by five times if the forest area is brought under cultivation.

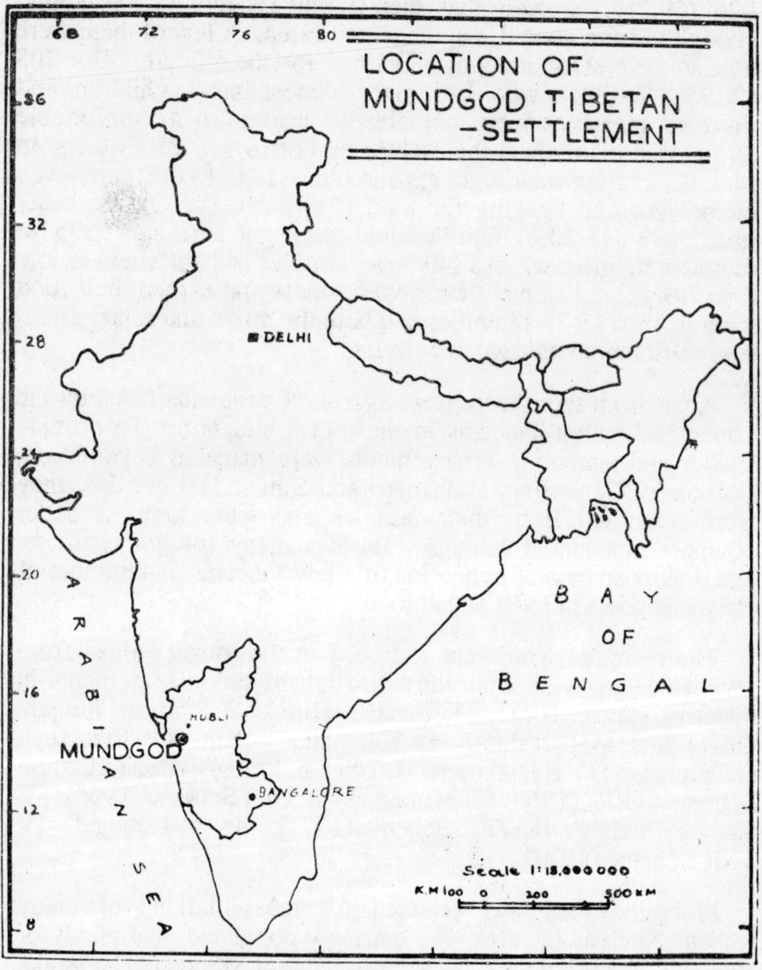
LOCATION OF
MUNDGOD TIBETAN
-SETTLEMENT
68
72
76
80
36
32
28
24
20
16
12
8
DELHI
HUBLI
MUNDGOD
BANGALORE
ARABIAN SEA
BAY
OF
BENGAL
Scale 1:15,000000
K.M 100 0 200 500 KM

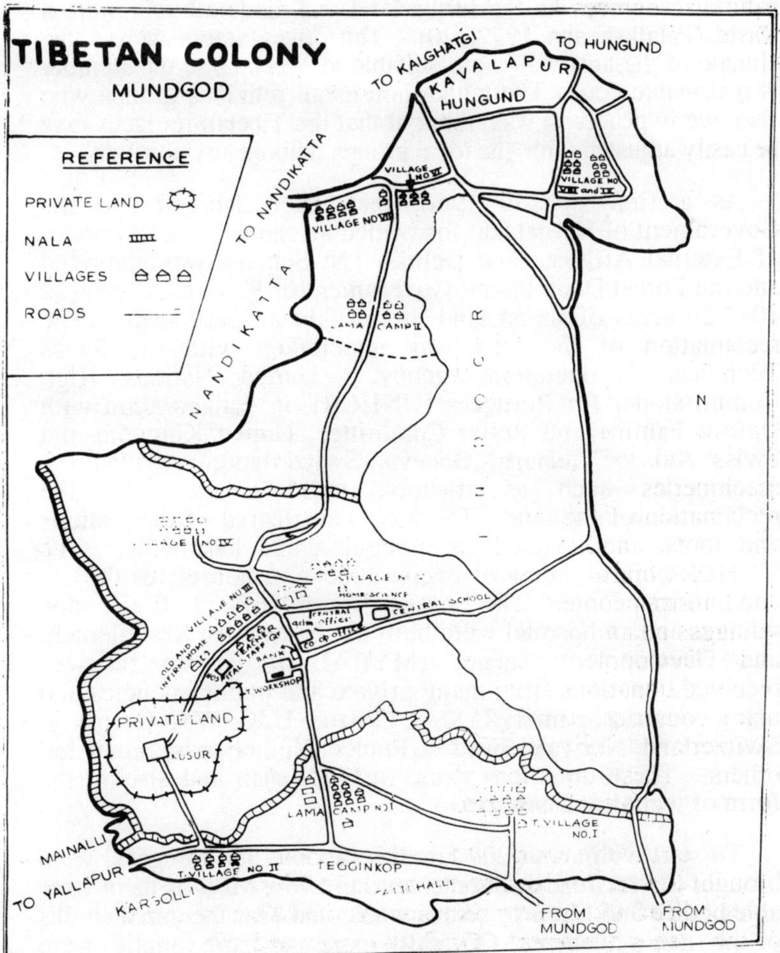
TIBETAN COLONY
MUNDGOD
REFERENCE
PRIVATE LAND
NALA
VILLAGES
ROADS
TO KALGHATGI
TO HUNGUND
KAVALAPUR
HUNGUND
TO NANDIKATTA
NANDIKATTA
VILLAGE NO VI
VILLAGE NO VIII and IX
VILLAGE NO VII
LAMA CAMP II
N
VILLAGE NO IV
HOME SCIENCE
CENTRAL SCHOOL
CENTRAL adm office
co-op office
OLD AND INFIRM HOME
VILLAGE NO III
TEACHER STAFF QT
BANK
HOSPITAL
T. WORKSHOP
PRIVATE LAND
KUSUR
LAMA CAMP NO I
T. VILLAGE NO. I
MAINALLI
TO YALLAPUR
T. VILLAGE NO II
TEGGINKOP
KARGOLLI
FROM MUNDGOD
FROM MUNDGOD

The initial reason for the establishment of the Tibetan colony in Mundgod was to develop the forest land and bring more land under cultivation. This type of settlement was urgently needed as natural resources like the fertile land and moderate rain were a waste (Palalkshappa 1977: 20). The other factors were - the climate of the area was more suitable to Tibetans as the summer is reasonable cool. The taluka houses all religious groups who also live in peace. It was thought that the Tibetan refugees may be easily adjusted with the local groups without any conflicts.

As a first step in 1966, the Chief Secretary to the Government of Karnataka, forwarded a scheme to the Ministry of External Affairs, New Delhi. The Scheme was approved and the Forest Department, Government of Karnataka released 4045.29 acres of forest land to the Tibetan Settlement. The reclamation of the land was undertaken with the Swiss Technical Co-operation agency. United Nations High Commissioner for Refugees (UNHCR), in collaboration with Oxford Famine and Relief Committee, United Kingdom and Swiss Aid to Tibetans, Geneva, Switzerland; provided the machineries such as tractors, bulldozers,etc., for the reclamation of the land. The area was cleared of tree stumps and roots, and levelled by ploughing and harrowing. The UNHCR built a colony of twelve blocks of houses for the old and infirm people. The houses for refugees in all the nine villages and an hospital were built by the Mysore Resettlement and Development Agency (MYRADA). Tibetan refugees received donations from many private and public agencies and many countries, namely U.S.A., Canada, U.K., West Germany, Switzerland, Norway, Sweden, France, Netherlands, Japan and others. These donations came in kind, cash and also in the form of technical assistances.

To start with about 200 families (about 1000 refugees) were brought to the Mundgod Settlement, in 1966. Most of them were able bodied and healthy persons who could bear the initial strains of the new settlement. Gradually more and more families were brought in batches and as of 1977 there were 1015 families (see table 4). In 1978 another thousand of them were brought to Mundgod and this means further sharing of facilities within the Settlement, which were already inadequate. To provide each of them with land a scheme to redistribute the cultivable land was undertaken. It was also proposed to irrigate their lands from a dam specially constructed and financed by the MYRADA and the

**Table 4: Chronological Order and Number of Tibetan Families Entering Mundgod Settlement**

| Sr.No. | Village Number | The Year in Which the Families arrived in Mundgod Settlement | | | | | | | | | | | | |
|---|---|---|---|---|---|---|---|---|---|---|---|---|---|---|
| | | 1966 | 1967 | 1968 | 1969 | 1970 | 1971 | 1972 | 1973 | 1974 | 1975 | 1976 | 1977 | Total |
| 1. | I | 110 | 7 | 2 | 4 | 5 | 2 | 1 | 2 | 3 | 3 | - | 1 | 140 |
| 2. | II | 1 | - | 3 | 52 | 3 | 1 | 2 | 2 | 1 | 1 | - | - | 66 |
| 3. | III | - | 23 | 88 | 7 | 3 | 7 | 1 | - | 4 | 3 | - | - | 136 |
| 4. | IV | 48 | 29 | 45 | 68 | 4 | 1 | 4 | 3 | 4 | 2 | - | - | 208 |
| 5. | V | 3 | 6 | 30 | 4 | 2 | 2 | 3 | - | 7 | 2 | - | - | 59 |
| 6. | VI | 2 | 38 | 49 | 10 | 7 | - | 3 | 3 | 1 | - | - | - | 132 |
| 7. | VII | - | 1 | 107 | 11 | 10 | 6 | 6 | 5 | 5 | 6 | 2 | 2 | 161 |
| 8. | VIII | 1 | - | 44 | 1 | 29 | - | 1 | 1 | 1 | - | - | - | 78 |
| 9. | IX | - | - | 6 | - | 27 | - | 1 | - | 1 | - | - | - | 35 |
| | Total | 184 | 104 | 374 | 157 | 90 | 19 | 22 | 16 | 27 | 17 | 2 | 3 | 1015 |
| | Percentage | 18.13 | 10.24 | 36.77 | 15.47 | 8.87 | 1.87 | 2.17 | 1.58 | 2.66 | 1.68 | 0.20 | 0.30 | 100.00 |

required skilled manpower and technical knowhow given by the Agriculture Department, Government of Karnataka.

To sum up, the Tibetans lost their homeland and became refugees owing to the porcess of sinonization by China at all levels of the Tibetan culture. As its history shows Tibet has never been a part of China and the Tibetans had struggled hard to preserve identity of their culture, institutions, religion, etc. But as it remained isolated from the rest of the world it could not impress the outside world about its independent existence. What the free India could do at this juncture was to share the suffering of the p0eople of Tibet by giving them refuge on humanitarian grounds. Many of these Tibetan families who arrived in India have lost their family members, kith and kin and are in broken form. Most of them also lost their belongings and property. They lived in transit camps in miserable conditions. Many relief agencies and individuals from India and abroad helped in rehabilitating the Tibetan refugees in resettlement camps in various states of India. The help which came both in cash and kind was handled properly by dedicated social workers and officials drawn from both State and Central governments. The rehabilitation officials did their best to make the stay of the Tibetan refugees as comfortable as possible. Now what is more important for the Tibetan refugees is to preserve their identity, traditional culture and religion in this land of refuge under the guidance of their temporal and spiritual head H.H. the Dalai Lama who is their only faith for the future.

# 3

# Land And People

The people of Tibet refer their country with a respectful term *Po.* In early Arabian works Tibet has been referred to as Tobbat, Tibat, Tibet and other variants. The word Tibet is derived from the two Tibetan words *Tõ Põ*, meaning upper land (Bell, 1928:1). Tibetans recognize Tibet into two main regions — upper region (*Theywpa*) and lower region (*Mehpa*). For outsiders Tibet is known as the 'Roof of the World' because of its great elevation which ranges from 9,000 to 29,000 feet. It is also known as the "Forbidden land" since no body went there because of the difficult terrain and its leaders had traditionally opposed the entry of any visitors except on rare occasions (Lowell 1962:606).

Tibet occupies an area of about 4,71,700 square miles of the plateaus and mountains, of Central Asia. Tibet roughly lies in between the 28th and 36th parallels of north latitude and 79th and 99th of east longitude. It is surrounded by mountain ranges on three sides. On the north are the Kuen Lun and Tang La ranges; on the west the massif of the Kara Koram, and Ladakh mountains; and on the south for about 1500 miles, the Himalayan ranges.

The Byang-thang plateau is bordered on the north by the Kunlum Mountains with the highest peak reaching 25,338 feet. North of the Kunlum range lies the Tsaidam basin averaging 9,000 feet and bordered in turn by the Astin Tagh and Nan Shan mountains. The western and the southern border of the plateau of Tibet is formed by the Himalayan mass that stretches from Nanga Parbat (26,600 feet) in the northwest to Namcha Barwa (25,446 feet) in the southeast.

Lowell (Ibid: 607) divides Tibet into three parts. In the south is the Tsang-Po valley (upper Brahmaputra). The river flows almost parallel to the Himalayan range for about 900 miles, at an elevation of 12,000 feet. This region is also called Central Tibet consisting of three chief towns – Lhasa, Shigatse and Gyang-tse. Secondly the area of north of the Tsang-Po valley extending from the Trans-Himalaya to the Kunlum range, is the Chang Tang, a vast arid and a windy plateau. Mean elevation of this area is about 15,000 feet. The third distinct area is Kham in eastern

Tibet; a land of parallel mountain chains running north and south. The region has elevation between 9,000 and 13,000 feet above sea level.

Based on the land types, Bell (1928:1) divides Tibet into four regions. *Tang* are the uncultivable plains and valleys lying mostly at high elevations; *Gang* are the ridges which are like those round Gyatse as well as the uncultivated plains in which these ridges enclose; *Drok* are the upland grazing grounds, the areas around Nag-chu-ka, north of Lhasa, is an example of dark land; *Rong* areas are the valley regions.

The vast Tibetan plateau gives birth to seven major rivers of Tibet. The Indus in far-western Tibet, cuts its path through the Kara Koram mountains and flows through Pakistan to the Arabian sea. The Brahmaputra rises near the Indus, but runs east through the heart of Tibet, then turns south through Himalayan gorges, and continues through Assam and Bangladesh to the Bay of Bengal. The Salween rises in eastern Tibet and the Iravaddy rises in northern Burma. Yangtse Kiang and the Mekong, flow through eastern Tibet from its sources in Tsinghai where the Hwang Ho also originates. "The mountain barriers and the river gorges that provide the least difficult approach to Tibet; and there is no easy way out of the wide encirclement of mountains. Tibet, therefore, has never been a through route for migratory peoples, and the absence of easy communication facilities has tended to preserve not only the seclusion and conservatism, but also the independence and the national homogeneity of the Tibetans" (Richardson 1962:4).

Climate of Tibet is generally dry and receives around 18 inches of rain annually. The Himalayas act as a barrier to the monsoon (rain-bearing) winds from the south. Temperatures in the higher altitudes are low, but the lower valleys and the southeast are mild and pleasant. There occurs a greatest fluctuation in temperature and it varies during different periods of a day. Lhasa which lies at an elevation of 11,830 feet, has a maximum temperature of 45°F and a minimum of -18°F and sometimes comes down to -48°F. Generally climate of Tibet is cool, dry and pleasant without any dust in the atmosphere.

## Flora and Fauna

The highest elevated areas in Tibet - the Byangthang, does not receive any rain and so it is devoid of trees and larger forms of vegetation; except grass. However, the vegetation including larger plants is found in the river valleys and in the lower wetter regions of the south and the southeast. The various types of plants grown are poplars, junipers, spreading yews, pines, teak, oaks, birches, elms, bamboo, wild rose or other thorn trees. Few of the fruit bearing trees like peach, walnut, apple, appricot, banana are also found. Mushrooms, sweet potatoes, nettles, and certain edible roots, etc. are grown in the valley regions.

Animals found in the Tibetan forest are wild boar, wild goat, tiger, leopard, bear, langur, porcupine, jackal, wild buffallo. In the grass lands and dry bush areas, are found the brown bears, deer, wild and big horned sheep, musk deer, wild asses, wild yaks, foxes, wolves, rabbits, rats, etc. Certain fish like catfish and trout, frog, crab, tortoise are also found. The common domesticated animals are the yak, which is used as the transport animal; Zo, cow (*pachu*) and *dri* are the milk yielding animals; sheep and goat are wool yielding ones, horse as riding animal, etc.

Tibet is traditionally divided into three provinces - "*Chol-khã-gsum*" (*Chol-khã*, meaning provinces or the regions and *gsum* meaning three). The province of U-Tsang stretches from the border of Jammu and Kashmir to the town of Sog. The Khams or Dothey province consists of the territory between the Sog and the upper bend of the Huang Ho. The Amdo or Domey province reaches from the Huang Ho to Chorten Karpo in Kansu province. Tibetans have a belief that their best religion comes from U-Tsang, their best men from Khamba and their best horses from Amdo.

The mineral resources of Tibet are silver, gold, sulphur, copper, brass, pearl, aluminium, etc. Although the mineral resources were assumed to be of great importance they were never properly surveyed nor there has been any attempt to exploit them till recently. However, gold was mined rather haphazardly in Western Tibet and was produced by washing the sands of several rivers of the east. The Tibetan religious principles and the customs did not allow them to dig out gold.

The Tibetans who lived in such a physical location, and culture must be happy with their land in all respects. But with the advent of Communists and the 1959 revolt in Tibet disturbed the calm, and orderly society and many left their homeland and became refugees. They had cooler weather and customs and manners of their own. As such on becoming refugees they had to face considerable difficulties before they could adjust to the new environment.

Benyei (1960:69-70, 82-5) out of his own experience as a resettlement official, has postulated three stages in any rehabilitation work. They are; 're-settlement' — finding jobs and accommodation; re-establishment — the acquisition of more permanent accommodation, a more satisfying job, advanced technical or linguistic training, family reunion, and a reasonably satisfactory social life; and finally, the 'integration' – the stage following successful reestablishment when an immigrant becomes so identified with his new country that he decides to become naturalized (loc.cit. Charles Price 1969:200). Any resettlement programme, therefore, needs to take into consideration the ecological factors of the new home such as the nature of the land, climatic conditions, rainfall, vegetation, water resources, etc.

In settling the Tibetan refugees at Mundgod the above mentioned factors were taken into consideration. As the Tibetans entered Indian border they were housed in camps at the northern borders of the Himalayas. It was a problem for the Indian government to keep them in one place that too in a border area, and provide them with living facilities. To start with for a few years, though they were housed in transit camps in Himalayas, they were made to change their residence seasonally to places in Punjab, Uttar Pradesh, Arunachal Pradesh, Assam, etc., so that they can adjust well to the hot and cold climatic conditions. There was also a need for a permanent rehabilitation programme. The Government of India in co-operation with the State Governments, located areas which were comparatively cooler, and where adequate land and other resources were also available. Among the places selected in the Karnataka State, Mundgod is one which is about 548.79 metres above sea level and has a moderate temperature. The average annual rainfall is 1280 millimetres. The monsoon rains start in the second week of June and last till the end of October. Winter commences in November and lasts for about three months. The evenings are cool and the mornings shrouded by thick mist. The winter is followed by summer - from mid-February to May and during summer the temperature rises. Compared to the coastal areas in the State,

Mundgod remains much cooler throughout the year. Occasional showers in April and May bring down the temperature considerably, especially during nights.

Precaution and care was taken to select suitable places for the rehabilitation of the Tibetans. But it is noticed that the Tibetans at the Mundgod settlement are not happy with the summer months. They find it rather difficult to work in the hot Sun. Therefore, they choose to work during the evenings and early morning. But cultivation demands work round the clock and in all the seasons, thus Tibetans who cannot face the hot Sun are compelled to engage the local labourers to help them in their work and they do the supervising. Heat does not agree with them, so much so many of them get blisters during summer. Several of them naturally, therefore, recall the memories of the pleasant climate of their motherland, because the hot climate has made them suffer very often with endodermic and exodermic afflictions. However, they are gradually adjusting to the new climatic conditions though it is difficult and uncomfortable.

Regarding the type of soil over here - except a very few Tibetans who have received less fertile land at the low levels, others got fertile land which gives good yield. As this area was under thick forest and reclaimed very recently, the land has retained its fertility to the fullest extent and also gives better yield. Tibetans even opine that this land is much more fertile than the land in Tibet.

Suitable rains have helped the Tibetans here to take a good yield of crops. In their motherland rains are scanty and uncertain and many times it was difficult for the Tibetan farmer to grow even the required food crops. So they had to depend on the sources of irrigation such as rivers, water streams from snow melting (*Kongro-tsu*), natural fountains or springs (*tsu-mey*) and the wells (*tromba*), wherever it was possible.

The Tibetan resettlement villages are provided with bore wells, digging of which were financed by MYRADA, to provide drinking water. The water from bore wells is lifted to the overhead tanks, and the same is supplied through pipes laid down throughout the village. The water supply section, - a body working under the management of the Tibetan Co-operative Society, has appointed a person in each village to look after the water supply to the villagers. The Tibetans pay certain amount of money as the water charges, on the basis of number of individuals in the family. A few families have also taken private tap connections to their individual houses for which they pay little more and seperately. This payment is something unusual to them since water is a natural resource and say they have to 'pay for the God given water'. The Tibetans also feel that the water supplied here is contaminated and is responsible for several diseases. However, a few of them have realized that precautionary measures like - boiling the water, etc., can protect them against contamination.

## Flora

The Mundgod Settlement area comes under the Hilly (Malenad) region and receives adequate rain. This has helped the growth of a variety of trees, plants and shrubs. The valuable trees namely, sisum, teak, *honne, nandi*, etc., are grown in plenty. There are also a few soft wood trees like *devdari, boorala, maddale, gulamavu*, etc. The commercially valuable items are the sandal, teak, bamboo, etc. The fruit yielding trees are mango, guava and these are grown in plenty in the Tibetan settlement.

A few Tibetan households have kitchen gardens where they grow plantains, papaya, mango, etc. The vegetables like lady's finger, brinjals, beans, gourds, radish, onion, tomato, pumpkin, etc., are also commonly grown for domestic use. A few younger Tibetans have also taken interest in growing varieties of flowers like jasmine, sunflower, etc., in their kitchen gardens.

## Fauna

The forest in the Mundgod area is not rich enough now to provide shelter for wild animals like tiger, leopard and elephants. It was said the tigers are found only in the eastern part of Mundgod forests and they are also not easily spotted. Sambar, spotted deer, wolf, jackal, porcupine, wild boar, wild cats, black monkeys, etc., are common. The place is infested with poisonous as well as non-poisonous snakes. Cobra, pythons are commonly found. Tibetans are very much afraid of snakes because they never had them in Tibet. Birds commonly seen in the area are parrots, crows, blackbirds, cuckoos, sparrow, *ratna pakshi*, etc.

In Tibet the Tibetans raised livestocks such as yak, *dri*, *Zo*, *pachu* (cow), *ra* (goat), *lu* (sheep). They now rear livestocks like the cows, goats, buffaloes, bulls and bullocks (see Table 23 for details).

## Transport and Communication

Tibet is a mountainous country and transport and communication facilities were meagre. So much so it is said that contact between people from two adjacent districts was limited. However, merchants and nomads managed to travel and trade was maintained. The merchants visited places like Kalimpong in India, and they reached even Khamba province which is on the borders of mainland China. Mules, yaks, Zo, horses, etc. were used for transport. Except the difficult passages through the mountains, there were no good roads and the travel was beset with robbers and thieves. Hence the traders used to form caravans for safety. Tibetans never had the common communication facilities such as the newspapers, radio and so on. A few reports and bulletins which were old were available only at Lhasa city. With regards to communication, as reported by some Tibetans, there was only one wireless set in Lhasa, Modern vehicles and machinaries had no place in Tibet. The two cars in Tibet were owned by the H.H. the Dalai Lama and were used only in the city of Lhasa. Thus Tibet's whole transport system was based on the animals. This also lead to their cultural differentiation from region to region which can be seen in their customs, manners, food habits, rituals, folk life, etc., however, within the Tibetan Buddhist cultural umbrella. Life out of Tibet has now exposed the Tibetans to modern means of transport and communication, which have almost changed their life style.

Tibetan settlement under study is situated about eight Kms. to the west of Mundgod town. This includes eleven villages dispersed on either side of two adjoining roads, Mundgod to Yallapur and Mundgod to Kalghatgi, They are inter-connected by unmetalled roads and they are dusty in summer and muddy in rainy seasons. The Settlement has also its wider contacts with the Hubli city which is at a distance of 55 Kms. Though Mundgod is their main centre of trade, commerce and recreation, the Tibetans do visit other towns nearby which are at a distance of 13 to 58 Kilometers. They also visit distant places for selling woolen goods, which is one of the major source of family income. The Settlement is connected with Hubli on two sides. The residents of the villages one to five and the Lama village No. 1, are close to the state owned road and make use of the state transport buses plying on them. The residents of villages from six to nine and the Lama Village No.2, walk a few Kms. to take buses.

The Settlement has state transport facility from Mundgod which facilitate the Tibetans to go for marketing. Their most popular and prestigious mode of transportation is the bicycle which most of the Tibetan families including the Lamas, possess. In addition 113 families owned bullock carts, a few motor bicycles and a car owned by Tibetans which also serve as modes of transport. Apart from this the Tibetan Co-operative Society has two trucks and a jeep for the transport of men and materials in times of need. The Settlement hospital owns an ambulance van which transports patients to hospitals in towns and cities. Very often the Tibetans walk the distance from the Settlement to Mundgod with the loads of luggage and children. By this they save money and also get an opportunity to meet relations and friends; who are spread in different villages.

Comparatively easily available and quick transport facilities over here in India helped Tibetans to have more and frequent contacts outside. Often young men visit Hubli either to see a movie, or for shopping. The easily available and cheap transport facilities have made it possible even for the middle class people, to go on business, pleasure trips and on pilgrimage to distant places and they have become more mobile. Such movements were not possible in Tibet.

In terms of communication, almost all families own radio sets. They listen to Tibetan and Hindi music and news from distant places. A few have taken active interest in knowing the Indian and world politics. Tibetans also subscribe to magazines and news papers; which arrive from Mundgod, Hubli and Dharmasala. Those who can read only Tibetan language subscribe to weekly and fortnightly magazines like *Sheja* published in Tibetan language, by the office of the H.H. the Dalai Lama, Dharmasala, Those who can read English buy the magazines published by Indian and Tibetan publishers. A few educated ones are regular subscribers to popular Indian magazines and dailies. The Tibetans also get news papers and, magazines as gift from many foreign countries.

In terms of audio-visual facility the Tibetan Co-operative Society and the Department of Publicity, Government of

Karnataka arrange for the screening of films about different countries, their geographical features, plants and animals, lakes and seas, games, wars, present scientific advancements, industrial developments, new methods of agricultural practices namely the use of chemical fertilizers, improved seeds, machinaries and so on. All these have helped the traditional minded Tibetans to learn many things about other cultures, present scientific advancements, improved methods of agriculture, health, hygiene, sanitation and family welfare programmes. These have also served them as a means of recreation but and to know about many new things outside the Tibetan world.

## Postal System

No regular postal system was prevalent in Tibet. A postal service was arranged from the Indian borders to Lhasa and extended beyond that to the northern most part of Tibet passing through the district headquarters on the way. A post office (*Dhā-kāng*) was maintained in these district headquarters. Horses and recognized servants (*Dhāk-pā*) were used in transporting the postal bags. For every five miles a batch of such servants were stationed to lift the postal bags. The officers and the rich people sent letters through their own messengers; on horsebacks.

The Tibetans in the settlement have now access to the facility of the well established Indian postal system. A branch post office was specially opened in the Settlement in April 1975, with telegraphic and telephonic facilities. The other postal facilities made available are the Money Orders, National Savings Certificates, Foreign money exchanges, deliveries of parcels and savings deposits.

The postal establishment consists of one sub-postmaster, two postmen and one extra departmental mail carrier (EDMC) from the staff of the postal department. The post office caters to the needs of all the eleven Tibetan villages including a few Indian villages in the area. The postal delivery and clearance will be once in a day. Telegraphic and telephone facilities are available round the clock. The post-master receives quite a number of telegraphic messages in a day and Rs.40,000 to Rs.45,000 in the form of M.O. transactions in a month. It was found that not a single Tibetan had his fixed deposit or savings account in the post office.

## Electricity

The electrification of the villages has brought a few changes in the life of the Tibetans. In Tibet only the mustard oil lamps were used for the night hours. A few rich families used kerosene oil and petromaxes imported from India. Here, all the villages in the Settlement have electricity. The village leaders played an important role in bringing electricity to all the households in their villages. They collected the necessary amount from each family, to get the electrical line upto their villages and also to get connections to their homes from the main line. The villages also have street lights for which the residents pay. It is found that the Tibetans use electricity only for lighting purpose.

## Health and Medical Facilities

Mundgod Tibetan Resettlement Hospital (MTRH), was run by the Central Relief Committee (CRC) from the year 1966 to 19-12-1969 and was housed in a temporary building. The new and permanent hospital building which is in the Village No.III, was donated by MYRADA, and was occupied in 1970. Both the male and female wards have sixteen beds each and the maternity ward has two beds. There is an isolation ward for patients suffering from infectious diseases. The patients suffering from serious infectious diseases like tuberculosis, are accomadated in the 12th block of the old and inform camp, which is isolated from the main camp, but nearer to the hospital building. A separate twenty roomed ward for tuberculosis patients was also built, with separate rooms for each patient. The patients who are in very advance stage of tuberculosis are admitted here and provided with free treatment and food.

Separate residential quarters have also been provided to medical and para-medical staff of the hospital. The hospital is also equipped with an X-Ray machine donated by Central Relief Committee (CRC), Delhi. The staff of the hospital consists of a doctor, a female head nurse, a pharmacist, a mid-wife, a clerk, a typist, a laboratory technician, nine nursing aids, two social workers, an O.P.D. record keeper, an X-Ray assistant, a kitchen assistant, a peon, three sweepers and a driver. All these staff except the X-Ray technician and a female headnurse are Tibetans. A few of them were trained in Karnataka Medical College Hospital, Hubli and others in the settlement hospital itself.

Till recently this hospital was financed by MYRADA, Bangalore. Now the hospital is run with the help of donations from the charitable institutions and token collections from the patients. The hospital also receives donations and loans from overseas agencies namely the Norweigian Refugee Council, Canadian Aid to Tibetans, Swiss Aid to Tibetans, UKIKION, Switzerland, etc. It also receives money from individual donors from abroad. During 1975 the hospital received grants and loans from foreign agencies and also in the form of collections from the Tibetans in the Settlement, to the tune of Rs.3,25,361.93. It also received individual donations amounting to Rs.8,386.09. The administrative body of the hospital collects Rs.10.00 from each Tibetan (above the age of 8 years) per year. A nominal consultation and other fees are also collected from the indoor as well as outdoor patients.

The indoor patients are provided with free meals, medicines, nursing care, and bed. They are also provided with a cup of milk in the morning and afternoon. Lunch and dinner are provided free of cost, which consists of cooked rice and porridge. Patients suffering from tuberculosis are provided with eggs, milk, and meat in addition to normal diet.

The MTR Hospital undertakes treatment of all diseases. The difficult cases are referred to Karnatak Medical College Hospital, Hubli a State government run Institute. The Hospital has at its disposal an ambulance van donated by MYRADA, Bangalore; and a jeep donated by Central Relief Committee, Delhi. The hospital also has its branch in Village No.VI, to facilitate patients from Villages 6 to 9 and the Lama Village No.2, for their minor ailments. For the major treatments they come to the main hospital at the Village No.III. The doctor visits this branch hospital on every Wednesday and Saturday. A medical assistant will attend to the needs of patients on other days.

A few outside medical agencies visit the Settlement occasionally. The Mobile V.D. Clinic, Karwar, surveyed the colony in 1976, and conducted blood tests for all the men and women in the Settlement above the age of twelve years. They found about 15 positive cases and these were referred to the MTR Hospital for further treatment. The T.B. Unit of MYRADA, visits the Settlement once in two years. In the year 1975-76 it took X-Rays of all Tibetan refugees to detect the cases of T.B. and was able to identify 210 positive cases. Out of them 30 were open positive cases, i.e., cases of easy infection to others. The team recommended the T.B. patients to the MYRADA for free medical aid. According to the latest statistics available 70 patients out of the totally infected (210) were completely cured. The T.B. Centre, Karwar, provided patients with the medicines. Staff of Central Relief Committee (CRC), Delhi, visits the Settlement once in a year and gives B.C.G. injections. The worker from the Public Health Centre (PHC), Mundgod, also visits the Settlement fortnightly and helps to locate cases of malaria, small-pox, chickenpox, etc., and vaccinates children against these diseases.

Modern medicines are very well accepted by the Tibetans. Side by side the Tibetan type of magico-religious practices and the use of the traditional Tibetan medicines are still in practice. For all types of diseases they consult a monk medicineman, to know the disease, its cause and cure. Among them offering of worship to the family deity and fulfil the wishes of the bad spirits, are common to get the cure. It is found that after trying all these local medical treatments, the patients come to the doctors. The Tibetans believe that their traditional system of medicine is very effective in curing the diseases affecting the internal systems of the body. They also say the allopathic medicine bring immediate cure but this will not be permanent in several cases.

The experience of the doctors of the hospital is that Tibetan patients come for treatment after a tremendous delay, but expect immediate relief. Another problem with them is the recurrence of disease. Owing to lack of education regarding general health and hygiene, many of these diseases occur often. Further many of these diseases were not found in Tibet. Due to their exposure to new geographical, climatic and environmental conditions and not changing their traditional values of health and hygiene, habits, etc, in the new land have resulted in their suffering by many diseases. It is, therefore, suggested that the Tibetans be educated in the prevention of diseases more rather than their cure.

## Business Establishments

Tibetan Co-operative Society has provided the Tibetans with a hotel and a shop with necessary provisions, in Village No.III and another shop in Village No.VI. Apart from these there are also two grocery shops and three hotels owned by private individuals in Village No.III and there is one shop each in Village Nos.II, IV and VI. These serve the immediate needs of Tibetans who are weak and, old and live alone. Hotels also serve as places for gossip and recreation, for some. Men and women enjoy eating meals and snacks both vegetarian and non-vegetarian, prepared in Tibetan style and taste. The Tibetan Co- operative Society also runs four flour mills in different villages. In addition there is a flour mill and a huller privately owned by a Tibetan. All these cater to the needs of the Tibetans in the Settlement. For other facilities the Tibetans go to the neighbouring Indian villages or the nearby towns.

## Education and Educational Facilities

Though Tibet lacked adequate educational facilities and formal education was not widely spread, it is noticed that among the Tibetans the ability to read and write is fairly widespread. The children of noble family used to learn to read so that they could spend their leisure reading Tibetan history, the lives of holymen and so on. Many of them joined the official schools to become the officials in the secular as well as ecclesiastical orders. "The monks in the monasteries had more intensive course of education beginning with years of memorizing religious books and moral percepts and progressing to the study of philosophy, logic and debating - all, of course, within the limits of the religious canon" (Richardson 1962:14). Further, Richardson writes that in Tibet a landlord used to set up a school for his own children; and the children of his servants, village headman and substantial peasants in the neighbourhood, also learnt there. This education gave them sufficient knowledge, to enable them to keep rough accounts, write letters, and read the sacred books.

A Lama is consulted for knowing the future of a child and also for finding an auspicious day, for sending a child to school. Dawa Norbu (1974:118-119) describes the days of his childhood in school as follows.

"When the long awaited Monday (the auspicious day chosen to send him to school which also happens to be his birth day) dawned, he was scrubbed, and dried before the fire, his face and hair liberally oiled; was taken then to a temple of Manjusri, the God of Knowledge. He prostrated before the God three times praying silently to 'Strike open the eye of wisdom with your dagger'. A few presents and a *Kha-dar* were given to the teacher. There were no fixed fees: the amount depended entirely on the means and generosity of the parents. Nobody went to a teacher unless he had specific use for education, i.e., aristocrats took education to inherit their father's places; teachers, others to help in their business matters, etc., and the monks were to read only the printed forms and were not allowed to learn the second form, i.e., hand writing."

After coming to India as refugees, the Tibetan children had problem with their schooling. Therefore, the Government of India started schools for them in various centres in Dharamsala, Simla, Dehradun, Pachmari, Delhi, Dalhousie and Mount Abu. The children above five years and below ten years were taken to these schools. As a result today a few children are studying in schools and colleges of towns and cities mentioned above. A few families after coming to this Settlement, were also able to send their children, to these schools on their own, or through a sponsorship agency, since they think these schools are better and are also situated in cooler places.

The Total number of students staying in the schools away from the Settlement during 1978 was as follows:

| S.No. | Institution | Boys | Girls | Total |
|---|---|---|---|---|
| 1. | In Schools | 90 | 38 | 128 |
| 2. | In Colleges | 34 | 8 | 42 |
| 3. | Abroad for training | 3 | 5 | 8 |
| 4. | Nursing training (India) | - | 8 | 8 |
| | Total | 127 | 59 | 186 |

Education of most of these students was sponsored and financed by individuals and agencies - both from India and abroad.

Today, every Tibetan village in the camp has a nursery school and children between 2 and 5 years usually attend it.Their parents contribute a certain amount per month to maintain the school and to pay salary of the teachers. Free mid-day meal is given to the children using the ration donated by the CARE. This facility was later extended to the primary schools also

There are two Primary Schools and a Central School run by the Central Tibetan Schools Administration under the Ministry of Education, Government of India. Primary School No. 1 is situated near Lama Village No. 1 which is convenient for the children from Villages No. one to five. Primary School No. 2 is situated in Village No. six which is attended by children from Villages six to nine. Each primary school caters to the needs of about 150 students. Here the children are admitted at the age of 6 and are provided with education upto VIth Standard. After that they go to the Central School for Tibetans located in Village No. III where they get education upto Xth Standard. Initially the schools came directly under the administrative control of the Tibetan Co-operative Society and the funds for their maintenance till 1977-78 came from the World Children Welfare Fund. Later they are now taken over by the Central Tibetan Schools Administration, Ministry of Education, Government of India.

In the primary schools the children learn three languages - Tibetan, Hindi and English. They also learn elementary mathematics and religion. The school activity starts with prayers. The prayers recited are *Kyamtõ*–Buddha, his word and church; *Konchog-sum* - prayer for the three Gods; *Khankhey* - The prayer for the God of Intelligence; *Khanyemã* - the prayer for the previous lamas; *Drolmã* - prayer for the Chejen Drolma - the protective deity; *Shaptden* - prayer for long life of H.H. the Dalai Lama; *Tsemey Yõndhen* - Prayer for those who have died for the freedom of Tibet and her people; *Dashik Relna* - prayer for family deity; and the *Indian National Anthem*. When they eat their mid-day meal they offer food to god and also pray (*Tsõpha*).

The children are provided with free text books and other stationary articles. They are taught not only the school subjects including English and Hindi but also the Tibetan language, religion and culture, in the form of prayers, stories and biographies of great lamas. They are also made to partake in extra-curricular activities which includes learning of Tibetan and Indian dances and songs. A few dances such as *Tsona palmo* - prayer for H.H. the Dalai Lama, *Tsuney Sangbo* - prayer for good luck, *Tamak* - horse dance, *Pheley* - art of Tibetan clothing, *Drogley* - life patterns of nomads, *Shingley* - life of peasants in Tibet, etc. are commonly taught. The Indian dances accompany Hindi and Kannada songs. The subject matter of songs they learn include knowledge about the Tibetan land, geographical features like lakes, mountains, snow fall, flora and fauna, life of the people of various classes and groups, freedom of their country etc. All these help them to know about their land, home, traditions, values, customs and beliefs. They are also taught about Indian and Tibetan festivals and their importances. These have helped them not only to know about their own religion and culture, but also the Indian gods and festivals.

The children also arrange for group dances and songs from time to time, in a village centrally situated so that people from all the Tibetan villages in the Settlement can witness the programme. It is very interesting to see the children performing Tibetan dances in their traditional dresses. These programmes are well attended and the people look forward to see them again. These activities bring emotional attachment towards one another and their culture, which they fear to have lost and reminds them of their traditional land. A few teachers from the primary schools are of the opinion that a good number of parents do not give their full co-operation as they lack interest in formal education for various social and economic reasons, and thereby the progress is hindered.

The Central School for Tibetans takes care of further education of the children. This School was established on 22nd October, 1969 in Village No..III. Its staff consists of a Vice-Principal and 23 assistant teachers (1977-78). Here education is given from First to the Tenth Standard. After this the students go to colleges in places like Hubli, Dharwad and so on. A few of the meritorious students are sponsored by foreign agencies in their education.

The school curricula includes subjects like Mathematics, Geography, Science, Social Studies, Civics, Drawing, Tailoring and Dances. Languages like English, Tibetan and Hindi are taught. The students are also taught about Tibetan religion by a lama teacher of the school. This is more or less a class of moral lessons and religion. The lama teacher gives more importance to discipline, cleanliness, good character, and enlightens them on Tibetan religion, culture, etc.

The students from Ist standard to Xth are divided into four groups and are called as houses. These are named after the Tibetan kings, gods and goddesses such as Tissa House, Shiva House, Thisung House, Pema House, etc. Each house will have one elected leader. Each class also chooses its leader (*Churpyun*). The leaders of all these classes vote and select a General Secretary (*Gendhā*) of the student union. All these house leaders, class leaders and the general secretary of the school are responsible for maintaining discipline, and cleanliness in and around the school. Every Sunday the students meet in a place and discuss about cleanliness, discipline, progress of education, etc. They also arrange for sports and games like volley ball, foot ball, cricket, table tennis, ring, hockey, kabaddi, dumb bell, etc. The different houses are made to compete with all their seriousness and show progress in all respects both in curricular and extracurricular activities. The house which scores highest number of points is awarded a prize at the end of the year. This type of competitive activity brings group feelings, team spirit, etc., and helps them to develop a strong will to live well in a new land and environment.

Girls in this school are taught useful arts, namely, tailoring and embroidery in addition to usual caricula. The school is also equipped with ten sewing machines and materials needed for embroidery. The students are taught to stitch frocks, shorts, jubba, handkerchief, aprons, table cloth, pillow covers, blouse, etc. Some students, however, do not seem to be happy because the Indian craft teacher is unable to teach them Tibetan pattern of sewing and embroidery.

The students are also taught Indian as well as Tibetan dances and songs. Competitions are arranged on days like the 15th of August and, the 2nd October and the winners are given prizes. The students also take interest in debates in all the three languages - Hindi, English and Tibetan. A few of them can sing Kannada songs and also dance to their tunes. They also stage dramas of both mythological and historical themes in Hindi and Tibetan languages.

In the school there is the committee of parents and teachers. The Vice-Principal who is the secretary of the committee arranges for occasional meetings of the village leaders and teachers to discuss the matters pertaining to the problems, activities and progress of the school. In turn the village leaders are made to conduct meetings in their villages to make the people know the importance of education, and their respective duties regarding the same. Table-5 shows that out of the total population of 4267 only 467 (10.96%) were able to get Tibetan education. Presently the situation has changed. The Tibetan refugees have taken interest in sending their children for formal education not only to the local schools but also to schools in other cities and towns of India. Many of them are worried about their

**Table 5: Literacy According to Age and Sex (1977-78)**

| S.No. | Age Group | Sex | Children not attending School | Illiterate | Tibetan Education (informl) | Nursery | Primary | Secondary | Xth Std. | Technical | Medical/ Nursing | Total | Grand Total | Percentage |
|---|---|---|---|---|---|---|---|---|---|---|---|---|---|---|
| 1. | 0 - 5 | M | 293 | - | - | 64 | - | - | - | - | - | 357 | 715 | 16.74 |
| | | F | 279 | - | - | 79 | - | - | - | - | - | 358 | | |
| 2. | 6 - 10 | M | 34 | - | - | 81 | 132 | 2 | - | - | - | 249 | 471 | 11.12 |
| | | F | 35 | - | - | 81 | 104 | 2 | - | - | - | 222 | | |
| 3. | 11 - 18 | M | - | 42 | 26 | 2 | 123 | 58 | - | 1 | - | 252 | 531 | 12.54 |
| | | F | - | 58 | 1 | 3 | 145 | 72 | - | - | - | 279 | | |
| 4. | 19-26 | M | - | 36 | 14 | - | 19 | 76 | 9 | 9 | - | 163 | 422 | 9.89 |
| | | F | - | 93 | 10 | - | 32 | 110 | 3 | 6 | 5 | 259 | | |
| 5. | 27 - 34 | M | - | 100 | 52 | - | 4 | 35 | 5 | 7 | 2 | 205 | 440 | 10.30 |
| | | F | - | 188 | 15 | - | 7 | 21 | 1 | 1 | 2 | 235 | | |
| 6. | 35 - 42 | M | - | 170 | 103 | - | - | 2 | - | 3 | 3 | 281 | 536 | 12.46 |
| | | F | - | 240 | 9 | - | 2 | 2 | 1 | 1 | - | 255 | | |
| 7. | 43 - 50 | M | - | 174 | 101 | - | 1 | - | - | - | - | 276 | 476 | 11.13 |
| | | F | - | 191 | 9 | - | - | - | - | - | - | 200 | | |

| S.No. | Age Group | Sex | Children not attending School | Illiterate | Tibetan Education (informl) | Nursery | Primary | Secondary | Xth Std. | Technical | Medical/ Nursing | Total | Grand Total | Percentage |
|---|---|---|---|---|---|---|---|---|---|---|---|---|---|---|
| 8. | 51 - 58 | M | - | 136 | 66 | - | - | - | - | - | - | 202 | 361 | 8.45 |
| | | F | - | 153 | 6 | - | - | - | - | - | - | 159 | | |
| 9. | 59 - 66 | M | - | 82 | 39 | - | - | - | - | - | - | 121 | 227 | 5.31 |
| | | F | - | 103 | 3 | - | - | - | - | - | - | 106 | | |
| 10. | 67-74 | M | - | 22 | 9 | - | - | - | - | - | - | 31 | 73 | 1.71 |
| | | F | - | 39 | 3 | - | - | - | - | - | - | 42 | | |
| 11. | 75 and above | M | - | 9 | 1 | - | - | - | - | - | - | 10 | 15 | 0.35 |
| | | F | - | 5 | - | - | - | - | - | - | - | 5 | | |
| | Total | M | 327 | 771 | 411 | 147 | 279 | 173 | 14 | 20 | 5 | 2147 | 4267 | 100.00 |
| | | F | 314 | 1071 | 56 | 163 | 290 | 207 | 5 | 8 | 7 | 2120 | | |
| | Percentsge | M | 7.66 | 18.11 | 9.65 | 3.46 | 6.45 | 4.05 | 0.33 | 0.47 | 0.12 | 50.31 | 100.00 | |
| | | F | 7.36 | 25.09 | 1.31 | 3.80 | 6.80 | 4.86 | 0.12 | 0.19 | 0.16 | 49.69 | | |
| | Grand Total | | 641 | 1842 | 467 | 310 | 569 | 380 | 19 | 28 | 12 | 4267 | | |
| | Percentage | | 15.02 | 43.20 | 10.96 | 7.27 | 13.25 | 8.91 | 0.45 | 0.65 | 0.28 | 100.00 | 100.00 | |

future. A few of them are of the opinion now that their children should get modern education so that they can get employment and settle in urban centres. They feel their children so educated should work for the upliftment of the uneducated masses of their community and find a better way to struggle to achieve independence of Tibet. This attitude towards the modern education has also brought about a few changes in the traditional way of life of the people and many of them now have new aspirations and aims in life.

## Settlement Pattern

The different villages of the Mundgod Tibetan Settlement are scattered along the length of about 7 kilometers starting from the 4th kilometer from Mundgod side and end near Nandigatta, a village above 11 Kms. from Mundgod. As we go from Mundgod at the 4th Kilometer to the right, we come across Village No.1. Next to that on the same line we come to the lama village No.1. To the west at a distance of about 2 Kms. from the lama village, lies Village No. 3 where we can find the banks, post office, Co-Operative Society office, the Office of the Representative of the H.H. Dalai Lama, the Indian Administrative Offices, Central School, etc. The workshop owned by the Tibetan Co-operative Society, residential quarters for the teachers of the Central School for Tibetans, hospital and quarters for the medical staff are also located in this village.

The village houses also the settlement hospital and the camp for the old and the infirm. The twelve blocks of the camp each consisting of 28 rooms, can house 630 persons. Each room accommodates two persons. They may be husband and wife, brother and sister or friends. Each inmate is provided with Rs.45.00 per month by the Government of India to meet their food and clothing. They are also provided with 13 Kg. of dry ration per month, milk powder, oil, clothing, etc. donated by Catholic Relief Services, U.S.A. Each block has a kitchen and the inmates pool their ration and cook their food in common. They have a common prayer hall in the camp.

The old and infirm home is managed by a male member and two lady supervisors. They look after the payments to the inmates and also run the common mess by in turn collecting money from them. Care is taken to see that old people coming from one ethnic background are housed in a single block. Owing to their advanced age and weakness they need constant assistance from others. So they are helped by care takers. The able ones help in the kitchen and also in washing clothes. However it is found that they are not happy since their problems are not only of physical comfort but also mental as many of them have lost their family members, close kith and kins etc, during their flee from Tibet, lost their home land and now with none to share their happiness and sorrow of life. During the interviews with them the researcher found that many of them cried, shared their sorrow with him and the researcher had to comfort and console them. These people who really need the mental comfort and consolation, found so much warmth with the researcher because he could speak to them in Tibetan, their own language, which brought them so close, as if they are talking to a family member. Most of them are undernourished and suffer from diseases like leprosy, tuberculosis, paralysis, itches and so on. They also lack proper medical care. With the meagre pension they get it is not possible for them to lead a comfortable life.

Those old and infirm, who have children and other relatives living in the same settlement/village or away get some amount of money from them. A few of them save some money for their death rituals and utilize the rest for personal uses like purchase of clothes, utensils, materials for distribution at the monasteries to get merit (*ge-wa*). Those who did not relish the food supplied by the common kitchen, cooked something extra to supplement it.

The people from the old and infirm village also attend the rituals and worships conducted in different monasteries at the settlement, public meetings to pass their time. There is a small temple (*Gum-bã* ) and a *Cho-rten* near their village and they spend much of their time here.

The *Po-ta-la* the official place for the stay of H.H the Dalai Lama is also located in Village No.III. His Highness stays in this building whenever he visits the Settlement and during the other times it remains closed. A few rooms attached to the *Po-ta-la* are used whenever a distinguished guest visits the Settlement.

Every Tibetan village is provided with two important things - the community hall and a temple for the protective deity of the village — *Palden Lhamo* or the head lama of a sect. The community hall is built by the contributions of the residents. This hall serves as a meeting place for the villagers where they

(i) A Tibetan Village Settlement

(ii) Local Indian Labourers Working in a Tibetan Farm

(iii) Stock of Paddy and Maize in a Godown in the Tibetan Settlement

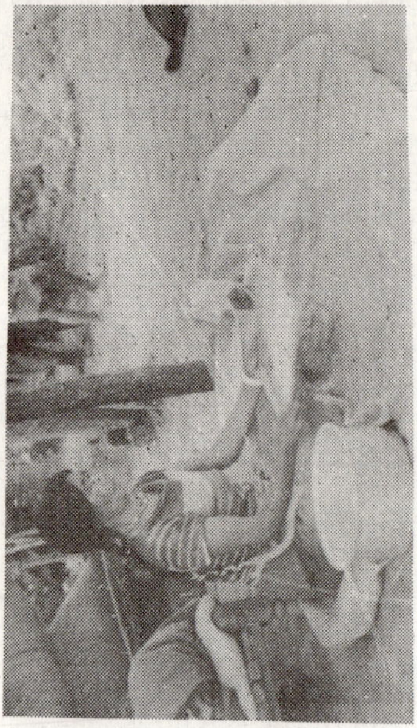

(iv) A Housewife Cleaning the food grain

meet to discuss the welfare matters concerning the village as a whole. They also discuss about the future plans and programmes to liberate their country and return to their mother land. Owing to the scarcity of accommodation this building is also used as the village nursery school.

The temple (*Gum-bã* ) in each village is looked upon as an abode of the patron deity of the village. The monks residing in the village look after its up-keep and offer the worship. Sometimes they stay here by turns, and attend to their duties. The villagers assemble in the village temple on all festival celebrations and on the four auspicious days in a month, i.e., the 8th, 10th, 15th and 25th day according to the Tibetan Calendar. They may come to perform rituals or simply to listen to the recitation of sacred texts by the monks or to meditate with a rosary and a prayer wheel. These village temples attract and bind them together with regard to religion, customs and traditions. On auspicious days religious minded Tibetans sit in the temple throughout the day from Sun-rise to Sun-set, chanting the holy or sacred syllables 'Om-Mani-Padme-Hum', and turn the prayer wheel. They also fast (*Nyungney*) on these days. The traditional minded observe fast so strict that they do not take even water.

Lama Village No.1 consists of monks of *Gan-Den* and *Nyingma-Pa* sects. Among the *Gan-Dens* there are again two sub-sects – *Shar-tse* and *Shang-tse.* They have separate monasteries, but a common hall to meditate. There are 16 blocks of quarters each having ten rooms. Each room is shared by two monks. The blocks are allotted on the basis of sects and sub-sects to which they belong. Care is taken to see that monks belonging to the same sect and sub-sect are put together.

Lama Village No.2 consists of monks belonging to sub-sect *Dre- Pung.* They are further sub-divided into two groups: *Loseling* and *Gomang.* There are monks who belong to *Saskya-pa* sect also. All of them have their separate monasteries. There are also 16 blocks of quarters each with 10 rooms built for monks. Each room is shared by two monks. Here also care is taken to see that monks belonging to same sect and sub-sect are housed together.

The two lama villages are so located that Lama Village No.1 is nearer to the Village Nos. I, and II and Lama Village No.2 is closer to the Villages Six and Nine. Resident of III, IV and V villages which are in the centre, are at liberty to visit any monastery either in Lama village No.I or II. It was observed that the people of all the villages assemble in the monasteries either in Lama Village No. 1 or 2, irrespective of their sects practised in Tibet. In Tibet devotees of a particular area had their own sect, family gods and goddesses, etc., and their allegiance was rigidly maintained. While at Tibet the different geographical areas had their own impact on the customs, culture, religious sects. Therefore the influence of one monastery or sect on the other was minimum. This was also due to lack of communication between them. Now this distinction is lost and people visit and partake in the rites and prayers arranged in any monastery of the Settlement.

A few Tibetans claim that the monasteries have good effect on the commoners, but wished the monasteries to be located far away from their dwellings. In Tibet they were far away on hills, and the monks were free from the worldly attachments. Commoners and especially women were not allowed to go near the monasterial area. But here the monasteries are very near to the commoner's camps and this they say disturb the religious life of monks.

The eleven villages including the lama villages of the Settlement, are built on elevated areas so that rain water drains away. Each village is made up of a cluster of houses built in rows. These houses are separated by wide open space in the middle. Each block of houses has its own fenced compound and this is used for keeping live-stocks, and for storing hay stocks, manure, fuel, etc. There are wide and straight roads in the Settlement. Owing to lack of repairs the village roads are too muddy during rainy season.

Each block is a twin house, and each house normally accommodates a family of five members. If the family has more members they get more number of rooms in the block. If there are 10 members in a family they get the entire block. In most of the cases owing to small size of families, a block is divided between two families and in a few cases even between three or four families. Of the 404 blocks in the Tibetan Settlement, 11 are occupied by individual families, and the remaining 393 blocks accommodate two or three and even four families each.

The details of the distribution of the 1015 families in the nine villages is shown in Table 6.

## Table 6: Villagewise Distribution of the Families and Population in the Settlement

| S.No. | Village No. | No. of twin quarterts | Total no. of families accommodated | Percentage | Population Male | Population Female | Total Population | Percentage |
|---|---|---|---|---|---|---|---|---|
| 1 | I | 52 | 140 | 13.79 | 288 | 302 | 590 | 13.83 |
| 2 | II | 33 | 66 | 6.50 | 146 | 155 | 301 | 7.06 |
| 3 | III | 52 | 136 | 13.39 | 285 | 259 | 544 | 12.75 |
| 4 | IV | 80 | 208 | 20.49 | 426 | 437 | 863 | 20.22 |
| 5 | V | 29 | 59 | 5.81 | 161 | 139 | 300 | 7.03 |
| 6 | VI | 54 | 132 | 13.00 | 287 | 278 | 565 | 13.24 |
| 7 | VII | 60 | 161 | 15.86 | 320 | 311 | 631 | 14.77 |
| 8 | VIII | 30 | 78 | 7.68 | 167 | 170 | 337 | 7.90 |
| 9 | IX | 14 | 35 | 3.44 | 67 | 69 | 136 | 3.19 |
| | Total | 404 | 1015 | 100.00 | 2147 | 2120 | 4267 | 100.00 |

The Tibetan refugees when they arrived in India were brought to the transit camps, where they were grouped under a leader and given permanent identification numbers. This helps identifying individual refugees. This had also made it convenient for the Indian administrators to have control over the number of refugees in the transit camps. When refugees were shifted to other places or rehabilitation camps they were sent in similar groups. The grouping was not based on ethnic or any such traditional grouping of the people. As a result people coming from different provinces (U-Tsang, Amdo and Khamba) and districts with different socio-cultural background, were brought under one group and leader. Later they were settled in resettlement villages in the same manner. As a result it is now seen a mixed type of population in one village. Table 7 shows the ethnic diversity and number of districts from which the refugees came and their resettlement in each village in the camp. Table 2 also shows that seventeen families coming from Amdo province are distributed in six villages and 43 families from Khamba province in eight villages.

The distribution of people belonging to a single ethnic origin in different villages or vice versa has brought some stress and strain in the life of the Tibetans. A few informants said that in the beginning they felt insecured to live next to people of other ethnic origin. Tibetans as a whole though belonging to a single racial group and face a common problem and have the same values of life, they differ much among themselves. Compared to the Indian neighbours they have, however, more attachments among themselves. This becomes stronger with persons coming from the same ethnic origin, irrespective of their stay in different villages and settlements.

**Table 7: District, Sub-districtwise Distribution of Tibetan Families in the Settlement**

| Sl.No | Village No. | Total No. of Families | No. of district, sub-districts the residents belonged to originally in Tibet |
|---|---|---|---|
| 1 | 2 | 3 | 4 |
| 1 | I | 140 | 18 |
| 2 | II | 66 | 17 |
| 3 | III | 136 | 35 |
| 4 | IV | 208 | 30 |
| 5 | V | 59 | 18 |

Contd.....

| Sl.No | Village No. | Total No. of Families | No. of district, sub-districts the residents belonged to originally in Tibet |
|---|---|---|---|
| 6 | VI | 132 | 24 |
| 7 | VII | 161 | 21 |
| 8 | VIII | 78 | 13 |
| 9 | IX | 35 | 9 |

While performing the social or ritual activities the Tibetans go searching for the people of their own district or eco-cultural zone. But they do not show the same attachment with persons of other ethnic origin even though they are their immediate neighbours. Since they are separated structurally from each other, the Tibetans seem to face stresses and strains in all walks of their life. Presently owing to the long duration of stay in this Settlement as neighbours, they have developed cordial relations and mutual understanding and also co-operate with one another in each others activities. The people belonging to different ethnic groups speak their own dialects. When they converse with people belonging to other ethnic groups they use the language of Central Tibet, which is commonly spoken by all the Tibetans. Even today the Tibetans love their dialects and would like to live with their own people sharing a common socio-cultural, religious and linguistic atmosphere, which however, has not been possible under the refugee situation.

## Settlement in relation to Social Order and ritual status

In Tibet, the Tibetans were organized into two main divisions: Pure and impure bones, based on their ritual status. There were strict customs enforcing the laws of purity and pollution between them. The low groups used to reside in separate localities meant for them; away from the locality of the high bones. In the present Settlement this type of distinction has not been maintained because while allotting the houses the authorities did not consider this point and allotted as and where they were available. This has created a mixed settlement of different social orders and hierarchy and has brought some stress and strain among a few traditional minded Tibetans belonging to high status group. When enquired as to how they find their low caste neighbours they said that they are not only ritually low, but also complained that the mere appearance of them brings ill-luck during the day. Majority of the Tibetans on the other hand said that they have accepted it as normal under refugee conditions. Owing to the longer duration of their stay with low caste people as neighbours, and also owing to the changed trends, the rules dividing the groups into high and low based on their socio-ritual status, are now loosening. Closer living, sharing common problems and mutual dependence among the members of a settlement, have now brought closer ties among them. Their living in an alien land has made them to come closer and have a sense of security, mutual help and confidence amongst themselves.

## Community feeling among refugees

The family with its significant social interaction, with others, can be identified as a unit of the community. The people in a community may also be affected by some factors like native place, racial features, etc. The people residing in a community interact regularly to be recognised as a social entity. The sentiment of community among the Tibetans who have been settled amidst the Indian community has become very strong. This is owing to the main difficulties they have among themselves namely the widely different racial features, and the isolation or the geographical barriers between them. The community as a whole sharing the common language and sub-culture, kinship, equal socio-economic, political and religious interactions, has brought closer affinities. Common ceremonies, gift exchange, community leadership, etc., have also brought their effects on the community sentiment. Tibetans though had different ethnic origins in Tibet, their stay nearer to each other here has now brought them closer, to have social interactions, playmates, and facilities of mutual help among themselves. This has rendered a rich social life away from traditional home. The common religious performances also have their effects on the sentiment of the community. Quarrels, thefts, might have disrupted their social life. But their society has regained much of its control to deal with such things.

## House structure, traditional and the present situation

Tibetans in Tibet had several modes of living namely nomadic, peasant, trading and outcastes. Nomads wandered from place to place in search of pastures for their livestocks and lived in tents. They changed their dwellings seasonally and as and when the grass exhausted. The other categories of people usually stayed in one place and lived in their well constructed houses. Waddell (1975:421-422) describes Tibetan houses as "buildings ranged round a central courtyard, the cattle being stalled underneath; together with a balcony and open verandah, are the human dwellings and cooking rooms. Windows are few and small to keep away the winter cold and wind, the interior is more or less tanned by the smoke due to the lack of chimneys". Dawa Norbu (1974:19) describes the structure of his house in the village of Tashigang, which was situated five miles outside the town of Sakya, as - "a simple and strongly built one. It had a broad stone base, about three feet high, and above this six feet of walling made of mud bricks cemented by cow-dung and straw. The main room had very few windows and a low chimney to obstruct cold air, and a massive door both for men and animals. The ceiling of the house made up of wood transported from the foot hills of the distant Himalayas and so was more expensive. It consisted of a large log across the house, supported by a central pillar. Across the log beams were laid a foot apart, and above the beams were slates". Further, regarding the furnitures, he (Ibid:20) says - "two oblong platforms made of mud, six inches thick, served as seats for the whole family during the day and as beds for his parents at night. A table was placed in the middle of the room. In the left hand corner of the room was the sooty stove made of stone and clay and about three feet square. Infront of the oven was a small container for dry fuel which also served as a seat. Behind it were two shelves filled with earthenware. The kitchen space was dominated by a huge copper vessel, holding about 20 gallons of water, brought from the river half a mile away. The other rooms consisted of a chapel furnished with images of the Buddha and Bodhisatvas, a store room with an underground granary, and a big bleak room, with a ceiling supported by pillars, where the children slept."

Sketch No.1 shows an exterior view of a middle and a high class Tibetan house and Sketch No.2 shows the arrangement of rooms and their use for different purposes inside a Tibetan house.

The traditional Tibetan houses were built usually on an area of 40' X 50' or 60' X 80' or even bigger than these in case of the big landlords. The house had a main gate on the longer side of the quarter. To the right side of this entrance was the longer space uncovered at top but built around a wall, where the livestocks were kept. To the left side was the ground floor, elevated to some height from the ground level to keep the flour

SKETCH NO. 1

**Exterior View of a Traditional Tibetan House**

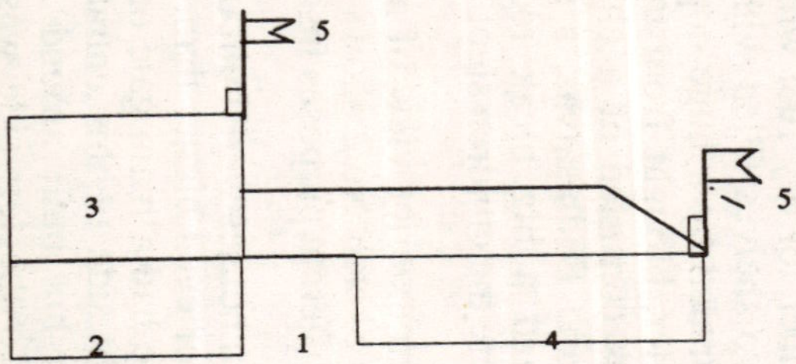


1. Main entrance

2. Ground Floor

3. First Floor

4. Space for keeping livestocks ( without ceiling)

SKETCH NO. 2

**The Arrangement of Rooms in a Traditional Tibetan House**

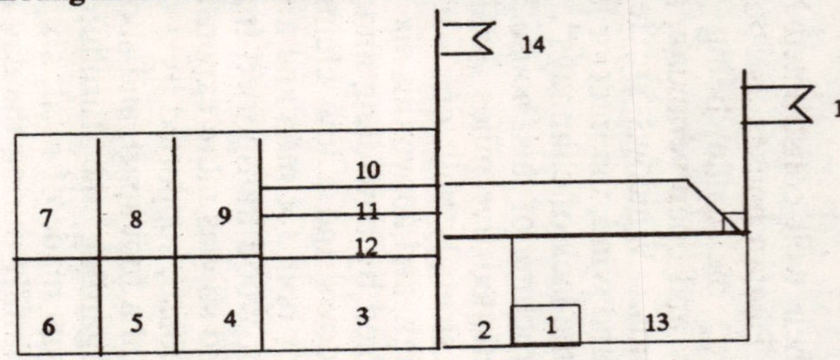


1. Entrance to the house.
2. Main Kitchen (*Chulā* )
3./4. Accessory Kitchen rooms (*Tap-sang* )
5. Store room for the food stuffs.
6. Godown for keeping food grains.
7. Place for keeping meat and mutton (*Shogāng* )
8. Prayer hall and gods' room (*Cho-gang* )
9. Room for arranging party and sleeping ( *Se-mjung* )
10./11. Rooms to be rented to traders (*Tsongāng* )
12. Sleeping rooms for Children
13. Space to keep the livestocks ( without ceiling )
14. Flags

away from moisture. In a few cases where the family owned shops, etc., doors were kept in such a way that they faced the road. A stair way from within leads to the upper floor. It had small windows to keep out the cold winter wind. Windows opened towards the front yard and also to south.

A house built by a richer Tibetan family will have more than one floor and many rooms used for different purposes. They also had smaller houses attached to the main house and used by the serfs attached to the family. The poorer section of the community owned smaller houses with 4 to 5 small rooms. The rooms had no adequate ventilation facility except small openings through which kitchen smoke passed through. This opening also served as a passage to let the sunlight in. The bigger houses also had a large verandah, which was covered by a thick sheet of cloth. This space was used by the family to take their meals, to sleep, and to sit and gossip.

Bell (1928:20) describes a nomad's tent as a structure made up of yak-hair and prepared by the nomad family itself. It is rectangular in shape, often twelve feet in length, but in some cases upto fifty feet. An aperture about two feet in width, along the middle of roof, lets the smoke out. The tent is supported by a horizontal pole supported by vertical poles at each end. The roof is stretched by cords fastened to the sides and corners, pass over short poles some distance from the tent, held by iron pegs, or by horns of animals. To keep off wind and snow a low wall of mud and stones or of dry dung is built round the tent.

As visualised by an informant, Sketch No. 3 shows the arrangement of poles and ropes of a Tibetan tent which is suported by eight poles, some to keep it erect and others to prevent it from folding. A tent is made up of heavy and thick woolen cloth. Ropes used for fixing a tent are made up of yak hair or skin and are eight in number. A tent is also supported by eight shorter ropes tied from the middle ends of the tent and fixed to pegs. The tent had an opening on the top of 2' X 4' to 3' X 5' depending upon the size of the tent. This cover was kept open to let out the smoke, and was closed with a flap during winter and rainy seasons. A tent was surrounded by stone or mud heap to prevent rain water and wind from entering inside. Size of a tent varied according to economic status of the owner; ranging from 40' X 60' or 20' X 40'. The poorer sections of the community had still smaller ones.

## Arrangement of materials in a tent

Tents used by Tibetan nomads provided a rectangular space inside (see Sketch No. 4). The interiormost place served as the space for the altar, and was separated from the front domestic space by a curtain. Right infront of the altar, to the other side of the curtain, was an elevated seat for the headman. On both sides in his front, were two rectangular and elevated structures used by family members and visitors for sitting. At night these were used for sleeping. The extra household things were also stored under them. Just at the entrance of the tent was the kitchen, closed by screens on all the sides and opened only towards the main entrance. On both sides of the kitchen were entrances to the tent which, on entry lead to the central area of the tent.

The Tibetans feel very proud of their tent. They were not only very big and served their purpose, but also very strong to withhold the occasional snowfall and heavy winds. Above all it was easy to erect and to dismantle and pack them during shifts.

In the Tibetan settlement under study all the refugee families are provided with stable buildings. Each block of house built in an area which measures 60' X 90', consists of five rooms meant for a family of ten members. In case of smaller families a house is shared by 2, 3 or even 4 families. There is no new allotment of houses made and so a few families whose size has increased, are facing problems. A few families have built extension rooms to solve this problem.

The houses given to Tibetans are in no way similar to traditional Tibetan houses either in shape or plan and arrangement of rooms. The plan of a present house is in Sketch No.5 and used for different purposes though they are planned for that.

All the houses are built with bricks and cement. The floor is elevated from the ground level to keep the house free from dampness. All the rooms are fitted with wide windows to facilitate adequate ventilation. These windows and doors are covered with thick curtains in the summer to check the hot weather entering inside the house. All are tiled houses and the roofing pattern helps the rain water to roll down easily.

In the open area around the home, the Tibetans have grown trees for shade, where during hot noons they rest and attend to

## SKETCH NO 3

**The arrangement of poles and ropes of a Tibetan tent.**

### View from side

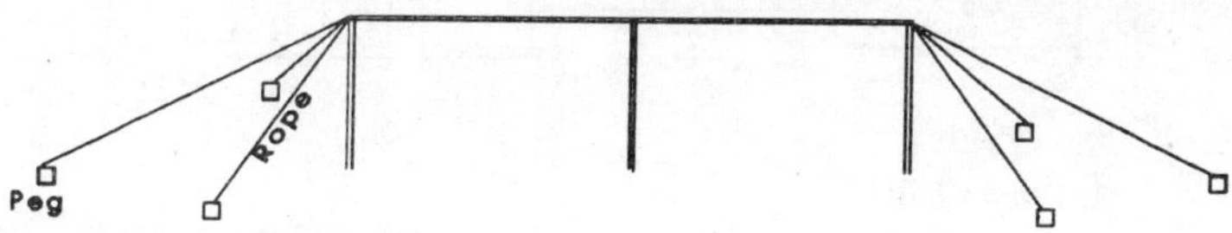


### View from Top

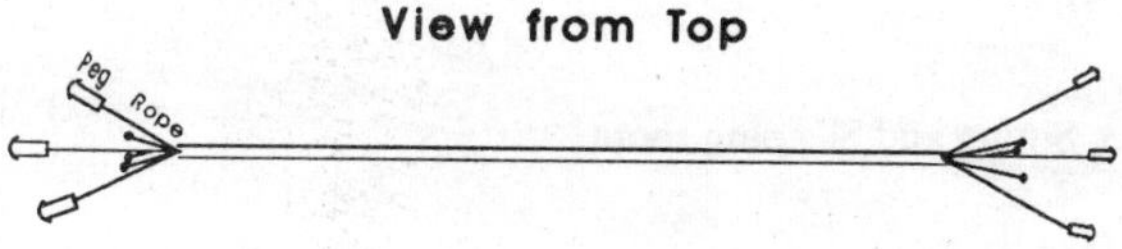


## SKETCH NO. 4

**The arrangement of domestic materials in a Tibetan tent**

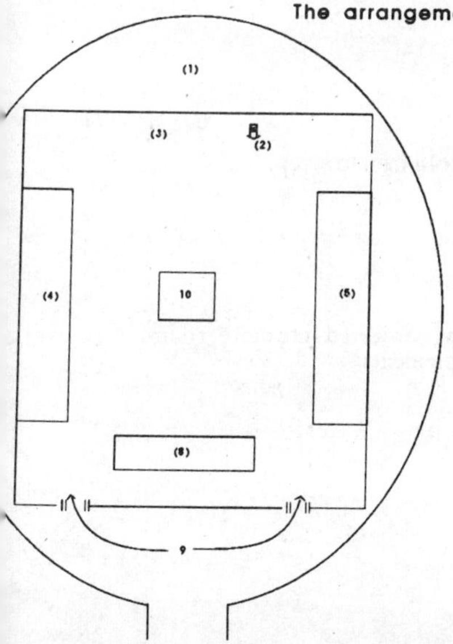


1. Alter
2. Screen seperating god's place and the domestic space.
3. A seat for head of the family.

4&5. Two feet elevated space for sitting as well as for sleeping for the family members.

6&7. Space for storing the household materials

8. Kitchen.
9. Entrance to the tent.
10. Lit firepots to maintain warmth in the tent.

SKETCH NO. 5

**Ground plan of a house in the Mundgod Settlement**

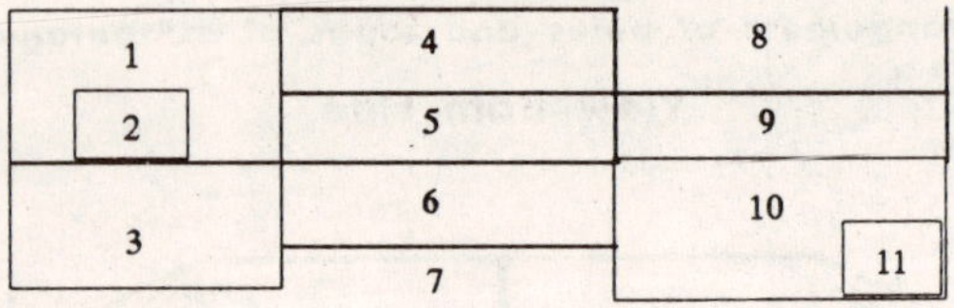


1. Prayer hall.

2. Altar for God.

3. Sitting and Sleeping room

4. Store room ( food grains )

5. Store room ( food stuffs)

6. Room for wed-couples or the old men to sleep.

7. & 8. Varandah

9 . Lavatory and bathrooms now converted into store rooms for fuel and agricultural implements.

10. Kitchen

11. Hearth.

some domestic duties. A few have also planted flowering plants, and fruit trees. At one corner of the compound a pit is dug where cowdung and other waste materials are disposed off.

The quarters given to Tibetans have bath rooms and lavatories. The lavatories are not used by the Tibetans since they are indoors. They preferred open area to answer their natural calls. Owing to this reason and because of lack of space in the house they have filled up the pan with earth and use the lavatory room to store household things and the rehabilitation authorities came to know about this very late. Learning from this incident when houses in village No.IX were built the lavatory rooms were planned away from the main house but within the compound. The Tibetans did not use them also and instead used them to store fuel needed by the family. Taking all these into consideration in Village No.III, common lavatory rooms were built outside the village area for sanitation and health purposes. These were used for some time and since they had no running water connections, and also Tibetans do not use water for cleaning their bottom, the place soon became very dirty. After a few days these lavatories were also not used. Now the open space around the village is again being used and this has created a problem in maintaining good hygienic conditions. Only five families in the Settlement claimed to be using the lavatory constructed near their houses. In Tibet only in the towns there were lavatories and the night soil was removed by *Khe-pa*, a low caste group. The others used open space for this purpose.

Tibetans in Tibet had separate rooms for various purposes; especially the rich who had two or three storied buildings with many rooms. The room for the family altar was at the top and in case of poor families one corner of a room was reserved for religious activities. The room with the altar was supposed to be kept ritually clean and so it was forbidden to enter or undertake polluting activities here. The girls in menstruation, ritually polluting objects such as foot wear, were not allowed there. Birth of a child polluted the entire house and so was to take place in a separate and small hut or tent erected near the main house. Now all these practices have lost their importance since they cannot afford to observe them owing to lack of space. The same room is used for sleeping even by the married couple. Those families who have two or more rooms can observe these purity and pollution rules and others have chosen to ignore. However, they put a curtain infront of the altar to separate it from the group engaged in polluting activity.

In Tibet the individual families invited lamas to perform domestic worships. On such occasions they worshiped in one room and took meals in another room, since it was forbidden to eat non-vegetarian food infront of the altar. Now, in the Settlement camp owing to lack of space, they are forced to perform worship and also eat their food in the same room. They perform, however, a short prayer(*Thōlōshā*), whisper three times the mantra - *Om Benzar Sato Hoom*, to the family deity begging for excuse for violating the rule.

In the traditional Tibetan home the kitchen formed the interiormost room and was also closed to the people of low class and impure bone. Over here these traditional practices are not maintained owing to lack of space. The entrance room of the house is used as the cooking place and all those who enter the house have to pass through it. The womenfolk feel ashamed to cook food in presence of outsiders who visit the family. On the other hand the food prepared is also rendered ritually impure and brings many ill effects on the consumers.

The families which do not have a bath room have constructed temporary structures near their houses to take bath. A few men take bath in open, infront of their house. Women also take bath in open at night. The Tibetans are not habituated to take bath daily and it is also not ritually required of them. In Tibet also, they took bath once in a month or two. In a few places like the districts of Phari, Tibetans went in groups to the nearby valleys such as *Laghang, Yishu*, with *chāng* and tea and enjoyed taking bath. It was a type of outing for them. In Mundgod also during summer months the Tibetans go in groups, to nearby streams to enjoy such a bath.

A traditional Tibetan house used to have its main door open to East or West. When it is not possible to build the house in that manner due to lack of space, etc., they next preferred the south. They know the Sun (*Nyima*) moves more towards south in winter and a house with doors and windows to the south receive more Sun rays and warmth to them. Over here they are facing problems with doors and windows which are too many and too wide and also open to untraditional directions. So the Tibetans keep most of these doors either permanently closed or cover them with heavy curtains. The curtaining of doors and windows is followed more as a custom than a necessity. While in Tibet heavy curtains were used to check the cold winds. On the contrary here the curtains are meant to check the entry of warm air into the house.

Tibetans clean their houses and white wash the walls every year, during the New Year Festival, in the month of February. The entire house and the household articles including the clothing, beddings, furniture, family altar, utensils of wood and metals, are all cleaned. In addition to this they do daily routine cleaning for ritual or hygienic purposes.

Traditional Tibetan houses had very little furniture. The common items were wooden cots used for sleeping as well as sitting. This scarcity was due to lack of wood, which was too costly to be imported from the low lands of Himalayas. Comparatively they have more furniture here. This was because when they came to this Settlement, it was surrounded by dense forest and so they got many items namely, cots, tables, chairs, made.

Another notable thing is wall decorations in Tibetan houses. Now we can see photos of family members, calendar pictures of gods and goddesses which decorate the walls. Similarly photos of Indian film actors and actresses also serve this purpose. When asked about this the older generation told that it is the work of the younger generation who are very much influenced by the Indian situation here. Except these there are no traditional or modern Tibetan art found on the walls or doors. Informants also told that even in Tibet there was no such custom to decorate the walls of homes except by a few ritual symbols and syllables written on the walls.

To sum up, though every precaution and care was taken to select a suitable place for the rehabilitation of the Tibetan refugees, but they find it difficult to adjust here in summer months. It also goes difficult to them to work on their agricultural fields in the hot sun. However, they are now slowly getting adjusted and rains for most of the year bring much relief and also good yield of crops. They are at present exposed to modern means of transport and communication facilities which have changed their life style. They have become more mobile who go on frequent business trips, pilgrimage or pleasure tours.

They have now easy access to modern communication facilities such as radio, television, news papers and have come to know the outside world, other cultures, scientific and technological advancements, etc.

The Tibetan refugees have now access to the postal facilities, electricity, modern health and family welfare programmes, modern medicines, etc. The magico-religious practices for curing ailments are being gradually replaced by modern medical facilities. However, owing to lack of education regarding general health and hygiene, the exposure to the new climatic conditions and not changing their traditional values about health and food habits, have resulted in their suffering by many diseases. It is therefore, essential, that Tibetans be educated, to help in the prevention of diseases. They have free access to modern education facilities in the Settlement. Many children have gone to educational institutions at distant places for higher education. Even many children have been sponsored by foreign agencies abroad. The schools not only provide them the formal education but also the knowledge of Tibetan language, religion and culture which help them to preserve their traditions, mythologies, folklores etc. The modern education has opened them to new aspirations and aims in life.

The settlement of mixed type though has brought some stresses and strains between the people of different ethnic origin, province, pure and impure bones etc., but now such distinctions are losing importance. Closer living with long association, sharing common problems and mutual dependence have brought closer ties among the ethnic groups of different provinces and have started understanding each other's culture, language, etc. However, the deeper contacts and inter-actions take place only with the people of the same province or origin. The houses in the Settlement are very much different from the traditional Tibetan houses in ground plan, arrangement of rooms, etc., and this has brought a few problems.

# 4

# Social Organization

Social organization of a society can be seen through the functioning of different institutions. Each institution is a make-up of social statuses and roles of individuals. These are again controlled and guided by values of that society. The Tibetan social organization is based on class system with its traditional economic, social and religious values.

The traditional Tibetan society is divided into two major classes - aristocrats and serfs. This division is based on the pattern of land holding, economic and political statuses. The landed property was shared by three institutions: the Church (*Gum-ba*) - lands granted to the lama dignitories; the state (*Ku-dra*) - the public properties, mainly assigned to different offices in the government and the family estates. All these had the attached serfs to work on them. In reality the serfs and their belongings together formed the estate. The family estates are further divided into: (1) official feudal estates (*Ge-ri-kh*) and private holdings of the nobility (*Jeo-rikh* or *Ger-Pa*); and (2) small percentage of land owned by commoners, subjects of the state, church or the nobility (Tsung-Lien Shen and Shen-Chi Liu, 1953:103). The landholding pattern therefore signified a person's status in the society.

According to Turnbull and Turnbull (1968:68) "A Tibetan noble is accorded respect because of the responsibility he shoulders and not because of his birth in the nobility. This is because any person can become a noble by entering Government service and acquiring an official position. Frequently it is the sons of these officials who enter service. This, however, is not always necessary. The nobility is not strictly a hereditory class. Children who enter Government service eventually may lose their noble status and return to the land as farmers". But usually it was not the case. The nobles who trace their descent in several ways continue to hold the status for ever. They may be the members of Dalai Lama's family and right from the 7th Dalai Lama (1708-57) the father and brothers of the Dalai Lama who were commoners were ennobled and given patrimony estates (*Yab-gzis*).

The next important group among nobles are *de-bon,* who trace their origin to early royal families such as Lha-rgya-ri and Rag-kha-shang. The early territorial rulers such as the Mdo-mkhar-ba, Rdo-ring, Bla-brang rnying-pa and Thon-pa families also come under this category. The third category *mi-drã*, are those who trace their origin to the ennobled ones by the Dalai Lama, for their services to the country. Lastly the *gyu-mã*, are considered as the common lords depending on the residual character of the ancestral property.

Of the three types of estates: Government, religious and private, the total tax from the lands except the land held by the monastery, went to the Government. The *Ger-pã* and the *Mi-Sɛr* who hold the land from the monastery paid tax to the monastery. In case of private estates, the nobles paid tax to the Government for the land they took from the Government and the serfs who in turn took land from them paid taxes to the nobles. A noble family maintained its claim to the estate as long as at least one male member in each generation served the Dalai Lama Government as a lay official. In the event of a nobleman having only daughters, the bridegroom of the eldest daughter adopted her family name and would thus serve the Government, thus keeping the estates for her family. So one need not, therefore, assume that the lineages of these noble families of Tibet are of a single continuous blood line (Turrell 1969:1109-1110). when such a heir was not available or he was too young to assume his duties, the family paid an exemption fee to the Government until the vacancy was filled (Tsung-Lien Shen and Shen-Chi Liu 1953:110). Thus noblemen could retain their nobility without much difficulty.

Nobility brought a high social, economic and political status in the society and so no one liked to part with it. However, they had heavy responsibilities and very little freedom. They were also always at the back and call of the Central Government when in session or not. For their services they received a vast area of landed property, attached with serfs, from the Central Government.

The nobility was most respected by their serfs and the common people. A noble was addressed in a respectful vocabulary, other than used among themselves. The noble and the serfs thus formed two hierarchical endogamous strata. They were hereditory for most part and were continued through a patrilineal descent.

The hereditory link between the lord and a serf occurred through a landed estate and if that estate changed hands (lords), the serf remained a part of the estate, coming under the authority of the new lord. As Goldstein (1971:522) says - "it was fundamental to the Tibetan system of society that serfs were linked primarily to an estate rather than to the families or institutions. The ties of loyalty and affection between the serfs and lord played an important role in the operation of the system". Serfs were divided into tax payer (*Khral-pa*) and small householder (*Dud- chung*). The latter were again divided into two groups - bound and unbound.

The village lords were under the control of the Central Government through the authority of the District Officer (*Dzong-pon*) and were called as *Rgyus-pa* and *Ger-pa*. They took land on lease basis (*pho-ma*) from Central Government and in turn gave to a number of *tre-ba* families, in the form of corporate family units. This was called *she-ga* for which the *tre-ba* were obliged to provide service and tax, to their master. "As a bound, and holding land from his master, the *tre-ba* was a hereditory post and the title holders were unable to leave it permanently at any cost. This was because they were subjected to heavy tax obligations to their lord in the form of cash, kind and labour. At the same time these families could not be evicted by their lords as long as the *tre-bas* fulfilled them with their specified obligations" (Goldstein, 1971:66). The taxes were paid by the corporate as a whole rather than on individual basis.

The second type of serfs, *dud-chung*, are of two types - bound and the unbound. The bound type held small plots of land under obligation from their lords on individual basis, which are non-hereditory. He could, however, increase his holding in the most productive years. Even then the lands could not be inherited but they could be transferred to the next generation by the permission of the noble. They had a very less tax obligation to their lords such as providing human labour. In case of *tre-ba* the family as a whole was under the obligation of the noble and performed duties towards the noble. Whereas under the *dud-chung* bondage the obligations and duties were on individual basis.

The unbound serfs were termed *mi-bo* (human lease) and were not bound to estates. They were free enough to go wherever they wanted and work for whomever they desired.

Even then they were linked through some obligations of giving small taxes in cash and kind to the leader. They worked their entire life helping the lords, rich people and the leaders, in trading, rearing the herds and livestocks and in agricultural operations. In return for these services the serfs received a piece of land and a house. A number of livestocks may also be given to them. Sometimes they were given additional rewards for their good services to the noble.

The unbound *dud-chung* was a free member and worked on human lease basis for any number of days in a place. He could shift his labour from one lord to the other according to his liking. He was like a wage labourer and got his wages in terms of cash and kind from his lord. Whenever the *dud-chung* worked for a nomad rearing livestocks, usually for one year, he received the new born ones of that year as his pay and the livestocks given to his care were returned to their owner safely.

The three major groups in the Tibetan society – *ku-dra, tre-ba* and *dud-chung* mutually depended upon one another for their food and service. The nobles held large landholdings and to enable them to continue as nobles the *tre-ba* systems came into existence. The *tre-ba* had large holdings and also fulfilled heavy obligation of taxes in the form of cash, goods and labour to their lords. To help the *tre-ba* groups the bound and unbound *dud-chung*, the lowest and the working groups came into existence. Owing to acute scarcity of labour, the lower and working groups came into existence securing food, shelter and protection from their next adjacent head.

The serfdom and the lord relationship was maintained through parallel descent, i.e., daughter serving the lord of the mother and the son the lord of the father. Thus the lord and the serf were interdependent on each other, where the needed labour was provided by the bound *dud-chung* in return to certain amount of land received from the lord. The serfs of unbounded type, had to pay very small amount of tax in terms of cash which varied from lord to lord in terms of sex, age and the serf's productivity. This structure of Tibetan society was formed on the basis of fulfilling one's livelihood in that society.

The Tibetans claim that their traditional system was much better, wherein they had no troubles in earning their livelihood. They were also happy regarding protection, food, shelter, law and order they received from their immediate superior group. Ritual and social obligations of each other were also fulfilled properly. In very rare cases the lord used to be very cruel and selfish, and demanded heavy taxes and the serfs were made to work like animals. When this happened the serfs ran away to other places. It was one of the duties of the local officials to see that the serfs were looked after well. The serfs never ran away from a lord. Whenever they did they neither got job nor security and also the law on their side without the lord. Further they were heavily punished if they were traced. On the other hand, run away serfs were never accepted by any leader or a noble of another village suspecting them to be thieves (*Ku-ma* ). Thus the attachment of a serf to a noble was strictly maintained.

The report of the Legal Inquiry Committee on Tibet appointed by the International Commission of Jurists (1966:114-116) has thrown some light on the lord and serf relation. According to the report, the serfs were to give gifts to lords every year, during marriages, festivals, etc. If the lords thought that it was small they rejected both the gifts and the serfs. The land provided by the lord to the serfs was insufficient for a large family. Sometimes the land was far away and unsuitable for cultivation. However, the serfs were allowed to work for other lords and supplement their income when there was no work on their lords' establishment. They had no chance to get education and also freedom of movement. Even to get marry, they were to take permission from their lord. Any violation resulted in torture and even a death penalty. Serfs were very often sold by their lords, and the pretty girls of the serfs were taken away by their lord. If the lord wished even he would separate the married serf couple and take away the serf's wife to be his concubine.[1] A bright serf boy liked by his father's lord, may be adopted by the latter and he could become his son and may get a chance to enter the monastery.

Contrary to these statements Shakab-pa (1966:76) writes that the laws prevalent in Tibet did not sanction any inhuman or cruel

---

1 Chang-Lu (1966:69-70) adds some more to it saying that serfs enjoyed no freedom. With the change of feudal lords or transfer of estates the serfs were also transferred. If they ran away, they were traced and fined heavily or punished cruelly. They were given very cruel and primitive type of punishment. Rifles, leather whips and leather palms were some of the instruments used for torture.

punishments, even to criminals. In 1898 a law was enacted with the sanction of the Thirteenth Dalai Lama to abolish capital punishment to criminals. Richardson (1962:77) also holds a similar opinion and says that in the more remote districts mutilation and torture were occasionally and illegally inflicted by district officials or by landlords who enjoyed magisterial powers over their peasants. However, none of the Tibetan informants from the settlement camp agreed with the capital punishments except in a very few cases. Or else the traditional Tibetan society would not have functioned properly without the co-operation between the lords and serfs.

Richardson (1962:27) says that the Tibetans accept their long established way of life and their social inequalities with active contentment. The sincerity of the Tibetan feeling was seen when recent foreign attempts to introduce change. An alien conception of social justice was strongly resisted, and it could be carried only through force. This does not mean that Tibetans were opposed to changes but they tended to progress in their own way, and they resisted attempts to impose changes on them from outside either by force or compulsion and intended to progress in their own way.

Charles Bell (1928:64) writes that when Tibet was in the feudal stage and nobles exercised enough power and influence with the priests, they shared the higher posts in the administration. They also exercised magisterial powers over their tenantry the extent of which varies from place to place. Punishments which were severe in nature were to be discussed with the Central Government in Lhasa and had to take permission before it was effected by the nobility or the district officers. At the same time people were free to write to Lhasa against any of the lords or district officers for any kind of injustice done to them.

In Tibet the Government policies as well as manners and customs of the people were powerfully influenced by the Buddhist ethic. All the lords and people of ranks were ruled by the Buddhist traditions and customs and its institutions of which the monastic order was the normal trustee and every family wished to dedicate at least one member to the church, and the sense of social participation among the people was very strong.

## The present situation

Now, at Mundgod Tibetan Settlement, there is no noble and

serf relationship and all are treated as equals. But to some extent the village authority and leadership, and ecclesiastic powers are with the 'lords'. It was also noticed at some instances where the 'lords' claiming original status and power here in the Settlement.[2] Here we can take note of two things. First the secular and the ecclesiastic seems to be two separate administrations under the authority of H.H. the Dalai Lama; they are mutually interconnected. They also need the recognition of each other for their functioning since the Tibetan Government is dualistic in nature. Secondly, it is observed that the distinction was made between the officialdom and the lay in the recognition ceremony of the abbot. Where the former held the priority while the latter were just called for a worship on the second day. This indicates that their recognition was also necessary. This naturally indicates that the lords or the people of officialdom here at the Settlement continue to hold the priority in governmental matters as in their traditional Tibetan society. However, common people also possess a democratic right to claim their role in governmental matters at present. In this way though the nobility has lost much of its significance in the present democratic Tibetan society, it tends to reappear and claims its traditional position in ritual and political aspects, and the commoners seems to accept the situation.

Forty-two families of this Settlement claim that they are 'lords' and the rest as commoners. The details are shown in Table 8.

**Table 8: The Mundgod Tibetan Families and their Social Status in Tibet**

| S.No. | Status / Village No. | Lord families | Commoner families | Total |
|---|---|---|---|---|
| 1 | I | 9 | 131 | 140 |
| 2 | II | 7 | 59 | 66 |
| 3 | III | 7 | 129 | 136 |

2 In one case, during the ceremony arranged to recognise a senior Abbot for the Shartse monastery (sub-sect of *Ge-lu-gpa*) who was appointed by H.H. the Dalai Lama, on the first day of the ritual it was observed, only the persons who held the official positions of all ranks and the appointed leaders of the nine villages and the members of the 'lords' families in the Settlement, were present. All of them garlanded the senior Abbot with the sacred scarf (Kha-dar) to show their respect and willingness to accept him as the highest official of the monastery. On the contrary the layman were invited to the monastery the next day, for a common worship.

| S.No. | Status / Village No. | Lord families | Commoner families | Total |
|---|---|---|---|---|
| 4 | IV | 5 | 203 | 208 |
| 5 | V | 2 | 57 | 59 |
| 6 | VI | 3 | 129 | 132 |
| 7 | VII | 7 | 154 | 161 |
| 8 | VIII | 1 | 77 | 78 |
| 9 | IX | 1 | 34 | 35 |
| | Total | 42 | 973 | 1015 |
| | Percentage | 4.14 | 95.86 | 100.00 |

Social hierarchy and class systems in Tibetan society are based on economic, social and the occupational factors enlightened by the ritual factors of Buddhism. The people on the ecclesiastic side are divided into two kinds - those who stand on the top level to the lay or secular people, the high born wealthy or learned ecclesiastics contrast with the improverished lower clergy, who are generally illiterate and burdened with all types of tasks. Alongwith them a small class of meditators (*yogins*) is marginally associated with these monks. There is no middle class in Tibetan society (Stein, 1972:92-93). Shakabpa (1974:374-375) says majority of Tibetans have the same ethnic origin, and have traditionally practised the same religion and spoke the same language. The population was divided on social and economic strata namely, the nomads (*brog-pa*), semi-nomads (*Sa-ma brog*), agriculturists (*zhing-pa*), forest dwellers (*rong-pa*) traders (*tshong-pa*), craftsmen (*lag-shes-pa*), government officials (*gzhung-zhabs*), monks (*graw-pa*), nuns (*a-ne*), and the outcastes (*ro-rgyab-pa*) who earned their living by begging and by disposing off corpses. Further he mentions that these were not the rigid groups like castes. However, nobles were clearly distinguished from peasantry.

## Hierarchy and Stratification

On the basis of socio-economic and ritual factors, we can classify the traditional Tibetan society as follows:

Division I: Priestly Class - The Lamas

(a) The high born wealthy or learned monks,
(b) The lower clergy-illiterate ones.

Division II: Nobility

(a) Descendents of early kings,

(b) Descendents of H.H. the Dalai Lamas' kin,
(c) Descendents of those who are ennobled for their services to the country.

Division III:

Descendents of yogins, meditators and nature controllers, or the descendents of the Senior Lama (*Ngak-pā*) in whose case marriage is legally allowed.

Division IV: Rich people -Lords and officials (*Jindā or Ge-ri-kh* and *Ger-pā*).

Division V: Common men (*Phā-lbā* or *Me-mong*)

1st Stage: (a) Peasant (*Shing-ba*)
(b) Nomad, (*Drok-pā*)
(c) Trader (*Chong-bā*)

2nd Stage: (a) Idol worker (mud), (*Jim-sõ--wã*)
(b) Stone cutter (*Do-sõ-wã*)
(c) Potter (*Zan-khem-bã*)
(d) Tailor (*Chem-sõ-wã* )

Division VI: Craftsmen

1st Stage: (a) Goldsmith (*ser-sõ-Che-mo-lã*)
(b) Silversmith (*Ngu-su Che-mo-lã*)

2nd Stage: (a) Coppersmith (*Sang-sõ-wã*)
(b) Blacksmith (*Ghar-Shãn*)

Division VII: Lower Castes

1st Stage: (a) Fisherman (*Nya-pã*)
(b) Hunter (*Ling-bã* )
(c) Ship builder (leather) ( *ko-bã* )

2nd Stage: (a) Descendents of ex-prisoners (*Ku-mã*)
(b) Beggar (*Pangõ/gyãwã*)

Division VIII: Outcastes.

(a) Butcher (*Shem-bã* )
(b) Corpse dispatcher (*Tam-den*).

Though the ecclesiastic group appears to be a separate institute from the lay, it cannot be separated from the secular group. It plays its dominant role on the secular side in the ritual aspect. As the religion is kept at the top of all aspects of the Tibetan life, the ecclesiastic group holds its privilages over all other subjects. The ritual group always has its members from the upper strata. The outcastes are never taken in the monastery because the impure bone cannot share a cup in drinking tea with a high class person as his touch of lips pollutes a cup and because they prepare tools for violence and kill animals which is against the philosophy of Buddhism. Therefore they are considered and treated as wicked according to the theological opinion. As Buddhism became the main religion and a basis for Tibetan society, the things considered to be bad in ritual aspect became bad in the social aspect also. Monks who belong to higher castes stand at the top of hierarohy. They readily visit all the households (high and low classes) to conduct rituals and worships and accept all types of foods; even meat preparations. Monks ask for parden from the divine deities by saying a short prayer before they accept meat. They, however, do not share a common plate in any of the households except with their own group of ecclesiastical standing and of the same ritual hierarchy. They feel there is nothing wrong in accepting cooked food from people of lower starta. Among the monks the wealthy or learned monks who most of the time function as officials, claim superiority over the lower clergy who are generally illiteratee, and are entrusted with manual jobs of the monastery.

Nobility claims the second topmost position in the traditional Tibetan social hierarchy. There are again three hierarchical groups among them–*Yab-gzis*, *de-bon* and *mi-drã* as discussed earlier. However, they are considered a single group by others. In social hierarchy they not only claim the highest position but also a higher seat. They are given priority over all others in performing communal rituals. The nobles do not share their cups while drinking *chãng* with the persons of lower categories. In terms of marriage they form an endogamous group. They do not accept cooked food and even water, from persons belonging to the divisions sixth, seventh and eighth. However, they accept water and cooked food from members of divisions third and fourth. A commoner respectfully salutes the noble. A person belonging to low caste not only steps aside to make way for the noble but also bows stretching his tongue out of his mouth and salutes him respectfully putting his right hand on the head.

Though the nobility maintains class endogamy, it can take brides from rich traders and peasants, the groups immediately below them. Under such circumstances children born by such a union cannot claim the status of nobility. Because a women of lower group is always taken as a second wife and her status will be consequently lower in relation to the first wife who always comes from a noble family. The second wife and her children are given lands separately for maintenance. Eventually the children returned to the class or group to which their mother primarily belongs. Tibetan nobility was highly endogamous in nature and gave much importance to its patrilineal stock (*brgyud*).

The division three claims its origin to a yogin, a meditator of the descendents of the senior lamas who are allowed to marry (*Nying-ma-pa* sect) and have children.

Division four includes the *Ger-pã* or the *jin-da* who hold the land in tenancy (*Phu-mã*) from the state or the church. He is rich enough and claims a higher position than all the common people (*Me-mõ-ng*). Occasionally a bride from Divison V the commoners is accepted but the claims of superiority over others continue.

The fifth Division includes *me-mõ-ng*, the common people of the strata. This in itself contains the three groups: peasant, nomad and trader at the upper level and the artisan castes like the potter, stone cutter, tailor are at the low level. They consider the ritual level of the three groups at the first stage as equal and higher than the groups lying at second stage. Since the peasants produce food from their lands and the nomads provide shelter and food by their livestocks resources, the trader forms the interlink between these two. Thus, they stand at the same level. A trader, if very rich, can claim superiority over the other two in his economic strata. These three groups also accept food from the group next to them i.e., the sixth group. However, they will not share their eating plate, drinking glass and the woolen rugs. No marriage relationships will be established with the group lower to them–the sixth group.

The artisan castes stand below the peasant, trader and the nomad. Because the latter group produces food while the former, the artisans do not. Thus the ritual value of their occupation has brought them down, below the groups at 1st stage. In all the other aspects of life including acceptance of food and sharing a single cup, marriage relations, etc., all the artisan castes stand at the same level.

Division VI consists of smiths. Their position is lower since they are considered having impure bone in them and therefore, have less ritual value in the hierarchy. They may be very rich, in material wealth, but they cannot claim a higher position in the social hierarchy. As smiths they are to work with metals and also some prepare weapons to take life, this is against the teaching of Buddhism. They are, therefore, considered low (impure bone) irrespective of their economic status.

Division VII, which includes fishermen, hunters– the *Ko-ba*, who kill animals for food are considered belonging to the lower caste. Ex-prisoners and their descendents have no social, political or ritual status because they have committed serious crimes such as murders. Beggars accompanied with their family and dogs, always beg for their food and depend on the upper classes. Tibetans consider it a sin to eat food without earning it. Beggars who get food by begging acquire lower status. Next to the beggar in the hierarchy stands the butcher who slaughters animals. He offers his service to the nomads who rear livestocks—sheep, goat, yak, etc., in butchering them for meat. For this he receives food and money from the nomads. Killing which is against Buddhism and making a living on this profession, further lowers his status in the hierarchy. One cannot understand the logic behind considering nomads higher in status because the butcher kills an animal which is identified for killing by nomad–the owner. However, the nomads say that they do not actually indulge in taking life and so they are free from such a low status to that of butcher.

*Tam-den* — the one who disposes off the dead, occupies the lowest position in the hierarchy. This is because he depends primarily on this job to earn a living. Tibetans view him as a person waiting for some one to die so that he can earn his living. His presence is considered a sign of ill luck. Irrespective of his economic status his socio-ritual position is low and he belongs to the lowest rung of the social hierarchy.

The Tibetans belonging to the sixth, seventh and eighth divisions do not own any landed property. They have to depend solely on their traditional occupations and the income from it. These groups functioned as service classes which always rushed to the needs of higher classes, and in return receive money, food and on some occasions clothing, as well. Smiths, when called to serve upper castes, stayed with the client's family which provided them with food and shelter. On such trips the smith never carry his tools himself but the servant sent by the patron family carry them because it is considred to be below his dignity. This practice is still in vogue even today among the Tibetans settled in India.

The Tibetans of the group six, seven and eight without lands or livestocks have to depend entirely on the support of the higher classes for their subsistence. Owing to their total economic dependence and being considered impure bone they have low social and ritual status. The lower groups, though debarred from ecclesiastic life in monasteries, are not barred from studying the sacred scriptures. They can also freely join the social and ritual functions celebrated in the community or the monastery, without fear of discrimination.

Tibetan hierarchy resembles that of Hinduism in concepts of purity and pollution. Few notions of purity and pollution regarding commensality are also observed. A noble as a man from the very high strata accepts cooked food and *chãng* from a common man (*phãl-bã*), only if served in a separate plate and glass.

Like the Indian caste system the Tibetans also have the notion of the purity of blood etc. Bougle, a French scholar writes —"In a society the different groups, of which that society is composed repel each other rather than attract, that each retires within itself, isolates itself, rather than attract, that retires within itself makes every effort to prevent its members from contracting alliances or even from entering into relations with neighbouring groups": (loc. cit. Madan, 1977:106). It means members of a particular caste will have relations only within themselves in socio-economic and political aspects. This is not so in complete form among the Tibetans, though their class groups are based on the rules of marriage preferentia and economic standing. For example, marriage of an aristocrat and a commoner is possible and is even allowed by social norms. The differentiation is only of economic in nature. The notion of purity of blood forces them to marry within their endogamous unit. A few rules which govern the notion of commensality in caste system does not prevail here. Thus only a few features of caste system prevails in the Tibetan society. This is because of the Buddhism, which holds true to its ritualhood in all aspects and walks of life. In this way to some extent, social mobility is possible in Tibetan society.

Tibetan society can be divided into eight social groups based on their economy, occupation and land ownership statuses and can be conveniently clubbed into two main groups: (1) high classes – from division one to five — the 'pure bones; and (2) lower classes from division six to eight— the 'impure bones'. We can consider these groups on the lines of caste system, since social mobility between these two was virtually impossible. Though they scrupulously maintain distance, in social relationships, they come together in ritual ceremonies. However, they lack the characteristics of caste system in many respects such as the social and political. The Tibetan society was not only based on class groups of occupational levels, traditional pattern of land ownership, but also based on the fundamental laws of the Buddhist philosophy of good and bad. Based on this we see a stratification practised in the Tibetan society. First, the priestly class – spiritualistic in nature; secondly, the nobility which is administrative and aristocratic in nature; thirdly, the middle class people (*me-mong*); lastly the 'impure bones' or lowest class of people who are reportedly un-Buddhistic in their traditional calling. Therefore, the main determinant of class in Tibetan system is the birth order of an individual rather than his economic position. Even then we have to take into consideration the social classes which share a few similar characteristics with castes in classifying classes into higher and lower order.

The new land holding pattern among the Tibetans in India, has brought considerable change in their social organization. Now, as refugees, all Tibetans are provided with equal amount of land on individual basis. Each one has a right to cultivate the land. However, after the land holder's death the land is returned to the Settlement Corporation, and cannot be inherited by his children. Lord and the Serf type of relationships have gone once for all. Each one is independent with his land, home and income irrespective of his class status as in Tibet. On the other hand, Tibetans are distributed evenly in the settlement, irrespective of their earlier status such as nobility, serfdom, and coming from a village, district, tribal region or province. They are also housed in proto-type houses. This type of shake up has broken many traditional ties and status position among the people.

All Tibetans unlike as in Tibet now have an almost equal

status and position in the society except those who belong to the category of impure bone. Informants say that a few persons who were impure bone, have used this confusing situation to hide their original identity. Marriages have also taken place with persons coming from two polar groups. In two cases people with lower status passing for pure bones were traced. Nothing could be done about this since the marriages were already consummated. A few have passed off for nobles of their native district and are now respected by others as nobles. Others who managed to bring wealth with them, have now become very rich and claim superiority over the rest who arrived here poor. Still others who were once nobles and had lot of wealth, land and sheep with them being taken away by the Chinese army have now become very poor. They now cultivate land and sell woolen garments to earn their living.

The traditional groupings which existed in Tibet have also undergone change. For example, the beggars, artisans, etc., groups are not found here. A few families have taken to new occupations such as carpet making, farming, trading, etc. This has brought them enough money. The Tibetans here do not think themselves in terms of old groupings like peasants, nomads, traders, artisans, etc. but are categorised into high and low class on new grounds. The peasantry is considered to belong to higher class and the smiths who follow their traditional occupations consider themselves of lower category.

In the traditional Tibetan society education was given only to higher strata. Now every child receives education. People of lower social strata, of impure bones, can also join monastery as monks. As householders they can now invite lamas and monks to their homes and provide them with food and *chãng*. They can also take part in community level rituals and functions freely. One of the informants who originally belonged to goldsmith caste now working with other metals such as silver, copper and iron, said that now people over here do not treat him as in Tibet. He is not kept out of the main settlement. He said this is due to the changed attitude in a new situation and also because of the advice given by the Dalai Lama to his people that the artisans and the craftsmen should not be looked down upon. They should be encouraged in this democratic society, so that the traditional art of Tibet will continue to flourish.

The educated younger generation as a result of all these

changes, is more susceptible to the rapidly changing world. As a result, a gap between the older and the younger generations has appeared. This is explained by the two groups in their own way. The old with their conservative background, view this as the result of lack of proper authority such as the nobility like in the traditional Tibetan society. The young who are educated and aware of the facts as to what happened to their country, think they should drop the old customs and adopt to more useful ones which will suit to democratic set-up like that in India. The Tibetans of older generation are also trying to adjust to new trends. During Dalai Lama's visit to Mundgod Camp in September 1977, he advised that all are equal in the modern society, especially in the present situation as refugees settled in India. This advice seemed to help the older generation to reconcile. The Dalai Lama also advised that all should work with equal strength for their community as a whole and ultimately should aim at the only goal — the liberation of their country (Public Speech, 29th September, 1977).

## Social Organization and New Residential Pattern

We already know that the Tibetans of Mundgod are settled in nine villages. The houses are of twin type and a family of five can comfortably live in each of them. In distributing settlers to different villages and localities their opinion and option to settle with mixed group were not considered. Owing to this the people have lost for most part their traditional group feelings and identities based on ethnic or geographic factors and are forced to develop new type of group feelings. The older ties, however, are still strong and we can see the new and formal groups such as labour co-operation, ritual groups, etc., formed on these lines.

The folk dances were performed, during marriages and New Year festivals, while in Tibet by people who belonged to one group and one region. Now, they are scattered in different villages and localities. However efforts are made to bring them together and make them to dance on such occasions. Now-a-days the younger generation, which is capable of adopting to new situations have learnt dances and songs from all regions of Tibet. However, the 'We' feeling is still strong among the people who belong to one district or a tribe. This can be seen during the celebrations of life cycle rituals where only people from common tribal and regional origin in Tibet, are invited. A few outsiders may also be invited on friendship basis. But the ethnic or geographic factors dominate in such group formation.

Customarily people belonging to a region meet for community meal during festivals such as the New Year Festival arranged daily on turn in each of the houses. They also consider it their obligation to visit people coming from the same region in Tibet even without invitation and especially at the time of New Year Festival. On such visits the guests are coaxed to drink *Chãng* to their maximum as elderly women fill their cups with *chãng* from a kettle and compel them to drink some more.[3]

Chese is applied to the rim of the *chãng* cup to indicate goodluck and only when a drink is offered during auspicious occasions. All those who belong to one class or group drink *chãng* from a common cup on turn. When they drink with impure bones then alone separate cups are used to avoid the touch of pollution. Tibetans when they drink in a mixed group, use a different type of cup - *phãwã Kãptchu*, a wooden one into which a silver or copper cup is fitted, to form the inner wall. At the bottom of this cup a small piece of gold is fixed and it is believed that the gold ritually purifies the *chãng* in the cup in case it is polluted by the accidental touch of a low born. They also believe that the gold has the capacity to absorb poison which may have been put by their rivals into the *chãng* offered to them. It is customary therefore, for the Tibetans to carry this type of a cup with them whenever they go out for trade and pilgrimage where they are supposed to drink with strangers and business rivals.

As already described as a custom a house wife compels the family guests to be free and have more of *chãng*. When a guest needs some more *chãng* she gracefully kneels before him with the

---

The Tibetan custom of treating a guest for a drink of *chãng* is well known. The house-wife personally serves the drink as the guests and male members of the family sit together. To start with, the house lady brings the kettle filled with *chãng* keeping a piece of cheese on its nozzle. She pours a small quantity of it as the offering into the cup placed infront of the family deity. Later she brings a cup with its rim applied with cheese at three places, and pours *chãng* and offers it to the guest. He inturn offers a few drops of it to the god by sprinkling in the direction of the altar, with his fourth finger for three times. A decent guest has to drink two glasses of *chãng* completely and at a stretch. Then a third is filled and placed infront of him. A guest in attending the ceremonies like marriages is forced to take three cups of the drink, like this. If he fails to do so he will be later, made to drink one or two more cups, as a penalty.

kettle and fills his cup. A guest after accepting the drink, is honoured with a sacred scarf - the *Khãtã*. He inturn offers one to the host (*trokh-po*) and also pays a token amount of money to the children of the house. He should also part with a very proper behaviour and should speak respectfully to his hosts; and his friends. *Chãng* is used in all the public ceremonies, meetings and life cycle rituals. Tibetans who are trained in ceremonial drinking of *chãng* since their early age will normally avoid getting drunk. So to them drinking *chãng* is both a social and a ritual act.

Today among the Tibetan refugees, marriage and other ties are established on regional basis of their homelands, so that after their return to Tibet they can be together and help each other. Moreover the people of common tribal origin with one cultural background will have fewer problems to adjust. In the field of economic activity also they have reciprocal relations only among themselves. Owing to these factors generally minimum contacts are established with the people of other ethnic origin even though they are their good neighbours in the settlement.

Tibetan refugees as a whole face many and common problems and to fight them they perform a number of rituals. During *Lo-Saar* - the New Year's Day, all the people irrespective of their class and creed come together, perform rituals and chant common spells to renounce this world. During the *Lhã-psõ* rituals performed to control spirits (which takes place on a hillock -*rẽy* specially meant for that), all the Tibetans in common offer the flour of roasted wheat or maize (*tsam-pã*) to the fire god. They also sit together in one line, without any discrimination of class and creed and chant spells.

When the Tibetans have disputes with non-Tibetans (local Indians), they form a common front and face the situation. This 'We' feeling has brought unity among them. At the community level they talk in terms of Tibetans and Indians, and each one shows a territorial and a racial loyalty. The Tibetans consider themselves to be a distinctive racial group when compared with the Indians who live around them. The researcher himself faced many difficulties while conducting the field work. The local officials say the Tibetan society is a closed and secretive one. They are closed even for innovations and changes connected with development. Among themselves they are very co-operative and helpful. They never do injustice to others and are also deeply

(i) Tibetan Children in a Nursery School

(ii) Celebration of Indian Republic Day in the Central School for Tibetans

(iii) Tibetan and Local Youth at a Volleyball Match

(iv) A Lama Teacher in the Settlement School

religious. Their faith in Buddhism and the Dalai Lama, are very strong and they are prepared to face any situation. A few informants told that they live for H.H. the Dalai Lama and trust him whole heartedly. It is with this faith in him that they followed him to India and hope that one day they will return to Tibet with him.

## Family and Kinship

Family is a social group characterized by common residence, economic co-operation and reproduction (Murdock, 1965:1). In a family which includes adults of both the sexes, at least two of the members of the group maintain a socially approved sexual relationship and have one or more children, their own, or adopted by the sexually cohabitating adults (Ibid). MacIver and Page (1971:238) write that family is a group defined by sex relationship sufficiently precise and enduring to provide for the procreation and upbringing of children. This preciseness refers to biological relationships and the social values. Beals and Hoijer (1953:382) define family as "a social grouping of members which are united by bonds of kinship". Another type in which the household of the above type may again include some of the extra members in the structure (dependents) who hold a consanguineal or affinal relationship to the main family. Lastly the household is of the type in which the nuclear family may be missing one of the spouse, or the children, either because they are not born or are dead after the birth. In all these cases though the household may not be having the full structure of a nuclear family according to the above said definitions, we may consider them as some variations from the ideal nuclear family type. Such a family lacking more than two of the structural positions with or without its dependents, it cannot form a nuclear family, it can be said to be merely a household.

An extended family consists of two or more nuclear families affiliated through an extension of the parent child relationship (Murdock Ibid;2). A patrilineally extended family is thus formed by a custom whereby sons remain in their father's family with their wives and children; and matrilineally extended family consists of a man and his wife with their daughters and husbands and children of the latter (Radcliffe Brown and Forde, 1950:5-6). Extended families are of two types; horizontally extended and vertically extended. Iravati Karve (1965:8) defines joint family as "a group of people who generally live under one roof, who eat food cooked in one kitchen, and have property in common, participate in common family worship and are related to one another as some particular type of kindred".

In a polygynous family a man is married to more than one wife and in polyandrous type a woman is married to two or more men at a time. Polyandrous family may exist in two forms - fraternal - wherein several brothers share a common household with one woman and; non-fraternal, where a number of unrelated men join the household of a woman and participate jointly in economic responsibilities and have sexual privileges. Though the traditional Tibetan society had a few typical type of families, now as refugees the Tibetans have a wide range of family types.

In the Mongol censuses of Tibet in the thirteenth century, a family was defined as a house, four pillars in size, containing six persons: the married couple (their children), man servant and maid-servant. The household also included domestic animals and fields (Stein, 1972:120). This definition tends to define a household rather than a family.

A Tibetan family, based on kinship structure, can be divided into two main types - (1) elementary family, and (2) extended family. In Tibet by the necessity of the economic co-operation, joint families were more advantageous and were more in practice. Tibetans, who lived as peasants, nomads and traders, had many functions to perform simultaneously. Different occupations in the family, such as peasantry, nomadism, trade made the male members to go away from their main household for longer periods of time. During their absence it required others to maintain their family and it was their own brothers who could do it. This factor necessitated them to bring into existence the marriage of all brothers to a single wife to hold the family jointly in economic co-operation. The same is known as fraternal polyandry. This is seen among all classes in Tibetan society. The possible reasons for all the classes can be noted as below. The nomads had a dualistic system of life, i.e., came back to their homes only during winter season, and during the other seasons they were away looking after their flocks of sheep and herds of cattle.

Another factor which relates generally to all the classes and mainly to the peasants, was that they held land from their nobles and had an obligation to pay heavy taxes in terms of services and cash needed by their immediate master. It was necessary for them not only to maintain a joint family but also the practice of polyandry so that the family and its property are inherited through a single line. The unity of the family was also sought to be maintained. Among the nobles, who were more interested in keeping the family property intact so as to stand high in socio-economic and political position, maintained joint families and; elementary families were not preferred. Landlords or nobles holding big estates and large number of serfs attached to them, tried to retain them intact by maintaining a single line of inheritance of property. Breaking-up of family property, therefore, was strictly forbidden among the Tibetans.

In the cases where polyandry was not practised many other methods were adopted to keep the family inheritance in a single line: wherein the eldest son inherited the entire property and also married to continue the family pedigree so as to inherit the family and its property in the next generation. Among other sons of the family a few of them joined the monastery, accepting celibacy and a few others married matrilocally to other families (*Mag-pa*) and became members of those families. Brothers who enter a *mag-pa* marriage were sent out of the main family in marriage, without any property. And expenses of brothers who had joined the monastery were to be borne by the eldest brother of the family where he continued the generation. There was also another practice wherein the younger brothers married girls from other families and were sent out of the main family to reside neolocally. They were not allowed to have equal share in the family property but were given just enough to maintain their subsistence.

Families without a male heir to continue family pedigree, accepted *mag-pa* in marriage for the eldest daughter of the family and others went to nunnery. If any or all of her sisters decided to marry in polygyny, they were married to the same *mag-pa* in polygynous union and the family pedigree was continued or if they liked to marry outside they were allowed to, and were married off at any time, even after the dissolution of their *mag-pa* marriage.[4] In a *mag-pa* household the woman holding the

4 In a *mag-pa* marriage husband moves to his wife's place and stay matrilocally to continue the family pedigree and property.

matrilocal residence after marriage also holds the matrilineal succession and matriarchal authority over the property of the family which she inherits.[5] The other type of family through the patrilocal residence, patrilineal succession and patriarchal authority, was much more in practice and was termed as *bag-ma* or *na-ma*. Value was always therefore attached to the continuation of the family name and family property without fail or break either through matrilineal or patrilineal descent.

In a *mag-pa* institution, all the rights of authority were with the woman, and had the option to take some more husbands into the union forming non-fraternal polyandry. In a matrilocal marriage, as Prince Peter says, 'the younger brothers of a *mag-pa* do not hold any access for the sexual rights in his wife because she does not belong to her husband but he belongs to her and her family. She however would allow them to have sex in fraternal polyandry in a *bag-ma* marriage. The heirness's children take her name and her bride-groom is really nothing more than the man she has chosen to enable her to have the children she needs to hand down the property, she has inherited and undivided' (1963:315-16). A *mag-pa* also had no right over her and her property. He could be turned out at any time without any obligations. Thus these two forms of residences — matrilocal and the patrilocal, with their preferred type of marriages in the system formed the authority and succession through their respective systems. This helped the family to bring stability and hold the family in elementary or extended form depending on the necessity of situation.

In the settlement camp at Mundgod the land holding pattern is not in the traditional pattern and is totally changed and each family is promised independence of its own with all its members holding the cultivable land allotted by government independently. The land, is temporarily owned, and goes back to the Settlement corporation after the individual's death. The traditional institutions of keeping property intact have not found favour. There are also changes in the residential pattern of the married persons. Households which lost their family members due to

---

5 This however was an arrangement for one generation but in the very next generation if they got male heirs the girls are sent off in marriage and the patrilocal residence with patrilineal descent and patriarchal authority was maintained.

death or capture by Chinese army have also changed in their structure. Owing to loss of key members in the family the ideal structure of the family is lost. Many families have been reduced to the status of broken families since their members were lost. Widows or those, who lost their spouse in flight joined the original natal family to which they belonged, for economic necessity. In contrast to the joint families in Tibet, here the members of a family live separately since they have their independent resources.

A few persons who lived in matrilocal residence (*mag-pa*) in Tibet have now separated from their wives also leaving the old parents of the woman in separate apartments. This is to get more land grants. Under such circumstances we can find lot of economic co-operation among them. Consciousness of the Tibetans regarding the maintenance of traditional family, its property, mainly its name and blood through descendents, is now shifted to the maintenance of their own individual families with their own independent occupations.

As already discussed the Tibetan social organization was based mainly on lord and serfdom relationship. Serf had to serve his master in all the transactions of his household such as the trading, rearing the ocks and herds, etc. They used to stay away from their families for a longer duration, thus leading a dualistic pattern of life. Marrying independently and having individual homes of their own, would have created problems since they could not have fulfilled the obligations of the family. Thus polyandry became more convenient to hold the family jointly in economic co-operation. Here in the Settlement, as each one of them is independent with his own piece of land received by the Settlement administration, the Tibetans have developed democratic tendencies and views. In Tibet they had the obligations of heavy taxes in terms of cash, kind and service to their immediate master. It was necessary for them to keep the family intact to pay the high tax due to their master. They need not do this, as no such system of taxation exist here. The Tibetans who were under the centripetal force of economic co-operation in Tibet have been now tended towards independent structures due to their independence in their economic life. In the present settlement there are 794 (78.33%) families with patrilocal residence (*na-ma*) and 149 (14.68%) families with matrilocal residence (*mag-pa*) there are six families which are both matri as well patrilocal in residence and this situation is a recent one. The brothers and brothers-in-law with their wives stayed together for economic co-operation and to take up different vocations all at one time. In also a few cases the sons-in-law who lost all their consanguineal kin joined their affinal family in *mag-pa* and stayed with their brothers-in-law. In few cases the families lack the traditional Tibetan ideal structure as their daughters with their children (pre-marital) are also staying with their natal family. About 66 families are broken families as they have lost all their family members during the flight from Tibet either because they were captured and taken away by Chinese army or death. Some of these members are staying alone and leading a monkhood/nunhood lives. (See Table 9 for details). Also many families have lost their key members in the family during the flight and thus the ideal structure of the traditional family is totally lost in such cases.

In Tibet, the households which were ruled by the authority of the senior member of the family, either the father or the elder brother, any property given away or rather lent by the lord directly or indirectly, is essentially indivisible and continued from generation to generation held by the eldest of the family. It is inherited, but possession is governed by a reciprocal obligation between giver and recipient, and the land cannot be taken back by the lord, as long as the labourer pays for it with his service.

As the headman of the family, representing the family in holding the lands and maintaining the family, he holds a high authority over his family members. His children were under his authority and they were not supposed to take a step further without the guidance and permission from their father. It was also necessary for them to keep the family intact for its traditional occupation, which the younger generation were to follow under the sole authority of the father or the headman. Stein (1972:100) however states that, "as soon as the eldest son married and so took the undivided family property into his hands, the parents who were already old were pushed into the background. They kept only a small allotment and their living quarters and were thus treated as sub-tenants on the same basis as the servants (*Khol-pa*). The father or the paternal uncle stood aside as soon as the son married and became the head of the family". But the informants did not agree with this statement. They said the father held control over the family estate as the representative of the family and also had a juridical control over the family members. As a more experienced person he played appropriate roles in

## Table 9: Traditional Occupational Groups Versus Type of Residence

| Sr.No. | Types of Family / Occupational Categories (Traditional) | Patrilocal | Matrilocal | Matrilocal as well as partilocal | Single individual staying | Monk staying alone** | Nun staying alone** | Total |
|---|---|---|---|---|---|---|---|---|
| 1. | Peasant (P) | 465 | 87 | 3 | 11 | 36 | 7 | 607 |
| 2. | Shepherd | 264 | 43 | 3 | 7 | 3 | 1 | 320 |
| 3. | Trader | 17 | 9 | - | - | - | - | 26 |
| 4. | Shepherd and Peasant (SP)* | 34 | 10 | - | - | - | 1 | 45 |
| 5. | Peasant and Trader (PT) | 7 | - | - | - | - | - | 7 |
| 6. | Other classes (O) | 8 | 2 | - | - | - | - | 10 |
| | Total | 794 | 149 | 6 | 18 | 39 | 9 | 1015 |
| | Percentage | 78.33 | 14.68 | 0.59 | 1.79 | 3.86 | 0.89 | 100.00 |

* Includes one family of shepherd and trader.

** Lost spouse and leading monkhood/nunhood life

social, political and ritual life of the community. The youngsters were rarely allowed to participate in these activities. When allowed they were made to do so under the direction of their parents.

Here in The Settlement, the situation is different. The traditional system has lost its values for most part and the youngsters have new values of life in the present changed situation. The present economic conditions have lead them to cease the lord and serf relations and made them to go out of the control of their lords, the parents and the old people. The new generation with its new perspectives and values are now moving away from the main family. Thus the consciousness to maintain the traditional family, its property, mainly its name and blood through descendents, is now shifted to the maintenance of their own individual families with their own independent occupations. The authoritarian dominance of the head of the joint family has also been disregarded by the younger members of the family. The emergence of modern education and the consciousness of their status and roles by the women have contributed to the preference of monogamous marriages and nuclear families. This has affected the joint family system since the women coming from different family background with different views prefer to live separately with their husbands. As a result, the number of elementary families has increased. When parents live with their married sons - this results in an extended family of second and third generations. However, the authority in the family lies with the married and eldest son and not with the father. Now-a-days the older people do not have much say in the field of political activity also. Their knowledge about the society and culture too has become obsolate in the modern situation. However, they continue to stay with their sons comfortably, concentrating on meditation. A few may attend to such jobs as looking after children and keeping a watch on fields etc.

Table 10 shows the number of nuclear and extended families in Mundgod settlement. The table shows that there are 721 (71.06%) nuclear families and 228 (22.44%) extended families. Of the latter, 27 (2.65%) are horizontally extended, 191 (18.81%) are vertically extended and 10 (0.98%) are both vertically and horizontally extended families. The figures also prove that the vertically extended families are more stable than the horizontally extended families. With the death of parents the brothers form nuclear families with their wives and children. In a few cases it

**Table 10: Traditional Occupational Groups Versus the Types of Families**

| Sr.No | Type of Family / Occupational Categories (Traditional) | Elementary | Extended: Horizontal | Extended: Vertical | Extended: Mixed | Polyandrous Families | Polygynous Families | Monk staying alone** | Nun staying alone** | Single individual staying | Total |
|---|---|---|---|---|---|---|---|---|---|---|---|
| 1. | Peasant | 389 | 17 | 114 | 4 | 15 | 14 | 36 | 7 | 11 | 607 |
| 2. | Shepherd | 207 | 8 | 57 | 6 | 17 | 14 | 3 | 1 | 7 | 320 |
| 3. | Trader | 20 | - | 5 | - | 1 | - | - | - | - | 26 |
| 4. | Shepherd and Trader* | 28 | 1 | 11 | - | 2 | 2 | - | 1 | - | 45 |
| 5. | Peasant and Trader | 4 | - | 2 | - | 1 | - | - | - | - | 7 |
| 6. | Others | 7 | 1 | 2 | - | - | - | - | - | - | 10 |
| | Total | 655 | 27 | 191 | 10 | 36 | 30 | 39 | 9 | 18 | 1015 |
| | Percentage | 64.56 | 2.65 | 18.81 | 0.98 | 3.55 | 2.95 | 3.84 | 0.89 | 1.77 | 100.00 |

* Includes one family of Shepherd and Trader

** Lost spouse and leading monkhood/nunhood life

is found that the parents stay with one of the sons, while others stay separate. The joint or the extended families through parents (paternal) are more stable compared to the families extended through siblings (fraternal).

The residential pattern of the members in a household is a basis for the structure of the family. The members in a family are linked by consanguineal and/or affinal relationships. These members in a household are grouped together to form a single family or have broken out into smaller groups owing to some factors based on the centripetal and the centrifugal forces acting on them. This may bring some changes in the structure of an ideal family in which the household consists of a man, his wife and children. If children are married their wives and children also live with them.

Nuclear or extended families have their own ideal structure. This ideal structure cannot be realised by some of the families. These families are affected by the biological or socio-economic handicaps, such as widowhood, desertion or divorce, bachelorhood, or barrenness. These have resulted in the inadequacy of self support for economic and the social means. These families which were living separately have now reunited with the families of their original consanguineal or the affinal ones to form either nuclear or joint families with dependents for economic co-operation. There are, therefore, a few deviations from the ideal types of families. The reasons which bring deviations in the ideal pattern of the families are also as follows. A person who married a girl from this camp and has no family of his own stays with his wife's family though the latter's family has male heirs to continue family line. This type of residence results in a dual structure of matrilocal and patrilocal residences. This, in a few cases, was also due to economic co-operation between brothers and brothers-in-law to take up different occupations such as agriculture, woolen garment business, etc., all at one time. Secondly a few, who are married while their place of residence is not finalised by the respective parents, are staying with their parents to support them economically. This situation might continue for long and in due course children may be born to the couple. This type of residence also pose a deviation from the ideal family structure.

Another reason is owing to premarital child births, which is reported among few Tibetans, daughters with such children stay with their parents. The status of such children pose a deviation since the marriage has not taken place, may be because the man did not agree for the marriage or for economic and other reasons the marriage was postponed. Under such conditions the status of the family will not fit into established and ideal structures. The new type of households sometimes lack members with definite relationship through consanguinity or affinity, among themselves but just live together for economic cooperation or other reasons.

Based on the residential patterns the different types of families may be divided into nuclear and extended families. A simple nuclear family ideally presents a structure of two adults socially approved for sexual cohabitation and their biological or adopted children. A potential simple nuclear family is a family of newly married or couple without children. They have the possibility to have children at any time. A broken family is one where the members constituting the complete structure are lost by death or by legal means of divorce. A polygamous family exists under two types: polygany any polyandry. There are 431, (42.55%) simple nuclear or the elementary families against only 47 (4.54%) simple vertically extended families. The horizontally extended families which were ideal in the Tibetan structure are found in small numbers and a number of these in broken form. It clearly indicates that extended families are on the decline.

## The Composition of a Few Important Types of Tibetan Families in Mundgod Settlement are Shown Below (1978)

| Sr.No. | | | Family Type | Total |
|---|---|---|---|---|
| 1 | *NUCLEAR OR ELEMENTARY FAMILIES* | | | |
| | (a) | **Simple nuclear families:** | | |
| | | (I) | Ego, wife and unmarried children | 426 |
| | | (ii) | Wife (ego) and children ( Husband working in some other place) | 5 |
| | (b) | **Simple nuclear families with dependents** | | |
| | | (i) | Ego, wife and children and brother (single) | 11 |
| | | (ii) | Ego, wife and children and wife's brother (single or monk) | 5 |
| | | (iii) | Ego, wife and children and wife's brothers (widowers) | 7 |
| | | (iv) | Ego with second wife and children of first wife | 1 |
| | | (v) | Ego married a widow and her children from previous husband | 1 |
| | | (vi) | Ego (single), brother's wife and children (brother employed elsewhere) | 6 |
| | (c) | **Potential nuclear families** | | |
| | | (i) | Ego and wife | 75 |
| | (d) | **Potential nuclear family with dependents** | | |
| | | (i) | Ego, wife and sister (widow or divorced) and her children | 4 |
| | (e) | **Broken nuclear families** | | |
| | | (i) | Ego (widow) and children | 109 |
| | | (ii) | Ego (divorcee) and children | 19 |
| | (f) | **Broken nuclear families with dependents** | | |
| | | (i) | Ego (Widow or divorcee) with children and daughter divorced or widowed and grand children | 5 |
| | | (ii) | Ego (widow) with children and classificatory brother and sister (single) | 4 |
| | | (iii) | Ego (single) with mother (widow) and sister (widow) and her children | 17 |
| 2 | *VERTICALLY EXTENDED FAMILIES* | | | |
| | (a) | **Simple, Vertically extended families** | | |
| | | (i) | Ego, wife, son, daughter-in-law and children | 47 |
| | (b) | **Vertically extended families with dependents** | | |
| | | (i) | Ego, wife and children with parents and sisters (single, middle and old aged) | 1 |

| Sr.No. | Family Type | Total |
|---|---|---|
| (c) | **Vertically extended broken family** | |
| (i) | Ego, wife, children and father or mother (widower/widow) | 6 |
| (ii) | Ego (widower), children and father or mother (widower/widow) | 2 |
| (iii) | Ego (widower), children and mother and father | 1 |
| (iv) | Ego(widower) with son (divorcee or widower) with grandsons and daughters (single) | 2 |
| (v) | Ego (widower) with daughter-in-law and grand children | 1 |
| (d) | **Vertically extended broken family with dependents** | |
| (i) | Ego (widower) with daughter-in-law and her children and sisters (widow) | 5 |
| (ii) | Ego (widower) and children, sisters, (single) and father (widower) | 1 |
| (iii) | Ego (widower), son, daughter-in-law (in her natal home) and sister's children | 6 |
| (e) | **Vertically extended matrilocal family** | |
| (i) | Ego, wife, married daughter and son-in-law (staying matrilocally) | 40 |
| (ii) | Ego, wife, children, married daughter and her husband living at his own home, i.e., still not brought into matrilocal residence | 12 |
| 3 | *HORIZONTALLY EXTENDED FAMILIES* | |
| (a) | **Horizontally extended broken families** | |
| (i) | Ego (widower) and brother (widower) with their children | 7 |
| 4 | *HORIZONTALLY AND VERTICALLY EXTENDED FAMILIES* | |
| (a) | **Broken horizontally as well as Vertically extended families** | |
| (i) | Ego (widower), son and daughter-in-law and children, father, and brother (widower) | 3 |
| (b) | **Simple horizontally matrilocal as well as vertically patrilocal extended families** | |
| (i) | Ego, wife, sons, and daughters-in-law, their children and daughter, son-in-law and their children | 2 |
| 5 | *POLYGAMOUS FAMILIES* | |
| (a) | **Polyandrous families** | |
| (i) | Polyandrous family with both the male spouses residing in the family with the relation - ego, ego's brother, wife and children with or without mother (widow) | 17 |
| (ii) | Ego, wife, children and father or mother (widower/widow), ego's brother in polyandry but in service elsewhere | 5 |
| (iii) | Ego, wife and daughter with her husband and children, ego's brother in polyandry | 9 |

| Sr.No. | | | Family Type | Total |
|---|---|---|---|---|
| | | (iv) | Ego, wife and daughter with her husband and children, ego's brother in polyandry and another brother in polyandry is in service elsewhere (trifraternal polyandry) | 2 |
| | | (v) | Ego, wife and children with ego's friend (trokh-põ) in polyandry (non-fraternal) | 3 |
| | (b) | **Polygynous families** | | |
| | | (i) | Ego, wife, children and daughters in the home and son-in-law in polygyny (matrilocal) | 2 |
| | | (ii) | Ego (widower), daughters and son-in-law (matrilocal) | 1 |
| | | (iii) | Ego (widower), son, daughters-in-law sororal and their children | 7 |
| | | (iv) | Ego with two wives (sororal) and children | 8 |
| | | (v) | Ego's one wife left in Tibet and another wife sororal with children of both the wives | 1 |
| | | (vi) | Ego, wives (non-sororal) and children and the ego's sister (widowed) | 3 |
| | | (vii) | Ego's one wife in sororal polygyny deserted, and another wife (sororal) with children of both wives | 4 |
| | | (viii) | Ego's first wife dead, married a woman as second wife and her daughter from her first husband as the third wife | 4 |
| 6. | *UNSPECIFIED* | | | |
| | | (I) | Ego (woman ritually not married) and her children | 1 |
| | | (ii) | Ego with sisters and their children (women ritually not married) | 7 |

With the absence of comparative figures on the types of families in Tibet we cannot however make this statement. The opinion of the informants has been taken as the base to make this statement. Here the changed pattern of land holding, traditional economy and absence of taxes of any kind to be paid to lord has brought change in the composition of the family.

Here individual members enjoy more freedom. There is also much social and spatial mobility. Individual members can go out and establish a family of their own independently. This has also changed the residential pattern. In the traditional order the residence used to be either patrilocal or matrilocal. Now the shift is towards patrilocal and neolocal. The latter type of residence has also brought rise in the number of elementary families. In case of families where elder parents are alive they tried to hold the family intact in the traditional form, more for the emotional and social reasons than economic. Under such cases the families will be of three generations. In Mundgod Settlement there are 47 such families. There are five families in which only father is alive. Among the other two, only mother is alive. Tibetans have a notion that brothers who come from a single parentage can stay together and work hard and not their wives, who come from different families, never care to merge their differences and try to live together. Brothers, therefore, initiate the move and go separate soon after the death of their parents or after their marriage. It may be observed here that patrilocal families are more stable than the fratrilocal families. Here as a custom the parents are taken care of by the eldest brother even though the other brothers separate out. In Tibet, the death of the father did not make any difference. The eldest brother had the full authority and control over the other members of the family and the family property. Here the authority of the eldest brother has completely disappeared. However, though they live separately they still try to maintain common interest and sometimes hold on land and other possessions of the family.

In some way we can also see unity among distant kin among the Tibetan refugees. As refugees, who lost many of their dearer and nearer ones and valuable belongings, they have developed emotional attachment with whatever category of kinsmen they have come across now. As a result, there are families of uncle and nephews, cousins, etc., who sometimes are orphans. These orphans are cared by the old as their own children. When they grow up the boys marry matrilocally and the girls patrilocally (*na-ma*) to other families in the Settlement so that both will get a home to live. To get such a home for the young ones the adopted elder kin however remote their kinship ties may be, struggle hard.

There are 52 (5.09%) families under monogamy and 3 (0.29%) under polygynous union with matrilocal residence. In these families the youngsters who are too young and are inexperienced, are guided by their parents-in-law in familial matters. This does not mean the sons-in-law consult elders in all matters and also always. Sometimes the youngsters owing to their exposure to the outside world, will have more experience to deal with a familial problem than an elder who is retired from active life and possesses minimum knowledge of the present situations. However, younger generation tend to consult and take help from their mother's brothers who sometimes will be of middle age and have experience of both the worlds - Tibetan and Indian. A Tibetan mother's brother plays a very prominent role in the matters of social, economic and ritual life of an individual.

In the absence of this person, guidance is taken from a classificatory maternal uncle.

There are 37 (3.63%) families which house only old men and women, 10 (0.98%) have divorced persons and 18 (1.79%) have only the unmarried individuals and are staying alone. With these individuals a household cannot attain its ideal structure and also function better. Other Tibetans consider that it is their duty to help such individuals. They cultivate lands of such persons on lease and in return provide them with required food and clothing.

There are two largest families in the Tibetan settlement, in the village number I. One has 18 members and the other 21 members. In case of the first family all the sons stay together, jointly with their wives and children. Two sisters who are married and have children also stay with them. The eldest brother acts as the family head. Two brothers have married in polyandry with one woman. The other family with 21 members includes three brothers, their wives and children. One of the brothers is in Indian para-military service. Two of their sisters are married in polygyny to a person whose family also resides in the same Settlement. Among the other daughters of the family, one who is still young, goes to school and the other is married out. The eldest brother, with full co-operation from his younger brothers and guidance from his old parents, functions as the head of the family. Thus the family is kept intact for economic and kinship factors.

There are many factors which have brought strain on the ideal structure of the Tibetan family. The families who have lost their family members in flight from Tibet or have broken due to widowhood, barrenness, desertion or divorce, face inadequacy of self support for economic and social means. Such families who were once separated have now united and formed a new family set up. Under the changed circumstances it is struggling hard 'to stay intact' and for this it has taken the help of kin ties.

## The Position of Woman:

The Tibetan woman is in general considered to have inferior status to that of the men. This gradation is maintained in all the aspects of life. However, they are not kept in seclusion and isolation. They mix freely with men and participate in all socio-economic activities. The status of a Tibetan woman varies according to her age and social status.

With the change in the status of a Tibetan woman her dress and ornaments also change. Unmarried and married women plait their hairs into two parts dividing right from forehead to back, and are tied by thread or ribbons. A married woman wears over her dress, a sheet of cloth around her waist. This is made of a nice coloured stripped cloth and it hangs upto her knee. This cloth signifies her marital status. A married woman's chief ornament is her head dress - *pa-truk*. This varied in shape from region to region. This is made up of a wooden chaplet and ornamented with gold, and studded with corals and seed pearls. She begins to wear this ornament from the day of her marriage. In traditional Tibetan society a woman who wears more ornaments was considered to have higher status. The ornaments of a married woman include rings of gold, silver or shell in her hair, earrings of gold and silver or of seed pearls, necklaces of coral and turquoise with seed pearls, necklaces of beads, etc. However, among the Tibetans in Mundgod one cannot find this status distinction since most of the ornaments are not found now, except a few earrings. They could not bring these ornaments while coming to India or a few who brought sold them later to support themselves.

A Tibetan girl is reared with love and affection by her parents. She is allowed to mix freely with boys in their community. She gets equal status and right to inherit family property and continue the progency. In case of absence of male child in the family she is entitled for the family property and prescribed to marry matrilocally.

A Tibetan woman of higher birth had a right for many servants, to help her; and she used to manage the household. At present owing to their changed economic status most of them are unable to maintain servants any more. A few of them have brought their servants alongwith them from Tibet and even today they stay with their mistresses and help them in their work.

In Mundgod settlement woman has duties of cooking, house keeping and rearing children. They also have an important role to play in the economic activity of the family. Being well built she participates in spinning cloth, weaving carpets, working on the farm - in sowing, weeding, harvesting, threshing and transporting the corns and hay. They can easily carry paddy bags on their back like men, even for a long distance. They go on business tours with their husbands or work for a rich trader on monthly wage basis and can go alone to distant places in India. They are not discouraged by the distance of place of work and toughness of the task and help their family. A few Tibetan women have joined the paramilitary forces such as ITBP and here too they have proved that they are in no way inferior to men.

As housewives the Tibetan women have a more important role in serving the guests. With her charm and graceful appearance she can treat the guests well. When men are busy drinking *chãng* she can freely engage the guests in active conversation and keep the group lively. In the familial matters also she has a role to play. When important matters concerned to the family are discussed, she joins others and her opinions are considered with due respect.

With the advance of age a Tibetan woman acquires higher status in society. Tibetans address any elderly woman with a respectful term - *A-mã*, meaning mother. If she is of equal age she is referred to as *A-chã-lã* (respectful sister). Younger girls are referred to as *pu-mõ*, meaning daughter.

In religious sphere the Tibetan women hold a lower status. The word *Kye-meyn* meaning the "lower birth", is used to refer a wife. Women are considered a hindrance to monastic and spiritual life and so they were always kept away from monasteries. Bell (1928:163) says that 'although many years have elapsed, since the monastery was first founded, yet even till now the strict priestly rules are so well observed that no female is allowed to enter the monastic premises nor indeed does any female even dare to look towards the monastery'. The women are strong, intelligent, capable of maintaining their position, though they are not given importance in religious affairs, hold a position, in the nunnery and a place in ritual aspects.

The religious services are held on the eighth, tenth, fifteenth and the twentyfifth day of Tibetan calendar of every month, and also on the full moon and the new moon days. On these days all men and women visit monasteries to take part in religious service and to observe *nyung-ney* (fast). They are prohibited to take even a drop of water from sunrise to sunset and are made to sit in the village temple listening to the chants of monks who conduct the rituals. They too chant the syllable - *Om Ma Ni Pe Me Hum* and count the beads on the rosary. Many women have risen to the highest position in the field of religion by their own exertions. A few women in the past have claimed as the reincarnation of *Dor-je Pal-mo* - the thunderbolt snow, and were also great meditators.

Women play a more important role in Tibetan socio-religious ceremonies. On the New Year's Day they visit all their relatives and exchange gifts. Together with women belonging to the locality, kin and ethnic background they sing and dance. On festival days and on full moon days they sing and dance with male members of their groups. When men dance for recreation and to pass time after the harvest period, women join freely with them and dance throughout night.

Tibetan women have two phases of life; one in her natal family and another in her conjugal family. She spends her adult life amidst her conjugal family members. They wield considerable influence as wives and mothers in their conjugal houses. In Tibetan society, the women, once married into another family, are not allowed to visit their natal family frequently. When they visit for festivals or rites, they can utmost stay for a day or two and not more. The first and the subsequent child births also take place at their conjugal family. As daughters-in-law they also have important roles to play in their daily life. Right from her childhood days she is advised by her elders to co- operate with different members of her conjugal family, and bear good manners so that there will be no conflict among her family members. Woman is the centre of familial activity and her co- operation and willingness is important for the family to continue in joint form. She has to share the domestic work under the close supervision of her mother-in-law. Both the mother-in-law and the father-in-law have obligation to take care of their daughter-in-law since they come away from their parental family parting from her consanguineal members in the natal family. The Tibetan woman though holds a low status in the ritual aspect, holds an almost equal status in the social and economic aspects and plays an important role in decision making.

The women are free to take part in political activity. They attend public meetings in the village. They also take part in the meetings of the village elders, leaders, etc., held with the Representative of H.H. the Dalai Lama of the Settlement.

To sum up the noble and serfdom relationships have now almost gone and all are treated as equals. But to some extent the village authority and leadership, and ecclesiastic powers are with the erstwhile lords. The new landholding pattern has brought a significant change in the social organization of the Tibetans as each family possesses its share of land and right to cultivate. Each one is independent with his land alloted by the settlement corporation irrespective of his class status in Tibet. Their housing in proto-type houses also has broken many traditional ties and status position of the people. Except the pure and impure bone no other social distinction is now maintained. The old groupings such as peasants, nomads, traders, etc., have vanished and they have taken up various occupations to earn enough money depending on one's own individual capacity. Now they all think as one group and try to withstand the situation with deep faith in Buddhism and H.H. the Dalai Lama.

The ideal family structure is lost in many cases as they might have lost their key family members during their flight from Tibet. In few other cases some families who have broken due to widowhood, divorce, barrenness, etc, face inadequacy of self support, and have now joined to form new family setup which has no ideal or definite structure. These have joined together either for economic reasons or for social reasons such as establishing social fatherhood for a child born of a premarital union, etc. Conciousness to maintain the family and its property by traditional means of joint family or marrying in polyandry is now shifted to the establishing of their own independent and individual families as the land holding pattern has completely changed or there is no immovable property to hold intact. Thus the joint families have lost their significance in the present set-up.

## 5

# Marriage And Marriage Practices

Traditional Buddhist teachings of the renunciation of the worldly things, have influenced the Tibetan way of life. Worldly affairs like marriage are also normally rejected and usually some young men and women are attracted to celibacy and opt to become monks and nuns. The Tibetans view life to be full of misery and sorrow and they prefer to end the cycle of birth and death and attain the godhood. However, the eldest son of a family is under an obligation to marry and lead a family life so that the world will also continue. Others can join monastery as monks and nuns. Informants belonging to older generation see change in the present situations. The people are now attracted by the worldly things rather than other-worldly ones. There are cases of monks who have left their monkhood and entered into family life after coming over to India.

The Tibetans in Tibet joined monasteries for many reasons and one among them was to get education. In Tibet to get education one has either to join a monastery or to hire a tutor. The rich only could afford to hire a tutor and the commoners joined monasteries for education. Here, in India, the Tibetans have ample and free facilities to get modern and secular education. There is now a trend towards modern education in secular schools instead of religious education of monasteries. While in Tibet the regulations of monasteries were strict and there were usually no dropouts. A dropout from a monastery not only degraded himself, but also his family. With a laxity of regulations here in India a monk candidate may drop out of a monastery and his family is not worried of the degradation thereby. It was found that as good as twenty seven monks in the Settlement relinquished their monastic life and married to enter worldly life. In Tibet monks discontinued monastic life and got married only under the situations of the need to continue the family progeny. Secondly, in Tibet, it was essential by the traditional customs that a certain segment of men and women joined monasteries and this helped to maintain the population at a low level. Now they are free to marry and think that they can afford to marry and establish a family of their own. The economic position has also enabled them to educate all their children. All these factors have influenced their values in life here. Their attachment to the spiritual life according to a few informants is somewhat lessening.

Tibetan society as already discussed, can be divided into several divisions namely high and low classes - on the basis of economic status; pure and impure bones on the basis of ritual status, ethnic groups on the basis of origin of the tribal groups and on their geographical location; and finally the occupational groups - on the basis of the occupations they follow. In case of marriage alliances all these factors come to play an important role and the Tibetans are strictly endogamous in nature.

Marriage brings affinity between two groups of kinsmen. Members belonging to a class group will be under obligation to attend a marriage celebrated in their group and perform duties which are customarily assigned to them. In Mundgod settlement today, the ethnic background namely the tribal rather than the economic one, plays an important role in marriage alliances. The people of one tribal origin as a rule attend marriage ceremonies and perform their obligatory duties. Kinsmen of all categories also attend marriage and other ceremonies and perform their obligatory functions. These include preparation of food, arranging for the stay of guests — providing them with *Chãng* and participate in the dances performed throughout the three nights during the marriage, etc. They also contribute in cash and kind, towards the marriage expenses. Kinsmen and members of the group cooperate with each other and show solidarity.

Among Tibetans a marriage unites not just two persons but two kin groups as well. Through marriage several bonds of kinship—cognatic and affinal, are produced. Marriage brings a change in the social personality of the bride and the groom. After marriage they acquire more responsibilities and higher position and also more rights and obligations in the social system of the society.

Marriage rites are considered auspicious. A social importance is given to the ritual acts in a marriage and therefore marriages are performed at a very auspicious time. An astrologer is consulted to find an auspicious time for the marriage. Early morning is considered the most auspicious time to conduct a marriage ceremony. In the traditional Tibetan society marriages were arranged by parents. Older informants claimed that their children obeyed them respectfully in this regard. They also said that now-a-days the situation is changing and the younger generation select their spouses themselves.

## Rules of marriage

A Tibetan must not marry in his patri family which is his patriclan. He should also avoid marrying in his matri family, which is his matriclan upto seventh generation. The brides should be brought from families which are not related by blood. Now a days, the name of the clan has disappeared and is replaced by either the name of the territory, ancestral house, estate, monastery, or a religious teacher. Appendix-A gives the names of clans claimed by a few Tibetans. Most of the Tibetans now say the clan is loosing its significance. However they try to trace their clan membership upto seventh generation. The contacts between the consanguineals or the clan members are maintained through frequent visits during rituals and festivals, exchange of letters and photos. This mode of identifying the members is extended to cognates and agnates from generation to generation - irrespective of the distance of their stay.

Tibetans strictly observe clan exogamy upto seventh generation. They compare their clan organization to a human hand which has seven joints - from shoulder to the tip of the fingers. Each joint is a separate piece but connected with one another in a continuous and single line. Tibetans also consider that blood flows continuous in a single line upto seventh generation. After the fourth joint like in the human hand the clan branches into separate divisions. In exceptional cases one is permitted to marry within his clan after a gap of four generations.

The Tibetan population on the basis of pure and impure bones i.e., high and low castes, are divided into two main endogamous groups. A high caste man taking a spouse from a low caste was punished by outcasting. Such couples were also looked down upon in the society. Today, to some extent, these rules have become weak. Making use of the confused situation, now, a few persons originally belonging to low castes reported to have claimed to belong to high castes.

Among the pure bones themselves there are again groups-high and low. They again are endogamous in nature. A noble, who belongs to the highest stratum, is supposed to marry only in his group. Under exceptional cases he is allowed to take a bride from a lower group, but it should be only from among the pure bones. This woman, and her children cannot inherit or claim the status or property of their father. After the death of the person the woman and her children return to the mother's class. However, if the man was very rich, they were given a piece of land or the *phoma* - the estates attached with serfs. Among the commoners (*Phā-lbā*) there are again many groups such as peasants, nomads, traders and artisans, who usually marry within their group and also outside, except with the artisans.

## The age at marriage

The age at marriage in Tibetan society, is decided mainly on three factors - physical, social and economic. For girls the age at puberty is taken as the suitable age for marriage. Child marriages were not practiced and late marriages were the order among the Tibetans. For marriage, they believe that not only the physical but also the mental development is necessary. Marriages are arranged late so that the youth will know the meaning and responsibilities of a marriage and also the rules which govern them. They thought this will contribute to stability and happiness in married life. In settling a Tibetan marriage though the partners had very little choice to make in their traditional society they are now permitted to choose their partners for themselves. The Tibetans believe that the marriages arranged with the consent of the spouses will be more stable.

Table 13 shows that 120 males and 97 females belong to 19-26 years age groups, are unmarried. Further there are 43 men and 13 women in the 27-34 age group who are unmarried. Here late marriages are not necessarily taken to be preferred. It may be due to lack of finance, suitable match and such other factors. Obligations of looking after their old parents, the marriage of their siblings, etc are others. There are 28 males and 14 females in the age group of 35-50 who are single. About thirty persons married while in Tibet but left their spouses behind or lost them during the flight and never remarried. Others who lost all their kith and kin have also lost interest in worldly life and remained unmarried. A few who had no welwishers to arrange for their marriage during proper age, now think that they have already passed the stage of marriage. They could not also become monks or nuns since they were not fit to do so without having moral courage etc. Once they accept the life of a householder they cannot go back to the monastery or for the life of celibacy. So they live with their nearer kin without marriage and family of their own.

The lowest age at marriage recorded was 13 years, in case of a girl. There were other 8 girls married when they were between 13 and 18 years old. Lowest age recorded for men was as 19 and there were 38 men and 149 women in the age group of 19-26 years among the married. For details see Table 13.

Though a bride younger to the groom is preferred it is not uncommon to marry a woman who is of equal and even older in age. It is observed from Table 11 that of the 925 marriages and other unions, 38 (4.00%) marriages took place between the spouses who were of equal age, 553 (59.82%) married women younger than them and 240 (25.92%) married women older than themselves. In cases, where the wives were older than their husbands may be because of the polyandrous unions and the youngest brother sharing the same wife may be the present husband is much junior in age. The elder brother in the union might have died or lost during the fight. Also in a few cases the elder brothers left their wives in polyandry to the younger brother and married separetly. It is also because many persons who had lost their spouses, during the flight were eager to marry. The circumstances for them at the transit camps also forced them to accept the persons they came across as spouses irrespective of the considerations for the age etc. Marrying a wife younger than oneself is a common form of marriage, in 45 (4.86%) cases it was observed that the wives were younger than their husbands by 13 to 18 years. In 30 (3.25%) cases wives were 19 to 24 years younger and in 7 (0.75%) cases they were 25 to 30 years younger. This age disparity between the spouses is found because of the following reasons: a few who came to the settlement from the para military service or after woolen garment business etc., were not only rich but also fashionable and the young girls were attracted to them and married them. In four cases the marriage was between the 'step fathers' and 'step daughters' and so there is much gap in their age. However Table 11 on marriages which took place in Tibet shows 21 (2.27%) marriages were with spouses of equal age, 112 (12.11%) with elder wives and 236 (25.51%) with younger wives. This ratio clearly shows that the age of husband and wife are not the complete criteria in a Tibetan marriage but the importance was given to the socio-economic and

## Table 11: Marriage Types Versus the Difference of Age between Husband and Wife

### (a) Patrilocal marriages

| | | Difference of Age of the groom from his wife showing the groom elder or younger than his wife (in years) | | | | | | | | | | | | | | | | | Age difference is not known | | | | |
|---|---|---|---|---|---|---|---|---|---|---|---|---|---|---|---|---|---|---|---|---|---|---|---|
| 1 | 2 | 3 | 4 | 5 | 6 | 7 | 8 | 9 | 10 | 11 | 12 | 13 | 14 | 15 | 16 | 17 | 18 | 19 | 20 | 21 | 22 | 23 | 24 |
| In Tibet | P | - | - | 6 | 8 | 16 | 27 | 12 | 52 | 32 | 23 | 10 | 6 | 3 | 1 | 1 | - | - | - | 1 | 198 | | |
| | S | - | 3 | 5 | 5 | 13 | 18 | 6 | 26 | 19 | 12 | 12 | 4 | 1 | - | - | - | - | 7 | - | 131 | | |
| | T | - | - | 2 | - | - | 2 | - | 2 | - | 1 | 1 | 1 | - | 1 | - | - | - | - | - | 10 | | |
| | SP | - | - | - | 1 | 1 | 2 | 2 | 5 | 2 | 3 | 1 | - | - | 1 | - | 1 | - | - | - | 19 | | |
| | PT | - | - | - | - | 1 | - | - | - | 3 | - | 1 | - | - | - | - | - | - | - | - | 5 | | |
| | O | - | - | 1 | - | 1 | - | 1 | 2 | - | - | 1 | - | - | - | - | - | - | - | - | 6 | | |
| Total | | - | 3 | 14 | 14 | 32 | 49 | 21 | 87 | 56 | 39 | 26 | 11 | 4 | 3 | 1 | 1 | - | 7 | 1 | 369 | 369 | 39.85 |
| In transit camps | P | 1 | 1 | 1 | 1 | 7 | 16 | 3 | 15 | 16 | 15 | 13 | 11 | 2 | 2 | 2 | - | - | 2 | - | 108 | | |
| | S | - | - | - | 1 | 6 | 10 | 2 | 3 | 3 | 1 | 5 | - | 1 | - | 1 | - | - | 5 | - | 38 | | |
| | T | - | - | - | - | 3 | - | - | 1 | 3 | 1 | 1 | - | - | - | - | - | - | - | - | 9 | | |
| | SP | - | - | - | - | - | - | - | 4 | 3 | 1 | - | - | - | - | - | - | - | - | - | 8 | | |
| | PT | - | - | - | - | - | - | - | - | - | - | 1 | - | - | - | - | - | - | - | - | 1 | | |
| | O | - | - | - | - | - | - | - | - | - | - | - | - | 1 | - | - | - | - | 1 | - | 2 | | |
| Total | | 1 | 1 | 1 | 2 | 16 | 26 | 5 | 23 | 25 | 18 | 20 | 11 | 4 | 2 | 3 | - | - | 8 | - | 166 | 166 | 17.93 |

| 1 | 2 | 3 | 4 | 5 | 6 | 7 | 8 | 9 | 10 | 11 | 12 | 13 | 14 | 15 | 16 | 17 | 18 | 19 | 20 | 21 | 22 | 23 | 24 |
|---|---|---|---|---|---|---|---|---|---|---|---|---|---|---|---|---|---|---|---|---|---|---|---|
| In Mundgod Settlement | P | - | - | 3 | 1 | 36 | 7 | 4 | 28 | 23 | 19 | 13 | 5 | 3 | 3 | - | - | 1 | 8 | 3 | 156 | | |
| | S | - | - | 3 | 2 | 9 | 5 | 5 | 12 | 13 | 3 | 10 | 2 | 1 | 1 | 1 | - | 1 | 10 | 2 | 80 | | |
| | T | - | - | - | - | 3 | - | 1 | - | 1 | - | 2 | 2 | - | - | - | - | - | - | - | 9 | | |
| | SP | - | - | 1 | - | 1 | 1 | 1 | - | - | 2 | - | - | - | 1 | - | - | - | - | - | 7 | | |
| | PT | - | - | - | - | - | 1 | - | 1 | - | - | - | - | - | - | - | - | - | - | - | 2 | | |
| | O | - | - | - | - | - | - | - | - | - | - | - | - | - | - | - | - | - | - | - | - | - | - |
| Total | | - | - | 7 | 3 | 49 | 14 | 11 | 41 | 37 | 24 | 25 | 9 | 4 | 5 | 1 | - | 2 | 18 | 5 | 255 | 255 | 27.54 |
| Total | P | 1 | 1 | 10 | 10 | 59 | 50 | 19 | 95 | 71 | 57 | 36 | 22 | 8 | 6 | 3 | - | 1 | 10 | 4 | 463 | | |
| | S | - | 3 | 8 | 8 | 28 | 33 | 13 | 41 | 35 | 16 | 27 | 6 | 3 | 1 | 2 | - | 1 | 22 | 2 | 249 | | |
| | T | - | - | 2 | - | 6 | 2 | 1 | 3 | 4 | 2 | 4 | 3 | - | 1 | - | - | - | 1 | - | 29 | | |
| | SP | - | - | 1 | 1 | 2 | 3 | 3 | 9 | 5 | 6 | 1 | - | - | 2 | - | 1 | - | - | - | 34 | | |
| | PT | - | - | - | - | 1 | 1 | - | 1 | 3 | - | 2 | - | - | - | - | - | - | - | - | 8 | | |
| | O | - | - | 1 | - | 1 | - | 1 | 2 | - | - | 1 | - | 1 | - | - | - | - | - | - | 7 | | |
| Grand Total | | 1 | 4 | 22 | 19 | 97 | 89 | 37 | 151 | 118 | 81 | 71 | 31 | 12 | 10 | 5 | 1 | 2 | 33 | 6 | 790 | 790 | 85.32 |

## Table 11: (b) Matrilocal marriages

| The Place of marriage | Occupational Categories | Difference of age of the groom from his wife, showing the groom elder or younger than his wife (in years) | | | | | | | | | | | | Age difference is not known | | | Total | Grand Total | Percentage |
|---|---|---|---|---|---|---|---|---|---|---|---|---|---|---|---|---|---|---|---|
| | | -7 to - 9 | -4 to -6 | -1 to -3 | 0 | +1 to +3 | +4 to +6 | +7 to +9 | +10 to +12 | +16 to +18 | +19 to +21 | +22 to +24 | +25 to +27 | Husband is in military | Husband is in his home | Illegal Union | | | |
| In Tibet | P | - | - | 1 | - | 1 | - | - | - | - | - | - | 1 | - | - | - | 3 | | |
| | S | - | - | - | - | - | - | - | - | - | - | - | 1 | - | - | - | 1 | | |
| Total | | - | - | 1 | - | 1 | - | - | - | - | - | - | 2 | - | - | - | 4 | 4 | 0,43 |
| In Transit Camp | P | - | - | 1 | - | 3 | 3 | 1 | 1 | 1 | 1 | - | - | 4 | - | - | 15 | | |
| | S | - | - | - | - | 2 | 1 | 1 | - | - | - | - | - | 1 | - | - | 5 | | |
| | T | - | - | - | - | - | - | - | 1 | - | - | - | - | - | - | - | 1 | | |
| Total | | - | - | 1 | - | 5 | 4 | 2 | 2 | 1 | 1 | - | - | 5 | - | - | 21 | 21 | 2.37 |
| In Mundgod Settlement | P | 1 | - | 2 | - | 9 | 7 | 3 | 4 | - | 1 | 1 | - | 16 | 11 | 4 | 59 | | |
| | S | - | 2 | 1 | 1 | - | 4 | 3 | - | - | 1 | 11 | 2 | 15 | - | - | 40 | | |
| | T | - | - | - | - | - | 1 | - | - | 1 | - | - | - | 1 | - | - | 3 | | |
| | SP | - | - | - | - | - | 3 | 2 | - | - | - | - | - | 3 | - | - | 8 | | |
| | PT | - | - | - | - | - | - | - | - | - | - | - | - | - | - | - | - | - | - |
| Total | | 1 | 2 | 3 | 1 | 9 | 15 | 8 | 4 | 1 | 2 | 12 | 2 | 35 | 11 | 4 | 110 | 110 | 11.88 |
| Total | P | 1 | - | 4 | - | 13 | 10 | 4 | 5 | 1 | 2 | 1 | 1 | 20 | 11 | 4 | 77 | | |
| | S | - | 2 | 1 | 1 | 2 | 5 | 4 | - | - | 1 | 11 | 3 | 16 | - | - | 46 | | |
| | T | - | - | - | - | - | 1 | - | 1 | 1 | - | - | - | 1 | - | - | 4 | | |
| | SP | - | - | - | - | - | 3 | 2 | - | - | - | - | - | 3 | - | - | 8 | | |
| | PT | - | - | - | - | - | - | - | - | - | - | - | - | - | - | - | - | - | - |
| Grand Total | | 1 | 2 | 5 | 1 | 15 | 19 | 10 | 6 | 2 | 3 | 12 | 4 | 40 | 11 | 4 | 135 | 135 | 14.68 |

ritual status of the boys and girls and their family, character, education, skill in arts and crafts, behaviour and personal charm.

## Marriage types among the Tibetans

Tibetans practice three types of marriages: monogamy, polygyny and polyandry. Monogamy is more prevalent and ploygyny is mainly confined to nobility and polyandry is found both among the nobility and the commoners.

Of the 1015 families in the Mundgod settlement, 881 (86.86%) are monogamous, 30 (2.97%) are bifraternal polyandrous, 2 (0.20%) are trifraternal polyandrous and 3 (0.29%) are non fraternal polyandrous, 23 (2.29%) sororal polygynous, 3 (0.49%) non-sororal polygynous and 5 (0.49%) generational polygynous families; 18 (1.79%) families or households are composed of single and unmarried persons. There are also 39 (3.86%) households of monks and 9 (0.89%) of nuns who are leading a monkhood/nunhood life after losing their spouse during their flight from Tibet or due to death, divorce, etc. (See Table 12 for details).

In Tibet polygyny was practised for several reasons. Among them were ill health, incompatibility, barrenness, etc., on the part of the first wife. Similarly polyandry was practised by all classes of Tibetans for several reasons. There are three types of polyandrous unions. First, the brothers of a single family share a common woman resulting in fraternal polyandry. Some times classificatory brother may join them. Second type is that the father and the son/sons share a common wife, resulting in a generational polyandry. Thirdly, when friends (*Trokh-po*) share a common woman there results a non fraternal polyandry. On the basis of residence after marriage, these marriages can again be divided into two forms bride moving into bridegroom's family (*nã-mã*) and bridegroom moving into the bride's family (*mak-pa* or *mag-pa*).

## Monogamous Marriages

It is informed that now monogamous marriages are more in practice as they are more convenient in sexual relationships. Sex relations are expected to have the sanction of marriage. Some cases of pre marital sex relations leading to marriage are also reported. In some other cases the lovers have even children

## Table 12: Families According to Types of Marriages

| Sr.No. | Type of Marriage / Occupational Classes | Monogamy | Polyandry: Bi-fraternal | Tri-fraternal | Non-fraternal | 2 brothers born of the same mother but different fathers married to a woman | Polygyny: Bi-sororal | Non-sorroral | Ego married wth a woman and also her daughter | 1Married a woman and also her sister's daughter | Concbinage | Not married but staying single | Monk families** | Nun families** | Total |
|---|---|---|---|---|---|---|---|---|---|---|---|---|---|---|---|
| I | P | 520 | 15 | - | 2 | - | 12 | 1 | 1 | 1 | 1 | 11 | 36 | 7 | 607 |
| 2 | S | 279 | 13 | 2 | 1 | 1 | 10 | 2 | 2 | - | - | 7 | 3 | 1 | 320 |
| 3 | T | 25 | - | - | - | - | - | - | 1 | - | - | - | - | - | 26 |
| 4 | SP* | 40 | 2 | - | - | - | 1 | - | 1 | - | - | - | - | 1 | 45 |
| 5 | PT | 7 | - | - | - | - | - | - | - | - | - | - | - | - | 7 |
| 6 | O | 10 | - | - | - | - | - | - | - | - | - | - | - | - | 10 |
| | Total | 881 | 30 | 2 | 3 | 1 | 23 | 3 | 5 | 1 | 1 | 18 | 39 | 9 | 1015 |
| | Percentage | 86.86 | 2.97 | 0.20 | 0.29 | 0.10 | 2.29 | 0.29 | 0.49 | 0.10 | 0.10 | 1.79 | 3.86 | 0.89 | 100.00 |

* includes one family of shepherd and trader

** Lost spouse and leading a monkhood/nunhood life.

before marriage. Later they informed their parents and got married. In one case a couple lived together without any formal marriage ceremony but shared all the functions of a family including reproduction.

Regarding the rules of residence, after marriage the spouses are allowed to live together. When a bride moves to her groom's family, there results a patrilocal type of residence (*nā*-mã). When the wife's family lacks male members or when extra members are needed by it for economic cooperations or when the groom is alone without any affinal or cognatic kins, then the husband is accepted into the bride's family. This results in a matrilocal residence (*mag-pā*). The married couples stay away from both matri and patri families, having their own independent residences forming neolocal residences. Again in a few cases it was found the bride and groom were not co-residents. The reasons were being the formal marriage rites were not performed even though they had children, so their living together was not approved by the society. Secondly, even though the ritual ceremony took place, the bride and groom were to look after their respective parents who were old. However, they shared the economic, social and reproductive activities of their family.

Many changes have taken place in the ideal constitution of monogamy. The spouses under monogamy include the remarriage of even divorcees, widowed, marrying virgin girls or boys. Many Tibetans who lost their spouses, during the flight have now married to the unmarried or widowed or divorced. These unions and filling of vacant positions in the family have again brought stability in the family. These types of families also have all the relevant features of a family with reproductive, economic and educational functions.

Tibetans also acquire wives by exchange of brides. The marriages by exchange practised by the Tibetans are of two types: (a) exchange of a daughter for a sister and (b) exchange of sisters. Two brothers exchanging their sisters are common. In a few cases a sister is exchanged to her husband's daughter by his first wife. Similarly two brothers marrying two sisters is also common. There are cases of one brother marrying the mother and his other brother marrying her daughter from her previous marriage. The Tibetans consider that such marriages bring unity among the brothers in a family, since the mother and her daughter or the two sisters come from one family. When sisters are exchanged by two families, they will also be equally bound by obligations and duties to each other and always extend their helping hand in socio economic matters.

In Mundgod settlement out of 880 families married in monogamy 835 are still existing in complete form of an ideal family. The remaining marriages are either dissolved or broken owing to the death or the spouses took divorce. Among the 835 marriages 699 are patrilocal and 136 are matrilocal.

There is a case of a Tibetan who married an Indian woman. This man had left behind his wife in Tibet and while in transit camp he met this woman and married her. There are also two cases of Tibetan women marrying Indians. Among them, one was in the Indian Army. He was a Brahman and a resident of a village in Madhya Pradesh. They met when the woman was in transit camp and working as a labourer for road construction. This woman was already married in Tibet and had a child. During the flight she left her child and husband in Tibet. Now she has another child from her present husband. In another case an Indian had married a Tibetan in Tibet itself, and has now fled with his family members to India.

Table 13 gives the marital status of the Tibetans. There are in all 4267 persons in the settlement. Out of them 2033 (47.65%) persons (1053 males and 980 females) are single, 1609 (37.71%) (750 males and 859 females) are married, 27 (0.63%) are married monks (after renouncing the clergy life) 255 (5.98%) (108 widowers and 147 widows) are widowed, 61 (1.43%) (22 males and 39 females) are divorced, 15 (0.35%) (4 males and 11 females) divorced and remarried, 46 (1.08%) (26 males and 20 females) widowed and remarried, 24 (0.56%) (17 males and 7 females) lost their spouses in the flight and are remarried here, 30 (0.70%) (19 males and 11 females) lost their spouses in the flight and are single here, 13 (0.31%) females are concubines and 115 (2.69%) monks and 28 (0.65%) nuns are staying in the nine villages of the settlement.

Widowhood is considered the natural breaking of a marriage. There are 301 widowed persons in the Settlement. Of which 167 are widows and 134 are widowers (including those remarried). Men are found to be more prone to death than women. This is because of the hardship, burden and responsibilities men face in earning livelihood for the family. Presently there is no restriction

**Table 13: Age and Sex Versus The Marital Status**

| Serial Number | Age Group (in years) | Sex | Single | Married | Left Moonkhook and Married | Widow | Divorced | Divorcee and Married | Widow and married | Lost spouse in the flight and married | Lost spouse in the flight and single | Concubinage | Monks/Nun | Deserted | Total | Grand Total |
|---|---|---|---|---|---|---|---|---|---|---|---|---|---|---|---|---|
| 1 | 2 | 3 | 4 | 5 | 6 | 7 | 8 | 9 | 10 | 11 | 12 | 13 | 14 | 15 | 16 | 17 |
| 1. | 0 - 5 | M | 357 | - | - | - | - | - | - | - | - | - | - | - | 357 | 715 |
| | | F | 358 | - | - | - | - | - | - | - | - | - | - | - | 358 | |
| 2. | 6 - 10 | M | 249 | - | - | - | - | - | - | - | - | - | - | - | 249 | 471 |
| | | F | 222 | - | - | - | - | - | - | - | - | - | - | - | 222 | |
| 3. | 11-18 | M | 247 | - | - | - | - | - | - | - | - | - | 5 | - | 252 | 531 |
| | | F | 270 | 8 | - | - | - | - | - | - | - | - | 1 | - | 279 | |
| 4. | 19-26 | M | 120 | 38 | 1 | - | 1 | - | - | - | - | - | 3 | - | 163 | 422 |
| | | F | 97 | 149 | - | - | 6 | - | - | - | - | 6 | 1 | - | 259 | |
| 5. | 27-34 | M | 43 | 145 | 2 | 2 | 3 | 1 | 1 | - | - | - | 8 | - | 205 | 440 |
| | | F | 13 | 190 | - | 11 | 9 | 3 | 2 | 2 | - | - | 5 | - | 235 | |
| 6. | 35-42 | M | 21 | 198 | 6 | 8 | 6 | 1 | 5 | 6 | 6 | - | 24 | - | 281 | 536 |
| | | F | 10 | 210 | - | 15 | 6 | 3 | 2 | 2 | 1 | 4 | 2 | - | 255 | |

| 1 | 2 | 3 | 4 | 5 | 6 | 7 | 8 | 9 | 10 | 11 | 12 | 13 | 14 | 15 | 16 | 17 |
|---|---|---|---|---|---|---|---|---|---|---|---|---|---|---|---|---|
| 7. | 43-50 | M | 7 | 178 | 9 | 24 | 5 | - | 9 | 5 | 3 | - | 34 | 2 | 276 | 476 |
| | | F | 4 | 144 | - | 10 | 12 | 5 | 11 | 1 | 2 | 3 | 7 | 1 | 200 | |
| 8. | 51-58 | M | 4 | 113 | 8 | 34 | 4 | 1 | 7 | 2 | 6 | - | 21 | 2 | 202 | 358 |
| | | F | 5 | 92 | - | 37 | 5 | - | 2 | 2 | 5 | - | 8 | 3 | 159 | |
| 9. | 59-66 | M | 5 | 62 | 1 | 22 | 3 | 1 | 3 | 2 | 4 | - | 16 | 2 | 121 | 227 |
| | | F | 1 | 51 | - | 46 | 1 | - | 2 | - | 1 | - | 3 | 1 | 106 | |
| 10. | 67-74 | M | - | 13 | - | 11 | - | - | 1 | 2 | - | - | 4 | - | 31 | 73 |
| | | F | - | 14 | - | 24 | - | - | 1 | - | 2 | - | 1 | - | 42 | |
| 11. | 75 & above | M | - | 3 | - | 7 | - | - | - | - | - | - | - | - | 10 | 15 |
| | | F | - | 1 | - | 4 | - | - | - | - | - | - | - | - | 5 | |
| Total | | M | 1053 | 750 | 27 | 108 | 22 | 4 | 26 | 17 | 19 | - | 115 | 6 | 2147 | 4267 |
| | | F | 980 | 859 | - | 147 | 39 | 11 | 20 | 7 | 11 | 13 | 28 | 5 | 2120 | |
| Percentage | | M | 24.68 | 17.58 | 0.63 | 2.53 | 0.52 | 0.09 | 0.61 | 0.40 | 0.45 | - | 2.69 | 0.14 | 50.32 | 100.00 |
| | | F | 22.97 | 20.13 | - | 3.45 | 0.91 | 0.26 | 0.47 | 0.16 | 0.26 | 0.30 | 0.66 | 0.12 | 49.69 | |
| Grand Total | | | 2033 | 1609 | 27 | 255 | 61 | 15 | 46 | 24 | 30 | 13 | 143 | 11 | 4267 | |
| Percentage | | | 47.65 | 37.71 | 0.63 | 5.98 | 1.43 | 0.35 | 1.08 | 0.56 | 0.71 | 0.30 | 3.35 | 0.26 | 100.00 | |

on the number of remarriages for both men and women. It is observed that 26 widowers and 20 widows are now remarried. But the remaining 255 lead a saintly life, shaving their head after the death of their spouse.

In the traditional Tibetan society a widow was generally not permitted to remarry and a married widow was looked down upon. If a woman lost her first husband she was known as *ya-ksã-mã*. If her second husband too died she was known as *yo-gnã-mã*. After the death of her third husband, she was called a *nãm-thok*. A *nãm-thok* widow was considered an inauspicious person and was not allowed to participate in any rituals and ceremonies. Even the food cooked by her was considered impure and was not eaten by others. She was also considered to bring illuck and misfortune and so was not usually preferred in marriage any more. So they spent rest of their life in worshipping and such other religious activities. A few of them as a sacrifice shaved off their head and led the life of nuns. However things are changing and in Mundgod settlement twenty widows have remarried. When a widow marries no rituals are performed; but a feast is given. Accompanied by a few men and women she goes to her conjugal home and on arriving there men drink, dance and enjoy the occasion.

While in Tibet the widows were not allowed to remarry at least for one year and forty nine days after their widowhood. As a first degree mourner a widow mourned for forty nine days. During this period it is believed that the soul of the departed will be moving around to take its next birth. After this, for one year, the widow was not allowed to marry to prove that she was not carrying the baby of her deceased husband. However in the Settlement, widows do not observe this custom strictly. After the worship for the soul and mourning for 49 days she is permitted to marry. A few of them married so soon that at the time of remarriage they were found pregnant with a baby of their deceased husband. In such cases a male child born afterwards was given to the deceased husband's family and the female child was retained with the mother. In the traditional Tibetan society widows with babies in their womb were strictly prohibited from marrying. A woman after the death of her husband, usually stayed in her conjugal family itself. In exceptional cases due to the bad treatment by her parents-in-law, she went back to her parental family. If she remains unmarried, she will have a right for maintenance from her conjugal family, until her death.

Widowers can marry virgins and also can have all the rituals of an ideal Tibetan marriage. The marriage is also considered as an auspicious occasion. Marriage of a widower with a widow is not auspicious and so do not carry most of the rituals of an ideal marriage.

Divorces are a threat to the institution of marriage in the Tibetan society. There are 76 divorce cases in Mundgod settlement (including remarried). Out of these 26 are men and 50 are women. The main reasons for this are immorality, unfaithfulness and non cooperation, ill treatment on the part of the parents-in-law and quarrel-some nature of the women. On the part of the men heavy drinking, gambling, extramarital sex, inability to feed the family, ill health are the main reasons. In the traditional Tibetan society women were not allowed to return to her natal family unless there was a valid reason. When such an incident occurred leaders of the community tried their best to unite the couple instead of separating them. This was because family solidarity was always considered better than its dissolution.

In Mundgod settlement marriage between persons coming from the same village are recorded. In these cases there are direct and constant contact between the affinal groups for help and consultation. Sometimes such a wife takes advantage of the physical nearness of her parents and go away to her parental family even for minor quarrels with her husband and announces a divorce. Lack of an agency and authoritative persons with suitable social standing to settle such disputes has resulted in high rate of divorces and separations. Besides women here enjoy more economic freedom and are entitled to equal amount of land by the settlement authorities for their subsistence. The general administration in the society has now tended to be weak and on a few occasions people find it difficult to appeal to a suitable agency which can set the things right. In Tibet however, the situation was different and such cases were tried by their concerned lords and the offenders were strictly punished. In case of the dissolution of marriage the party found guilty was made to repay the bride price (*nu-rin*) or dowry. With the loss of lordship the leaders here have also lost their authority and powers to control their people and the old moral codes and conduct are losing their importance. Even the births due to premarital and extra-marital relations are becoming common.

In Mundgod settlement out of 76 divorce cases . Four men and eleven women have remarried. Like in the traditional Tibetan society, the divorcees have lower status than even the remarried widows. The Tibetans view widowhood a natural cause and divorce an unnatural act. It is also an evidence of disloyalty to her husband and the family. Thus a divorced woman carries a stigma in the Tibetan society.

On remarriage divorced persons loose their right to the movable or immovable property of the family of the first marriage. With the dissolution of a marriage the sons go with the husband and daughters with the mother. When a divorcee with daughter(s) remarries she can leave them with her parents or even take them to her new conjugal home.

There are 36 men and 18 women whose spouses were left behind in Tibet because at the time of flight they were away from the family either on trade or rearing livestocks in upland. A few who were together in the family deliberately did not reveal their plans of going to India fearing they might weep or reveal the news to others drawing the attention of the Chinese soldiers. Of them 17 men and 7 women are remarried and the others think that their spouses are alive back home and so are in two minds whether to remarry here or not, since they are intending and hoping to go back soon.

There are 14 cases of births without the ritual marriage of the women. They are of two types, children whose genitors are traceable and others untraceable. Among those whose genitors were traced eight babies are considered illegitimate because their fathers refused to marry the women in whom they begetted a child. This was due to their position in the social hierarchy, earlier marriage, bad reputation of the women and other reasons. Owing to these factors the social fatherhood of the children was not fixed. In Tibetan society the status of a woman with illicit relations and illegitimate children is low. However such children having a social father, have higher status than those who do not have.

## Polygynous marriages

Polygynous marriages usually took place among the rich Tibetans. They were both patrilocal and matrilocal in residence after marriage. In case of patrilocal marriages a rich man married more than one wife for status and also to supplement working hands. In case of matrilocal family, which has no male issue, a man who married the eldest daughter of the family also married her all other sisters if they agreed to be his additional wives. Or else they were allowed to join nunnery. If the first wife had incurable diseases or was barren, the sororal polygyny with patrilocal residence was adopted. Sororal polygyny was preferred to non-sororal polygyny since it was thought the sisters maintained unity in the family.

The permission of the first wife was essential, for a man to take another wife, irrespective of whether she was the sister of the first wife or not. Only the eldest son from the eldest wife was considered the legitimate heir for family headship and property.

Thirty two polygynous marriages have been reported in the Tibetan settlement of various types as shown in Table 14. A close study reveals that they have taken place mainly for economic reasons. An additional wife means an additional hand to earn. One of them can stay in the settlement to look after the farm work and also the children of the other wife. The other wife can accompany her husband on his business tour and help him. There are cases of ill health of first wife leading to sororal marriage.

In other cases a man had socially approved cohabitation with two sisters of another family. However, he did not share any economic activities of that family. In such cases one may or may not have married the women by ritual means but social fatherhood to the children born to the women were established by performing some rituals. The man also did not have any priority either on sex or economy of the women and their family. In such cases the spouses stayed separately because their respective families also needed their financial support.

Property and leadership rights were inherited by the eldest son of first wife. But presently the issue of inheritance does not arise as they do not possess any immovable property of their own. There is also no competition and conflict to inherit family property since sisters have more affinity for polygynous unions. Still the importance is attached to the economic position of the person to support his wives and children.

There is another type of polygyny the two generational polygyny, in which both mother and daughter share one man as

**Table 14: Marriage Types and their Composition According to the Change of Places.**

| Residence after marriage | Place of Marriage | Occupational Classes | Monogamy | Polyandry: Bifraternal | Polyandry: Trifraternal | Polyandry: Non-fraternal | Polyandry: Two brothers born of different fathers but same mother married a woman | Polygny: Bi-sororal | Polygny: Non-sororal | Polygny: Ego married a woman and also her daughter from first husband. | Polygny: Married a woman and also her sister's daughter | Total |
|---|---|---|---|---|---|---|---|---|---|---|---|---|
| 1 | 2 | 3 | 4 | 5 | 6 | 7 | 8 | 9 | 10 | 11 | 12 | 13 |
| PATRILOCAL | IN TIBET | P | 188 | 5 | - | - | - | 8 | - | 1 | - | 202 |
| | | S | 126 | 6 | 1 | - | 1 | 7 | 1 | 1 | - | 143 |
| | | T | 8 | - | 1 | - | - | - | - | - | - | 9 |
| | | SP | 18 | - | - | - | - | - | - | - | - | 18 |
| | | PT | 4 | - | - | - | - | - | - | - | - | 4 |
| | | O | 6 | - | - | - | - | - | | | | 6 |
| | Total | | 350 | 11 | 2 | - | 1 | 15 | 1 | 2 | - | 382 |
| PATRILOCAL | IN TRANSIT CAMP | P | 104 | 2 | - | - | - | 3 | - | - | - | 109 |
| | | S | 33 | 3 | - | - | - | - | - | - | - | 36 |
| | | T | 6 | - | - | - | - | - | - | - | - | 6 |
| | | SP | 8 | - | - | - | - | - | - | - | - | 8 |
| | | PT | 2 | - | - | - | - | - | - | - | - | 2 |
| | | O | 2 | - | - | - | - | - | - | - | - | 2 |
| | Total | | 155 | 5 | - | - | - | 3 | - | - | - | 163 |
| PATRILOCAL | | S | 63 | 8 | - | 1 | - | - | 1 | 1 | - | 74 |
| | | T | 7 | - | - | - | - | - | - | 1 | - | 8 |
| | | SP | 10 | - | - | - | - | - | - | - | - | 10 |
| | | PT | 2 | - | - | - | - | - | - | - | - | 2 |
| | | O | - | - | - | - | - | - | - | - | - | - |
| | Total | | 194 | 13 | - | 3 | - | 2 | 2 | 3 | 1 | 218 |

| 1 | 2 | 3 | 4 | 5 | 6 | 7 | 8 | 9 | 10 | 11 | 12 | 13 |
|---|---|---|---|---|---|---|---|---|---|---|---|---|
| PATRILOCAL | Total | P | 404 | 12 | - | 2 | - | 13 | 1 | 2 | 1 | 435 |
| | | S | 222 | 17 | 1 | 1 | 1 | 7 | 2 | 2 | - | 253 |
| | | T | 21 | - | 1 | - | - | - | - | 1 | - | 23 |
| | | SP | 36 | - | - | - | - | - | - | - | - | 36 |
| | | PT | 8 | - | - | - | - | - | - | - | - | 8 |
| | | O | 8 | - | - | - | - | - | - | - | - | 8 |
| | Grand Total | | 699 | 29 | 2 | 3 | 1 | 20 | 3 | 5 | 1 | 763 |
| MATRI-LOCAL | IN TIBET | P | 3 | - | - | - | - | - | - | - | - | 3 |
| | | S | 2 | - | - | – | - | - | - | - | - | 2 |
| | Total | | 5 | - | - | - | - | - | - | - | - | 5 |
| MATRI-LOCAL | IN TRANSIT CAMP | P | 15 | 1 | - | - | - | - | - | - | - | 16 |
| | | S | 5 | - | - | - | - | 2 | - | - | - | 7 |
| | | T | 1 | - | - | - | - | - | - | - | - | 1 |
| | Total | | 21 | 1 | - | - | - | 2 | - | - | - | 24 |
| MATRILOCAL | IN MUNDGOD SETLEMENT | P | 59 | - | - | - | - | 1 | - | - | - | 60 |
| | | S | 40 | - | - | - | - | - | - | - | - | 40 |
| | | T | 3 | - | - | - | - | - | - | - | - | 3 |
| | | SP | 8 | - | - | - | - | - | - | - | - | 8 |
| | Total | | 110 | - | - | - | - | 1 | - | - | - | 111 |

| 1 | 2 | 3 | 4 | 5 | 6 | 7 | 8 | 9 | 10 | 11 | 12 | 13 |
|---|---|---|---|---|---|---|---|---|---|---|---|---|
| MATRILOCAL | TOTAL | P | 77 | 1 | - | - | - | 1 | - | - | - | 79 |
| | | S | 47 | - | - | - | - | 2 | - | - | - | 49 |
| | | T | 4 | - | - | - | - | - | - | - | - | 4 |
| | | SP | 8 | - | - | - | - | - | - | - | - | 8 |
| | Grand Total | | 136 | 1 | - | - | - | 3 | - | - | - | 140 |
| GRAND GRAND TOTAL | | P | 481 | 13 | - | 2 | - | 14 | 1 | 2 | 1 | 514 |
| | | S | 269 | 17 | 1 | 1 | 1 | 9 | 2 | 2 | - | 302 |
| | | T | 25 | - | 1 | - | - | - | - | 1 | - | 27 |
| | | SP | 44 | - | - | - | - | - | - | - | - | 44 |
| | | PT | 8 | - | - | - | - | - | - | - | - | 8 |
| | | O | 8 | - | - | - | - | - | - | - | - | 8 |
| TOTAL | | | 835 | 30 | 2 | 3 | 1 | 23 | 3 | 5 | 1 | 903 |
| PERCENTAGE | | | 92.23 | 3.33 | 0.22 | 0.33 | 0.11 | 2.56 | 0.33 | 0.55 | 0.11 | 100.00 |

their husband. Here a woman who is a divorcee or a widow with a daughter from her first husband, when remarries, takes her daughter, to her new conjugal family. After attaining maturity the daughter is also taken as a wife by her mother's husband. However, this type of marriage involves no rituals. To symbolically convey it to the members in their society a few close relations are invited for the celebration where men and women drink *chãng* and dance, and the marriage is solemnised and declared. The situations which gave birth to such types of marriage are as follows: owing to scarcity of women to marry in one's own class group a man marries a much older divercee or a widow who has a grown up daughter from her previous husband, with the intention to marry the latter in due course of time. The step father looks after the girl and later when she attains the age of maturity she is taken in marriage by the man who is neither her biological nor a social father. There will be again lot of age gap between them. This did not matter because the man can also ask his younger brothers to join him in polyandary; which will also get him financial and other support from them. Secondly, divorcees or widows who had none to look after them got remarried, and later owing to their emotional attachment towards their daughters from first union never wanted to give them out in marriage. Instead asked them to marry their step fathers and stay with them. Away from him and no body to fall back the girls stayed with their mothers. Thirdly, there are cases of step fathers marrying their step daughters to give legitimate status to their illegitimate children.

In a few cases the step fathers thought that if their step daughters marry out and go away the family will lose one working hand. A few step fathers themselves were attracted by the young girls and took them as their wives. Not in all cases the girls agreed to marry their step fathers who were old or poor. Under such circumstances, the step fathers even forced them to have sex with them and later announced in the community that the girls have been already taken in marriage. The Tibetan society though criticize such men for their behaviour could not do anything since the girls were under the control and obligation of their step fathers. A few argued that they were alone and none to cook food and keep home for them and so married their step daughters. They said if they give these orphan girls in marriage to some one outside, their husbands may not care for them well, and to avoid these problems they themselves married them. There are also cases of girls taken for a young man paying bride price and later the young man died or refused to marry the girl arranged by his parents. Under such circumstances the father of the boy takes the girl as his wife if not to have sex but to establish his claim on the girl till one, of his younger brothers, cousins or nephews join him in polyandry. In other cases daughters had sexual relation with their step fathers and children were born to them. Later they married some other persons and went to their conjugal homes with their children. Most of this type of marriages were polygynous and without any formal rituals. The informants told that these types of unions are not totally approved by the society, but it continues to occur owing to the peculiar conditions existing in the Tibetan society especially away from their traditional home land.

However, one has to be careful in making any generalizations regarding Tibetan marriages. Because in some cases they were not real marriages but just arrangements to bring a legitimate status to the child of the unwed mother or to establish a claim on the girl for economic or other reasons. In some cases once the purpose is served the girls will be again at liberty to break her relations with such husbands and marry someone legally.

There are 29 polygynous marriages with patrilocal residences. Among them 20 are sororal polygynous; three are non-sororal polygynous; six are generational polygynous. It can also be seen that these marriages are found mainly among peasants and momads.

The practice of polygyny was widely present in Tibet. Our data also shows that eighteen such marriages took place while they were in Tibet, three in the transit camp and eight in the present settlement. Now the trend is on decrease in polygynous marriages. This is owing to the scarcity of women and the poor financial conditions prevailing in the settlement.

Sororal marriages with matrilocal residences are few. Only two marriages took place in transit camps and another has taken place in Mundgod. The sororal polygynous marriages were proved to be more stable than the non-sororal types, as the sisters come from the same family. In polygynous marriages many irregularities such as the elder sister after becoming a widow or a divorcee, joining the younger sister's husband or the reverse one found. And even a few of these marriages took place owing to the death or barranness of the first wife (elder sister of second wife).

It was also believed that the younger sister or the first wife, may look after the children of her sister well.

## Polyandrous Marriages

The Tibetan word for polyandrous marriage is *Sa-Sum- pã*, which means "the three who eat together". It is reported that the polyandry was more prevalent among those who came from the U-Tsang and the Kham-ba provinces. The composition of this type of marriage varies from one area to another and one class of people to other. It existed in all classes of people with varying composition. Sir Charles Bell (1928:193) wrote that monogamy was more prevalent in Tibet. Bell further quotes from the information collected by the Peak Secretary, that in the province of U out of every twenty households one might say that fifteen would be monogamous, three polyandrous and two polygynous. In the Northern plains he estimated, the proportion to be ten polyandrous, seven monogamous and three polygamous.

As it has been already described the polyandry takes three forms – fraternal, non-fraternal and generational. Fraternal and generational polyandry usually takes place patrilocally (*nã-mã*) and the non-fraternal polyandry takes place matrilocally (*mag-pã*). Fraternal polyandry takes place among the brothers born of the same parents. Polyandry among classificatory brothers is rare. It is the eldest brother who marries the girl on the condition that the girl should take his other younger brothers also in the union. The elder brother governs the entire authority of the family, inherits the family headship and its movable and immovable property from his parents and also priority of sex with the woman married in polyandrous union. The other brothers accept elder brother's supreme authority and function without any disapproval. The eldest brother takes decisions regarding all the family matters and assigns the duties to other brothers. Most of the time in a year they will be away from the main family as traders, herdsmen, etc., and all the profits they gain go to the common family purse held under the authority of the eldest brother.

The informants from the Kham-ba region told that there was no jealousy regarding sexual rights among the brothers. They further told that wife was shared on rotation. The brother who stays at home readily gave the wife to the other brothers who arrive after their tour of business. The sexual intimacy with the common wife runs by mutual understanding and cooperation among the brothers though as a mark of respect the eldest brother holds his priority in the sex as in other aspects of the household. The whole family as a group forms an indivisible unit entity which is represented by the eldest brother. Whoever among the brothers may be the biological father; the children born to the wife are counted as those of the eldest brother. The children address and refer the eldest brother as *pã-lã* meaning 'father' and all his younger brothers as *a-gu*, meaning 'uncle'.

Normally a polyandrous group accepted not more than three husbands in the union. Younger brothers if there are any and if they are too young to join the union, are either sent to monastery accepting celibacy or allowed to marry matrilocally to other families. It is rare to find them marrying independently and forming separate households. Monks joining monastery did possess potential authority over the wife and the land of the family they belong. So in case if a monk comes out of a monastery relinquishing celestial life he has a right to make a normal living in the society. Bringing of another woman into a polyandrous union was strictly prohibited. If any brother brings a new wife, he was seperated out of the family with his wife and a small amount of movable property. This is to retain family property intact and this shows the importance the Tibetans gave for the family property.

Non-fraternal polyandry was not preferred in Tibet. A Tibetan proverb says "*Chu-ma ja-mna Lu-dhang chees, Je -deu na trok-po Cha-la dees*" meaning, if you want to be equal, perform pooja to water gods; if you want to have problems in life, have marriage with friends. Friends who possess different bones (*rus*) never meet or agree with each other on many things the way the brothers of a common bone do. Therefore non-fraternal polyandrous marriages are not preferred by the Tibetans even today.

The bigenerational polyandry wherein a father and his son shared a wife, was also practiced in Tibet. In this union father who had lost his wife, brought in a wife for his eldest son instead for himself. Himself being still not very old had a right for sexual access in this woman. This was practised to avoid bringing in two wives, one for the father and the other for the sons. Sometimes he brought wife for himself and was shared by his children. This was to solve the problems in the matters of inheritance of familial property between the sons of first and second wives.

The reasons given for the practice of polyandry by the Tibetans in Tibet are as follows: (1) To maintain familial property intact or to avoid the division of property into smaller holdings which weakened the family economically. (2) To raise the family economy by maintaining unity and co operation among the brothers which ultimately brings higher status in their social and economic life in the society. (3) To maintain peace in the family by having only one woman instead of more. The Tibetans think that any number of men can meet but not two women. (4) Lastly, it minimizes familial worries and burdens since they will be shared by more than one man.

Most common among the polyandrous marriages through matrilocal residence, are the non-fraternal. As described already in a *mag-pa* marriage, it is the woman who has the sole right on her husbands. Even the elder or the younger brothers of a *mag-pa* will not have any right of access to sex with such a woman in polyandry. The brothers of a *mag-pa* lived separately, in their parental family. However, a woman in *mag-pa* marriage can take as many number of husbands as she wishes. She could even authoritatively force her first husband to accept some more members in the union so that they can be of some help to the family. Apart from this since Tibetans had a dualistic life in Tibet, they could not maintain individual families of their own. Because of these reasons polyandry was a preferred type of institution practised in Tibet.

In Mundgod today, no such situations are present and so there is also a change in the composition of the polyandrous marriage. Here we can see the institution of polyandry remaining the same in its structural aspect, but it is less common than in Tibet. The informants also told that polyandry is not necessary here since they do not hold the land in common. Their life here is also usually not a dual one. On the other hand the permanent stay of the male members with their family creates problems in polyandrous sexual union.

There were in all 36 polyandrous marriages of various types reported in the Tibetan settlement as shown in Table 14.

The investigations have revealed that the members are pressed by circumstances to accept this type of union. Important among them are to bring unity and economic cooperation among the brothers. Most of the polyandrous marriages in The Settlement are of bifraternal type, where one brother stays with the family looking after the dependent members and also attend to the farm work, while the other brothers join para military service or go on business and contribute to the family purse. Polyandrous union thus is based mainly on economic cooperation. Secondly, they cannot marry individually and establish a family of their own since most of the time in a year, they stay away from home in service or on business tours.

A significant change which has taken place in the institution of marriage after coming to India is in the authority of the eldest brother over his younger brothers. Though he totally shoulders the responsibilities of the family he cannot demand obedience and respect from them as in traditional Tibet. He cannot make them remain as his co-husbands. If a younger brother prefers to go separate, he cannot be stopped. Younger brothers also get equal rights for the movable property of the family such as cash, cattle and ornaments. They may even claim the wife in accordance with polyandry and take her away though she traditionally belongs to the eldest brother.

Under non-fraternal polyandry men who are not brothers share a wife in common. In Mundgod Settlement it is observed there are only three such cases where friends share a wife in common. It is observed that some men when they came from Tibet, had none to care or work with. So they entered into polyandry with some one already married and had a family but had problems to support it. In these cases the men reside separately in their houses and also keep their agricultural produce separate. The wife lives with her principal husband. When the principal husband is away or even at his presence in the home these accessory husbands have a right to visit her and have sex with her. These co-husbands do not hold sexual jealousy among themselves. Usually when an accessory husband arrives at night after his dinner to the house where his wife lives, it is understood he has come for sex. As a mark of her consent to it the wife offers him *chãng*. If the first husband is present he too gives him company in drinking. They drink and talk on day to day matters till they feel sleepy. Later the visiting husband is led to the bed room by the wife and the other husband readily sleeps in the varandah of the house. The men in non-fraternal polyandrous union help each other in economic activities like agricultural operations, business tours, etc.

It is observed out of the total polyandrous marriages, 35 are patrilocal and one is matrilocal. It can also be seen that polyandrous marriages are more among the shephards (20 out of 253 marriages or 2.2%). Comparatively the peasants have less (i.e., 14 out of 435 or 1.54%) number of polyandrous marriages.

The institution of polyandry is more important for nomads for the following reasons. First, the people of older generation among the nomads had less contact with outside world and so, they maintained their traditional value towards the polyandrous marriage intact. They were also able to force their youngsters to adopt the polyandrous marriage. Those of younger generation who are educated and serve in para-military services or work for wages in woolen garment business, cannot afford to have a family of their own. So they joined their brothers in polyandry. Thirdly, as nomads they are still to adjust to the agricultural life here. Facing the economic hardships they joined their brothers in a family, thus forming a joint marriage i.e., in polyandry. On the other hand the peasants who were well settled with farming as their profession in Tibet, are not finding it much difficult to adjust to farming life here. They are able to form an independant family of their own; based on the individual economy and prefer to marry in monogamous pattern.

It is forbidden for the Buddhist Tibetans to have sexual intercourse in the room where the family altar is put up. Usually the children, unmarried and the old people sleep here and the married persons share a separate room, may be the kitchen or the store-room. Under critical circumstances of lack of space, a couple can have sexual intercourse in the god's room but only after putting a curtain in front of the altar. Kissing and hugging are common among the sexes before coitus. It is forbidden for men to touch the breasts of a woman. It is said the breasts are the property of her children from which they get milk. The child is her flesh and blood and as a consanguineal kin it gets the right to touch breasts and drink the secretion. Whereas the husband who is an affinal kin, has no right to touch them. Thus Tibetans place children and husband at different levels. The Tibetan men are not excited at the sight of breasts of women since they are not sex symbols. However, in the present days, there is a change in the tendency among the younger generation. They say they cannot get satisfaction in their sexual intimacy without touching the breasts of their sex partners. It was informed that that this type of fondling with the breasts is a new habit learnt by a few youngsters from their Indian friends.

A Tibetan bed is a six feet by five feet sheet like quilt which is used for lying down as well as for covering the body. Tibetans never cover their face with this but during cold seasons they may cover the face with another woolen sheet. Among Tibetans, men, women, children and old use separate beds. Tibetan men never share their bed with their wives and always slept in their bed and went to meet their wives in the night. This is followed as a custom; may be to vacate the wife's bed so that other husbands may visit her the same night. This is a practice which was prevalent even in Tibet. However, in Tibet the younger brothers had to wait for the absence of their elder brother from the house to have sex with the wife since he had the sole right and authority over her and may come to his wife's bed at any time. Now his claim is weakened and the other husbands can sleep with her even if the elder brother is present in the house.

## The Marriage Geography

As on 1978, in all 903 marriages were contracted among the Tibetans of Mundgod settlement. Of them 387 (42.85%) were contracted in Tibet, 187 (20.72%) in transit camps and 329 (36.43%) after coming over to the Mundgod settlement. Out of 387 marriages which took place in Tibet 382 (42.27%) were patrilocal and 5 (0.58%) were matrilocal. It was also observed that 366 (39.7%) marriages were contracted taking spouses from within the same district and only 16 (1.76%) came from the neighbouring districts. Not a single marriage was contracted with persons outside the province. In case of the five matrilocal marriages 3 (0.33%) were contracted with persons within the district; while the other 2 (0.22%) were contracted outside the province. The marriages of the latter category were contracted when men were in that province on business tour.

Of the 187 (20.72%) marriages which were contracted in transit camps, 73 (8.03%) were with persons originally coming from the same district, 67 (7.37%) with persons coming from other districts and 21 (2.31%) with persons coming from different provinces. There are also 2 (0.22%) marriages contracted with Indians. Marriages with spouses from other districts are almost equal to the marriages of spouses within a district. Compared to situation in Tibet to the transit camps we can see a steep increase in this type of marriage from 16 (1.76%) in Tibet to 67 (7.37%) in transit camp. While in Tibet there was not even a single marriage contracted with person outside a province. While in transit camps 21 (2.31%) inter province marriages took place. Among the matrilocal marriages 8 (0.88%) took place within the district, 10 (1.10%) took place with persons coming from other districts, 3 (0.33%) took place with persons coming from different provinces, 1(.11%) with a person whose tribal origin is not known and 2 (0.22%) marriages took place with Indians. Contrary to the situation in Tibet there is an increase in the marriages with the persons coming from other districts and other provinces.

Of the 329 (36.43%) marriages taken place in Mundgod settlement, 218 (24.14%) are patrilocal and 111 (12.29%) are matrilocal. Of the 218 (24.14%) patrilocal marriages 108 (11.88%) were contracted with persons of the same district and 90 (9.90%) with persons from other districts and 15 (1.65%) with persons from other provinces. In case of matrilocal marriages, 49 (5.39%) married persons coming from the same district, 30 (3.3%) outside the district but from the same province and 4 (0.44%) with persons coming from other provinces.

Of the patrilocal marriages within the district, we notice, the ratio of the marriages contracted changes from 95.81% (Tibetan situation) to 44.78% (transit camp) and to 49.83% (Mundgod settlement). This ratio clearly shows that there was higher preference for contracting marriages within the district in Tibet. However, it came down to 44.78% in transit camps. It has again raised to 49.83% in Mundgod camp. The increasing tendency shows the increase in the Tibetan values towards the traditional type of marriage. Regarding the marriages contracted with persons from other districts the ratio varies from 4.19% (Tibet) to 41.11% (transit camp) to 42.78% (Mundgod). This ratio clearly shows while in Tibet marriage with persons outside the districts were minimal but in transit camps and in Mundgod settlement the number increased considerably. Regarding the marriages contracted outside the province there were none while in Tibet. Now we can see as many as 12.88% having taken place in transit camp and 5.46% in Mundgod settlement. These figures show that this type of marriages which were not at all preferred and practised in Tibet, have come into practice after they come out of Tibet. However the number of such marriages is decreasing now in Mundgod. This clearly shows that the Tibetans whose ideologies and values were broken, owing to their new status as refugees in transit camps have reestablished or regained them since their social and economic conditions have improved. while in Tibet the number of matrilocal marriages contracted within the district itself was as high as 60%. This came down to 33.36% when they were in transit camps and now it is 44.14% Mundgod settlement. The figures show that while in Tibet marriages with persons within a district were highly preferred. However, this was disturbed while they were in transit camps. Once again it is moving towards the traditional setup in the Mundgod settlement.

While in transit camps they had the worst time to support themselves. In this situation some of them came closer to the Indians and as a result four marriages have taken place with Indians. In Mundgod, of course, there are none and the Tibetans are trying hard to keep themselves away from the local population, in this connection.

Tibet being a land with geographical barriers, having no proper roads and communication net work posed problems in terms of transport of men and material. This brought some type of isolation and development of regional cultures and groups among the Tibetnans. There was very little spatial movement of common man and so there was very little communication between people coming from different districts and provinces. It was only the traders who moved about, had a little opportunity to travel and also marry outside.

When the Tibetans arrived at the transit camps, irrespective of their province and district, were housed together for nearly 7-8 years. This brought considerable contact among themselves and this was extended to marital alliances. The common problems they faced made them to forget their differences and come closer. As they are rehabilitated in the permanent settlements now they are able to revive their traditional values in selecting spouses, food, dresses, etc., of the people and district who share common culture. They also feel that when they return to Tibet, the conjugal families will be closer by frequent exchange of visits, gifts and other socio-economic activities.

In the traditional Tibetan society different groups stood in obligation to exchange bridges. On this basis two villages which had affinal ties mutually exchanged visits, help etc. These were receprocal in nature. When they come out of Tibet these relations were lost to some extent and new values and relations were adopted. Thus the original norms and values were relaxed to some extent. Now with the gaining of economic and social stability the original values and moral stability are also returning. The old customs and manners are also revived. As a result today, marriage between the members coming from the same place and or district in Tibet are preferred. Because on an enquiry it is understood that they prefer such persons so that on their return to Tibet they will be together to help one another.

To sum up, the traditional Buddhist values are for the renunciation of the materialistic world, this trend is now on decrease as good number of monks are reported to have left their spiritual life and married. The distinction between various class groups is now being weakened and only two divisions - the pure and the impure bones are recognised for selecting mates. Marriage and other ties are established on regional basis so that in case of their return to Tibet they can be together. Many more marriages with wider age disparity have taken place because of social or economic reasons. The customary authority and leadership, the old moral codes and conduct have lost their importance. The incidences of divorce, pre-marital or extra-marital unions and child birth are on the increase. Many instances of a man/woman marrying with divorcees, widows/widowers and also with their daughters/sons from previous husband/wife were reported showing much wider age disparity and peculiar type of marriages such as generational polygyny or polyandry are seen among the Tibetan refugees.

In the present set up here the elder brother does not hold the authority and power as in Tibet. So the younger brothers prefer to marry separately and establish their own separate household with their own land holding. This has resulted in the decline of polyandrous marriages, and monogamous marriages are on the increase. In rare cases two or three friends married together for economic cooperation –non-fraternal polyandry. In some cases polygynous marriages have taken place mainly for economic reasons as the additional wife serves as an additional hand to earn for the family. While in Tibet marriages with persons from different districts and provinces were practically nil. Such marriages which took place in more number in transit camps, have now considerably reduced and started marrying with people of their own district or province. Thus the traditional values which were once lost under the refugee conditions, are now regaining their importance.

Tibetan Children in a Nursery School

# 6

# Economic Organization

A report submitted to the International Commission of Jurists by its Legal Inquiry Committee on Tibet (1960: 66-67) says: "At present out of a population of 1.2 million people in Tibet the number of feudal lords and their government functionaries is less than 5 per cent while the peasants account for 60 per cent, herdsmen 20 per cent and lamas 15 per cent. There are in addition, a small number of craftsmen and merchants". The feudal lords either of monastery or of the local government of Tibet, controlled all the land in Tibet.

The Tibetans consider that the land belongs to the divine authority - His Holiness the Dalai Lama. He in turn they believe, has allotted the land to three agencies - monastery, state and nobility. These three institutions provide commoners with protection, and service and they in turn owe them tax and services.

Based on their economic activity the Tibetan population was divided into peasants, nomads or herdsmen, traders and artisans. Each group was in itself a separate cultural entity with different ways of life.

## A. Peasants (Shing-bã)

Tibetan peasants, or the cultivators, lived in countryside. Compared to the land area available for cultivation the tillers were few. As Bell (1928:30) says, "Tibet lacks men to till the land. Owing to their practices of polyandrous marriages and celibate life in monasteries, and also due to a high death rate owing to venereal diseases, there men were few and, therefore, most of the land was left fallow".

The monasteries were autonomous in nature and self administered. The land attached to these is known as *Cho-zi.* Monasteries in turn gave land to lay (*mi-ser*) for tilling and in return they paid land tax and also served their masters (*Jin-dã*).

Land owned by the state is the land given to the government

(i) Ploughing with the Help of a Tractor

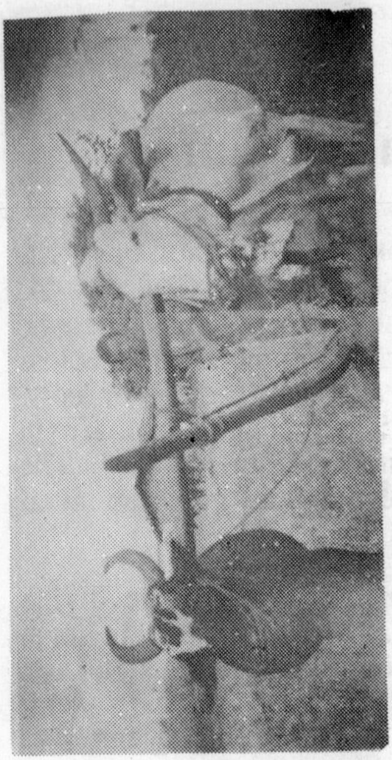

(ii) Local Indian Labourer Teaching a Tibetan to Handle the Native Plough

(iii) Local Indian Labourers Collecting the Harvested Paddy into Rikes

(iv) Arranging Maize Corn heads for Drying

(i) Tending the Calves of Cows

(ii) A Watch Tower in the Field

Tibetan Girls Learning Sewing and Embroidery in the Central School

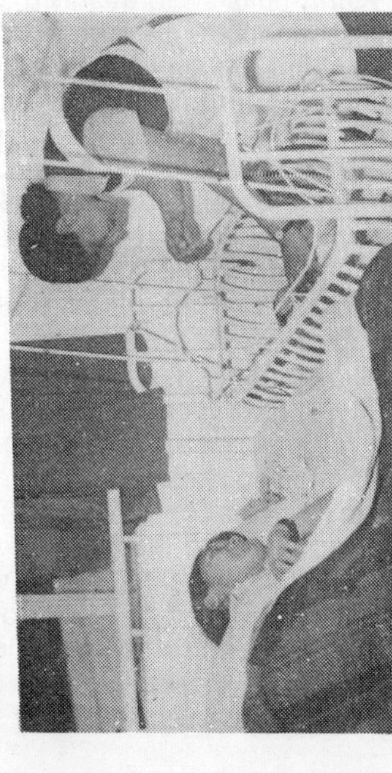

A Mother and her Baby in the Maternity Ward

officials for their services towards their fellow men and this is known as *Shu-ng ko-ng*. This land is also cultivated by the serfs. The land owned by the nobility is known as *Ger-pã*. It is made up of large domains handed down from generation to generation within each individual family of the ancient Tibetan aristocracy. The property owned by the nobility was unquestionable and the noble was the sole authority of the property and the serfs attached to him.

Serfs attached to the land were not allowed to move out of it without the permission of their lord. Those who go out with permission should return to his lord before the scheduled time was over. When he could not return he had to inform his lord and get the time of their stay extended. Otherwise he was liable to be traced, and was legally subjected to heavy punishment and high penalty. A serf who wanted to leave his place permanently had to get legal permission from the noble and also had to pay him a large sum of money. In addition he was also supposed to get the permission from the district officer to shift his residence permanently.

The land holding rights of the serfs were of three types: (1) the *Khral-pã* is a serf attached to any of the three estates. He was in possession of his lord's land permanently. As long as he fulfilled his obligations in terms of human and animal service towards his lord, the latter had no right to take away the land given to him. Under this type of cultivatorship the right to cultivate the land could be inherited by his descendents. (2) The *dud-chung* (bound) type of serf received the land from the lords, on individual basis. In this case a serf could enjoy the benefits of the land but it could not be inherited by his descendents. The serf also had no right to sell his tilling right to any other person and it was the right of the landlord. This type of land was normally returned to the lord after the death of the individual serf who held the land. However, the land tilled by a father could be extended with legal permission of the lord to his sons. This type of serfs owed taxes to their lords only in the form of manual labour and not on any corvee services. (3) The serfs of the human lease are the third type and they could work for any of the lords and were free to move wherever they wanted. The serfs here leased a certain area of land or a flock of sheep or herd of cattle. The lord had the full control over the leased property and the serf could not sell or give them away to others. However, he was free to utilise it in any way he liked in order to get more income. In return he was obliged to give a certain amount of the produce to his lord, every year, for the property given to him.

## B. Nomads (Drok-pã)

Tibetan nomads or heardsmen distinguish themselves into three groups: (1) **the richer class:** possesses its own livestocks - thousands of sheep, hundreds of yaks and scores of horses. They also own fifteen to twenty working men and women; and the serfs attached to them. (2) **a middle class** nomad holds two hundred to four hundred sheep, twenty to thirty yaks and five to ten horses. They may also possess one or two servants. (3) **the poor class** owns fifty to hundred sheep, two to five yaks and one to two horses and may not possess any servants. These groups of nomads may hold the property of their own or of lease from their lord. Bell (1928:25) recognized two types of livestock leases. First, shepherds employed by a family must pay one lamb yearly for every three sheep. Any thing produced over this may be kept for themselves and the deficiency must be made good. The wages for these serfs holding the livestocks, were provided by their lords. Under another form of tenure the owner may specify a certain amount of yak-hair, butter and cheese to be paid to him at the end of the year, and any other surplus goes to the serf holding the livestocks. One *sho* (about 4 paise) was also paid in return for collecting the wool. A tenure of this kind was nicknamed as "no birth and no death" system implying a number of cattle received should be returned and any increase in the flock went to the shepherd and any decrease owing to death or loss or theft, must be made good by him.

The nomads moved from place to place in search of food and shelter for their livestocks. Changes in the ecological conditions according to the variations in the season, compelled them to lead a dual way of life. Men went to grazing lands with their livestocks and came back only during the winter, to get protection against cold. Nomads divide a year into four seasons: (1) *Chegã* (winter): It commences from the eleventh Tibetan month (*Dawa Chuk-chik-pã*) and lasts till the first month (*Dawa Thãng-bõ*), i.e., from December to February. During winter the land will be covered with snow and grass will not be available for cattle anywhere. So they stay at home with all their livestocks and feed them with hay collected during autumn. However, during day time the livestocks are led to pasture lands, nearer to the village settlement and brought back during the night. (2) *Yer-ka* (summer): Tibetan summer commences from the second Tibetan month (*Dawa Nẽ-wã*) and continues upto the fourth month (*Dawa Shi-bã*), i.e., from March to May. Summer is the warmest season. Water from the melted snow starts flowing down in the form of streams. Since the land is cleared of snow now, grass shoots-up everywhere. The nomads who live in tents, taking this opportunity, shift their camps often to get good grass to their cattle. (3) *Thyo-ngã* (rainy season): The Tibetan rainy season starts from the Tibetan fifth month (*Dawa ngã-wã*) and goes upto the seventh month (*Dawa Dyu-mbã*) i.e., from June to August. During these months rains will be heavy and the nomads stay in plains. (4) *Ku-ngã* (Spring season): starts from the eighth month(*Dawa Gye-pã* ) and lasts till the tenth month (*Dawa Chu-pã*), i.e., from September to November. This is the cold season and there will be occasional snow fall. Now onwards the grass starts fading and finally gets covered up by snow. Hence the nomads foot their livestocks where they could take shelter against the cold winds and the occasional snow fall.

The peasants, it is observed, had certain number of livestocks and pasture lands also. A few peasants led the dual pattern of life of peasants and nomads in terms of their economic as well as physical stay. They were, therefore, called *Sa-mã Drok-pã*, literally meaning a combined life of peasants (*Shing-bã*) and nomads (*drok-pã*).

During winter the economic activities of shepherds include both food production and preservation. The livestocks now well fed with the plentiful supply of autumn grass, etc., will be slaughtered for flesh. The meat pieces were treated and stored well under the cover of snow. Women who cannot go out owing to cold weather, sit at home and spun wool and weave it into cloth. During the summer they cut the wild grass and preserve it to be used as fodder for animals during winter season. The Tibetans breed their cattle as dairy animals also. Male offspring born of the union of a bull (*lhã-ng*) and female yak are used for agricultural and as pack animals also. In trade and seasonal migrations these animals were of greater use compared to pure yak. While the female hybrid gave more milk than the ordinary cattle.

## C. Traders (*Tso-ng-pa or Cho-ng-bã*)

The trading community stood between peasants and the

nomads - who did not own any property - land or the livestocks. They served mainly as link between these two groups. They got animal products namely, meat, ghee, cheese, skin, wool, etc., from nomads and supplied them to the peasants. In return, from peasants, they received food products, namely, barley, wheat, etc. and gave them to the nomads. They also exported Tibetan products namely wool, yak-tail, musk, deer horn, salt, medicinal herbs, skins of yak and sheep, woolen cloth, blankets, etc., to India and China and imported metal wares, tea, porcelain, textiles, sugar, rice, dried nuts and also silk from India and China. Gold was found in the uplands of Northern Tibet. Tibetans believed that mining of gold took away the fertility of the soil and it also angered the earthly gods. A few informants viewed this ban on mining of gold to a different reason. They were of the opinion that extraction of gold brings more money and wealth to the Tibetans and this in turn leads the Tibetans towards materialistic living rather than a spiritual one. The basic principle of Buddhist philosophy is the renunciation of worldly things. This includes renunciation of metals like gold. Besides, the Tibetans were not aware of techniques and means to extract gold profitably and market it.

The main Tibetan trade centre was Lhasa; from which many trade routes were extended towards Ladakh, and Kalimpong. Traders were free from tax obligations towards the government. They were also exempted from paying taxes on their profession. However, they were obliged to pay tax on export of materials namely, salt (*tsãgã*), wool (*phey*), pig's hair (*phak-phã*), yak- tail and importing items namely tea. Loads of these goods were transported on yak and sheep back.

## D. Artisans

This group includes the metal workers like goldsmiths, silversmiths, coppersmiths and blacksmiths. They did not possess any lands in Tibet. They work for cash or kind or for both, for all classes of Tibetans. The serfs in order to take their services went to their houses and paid them mainly in cash. When the artisans served the nobles and monasteries they personally went to them to work and stayed with them for days and weeks. In return they received food, *chãng,* and cash payments and some times special gifts depending upon the nature of work done by them.

Artisans were exempted from the payment of all types of taxes. However, in a very few cases they were obliged to serve their masters as well as the religious heads whenever they were called.

There were a few marginal groups of people, namely, the beggars and robbers. Begging was not considered a sin for a monk since he begs not only for himself but also for the humanity. It is believed that he saves the humanity from the wheel of life by teaching them the religion, and its principles. Bell (1928:132) says that 'Tibetans firmly believed that a curse of a begger lama who is refused alms brings ill-luck to that family'. Hence householders readily gave alms to him. *Shem-bã* or *Ro-rgyap-bã*, the carriers of corpse, were an outcaste group. They lived on the alms given by people belonging to high castes. Robbers, form the last category of dependents on the society. They normally lived on high mountains and attacked caravans of traders for food and other needs. The robbers were also religious people and obeyed the sanctions of law and order of the state and they never attacked the monasteries in earning their living.

Table 15 shows the villagewise Tibetan families pursuing various traditional economic pursuits. As refugees now all the Tibetans are rehabilitated as farmers with cultivable land. Though majority of Tibetans come from agricultural background in Tibet, they had difficulty in adjusting to the new agricultural methods and practices since the land and weather conditions over here are different. This sudden shift in the occupation of the Tibetan population who were peasants, nomads, traders, outcastes and the mixed occupational groups in Tibet, and place of residence has brought lot of changes in their way of life and standard of living. Irrespective of their occupational background in Tibet they have been now forced to adopt themselves to the peasant way of living.

The Tibetan refugees rehabilitation Scheme No.II was started in October 1966 with an estimated cost of Rs.25 million. Forest Department of Government of Karnataka, released 4045.29 acres of land in favour of the scheme. The reclamation of the land was undertaken with the help of Swiss Technical Co-operation. Buldozers, needed for reclamation were provided by United Nations High Commissioner for Refugees, Geneva and the United Kingdom. Reclamation took place through removing and shifting of tree stems and roots, levelling the ground, ploughing

## Table 15: Number of Families According to Traditional Occupational Groups In Tibet

| Sr.No. | Village No. | Peasant (P) | Shepherd (S) | Trader (T) | Shepherd and Peasant (SP) | Shepherd and Trader (ST) | Peasant and Trader (PT) | Other classes (O) | Total | Percentage |
|---|---|---|---|---|---|---|---|---|---|---|
| 1. | I | 91 | 32 | 2 | 14 | - | 1 | - | 140 | 13.50 |
| 2. | II | 44 | 15 | 4 | 1 | 1 | 1 | - | 66 | 6.51 |
| 3. | III | 83 | 38 | 7 | - | - | 2 | 6 | 136 | 13.40 |
| 4. | IV | 114 | 90 | 1 | 2 | - | - | 1 | 208 | 20.50 |
| 5. | V | 42 | 9 | 4 | 3 | - | - | 1 | 59 | 5.81 |
| 6. | VI | 113 | 13 | 1 | 3 | - | 1 | 1 | 132 | 13.10 |
| 7. | VII | 53 | 87 | 4 | 16 | - | - | 1 | 161 | 15.90 |
| 8. | VIII | 36 | 34 | 2 | 5 | - | 1 | - | 78 | 7.79 |
| 9. | IV | 31 | 2 | 1 | - | - | 1 | - | 35 | 3.45 |
| | Total | 607. | 320 | 26 | 44 | 1 | 7 | 10 | 1015 | 100.00 |
| | Percentage | 59.81 | 31.54 | 2.56 | 4.34 | 0.10 | 0.69 | 0.98 | 100.00 | |

and harrowing the land. Of the total land provided, 3548.39 acres of land is used for cultivation. 461.5 acres are left fallow and 36 acres are used for village sites, roads, schools and office buildings, old and inform homes, hospitals, etc.

All Tibetans who are twelve years of age and above were individually given a land grant of thirtytwo gunthas and those who are below twelve years got twenty gunthas to make a living out of it. Care was also taken to see that members belonging to one family get their land in one area so that they can have it in one patch. During 1969 to 1974, the agricultural land was not permanently allotted to individual owners. Owing to this, every year, the land was redistributed by the Settlement Corporation and as a result a patch of land changed hands every year. This had its own impact on the settlement economy in those years. The land allotted to them was newly brought under cultivation and it needed a great deal of attention and hard labour in the form of levelling and clearing of roots and bushes. Since the land changed hands every year Tibetans took little interest in improving it. Money given to them to make the land more fertile by putting more labour and fertilizers, was rarely spent because they thought that the land would be given to others next year. They used the artificial fertilizers which were easily available to them from the Tibetan Co-operative Society, on credit basis but without much yield. Thus Tibetans at Mundgod incurred heavy expenses on agriculture and earned less profit out of it as they did not go for the basic need to improve the land.

The other reasons for getting lesser profit from agriculture were lack of sufficient knowledge about agriculture and lack of interest, lack of local agricultural methods and techniques, etc. Apart from supervisory work most of the Tibetans never undertook strenuous jobs in cultivation. As refugees they had the notion that sooner or later they will return to their home-land and thought there was no need to take extra pains to adjust to a new mode of earning. Some of them also knew that there was no problem for making a living with the available charity and did not bother for the meagre income they got from the land.

While they were in transit camps they were given many items free out of the donations received in the form of food, clothing and money, from foreign countries. For security reasons a few of the Tibetans were not allowed to go out of camps and were kept in camps for a few months and even a few of them were not allowed to go out even for years. However, the Tibetans were made to earn their bread by working as labourers in the projects undertaken by the Government of India. Owing to their special status they were not required to work compulsorily. Alms and charity received from the aid agencies both of Indian and other countries to help them, drove them to become lazy and dependent. Only a few of them who had some cash in hand while coming from Tibet, took up some occupations like woolen garment business, running hotel, maintaining grocery shops, etc., and they became independent to make their living. However, some socio-psychological factors inhibited them to lose their incentive to work hard to earn their bread.

Eventually, when they were settled as farmers in the rehabilitation camps, most of them continued to lead the dependent life. The loans given to these people by the Tibetan Co-operative Society to establish farming were not repaid for several years because of the dependent nature on their part. Realizing the reasons for the non-payment of loans the Society started giving them loans and other facilities for cultivation on credit basis (ploughing, fertilizers, seeds, etc.), and even today after many years of their stay in Mundgod Settlement, a few of them are not able to return the loans.

From 1974 the Tibetans were allotted lands on permanent basis and given many types of assistance -technical and financial, to see that, they will settle properly as agriculturists. In course of time they have learnt to live as agriculturists and have also adjusted to the local climatic conditions. They have also begun to understand that their chances of returning to Tibet may not be in the near future, and so are trying to settle well here itself. Now they are taking more interest in their lands and have started investing money in farming. They have also started planting some fruit yielding trees on their lands.

During the year 1971-73 an agricultural and home science training programme was introduced to train the Tibetans. About thirty five Tibetan men and women, who already had some basic education to become extension workers in agriculture and home science, were trained further to serve among the Tibetan refugee communities in India. Twenty candidates for agriculture and fifteen candidates for home science were trained from various Tibetan settlements in India. This training programme was financed by the Arbeiter Wohlfahrt Bundesverband, Bonn, a

West German firm. The training course was organized in consultation with the Department of Agriculture, Karnataka State and the Regional Home Economist, Government of India, Bangalore. An agricultural expert of Deputy Director's grade, was deputed from the Department of Agriculture, Karwar, as the principal for these training courses. Two women instructors were also deputed to conduct home science training. Two Tibetans who were already trained in agriculture extension in Norway, for five years, also assisted the agricultural trainees. A sum of rupees five lakhs was spent on this project. This training programme helped many young Tibetans to learn and adopt new agricultural methods and practices needed for cultivation in Mundgod Settlement. These pioneers later became models for others in their villages. In turn they also trained other Tibetans in new agricultural operations.

The local Indians from the villages around the Settlement, also helped the Tibetans to learn local agricultural methods and techniques. Indians regularly come to the Settlement as day labourers and taught the Tibetans about the agricultural techniques, ecological cycle, tools and implements and their operations. Even today, the Indians form the main labour force in their agricultural operations.

The Mundgod Tibetan Refugees Rehabilitation Scheme-II was planned with cooperation of many countries of the world. In the field of agriculture India was to give land and the Swatzerland Government to provide technical help. As a part of the help UNHCR also donated the Tibetan Cooperative Society with twentynine tractors with all accessories such as ploughing sets, harrowing sets, etc. Three machines of cone shelling and other agricultural equpments are donated by the Switzerland Government in collaboration with MYRADA, Bangalore. Apart from this the Swiss collaborators sent three agricultural officers and technicians to set up a fulfledged workshop to repair tractors and trucks owned by the Society. They also trained many young Tibetans as electricians, machanics, turners, fitters, etc., and taught them the operations skill of these machinaries.

To start with MYRADA donated money to Tibetans to purchase bullocks. Owing to the small amount of land owned by the Tibetans a group of five members received one ox. They in turn were supposed to join hands with five other people to have a pair of bullocks. Tibetans also received seeds and fertilizers free of cost, for the first two years of their stay in the Settlement.

The Churches' Accelory for Social Action (CASA) made a donation of Rs. 60.00 lakhs to construct a dam near Bachanaki, to irrigate about 2000 acres of land belonging to the Tibetan refugees. The dam was completed in the year 1966-67 and unfortunately till 1981 the water was not used by all the Tibetans owing to several reasons. First, the Tibetans say the land given to them is not properly levelled and so it does not facilitate the flow of water. However, when there is scarcity of rain water, this dam is utilized by both Indians from the neighbouring villages and Tibetans. It is said that the Tibetan refugees intentionally do not use this water and thereby take two crops according to the programme as they have to work hard and put more labour.

The Ministry of Rehabilitation, Government of India, had decided to accommodate one thousand more refugees in the Mundgod Settlement by 1978-79. Since they had to be accommodated within the land already provided to the Tibetan Settlement some amount of land already given to individual refugees was withdrawn and distributed to new entrants. To compensate this loss of land the Tibetans were advised to go for intensive cultivation by using water from the dam. To help them a pilot programme was undertaken by the District Agricultural Officer, Karwar. He hoped to irrigate about 2000 acres of Tibetans' land during 1981. The Officer said that if properly planned the Tibetans can even take three crops in a year. When the plans to irrigate the lands were pushed through the crop pattern would be in the following manner. Paddy and maize for four months from July to October using rain water; Carrot, chilly and other varieties of vegetables from the month of December to March, using the water from the dam; and food and oil seed crops such as soyabeen, wheat, sunflower, etc., from the month of April to June. To make this programme of crop patterning a success, two things were urgently needed: (1) levelling of the land to make it suitable for irrigation, and (2) training the Tibetans to grow new type of crops. Regarding the levelling of the land MYRADA had come forward with its donation of Rs. 40 lakhs. Using buldozers and tractors the levelling of land was started and in this way they were assisted by the Indian agricultural experts, surveyors and technicians.

To train the Tibetans in wet cultivation, a project was

The Old and infirm Tibetans

Tibetans in their village workshop

sanctioned by the Government of India with an estimated cost of Rs. 75,000/- and the training responsibility was taken up by the State Government. An Agriculture Officer, an Assistant Agriculture Officer, two Field Assistants and a peon were deputed to the settlment to undertake the project work. They implemented the programme through demonstration, exhibition and guidance methods. They also took an area of ten acres for demonstration cultivation. In this connection the officer deputed for job said, that there was not much co-operation from the Tibetans. Some of them even said that the Tibetans will not be benefitted much by this project, because now they will have to work hard and in all the seasons. The Tibetans would not have worked on agricultural lands especially in summer, since they were not used to this hot weather. They also said that there was scarcity of farm labours in the area and so they had to invest more money to make best use of the programme.

All these arguments may be true to some extent. A few Tibetans who were not used to this type of work, weather, etc., leased their land to others and live on whatever they got as rent. Others went out for woolen goods business or to work as labourers in Simla, Darjeeling, Dalhousie, etc., which are in higher altitute. A few Tibetans were of the opnion that the water from the Bachanaki dam was very inadequate and so could not meet the needs of both the Indian and Tibetan farmers. This scarcity they fear, would naturally spark bitterness among the two racial groups. Tibetans also feared that the Government of India was gradually withdrawing the land given to them instead of releasing some more land. They thought twentyfour gunthas of land was too small an area to support a person. Hence they prefered to work as labourers in hill stations where they would be at least living in a cooler place, instead of cultivating land here, without much yield.

The Tibetans, specially the nomads, do not favour cultivation. Peasants who were cultivators by tradition readily accepted agriculture and a few have even taken the lands of other Tibetans and Indians, on lease basis. Others who had no other means of livelihood, accepted agriculture and faced lot of difficulty in adjusting to the new professions.

Agricultural land was not and is not permanently allotted to a Tibetan and so he will not get the right to retain it with him, on his/her permanent migration to some other Tibetan village on marriage, divorce, etc. He cannot sell it or even lease it to a Tibetan or anybody else. So after death, marriage, divorce or even migration, the land held from the Settlement corporation automatically went back to it and later the same was allotted to a new member.

Table 16 gives the number of families according to the size of the land holding. However this type of temporary land holding by the Tibetans made it difficult to class it under any type of existing landholding patterns. The individual gets only the right to cultivate till his death. Legally speaking he was not the owner cultivator since the land was not owned by him, or it could not be inherited, and even leased out as he wished.

**Table 16: Mundgod Tibetan Families According to the Size of Land Holding**

| Sr.No. | Land holding in acres | Number of households | Percentage |
|---|---|---|---|
| 1 | Nil | 16 | 1.58 |
| 2 | Less than 1 | 118 | 11.63 |
| 3 | 1 to 2 | 225 | 22.26 |
| 4 | 2 to 3 | 339 | 33.57 |
| 5 | 3 to 4 | 194 | 19.10 |
| 6 | 4 to 5 | 82 | 8.09 |
| 7 | 5 to 6 | 26 | 2.53 |
| 8 | 6 to 7 | 11 | 1.08 |
| 9 | 7 to 8 | 2 | 0.19 |
| 10 | 8 to 9 | 2 | 0.19 |
| | Total | 1015 | 100.00 |

However there are a few types of unauthorised land leasing and mortgazing practiced among the Tibetans in The Settlement. These were in practice even in Tibet. The pricipal amount lent and the interest on it are collected by adjusting the produce from the land mortgazed or leased for a certain number of years. On the expiry of the term the owner got back his land. The other type of land leasing known as *te-ma*, under which all the produce from the leased out land, was adjusted towards the interest, and the principal amount was paid at the expiry of the term to get his land back. There was another form of leasing in which a fixed amount of money or grains was paid to the land owner and the lessee was responsible for the cultivation expenses of the land, etc. Under the other type the lessor and the lessee shared both the produce and also the expenditure.

The Tibetans have also taken lands on lease basis both from Indians of the neighbouring villages and Tibetans. The Table 17 shows that 26 (2.59%) families had leased out their land to other Tibetans, 104 (10.29%) families had both the land given by the government and also the land leased from both Indians (78) and Tibetans (26) and the rest have only the land given to them by the government. As already said legally the Tibetans were not entitled to lease-in or lease-out land and they were only the illegal transactions based on mutual understanding.

Among the Tibetans who had leased-out their lands to other Tibetans 13 were preasants, 8 nomads, 2 traders and 3 shepherds and peasant families. The land was leased out because of several reasons. One among them was that the family lacked male members to work. In a few cases the male members of the family were suffering from tuberculosis or skin diseases and their declining health did not permit them to work on the farm. In other cases the lands allotted were far away from their village and it became difficult for the family to manage it. A few nomads, owing to their cultural background, simply could not learn the local agricultural techniques and so it was less profitable for them. A few Tibetans showed their account books and proved their point. Instead, they leased out the land and got good returns. Above all when this was done he need not have to work in the hot sun and can also go on trade or as a labour, throughout the year and easily earn an additional income.

On the other hand some of the Tibetans were convinced that they were finding agriculture a profitable occupation. By keeping a pair of bullocks and working themselves on the land without hiring tractors or labourers, they could save enough. They also get loans on easy and low interest rates and other help from welfare agencies. Against this a few others argued that they do not have money to buy bullocks. The bullock given in common to five members by MYRADA, could not also be retained by them since all were not interested in agriculture. So its value was agreed upon and one or two bought it exclusively for themselves paying others their share of money. A few of them complained that the bullocks given to them were too old to work with and so they died soon. Both these versions are not fully justified. Thus though the Tibetans were provided with bullocks, they were not prepared to keep them, for they were not attracted by agriculture. So much so that even if a few who could afford to buy new bullocks did not do so.

At least in a few cases the Tibetans were not really having any money to purchase bullcoks. Even today they are poor and are not able to repay their loans and they continued to lease their land to other Tibetans. In the Mundgod Settlement during 1979 out of 1015 families as Table 23 shows, only 375 (36.9%) possessed bullocks.

Table 17 shows that there were 104 owner tenants who took land from 26 Tibetans, and 78 Indians from the neighbouring villages. Of the 104 families, 83 (13.67%) were peasants, 13 (4.06%) were shepherds and herdsmen, 4 (15.3%) were traders, 3 (6.8%) were shepherds and peasant families and one peasant and trader family. Leasing in of land was more among the peasants than the shepherds and herdsmen. This clearly indicated that compared to others the peasants have adopted well to the agricultural life.

Table 18 shows that some Tibetans had taken land from Indians on lease basis ranging from one year to twelve years. This clearly showed the Tibetans hope that they will stay here for atleast twelve more years. They have developed some sort of attachment to this land and agriculture. They have also extended their helping hands to the local population and have established good socio economic contacts with them.

The Indians who had leased the land can be divided into three types. The land given to the Tibetans and the Indians by the Karnataka government was just reclaimed from forest department and was fallow and full of wild growth of bushes and shrubs. The Indians who were poor and landless could not clear the land on their own. So their lands were left fallow; but the Tibetans who had enough technical and financial aid cleared their land and started growing crops. They also thought of taking the land which was next to theirs and belonged to the local Indians; paying money in some cases and free in other. When the agreed number of years were over, the land was returned to the Indian. Till that time he did not get any claim over the produce from the land. However, the land tax was paid by the Tibetan. In one way this was advantageous to the lessor since the land which was fallow was now cleared by the Tibetan and sooner or later returned to him. Under the second type the rich Tibetan peasants took cultivable land from the Indians for certain number of years paying a fixed amount of money. The lessee was at liberty to grow crop of his liking and also took all of it for himself.

## Table 17: Land Leased by Various Traditional Occupational Groups

| Sr.No. | Traditional Occupational groups | Families leasing -in Indian lands | Families leasing -in Tibetan lands | Total No. of families contracted in leasing -in lands | Percentage to Total No. of families in the category | Families not have leased -in/out lands | Percentage | Total No. of families |
|---|---|---|---|---|---|---|---|---|
| | | (a) | (b) | (a+b) | | (c) | | (a+b+c) |
| 1 | Peasant | 64 | 19 | 83 | 13.67 | 524 | 87.33 | 607 |
| 2 | Shepherd | 6 | 7 | 13 | 4.06 | 307 | 95.94 | 320 |
| 3 | Trader | 4 | - | 4 | 15.31 | 22 | 84.69 | 26 |
| 4 | Shepherd and Peasant | 3 | - | 3 | 6.80 | 41 | 93.20 | 44 |
| 5 | Peasants and Traders | 1 | - | 1 | 13.10 | 7 | 86.90 | 8 |
| 6 | Other classes | - | - | - | - | 10 | 100.00 | 10 |
| | Total | 78 | 26 | 104 | 10.39 | 911 | 89.61 | 1015 |

**Table 18: Amount of Land Leased-in by the Tibetan Families Versus the Number of Years Leased**

| Sr.No. | Land taken on lease basis (in acres) / No. of years leased | 0 - 2 | 3 - 4 | 5 - 6 | 7 - 8 | 9 - 10 | 11 - 12 | 13 - 15 | Total No. of families |
|---|---|---|---|---|---|---|---|---|---|
| FROM INDIANS | | | | | | | | | |
| 1 | 0 - 2 | 6 | 3 | - | - | - | - | - | 9 |
| 2 | 3 - 4 | 10 | 4 | 8 | 3 | - | - | - | 25 |
| 3. | 5 - 6 | 8 | 18 | 4 | 2 | - | - | 2 | 34 |
| 4 | 7 - 8 | - | 2 | 1 | 3 | 1 | - | - | 7 |
| 5 | 9 - 10 | - | 1 | 1 | - | - | - | - | 2 |
| 6 | 11 - 12 | - | 1 | - | - | - | - | - | 1 |
| Total No. of families | | 24 | 29 | 14 | 8 | 1 | - | 2 | 78 |
| FROM TIBETANS | | | | | | | | | |
| 7 | 0 - 2 | 5 | 4 | 2 | - | - | - | - | 11 |
| 8 | 3 - 4 | 5 | 3 | 2 | - | - | - | - | 10 |
| 9 | 5 - 6 | 3 | 2 | - | - | - | - | - | 5 |
| Total No. of families | | 13 | 9 | 4 | - | - | - | - | 26 |
| Grand Total | | 37 | 38 | 18 | 8 | 1 | - | 2 | 104 |

A few Indian land owners who were either government employees or lived in far away places, had leased it to Indian tenants. Later the Tibetans with better means took it from them paying more rent. Here the landlord got rent because his land was already cleared and under cultivation and there was no need for the tenant to invest further on that. This was the third type of land renting. Under this type the leased period was much longer, ranging from 8 to 10 years, and the landlords found it much profitable.

All the lease transactions with Indians were settled through the traditional headmen of the Indian villages to which the land belongs. He served both as a mediator and a witness. Since the rent for the land taken was paid in advance for years to come the borrower made a promising note on a stamped paper. In it the area of land, amount and number of years for which the land was leased was mentioned in Kannada and given to the Tibetan money lender. Though the Tibetans did not understand Kannada they accepted it with the faith in the mediators. But with the enactment of laws banning rural indebtness in 1976 all these documents became useless and the Tibetans like any other money lenders, had to collect their amount back using their good relations with the borrowers and the mediators.

Our investigations, have shown that in about 23 cases the Tibetans had terminated their transactions even before the completion of the tenure period. The reasons given for this are as follows: A few Indian landlords demanded for the vacation of their land or else they threatened to bring the matter to the notice of the government officials. Since the whole transaction was illegal and as refugees, the Tibetans got scared and vacated the land. During the 1976 emergency, when 20 point programme was strictly implemented, the lands leased or mortgaged were regained by the owners, the Tibetans who had taken lands belonging to scheduled castes, Lambanis, Muslims and other weaker sections, were hit hard. Secondly, there were instances of Indians cheating the Tibetans by leasing lands which were already mortgaged to some cooperative society or scheduled bank. Tibetans came to know about that only when the cooperative society or bank employees came to confiscate the harvest from the land when the Indian defaulter failed to return the loan. When the Tibetan lessees appealed to the cooperative society officials about this they did not entertain their claim since they were not informed of this transaction early and legally.

There were also instances where both the village leaders and the cooperative society officials jointly prepared traps to cheat the Tibetans who were alien and innocent of local manners.

An anatomical study of Tibetan victims evicted from their leased land, shows that they were weak financially and in tactfulness. Other Tibetans successfully managed to collect their money back and also retain their control on the land. But it was said the Tibetans lost over two lakhs of rupees in their land leasing transactions with Indians, during the year 1976-77. Tibetans say this should not have happened to them as they were poor refugees. When enquired about this, the representative of H.H. the Dalai Lama said that he was not aware of all these happenings. A few Tibetan and Indian informants said that he knew about this illegal money transactions, but he could not do anything to stop it. Other informants said that he not only knew what was going on but that he himself was behind these transactions. He knew the land given to the Tibetans by the government was insuffiicent whereas the resources at their disposal were more and so his people were also capable of managing it better than the Indians. So he "allowed" them to take land on lease.

## Agricultural Operations

In terms of its suitability for agricultural activity Tibet can be divided into two main areas upland and low land. The chief crops grown in the upland were barley. Peas, wheat, mustard, radishes and turnips. Wheat was grown as a main crop in the low lands and potato was grown in both the places. A variety of wheat known as buck wheat, was grown in very low lands, below the attitude of 11,500 feet. This was consumed mainly by the poorer Tibetans. Mustard, grown abundantly, was used to extract oil for lamps and for rubbing on the bodies of children. Maize was grown in very little quantity in Tibet.

In Mundgod the major crops grown are paddy and maize. Only one crop is raised in a year. Also, no mixed crop pattern is followed. About 344 (33.89%) families in the Settlement have raised kitchen garden, using tap water supplied for domestic use. Here they grow chillies, pulses and vegetables, namely, cabbage, cauliflower and sweet potatoes. A few varieties of fruit yielding trees, namely, mangoes, papaya, banana, etc., are also found. Apart from these, flower plants are also usually grown since they need flowers for daily worship. While in Tibet a few informants told, due to scarcity of flowers they offered sacred scarf (*Khã-tã*) instead.

Not all the Tibetan land was cultivable. In a few districts like Gerchey, Phari in the province of U-Tsang, land was not suitable for cultivation. These areas were occupied by only the nomads who for their food exchanged their livestock or dairy products with the traders who come from the other districts of Tibet. In the districts like Phari where the grass needed for the cattle was grown, the nomads exchanged it for food products with the traders.

The agricultural land given to Tibetans here in India can be divided into two varieties: black (*nak-põ*) and brownish (*pi- la sã-põ*) soils. Black soil is used for the cultivation of paddy, and the other variety to grow maize. Tibetans are of the opinion that not all the land they got is fertile and so they have to use chemical fertilizers to make them yield good crop. The two variety of soils are also not evenly distributed to all Tibetans. As a result a few Tibetans who have black soil grow only paddy and others produce only the maize. This has made the Tibetans to exchange rice for maize or vice versa.

The agricultural operations in Tibet can be divided into four main stages: (1) preparation of lands for sowing, (2) sowing the seeds, (3) weeding and watering and (4) harvesting the crop. There are also the operations namely weeding, building of protecting walls, repairing of bunds and canals, arranging for sites to blow the husk from the corns and finally storing the corns and so on.

In Tibet preparation of soil for sowing starts soon after harvesting of a crop, by ploughing land with the help of a plough (*Thong*), pulled by *dzo*. This type of ploughing helped in turning of soil. The informants said that in Kham-ba province the ploughing operation is made in criss cross lines. No systematic horizontal or vertical, lines are made. In other provinces such as *U-Tsang*, ploughing is made in circular lines starting from one corner of a plot. After the first ploughing fields are left like that and it is believed that this type of exposure increased the fertility of the soil. During winter season from December to April, all agricultural operations are suspended. As the summer sets in and snow starts melting, the fields are cleared of water and allowed to dry. As the women folk break the clods using sticks, men levelled the land using a flat and long plank like implement known as *Shãlã*, which was pulled by *dzos*. The operation not only helped levelling the land but also removed the stubs of weeds. Next activity was sowing. Melting of snow from the hill tops and blooming of flowers in trees indicated suitable time for sowing. Tibetans particularly used to watch the flowering of a plant known as *Hu-thung*, to mark the beginning of the sowing season. Other indication was the position of a particular star in the sky by name *Kar-ma min-duk*. This star was seen at the beginning of the sowing season, at the back of their district (zong) at about 7.00 p.m.

Sowing in Tibet, took place usually in the month of May (*Dawa Shiva*, the 4th Tibetan month) and continued upto the 5th month (*Dawa ngãwã*). There were three methods of sowing seeds. The first method was seeds were first spread on the ground and then the land was ploughed with the help of a light plough, drawn by *dzos*. In the second method lines were first made with the help of a plough. Later women folk dropped seeds into them. These lines were later covered with soil using a long and flat wooden plank, *Shãlã*. The third method of sowing was planting seeds at regular intervals. The Tibetans had both irrigated and dry cultivation in Tibet. Water coming from the hills due to the melting of snow was led to feeder canals and finally to the fields. This water was also collected in small reservoirs (*Kãng-Choo*) and later this water was used for irrigation. The management of water from the reservoirs was looked after by two persons known as *Lãs-pã* who were chosen for the post on yearly rotation basis, by the villagers.

Harvesting and collecting the crops starts in Tibet from the month of September and continues till the end of October (i.e., 8th to the 9th Tibetan months *Dawa gye-pã* to *Dawa gyu-pã*). Afterwards the crop is dried for one or two weeks, and then gathered in the form of bundles and finally into rikes. Later it was brought home with the help of yaks and *dzo*. The crop was left there, for 3-4 months if they were rich enough and had the stock of food of the previous year. But the poorer ones separted the corn within a month. The food grains cleared of husk, were collected in rectangular shaped stone structures the granaries, built in one corner of the house. It is told that owing to the dry weather in Tibet, the grains stored in such granaries could remain unaffected for 2-3 years and were also not attacked by insects.

The closure of the harvest activity marked the beginning of the socio-religious and economic activities of the Tibetans. Spinning and weaving of yarn for clothes, preparation and preservation of food products namely meat, cheese, ghee, milk products like chura were their main activities. One or two members from a few families went out on business tour and exchanging of materials; even to distant places. This was the time when they could meet their kith and kin in other villages and start negotiations for marriage and so on. This period also served as a leisure time and brought them opportunities to have some cultural activfities like singing and dancing. The Tibetan New Year celebration comes during this season and this marks many functions, and also socio-cultural activities like drinking, singing, dancing, exchange of visits by the kith and kin, and exchange of gifts.

The Tibetans at Mundgod grow only one crop in a year, between the months–May to December. During this period they get enough rainfall brought by the south west monsoon. This corresponds with the Kharif crop activity which is locally known as *Mungāru.* The Tibetans here at Mundgod follow the local Indians in their agricultural operations.

Immediately after the harvesting is over the village leaders assemble in a meeting with the representative of H.H. the Dalai Lama at the Settlement and discuss about the prospects of crops and agricultural operations for the year. In most of the cases these village leaders are also the directors of the Tibetan Co-operative Society and the representative of H.H. the Dalai Lama as its Chairman. In the meeting they also discuss about the profit and loss, prices for the crop, the ploughing rates charged by the Tibetan Co-operative Society, fertilizers, seeds supplied and so on.

During this meeting they also draw lots to fix priority numbers to plough the fields using the tractors owned by the Co-operative Society. There are about 15 young Tibetan men trained by the Swiss Technical Team, to operate the various agricultural machines, namely, the bulldozers, tractors, hullers etc. A supervisor who had trained in Agricultural Sciences, for five years in Norway supervise the activities. Ploughing of the fields starts soon after the harvesting of the crop. Since the ploughing had to be done before the moisture in the soil dries up and the soil become hard, they work day and night. The operation lasts for two months — October to November. It is the duty of the village leaders to see that all the lands of the village are ploughed. There is no need for the individual owners to supervise the work. So some of them go out on business tour. The rent for the ploughing will be collected when the individual owners sell their agricultural produce through the Co-operative Society.

The breaking of clods and levelling the lands is carried out in the month of April and May with the help of clod crusher (*Shālā*). With the coming of the first showers of rains the Tibetans start preparation for sowing of paddy and maize. Agricultural operations like sowing and harvesting are both economic as well as ritual activities. These activities are undertaken with the consultation of Lama or the almanac (*Letho*).

Though most of the Tibetans own cows, goats, sheep and buffaloes, hardly a few use the cattle shed manure. The dung and other waste material collected in a pit near the house was sold to Indian farmers. When asked about this a few Tibetans said that since they do not own carts to transport the manure to the fields, they sell it. Others said that they never believed in fertilizing the fields since it is the job of the fertility Gods. Still others prefer to use the chemical fertilizers supplied by the Co-operative Society. So one cannot expect them to hire a tractor or a cart to transport it to the fields and also spend on labourers to apply it.

## Sowing (*Shing-dyepa*)

Sowing takes place in the month of June. It is done by two methods —with the help of a plough (*thong*) i.e., lines are made in the soil and the seeds are dropped into them by a women by hand (and not through a seed drill). This is the Tibetan traditional method and also the local method of sowing seeds. The other method is sowing with the help of a special seed drill (*Koorige*). This has been adopted by only a few Tibetans, from the Indians. This type of sowing needs two persons a man to drive the bullocks and a woman to drop the seeds. This type of seed drill is used only for sowing paddy in linear fashion. With seed drill, at one time, seeds can be sown in three lines and the sowing will be faster. The fields need to be prepared well for the use of this implement. A plough is used to sow maize.

The seeds needed by the Tibetans are brought from the authorized seed dealers in Mundgod or Hubli or from the local

Indians. The different varieties of paddy grown by the Tibetans are the *Dodgyā, Andarsāli* and *Ginsāli.* Among these the Tibetans prefer both the plumpy veriety (*Hala dodgya*) and red variety (*Kempu dodgya*) of paddy the most since it requires very less watering. The variety is also less prone to diseases. The Tibetans know these varieties of paddy in terms of local terminology since they never had them in their traditional culture. A few Tibetans have taken interest in growing *Mysore Sanna* a fine variety of paddy from Mysore area. This variety not only gives a good yield but also a good price.

Paddy is grown in the low lands and plain lands since these variety of lands will be capable of retaining moisture for a longer period of time. Maize is grown in the slopy lands since it does not need much water. Transplantation (*Si-phney*) method of growing paddy was not known in Tibet. It needs ample irrigation facilities and labour. The agricultural officials advice them on application of fertilizers, which they get it on credit basis from Tibetan Co-operative Society.

There are different opinions regarding the use of chemical fertilizers. A few Tibetans are of the opinion that chemical fertilizers help in getting good yield for the first year, and during the subsequent years the dosage has to be increased. A few farmers, especially the nomads, underwent heavy loss since they could not get good yield from their lands. This was also because of failure of rains. A few greedy farmers did not follow the instructions given by the experts and applied excessive chemicals with a hope to grow more; but lost their crop. However, presently they have come to know the right use of fertilizers.

With the Tibetans also, there is a close relation between agricultural activity and religion. In a way agriculture is a ritual act for them. A worship is, therefore, performed to the family deity (*sun-gmā*) and earth gods before certain activities are undertaken. Rituals are also performed to bring fertility to the land.One can see a number of green coloured flags erected near the Tibetan fields at the time of sowing with short prayer for the family gods, printed on these flags. Most of the Tibetans do not know the meaning of these and simply follow them as a custom.

## Weeding (*Cha-nye Thok-pā*)

There are two types of weeding–with an implement and by

hand. Hand weeding is not preferred by the Tibetans because they feel that it is costly. However, they believe that the use of a weeding sickle not only removes the weeds but also helps in turning the soil. About twenty five days after sowing, the paddy crop is operated with a *dumma kunti* or *yade kunti,* weeding implement, depending upon the tool used for sowing such as a plough or seed drill. Weeding is undertaken atleast three times at an interval of one, two and finally two and half months after sowing. In Tibet weeding was done with the help of a hook like tool (*Lākhri*) by holding it in the centre. Operation of this was different from the *Kunti* used now and the Tibetans faced considerable amount of difficulty and loss by the time they got used to it.

Paddy crop also needs protection against wild animals like boars and rats. Hence the Tibetans watch the crop day and night, from a raised platform erected in the centre of the field. They also burn lamps in the middle of fields, throughout the night, to keep away the boars from the crop.

## Harvesting (*Shingā wā*)

The cutting (*Shing chye-pa*) of paddy starts from the month of October and through November. The harvest is left to dry in the field for 4-5 days. Later it is collected into stacks (*Chokgyapa*) and arranged into rikes (*Try-chek*) and kept for a month or two, till the rains are away. Or else soon after drying of the hay the paddy is separated and marketed.

Threshing of the harvest is done in two ways–by threshing the corn stocks to a hard surface and by operating a roller in a specially prepared threshing floor. When the latter technique is adopted, the hay is often shuffled with a stick having a hook at its tip (*Kong*). After separating the hay the hoof are collected in one place till the entire operation is over. Later the grains are separated by blowing the hoof. Finally the clean paddy is arranged into a heap and a ritual is performed to thank the environmental beings before it is taken home. This is a new practice adopted from the local population, who work for them. While in Tibet they offered a few paddy or maize stocks at the family altar when the crop was collected into rikes. This offering was left there throughout the year and replaced with the new crop next year. This indicates that home gods are responsible in bringing fertility.

The maize corn heads harvested and brought to threshing ground, are dried in the sun. They are also tied into bundles by using the sheeth and hang from the lines tied along the walls around the house. A required quantity of them are left there for seeds and the rest are brought down and the corns are separated with the help of a cone shelling machine available with the Co-operative Society and on rent. There are two such machines which are run with the help of motors in tractors and operated with the help of many hands. So neighbours and friends usually come together to undertake the work. The maize, after winnowing is stored in bags and kept in the varandah on the raised platform, and exposed to sunlight, to protect them against worms and insects.

The Tibetan women are physically strong and do not hesitate to help men in agricultural activities. Involvement of both men and women in different agricultural activities is thus found at all stages. Men do ploughing and levelling of land in addition to sowing, weeding and transport. Women also take part in levelling the land and in breaking the clods, sowing and weeding. They also cut and collect the harvest and later help in its transportation to the threshing ground.

During inadequate rains the Tibetans perform a ritual to the spirits of nature. On an appointed day the rite is performed on the top of a hillock. The hillock at Mundgod is called as *Norbu rey*, meaning the Norbu hill. The ritual takes place by an official accouncement of a high Lama and the representative of H.H. the Dalai Lama in the settlement, in all the villages through leaders and sub leaders of the villages. For the occasion all the monks and farmers from all the villages, assemble and chant spells and offer worship to the spirits. They also throw little flour in the form of offering to the spirits who bring rains. This goes on for three days. On the third day in the morning, all the villagers go around the village fields with the sacred texts, the images of the benovalent Gods or Goddesses, or of H.H. the Dalai Lama or the head of their sect. This act is believed to make the evil spirits go away from the fields and bring blessings for good yield for the year, by the benovalent deities.

## Incipient Economic Diversification

Tibetans have a strict division of labour based on both sex and age. They also attach importance for any secondary occupation other than agriculture, which serves them as a secondary source of income. Men and women join hands and work hard to improve the economic standing of the family. Though the trend, especially among the younger generation, is to change their traditional occupation and go in for easy and paying jobs, a few families still continue to have agriculture as their primary source of family income. The latter situation is found more among the families coming from peasant background. So both men, women and children concentrate on farm activity. It is noticed that the dropouts from the schools mainly belong to the families having the peasent background since they have taken up farming more seriously. They used all the labour force they have in the family. It is noticed that on the contrary, extra hands from families of non-peasant background have joined para-military services or are on business and trade to earn for the family.

While in Tibet *Pom-bõ*, the village headman, took care of all his people even in matters of their food and shelter. It was one of his duties to keep his subjects well fed and happy. As is already discussed the *tre-bã* and the *dud -chung* the bound, held lands from their lords and were self sufficient by producing things needed by them, in their own lands. On the other hand, the human lease serfs were entrusted with one or the other type of work by their lords, for which they received food, and shelter in addition to the usual remuneration. The original Tibetan society was a closely knit system with each fulfilling his obligations towards the other. In this way human and natural resources were under full control of the village leaders and this continued upto the national level. The society was enlightened with the Buddhistic principles and values and, therefore, the Tibetan government was rather interested in helping and taking care of its subjects than in exploiting them.

The Tibetan society as it is in Mundgod, is changed in its values. This is owing to circumstances forced on them as refugees. The change instead of being gradual, has leapt out from simple to complex, and from traditional to modern. For example, a traditional minded Tibetan was satisfied with what little he had. But in the new society a few informants complained that their leaders (*Po-mbõ*) have failed to bring more industries and modern methods so that they can earn more for themselves. They also complained that they have no secondary occupations which can bring them additional sources of income. They now insist that their authorities should start some projects like dairy and poultry farm or any other small scale industries, where the Tibetans can work and earn something instead of sitting idle for almost six months in a year. The poorer Tibetans who cannot till their land for themselves, due to scarcity of money, have leased their lands to others and do nothing throughout the year. Tibetans do not work as wage labourers either to Tibetans or Indians though they can earn quite a bit by this method. Using this situation hundreds of Indian labourers from neighbouring villages work for the Tibetans throughout the year, as day labourers. A few Indians have been also employed by the Tibetans on monthly wage basis and attend to domestic and farm work. In a way this is a loss to the Tibetan community since some part of their money goes outside while their own people are unemployed. Moreover, the leaders have lost interest in their subjects. A few are rich and lead a luxurious life while their followers are poor. Those who could bring wealth with them during their flight from Tibet, have business of their own and are leading a comfortable life. In addition, like other refugees they also continue to get benefits from the relief agencies. They are also influential and use the situation to exploit poorer Tibetans by employing them in their business. All these values are new to Tibetans and are the results of the changed situations.

A few informants however expressed that they took interest and planned their agricultural activity. In the course of time they formed smaller groups (*nam-dey*) among themselves to get mutual help at all levels, instead of employing labourers from outside the settlement. Secondly these groups had plans to contribute some amount of money to start a few smaller projects like dairy farm and poultry, in the days to come. They also had plans to do some welfare work among their people namely conducting literary classes for adults, helping the poor by providing them with loans without interest and to open well equipped nursery schools. They also thought of organizing cultural activities such as Tibetan dramas, songs and dances so that their people will retain their traditions, culture and values. It was thought that these things may help the Tibetans to maintain unity and cooperation in their efforts to free their mother land. But many of their plans remained on paper since the people did not come forward to make use of them. This was mainly due to their socio-economic problems. In addition to this the rich and influential persons did not like the commoners forming this type of groups. They thought the activities of the new group may weaken their position. However, the Tibetan Co-operative

Society was able to start a handicraft section, where about fifty men and women work on daily wages and knit carpets in the Tibetan art and style. This programme apart from serving as a means to earn income has also helped in keeping alive, the Tibetan art and craft and its related activities and values.

Tibetans, as already mentioned hold lands on individual basis which is brought together by the family members for convenience, and cultivation is their primary means of livelihood. Apart from this a few families have taken up a secondary occupations as shown inTable 19.

Those families come to the settlement as late as 1977 and have not yet received their quota of land are engaged in the following occupations as their primary source of family income : woolen garment business (4), labourers in hotels and shops (6), service (1) and monk depending on the alms(1).

Lot of shifts have taken place in the mode of earning by the peasant families with secondary occupations. Of the 607 peasant families (with 1290 males and 1206 females) 63 families (with 79 men and 55 women) have taken up woolen garment business as their secondary source of income. Similarly 27 families (with 36 men and 25 women) out of the 320 among shepherds and herdsmen ; 8 families (with 9 men and 5 women) out of the 26 among the traders; and 7 families (with 8 men and 7 women) out of 45 among the shepherds and peasants and 3 families (with 3 men and 4 women) out of 7 among the peasants and traders, have taken up woolen garment business as their secondary occupation. For details refer Table 20.

The Tibetans usually go on woolen garment business soon after the sowing of their land i.e., in July. They come back for about 15 days, during the harvest season i.e., in October. After this they again go out till the end of February. The garment merchants purchase sweaters, scarfs etc., individually and in bulk from woolen mills in Ludhiana, at a cheaper rate, and sell them in retail on the pavements of towns and cities. It is profitable since they spend very little on establishment and get more income from business than from their lands. They also hire a few Tibetan boys and girls as sales assistants by paying monthly remuneration, in addition to their food and shelter. There are 45 men and 39 women from this settlement who are employed in this way. A

**Table 19: Primary and Secondary Sources of Family Income of Mundgod Tibetan Families**

| Serial Number | Traditional Occupationl groups | Agriculture | Woolen garment business (owned) | Labour in woolen garment business | Office service | Government service | Working in handicrafts centre | Labour in floor mills, hotels, shops etc. | Hotel or shop business (owned) | Woolen garment busiess and working in handicrafts centre | Woolen garment business and Office service | Handicrafs centre and Office service | Only woolen garment business | Only as labour in hotels shops etc. | Only in office service | Monks getting gifts from others | Total |
|---|---|---|---|---|---|---|---|---|---|---|---|---|---|---|---|---|---|
| 1. | P | 424 | 63 | 27 | 50 | - | 22 | 8 | 4 | 1 | 2 | 2 | 2 | 2 | - | - | 607 |
| 2. | S | 233 | 27 | 25 | 11 | 3 | 4 | 10 | 2 | - | - | - | 2 | 3 | 1 | 1 | 320 |
| 3. | T | 11 | 8 | 1 | - | - | 3 | - | 1 | - | - | 1 | - | - | - | - | 26 |
| 4. | SP* | 28 | 7 | 3 | 3 | - | 1 | - | - | 1 | - | - | - | 1 | - | - | 45 |
| 5. | PT | 3 | 3 | - | 1 | - | - | - | - | - | - | - | - | - | - | - | 7 |
| 6. | O | 4 | - | - | 1 | - | 5 | - | - | - | - | - | - | - | - | - | 10 |
| Total | | 703 | 108 | 56 | 66 | 3 | 35 | 18 | 7 | 2 | 2 | 3 | 4 | 6 | 1 | 1 | 1015 |

* includes one family of shepherd and traders

**Table 20: Sexwise Population of Traditional Occupational Groups with Their Present Occupation**

| Serial Number | Traditional Occupational categories | Sex | Children | School going | Land/household | Labour in hotels, shops etc | Woolen garments business (owned) | Coolies in woolen garment business | Carpet making (Self owned) | Coolie in Society Handicraft Centre | Office Service | Working in hospitals | Tailoring | Hotel or shop owned | Goldsmithy | Blacksmithy | Carpentry | Working in Societ workshop | Art | Physically handi-capped, no work | Lama/Monk/Nun | Total | Grand Total | Percentage |
|---|---|---|---|---|---|---|---|---|---|---|---|---|---|---|---|---|---|---|---|---|---|---|---|---|
| 1 | 2 | 3 | 4 | 5 | 6 | 7 | 8 | 9 | 10 | 11 | 12 | 13 | 14 | 15 | 16 | 17 | 18 | 19 | 20 | 21 | 22 | 23 | 24 | 25 |
| 1. | P | M | 200 | 543 | 245 | 15 | 79 | 23 | 6 | 5 | 24 | 3 | 6 | 7 | - | 1 | 2 | 18 | 4 | 6 | 103 | 1290 | 2496 | 58.48 |
| | | F | 187 | 230 | 646 | 2 | 55 | 12 | 10 | 25 | 12 | 5 | 1 | 3 | - | - | - | - | - | 2 | 16 | 1206 | | |
| 2. | S | M | 88 | 305 | 137 | 10 | 36 | 15 | - | 4 | 3 | 3 | 1 | 2 | - | - | - | 7 | - | 4 | 22 | 637 | 1363 | 31.93 |
| | | F | 107 | 157 | 387 | 10 | 25 | 21 | - | 11 | - | 3 | - | 1 | - | - | - | - | - | - | 4 | 726 | | |
| 3. | T | M | 16 | 16 | 16 | - | 9 | 3 | - | - | 1 | - | 3 | 3 | - | - | - | - | - | - | - | 67 | 109 | 2.56 |
| | | F | 2 | 8 | 22 | - | 5 | 3 | - | - | - | 1 | - | 1 | - | - | - | - | - | - | - | 42 | | |
| 4. | SP | M | 17 | 38 | 28 | - | 8 | 4 | 1 | - | 1 | - | - | 1 | - | - | - | 1 | - | - | 3 | 102 | 203 | 4.76 |
| | | F | 11 | 26 | 44 | - | 7 | 3 | 1 | 5 | - | 1 | - | 2 | - | - | - | - | - | - | 1 | 101 | | |

| 1 | 2 | 3 | 4 | 5 | 6 | 7 | 8 | 9 | 10 | 11 | 12 | 13 | 14 | 15 | 16 | 17 | 18 | 19 | 20 | 21 | 22 | 23 | 24 | 25 |
|---|---|---|---|---|---|---|---|---|---|---|---|---|---|---|---|---|---|---|---|---|---|---|---|---|
|  |  | M | 4 | 6 | 11 | - | 3 | - | 2 | - | - | - | - | - | 1 | 1 | - | - | - | - | 3 | 31 |  |  |
| 5. | PT |  |  |  |  |  |  |  |  |  |  |  |  |  |  |  |  |  |  |  |  |  | 58 | 1.38 |
|  |  | F | 7 | 6 | 8 | - | 4 | - | - | 1 | 1 | - | - | - | - | - | - | - | - | - | - | 27 |  |  |
|  |  | M | 3 | 2 | 5 | 1 | - | - | - | - | 1 | - | 1 | - | 1 | 5 | - | - | - | - | 1 | 20 |  |  |
| 6. | O |  |  |  |  |  |  |  |  |  |  |  |  |  |  |  |  |  |  |  |  |  | 38 | 0.89 |
|  |  | F | 1 | 6 | 11 | - | - | - |  | - | - | - | - | - | - | - | - | - | - | - | - | 18 |  |  |
|  |  | M | 328 | 438 | 914 | 26 | 135 | 45 | 9 | 9 | 30 | 6 | 11 | 13 | 2 | 7 | 2 | 26 | 4 | 10 | 132 | 2147 |  |  |
|  | Total |  |  |  |  |  |  |  |  |  |  |  |  |  |  |  |  |  |  |  |  |  | 4267 | 100.0 |
|  |  | F | 315 | 433 | 1119 | 12 | 96 | 39 | 11 | 42 | 13 | 10 | 1 | 7 | - | - | - | - | - | 2 | 21 | 2120 |  |  |
| Grand Total |  |  | 643 | 871 | 2033 | 38 | 231 | 84 | 20 | 51 | 43 | 16 | 12 | 20 | 2 | 7 | 2 | 26 | 4 | 12 | 153 | 4267 |  |  |
| Percentage |  |  | 15.05 | 20.43 | 47.59 | 0.89 | 5.47 | 1.96 | 0.47 | 1.19 | 1.01 | 0.37 | 0.28 | 0.47 | 0.05 | 0.16 | 0.05 | 0.61 | 0.09 | 0.28 | 3.58 | 100.0 |  |  |

few of them who have more trade contacts in Karnataka, have even learnt Kannada, the language of the state.

The Society's handicraft section was started on 20th November, 1976. It received donations to organize itself as follows: Rs.60,000 from the office of the Finance Section of the Dalai Lama's Establishment in Dharmasala; Rs.10,000 from H.H. the Dalai Lama and Rs.62,000 from the MYRADA. This carpet weaving centre provides jobs to about 50 men and women belonging to 35 families. It is proposed to increase the number of looms soon so that many more can be benefited by this centre. These persons were initially given training in weaving for six months. In the beginning there were only five trained workers and they in turn have now trained another 45 men and women and all of them are now employed in the carpet centre itself. Though no financial assistance is given during training, immediate employment is assured to them in the carpet weaving centre after completion of their training. In an average 30 carpets of 6' x 3' and 7' x 4' were prepared by these craftsmen, in a month. These carpets were sent to CONTAK, a sales agency in Bangalore. From there, on order they are sent to different places, within and outside India.

There were also 16 families, with 16 men and 10 women among peasants, two families, with one man and one woman among shepherds and peasants and two families, with two men among peasants and traders, making carpets in their own homes. They buy yarn needed in the local market and sell the carpets through persons who go for sweater business. Not a single shepherd and herdsmen family has undertaken carpet making as their occupation. Their 26 men and 12 women, from 18 families, are working as helpers on daily wage basis in shops, hotels and flour mills in the Settlement. Around 54 peasants, 11 shepherds and herdsmen, one trader, three shepherds and peasants, one peasant and trader and one belonging to other castes, have taken up jobs in offices, hospital, workshop, school, etc., in the Settlement.

Lastly, seven families among the peasants, one among the shepherds, three among the traders and one among the other castes, have taken up tailoring as their subsidiary occupation. These persons stitch clothes in the traditional Tibetan style and earn their living. There are seven blacksmith and two goldsmith families who serve the community by undertaking respective metal works. They work for the commoners as well as the monasteries and get an additional income. They prepare artefacts in Tibetan style and a few have picked up the local type. There are also two carpenters who help those who need their services. But most of the Tibetans are capable of preparing minor wooden implements needed by themselves. The major implements are purchased from the local Indian agriculturists or carpenters. Apart from these there are four men among the peasants who have taken to the making of idols of Lamas in clay. The Tibetans need these in large number for placing on the altar in memory of the incarnate Lamas, and to worship. By this the craftsmen earn an additional income.

The Table 21 shows that 577 persons (465 men and 112 women) from the Settlement have migrated to as many as 32 towns and cities throughout India and abroad. Three men and five women among these have gone to Canada, England, Japan and some European countries in search of jobs or for higher education. Among those who have gone to other places in India - 330 are peasants, 172 are nomads, 33 are traders, 27 are shepherds and peasants, five are peasants and traders and 10 belong to other castes. The reasons given for migration to other places are as follows: Tibetans took more pride and interest in joining para-military or any government or private services since it brought them not only assured income but also status. They think with the salary they get, they can buy many modern goods, clothing, electronic goods and lead a luxurious life.

We have already noticed the fact that secular education was practically nil in Tibet. However, after their coming over to India, if the adults worked to earn a living the children were sent to different schools and colleges in different towns, and cities. A few welfare agencies and individuals from India and abroad also came forward to sponsor their education. As a result, a good number of Tibetan students are now studying in different branches of arts, science, commerce, medicine and engineering. In all 125 boys and 54 girls are studying in different towns and cities of India and three boys and five girls have gone to foreign countries, for their higher studies. After the completion of their education a few Tibetans are now serving as teachers, clerks, mechanics and nurses in different Tibetan settlements. Twentyfour men and twelve women have migrated to other places on employment. Apart from these, 14 men and 14 women

## Table 21: Members Residing Outside the Settlement

| Serial No | Village in Mundgod Settlement | Sex | In schools | Inl college | Abroad for training | Training in India | In para-military services | Coolie | In Govt./private service | Lama monk/nun | Total | Grand total | Percentage |
|---|---|---|---|---|---|---|---|---|---|---|---|---|---|
| 1 | 2 | 3 | 4 | 5 | 6 | 7 | 8 | 9 | 10 | 11 | 12 | 13 | 14 |
| 1 | I | M | 7 | 2 | 1 | - | 28 | - | 2 | 1 | 41 | 50 | 1.20 |
| | | F | 5 | 1 | - | - | 2 | - | 1 | - | 9 | | |
| 2 | II | M | 5 | 3 | - | - | 24 | - | - | 1 | 33 | 45 | 1.08 |
| | | F | 3 | | - | 1 | 6 | - | 2 | - | 12 | | |
| 3 | III | M | 15 | 3 | - | - | 31 | 1 | 4 | 9 | 63 | 79 | 1.88 |
| | | F | 9 | 1 | 1 | 1 | 2 | - | 2 | - | 16 | | |
| 4 | IV | M | 20 | 15 | - | - | 57 | - | 4 | 1 | 97 | 116 | 2.77 |
| | | F | 7 | 3 | - | - | 3 | - | 4 | 2 | 19 | | |
| 5 | V | M | 8 | 1 | 1 | - | 30 | - | 5 | - | 45 | 53 | 1.27 |
| | | F | 2 | 2 | 1 | 1 | 1 | - | - | 1 | 8 | | |

| 1 | 2 | 3 | 4 | 5 | 6 | 7 | 8 | 9 | 10 | 11 | 12 | 13 | 14 |
|---|---|---|---|---|---|---|---|---|---|---|---|---|---|
| 6 | VI | M | 18 | 6 | - | 1 | 29 | - | 4 | 1 | 59 | 70 | 1.67 |
| | | F | 2 | - | 1 | - | 2 | - | 2 | 4 | 11 | | |
| 7 | VII | M | 12 | 2 | - | - | 73 | - | 2 | - | 89 | 109 | 2.55 |
| | | F | 7 | 1 | 1 | - | 4 | - | 7 | 6 | 20 | | |
| 8 | VIII | M | 2 | - | 1 | - | 20 | - | 2 | 1 | 26 | 36 | 0.84 |
| | | F | 1 | - | 1 | 4 | 4 | - | - | - | 10 | | |
| 9 | IX | M | 3 | 2 | - | - | 6 | - | 1 | - | 12 | 19 | 0.44 |
| | | F | 2 | - | - | 1 | 3 | - | - | 1 | 7 | | |
| TOTAL | | M | 90 | 34 | 3 | 1 | 298 | 1 | 24 | 14 | 465 | 577 | 13.52 |
| | | F | 38 | 8 | 5 | 8 | 27 | - | 12 | 14 | 112 | | |
| Percentage | | M | 2.10 | 0.79 | 0.07 | 0.02 | 7.00 | 0.02 | 0.56 | 0.33 | 10.89 | | 100.00 |
| | | F | 0.89 | 0.19 | 0.12 | 0.19 | 0.63 | - | 0.28 | 0.33 | 2.63 | | |
| Grand Total | | | 128 | 42 | 8 | 9 | 325 | 1 | 36 | 28 | 577 | | 100.00 |

have also gone out as monks and nuns to monasteries in other places.

All the Tibetans at Mundgod have equal opportunities but it is however noticed that only the peasants have adopted well to the new conditions. It is because by tradition they are agriculturists and have adopted easily to the new agricultural operations and obtained a good yield. These people have also invested money on secondary occupations to earn more. On the contrary the shepherds and herdsmen who were nomadic in nature in Tibet, are still trying to adopt to the new ecological conditions.

## Livestock Economy

Though agriculture was the main occupation of peasant Tibetans in Tibet, they regard breeding of livestocks - yak, sheep, goat, dzo, cattles, etc., as a prestigious occupation. It was also a profitable occupation since it brought them wool, milk, meat, and skin; which served as materials for shelter and source of food. So Tibetans of all classes possessed livestocks. However, livestock rearing was the traditional and primary occupation of shepherds and herdsmen in Tibet. They took them to high altitude pasture lands and stayed there for months enjoying their dualistic pattern of life. Even a poor serf held the livestocks from his lord and went to pastures to raise cattle. In return he received additional livestocks of the year as his gift. There in Tibet they produced a cross breed of a bull and female yak; the female cross breed gave more milk and the male served as a tough animal for transport purposes.

Presently owing to change in the ecology and place of residence the Tibetans are now rearing local variety of livestocks which are useful in dairy industry and in agriculture. The Table 22 shows that out of 1015 families 375 (36.90%) possess bulls and bullocks, 743 (73.2%) possess cows, 40(3.94%) possess buffaloes, 29(2.86%) possess goats, five (0.49%) families possess the sheep and 171 (16.85%) families rear fowl. The total number of livestocks in the Settlement comes to 3160. The Table 23 shows that there are 735 bullocks, 1815 cows, 94 buffaloes, 100 goats and six sheep. Apart from these, there are 410 fowls reared by them.

It is also observed that in Mundgod Settlement however poor a person may be he possesses at least one or two cows, which

## Table 22: Occupational Background of the Families in Tibet Versus the Materials They Possess

| Sr.No | Occupational groups | Cattle-shed | Cart | Cycle | Sewing Machine | Radio | Number of livestocks | | | | | | Kitchen garden | Total No. of families in the catetory |
|---|---|---|---|---|---|---|---|---|---|---|---|---|---|---|
| | | | | | | | Bulls and Bullock | Buffalow | Cow | Sheep | Goat | Fowl | | |
| 1 | P | 318 | 68 | 186 | 22 | 98 | 216 | 28 | 455 | 3 | 14 | 112 | 230 | 607 |
| 2 | S | 181 | 34 | 75 | 7 | 37 | 124 | 5 | 226 | 2 | 11 | 39 | 96 | 320 |
| 3 | T | 13 | 3 | 16 | 5 | 10 | 10 | 4 | 14 | - | - | 7 | 7 | 26 |
| 4 | SP | 28 | 7 | 19 | 1 | 12 | 20 | 1 | 32 | - | 3 | 10 | 7 | 44 |
| 5 | PT | 7 | 1 | 5 | 1 | 3 | 3 | 1 | 7 | - | 1 | 2 | 1 | 8 |
| 6 | O | 5 | - | 3 | 1 | 1 | 2 | 1 | 9 | - | - | 1 | 3 | 10 |
| | Total | 552 | 113 | 304 | 37 | 161 | 375 | 40 | 743 | 5 | 29 | 171 | 344 | 1015 |
| | Percentage | 54.40 | 11.14 | 30.6 | 3.65 | 15.87 | 36.90 | 3.94 | 73.20 | 0.49 | 2.86 | 16.85 | 33.89 | 100.00 |

**Table 23 Traditional Occupational Background of the Family Versus the Number of Livestocks They Posses**

| S.No. | Occupational class groups | Number of livestocks | | | | | | |
|---|---|---|---|---|---|---|---|---|
| | | Bulls and bullock | Buffaloes | Cows | Sheep | Goat | Fowl | Total |
| 1 | P | 420 | 61 | 1083 | 3 | 48 | 244 | 1859 |
| 2 | S | 250 | 10 | 545 | 3 | 44 | 94 | 946 |
| 3 | T | 18 | 21 | 29 | - | - | 18 | 86 |
| 4 | SP | 35 | - | 107 | - | 6 | 24 | 172 |
| 5 | PT | 9 | 1 | 28 | - | 2 | 7 | 47 |
| 6 | O | 3 | 1 | 23 | - | - | 23 | 50 |
| | Total | 735 | 94 | 1815 | 6 | 100 | 410 | 3160 |

provide him with milk which is very essential to prepare the Tibetan tea. Tibetans keep on drinking tea upto 50-60 cups a day. Sometimes they prepare it as and when they need it or may prepare in large quantity in the morning and keep on drinking it as they work. The poor keep the tea filled kettle on the hearth to keep it warm. While the well-to-do ones have bought thermos flasks of family size, for the purpose. The cows give them not only milk but also male calves which are used as plough animal. By nature Tibetans are kind pastoral people and they care for the calves feeding them well with all sorts of foods like soft bread, *tsampa* and so on.

It is found that 40 families which possess about 94 buffaloes sell milk to the hotels in the Settlement. A few of them collect, buy milk and sell it in the Mundgod town. A few own even ten to fifteen buffaloes and sell milk to the tea shops in the settlement and at Mundgod town. Other families possessing one or two buffaloes sell their produce of milk in their village itself.

In this Settlement 34 families reared goats and sheep for milk, which brought them money. Poultry rearing was taken up by 171 families. A few of them have kept 50 to 60 fowls. Apart from chicken, eggs are sold to shops in the Settlement or in the weekly shandy at Mundgod.

Tibetans possess materials of domestic utility; 113 families possess a cart each, 37 families possess sewing machines. While 25 families use them only to stitch their family clothing, the other 12 families use them to earn their living by stitching clothes for others as well.

## Labour and Labour Exchange

The Tibetan family as a basic social unit, is also an economic unit. Human labour in Tibet, was derived from the leased serfdom. Most of the labour required by the lords was provided by the serf to gain economic subsistence for their family. Among commoners labour needed by a family was obtained through labour exchange (*saptok*), may be between two families or more. Men from different families collected together and helped each other at times of need. When they worked for a family the host provided them with food and tea during the day and *chãng* in the evening. In the present settlement this type of labour exchange is almost completely lost today. Only a few families who are agnates or the cognates come together and help each other and the host provided the food, tea and *chāng* needed by them for the day. This reciprocity extended to the bullocks, carts, ploughs and other agricultural implements also. However, most of the labour needed by the family was provided by the family members themselves. To undertake major agricultural operations they need extra and skilled labourers and this was provided by the Indian labourers who came in hundreds, during sowing, weeding and harvesting seasons.

The Indian labour force at the Settlement can be divided into three categories: those who come from nearby villages and serve throughout the year; seasonal immigrant labours and contract labourers. Labourers from distant Indian villages come to work during peak harvest season. They come with their family and stay in different Tibetan villages till the season is over. They are paid according to the agreed daily wages, either soon after the job is over or as advance in the morning of the day of work. The other category is the contractual labour groups. A group of Indian labourers come under one leader, who in turn negotiates with Tibetans and settle the contract amount and others work under his supervision. This is a popular local practice and the same is well received by the Tibetans. The local Indian labourers coming from the surrounding villages have their recognized Tibetan masters. The labourers attend their masters daily and carry on the agricultural as well as the domestic works for which they are paid in cash and he is also served with food and drinks like *chāng* and arrack. It was also observed a few Indian women work regularly for the Tibetans to help them in household duties for which they are paid both in cash and kind.

The wage for the labourers varies depending on the season, nature and urgency of the work. A few of them also received their day meal from the Tibetans. The labourers were paid in kind, paddy and maize. Payment of wages in advance for a week or even a month, was also common and often the Tibetans are cheated by the recipients.

At the Settlement it is common to hire bullocks and labourers together from surrounding Indian villages to do certain type of agricultural activities such as sowing, levelling, etc. Sometimes they are paid according to the nature and area of work. A few even undertake the entire work on contract basis and finish it according to their convenience.

Indian labourers are of the opinion that compared to the local farmers the Tibetans are more generous in paying the wages. They also found their Tibetan masters to be honest and good and provided them not only better wages but also food. At times Tibetans feel that they are blackmailed by the Indian labourers because they are indispensable. The Tibetans also know that they are paying them higher wages; but they are helpless in this matter. The Indian farmers in the surrounding villages also think that the innocent Tibetans have been fooled by the labourers. Sometimes they also complain that the Tibetans introduced many new factors such as payment in cash, advance payment, free midday meal etc., which the labourers have now started demanding from the Indian farmers also. It is said that owing to liberal payment, and good treatment, the labourers prefer working for Tibetans rather than for the Indian farmers. At times of need, they also said that the skilled labourers poses a problem.

## Redistribution and Exchange

Tibetans in Tibet contributed a part of their produce to the Tibetan Government in the form of tax. As a rule the peasants paid their tax in terms of food grains and the nomads gave wool, butter, mutton, and milk products like *chura*. The quantity of the tax to be paid by each householder was fixed on the basis of the land hold by him or by the quantity of livestocks possessed by each one of them. The Central authorities sent their representatives to all the provinces and the districts for tax collection. The tax collected by the village leaders was sent to the district officers and they in turn sent it to the Central Government. Those District Officers who did not hold any public land from the government, accepted tax from the commoners which served as their pay. However, they were obliged to send a part of it to the Central Government, at Lhasa. Food and other materials thus collected by the Central Government were in turn redistributed to the three big monasteries - Dre-Pung, Se-Ra and Gan-Dan. Some part of it also went to the military staff. A certain amount of the tax in grain was also kept aside in store in the capital city. This was distributed to poor or released to the people during draught years. Those who received such relief, however, returned it to the Central Government during the next year; adding some more to it.

The Mundgod Tibetans pay a levy of 20 kgs. paddy per acre,

and a rupee per head per month, towards the Freedom Society (*Rang-Zai*), which has its headquarters in Dharmasala. This society was started during the year 1972 and the amount collected is utilized for the maintenance of the Tibetan Co-operative Society's office and the Dalai Lama's establishment at Dharmasala. All Tibetans are members of this society. An amount of Rs. 10/- per adult member who holds 32 gunthas of land and Rs. 5/- from a child member who holds 20 gunthas, was collected as yearly donation towards the Mundgod Tibetan Resettlement Hospital (MTRH), located at the Settlement. Apart from these the Tibetans also contribute Re 1 or Rs. 2 per person per year to conduct worships in the monasteries. A few of them also contribute towards the firewood required as fuel in the monasteries for their daily routines and also for the special worships - for cooking as well as for the worship of the fire God. Tibetans in the Settlement are also expected to attend all the worships conducted by a senior Lama and contribute cash or a few other things like metal wares used in worshiping, packets of sweet etc. While in Tibet it was customary to contribute only in kind in the form of meat, firewood and butter for the lamps and to prepare ghee rice, to be distributed to the devotees. In return their pleasure was to receive blessings from the Lama.

Tibetans also have an obligation to contribute towards the life cycle rituals of their kin, non-kin, village or even the settlement members. They contribute both in kind and cash. When an orphan or a destitute dies everyone comes forward contributing towards the death rituals, which they believe will bring them good fortune (*Gewã*). They also contribute towards community level rituals, ceremonies and festivals.

In Tibet commodities were exchanged through the barter system. Traders formed a link between the peasants and the shepherds. Exchange was in kind and cash was used to the minimal extent. Tibetans did not pay any taxes for selling or buying of any goods except for tea and wool (*phak-pã*). Presently the whole system has been changed and exchange of materials exists only in a very few cases.

No weekly shandy gathers in the Settlement. Therefore the Tibetans visit Mundgod town every Monday for marketing. The town about three miles from the Settlement, not only serves them as the main marketing centre but also as a place for recreation. On market days they meet their kith and kin from other villages and together visit tea shops and cinemas. On Mondays a special bus service is arranged, from Mundgod town to the Settlement. Usually Tibetans arrive in Mundgod town by 9 a.m. and finish their marketing by noon. In the afternoon they usually go for a movie and return to their Settlement with their loads and usually by walk.

Tibetans produce enough and in some cases more food grains than they require for the year. The surplus is sold in the market. Those who do not have any secondary sources of income, have to sell a portion of their produce to meet their other requirements like clothing, vegetables, pulses, jowar, maida flour, oil etc.

The Tibetans are not allowed to sell their agricultural produces without the permission of the Co-operative Society. The Society which extends them loans and credit facilities to meet agricultural expenses on ploughing, buying seeds, fertilizers etc., retains the claim to sell the produce of their debtors through it so that the loan can be easily recollected. This arrangement facilitates the functioning of the society well and helps the collection of loans as well. Therefore soon after the harvest paddy and maize bags are stored in godowns owned by the Society, located in different villages. On producing the receipt to this effect the farmers are given fifty per cent of the value of the food grains stored. The remaining half of the amount is paid after the products are sold by the Society, to their commission agents at Hubli, Davangere, etc. A few Tibetans who are urgently in need of money sell their produce to Indian or Tibetan merchants and receive their amount immediately. This type of transaction is illegal but it goes on without the knowledge of the officials of the Society.

A Tibetan who is not holding any loan or credit facility from the Society may sell his produce directly. But he has to pay two per cent commission to the Society for the facilities like fertilizers, tractors etc., provided to him.

Some Tibetans because of urgency sell their agricultural products immediately after the harvest. But it is noticed that because of abundant supply of food grains in the market the rates go down and they are loosers thereby. If they can keep their produce upto March or April, they can get good prices. Further by the time the next sowing season starts they will have again to borrow money from money lenders and also the Co-operative

Society. However, a few who have planned their budget well, have earned enough and even give loans to others.

The marketing of food grains takes place at two levels. Those who are in need of food grains exchange their products with others. Tibetans also exchange their produce with the Indians who live in surrounding villages. In a few other cases those who need food grains take them from those who have in surplus. The same is returned after the harvest along with some amount of additional grain as a form of interest. Selling of most of their major products or buying of their requirements is done either in Mundgod town or Hubli city. Many of the Tibetans remember the problems they faced in the beginning in communicating with the local people in the market whom they did not know. Now the problem is solved to a major extent because most of them can converse in Hindi and a few also in Kannada. The local merchants consider Tibetans as good and honest customers.

Tibetans purchase agricultural implements from Mundgod and also from Indian farmers in the neighbouring villages. To settle the business they use local village leaders. Comparatively the Tibetans own less cattle and produce more fodder. So the surplus fodder is also sold to the local Indians. A few Tibetans also hold the local market in the Settlement selling the Tibetans the used clothes, bed sheets, slippers, shoes, china ware and such other materials. These things are bought by the Tibetan merchants from Bombay where the used things are sold cheap. The Tibetans who are unable to purchase new clothes buy these things and use them after alteration. A few Indian hawkers visit the settlement regularly selling fruits, vegetables and metal ware for cash as well as kind, and move about freely in the Settlement.

It is found that some Tibetans have started producing and selling liquor to the Tibetans as well as to the local people. The primary reason for this is economic and is usually undertaken by poor families in the Settlement. There is a lot of demand for the liquor produced by the Tibetans, by the Indian neighbours since it is cheap and is of better quality when compared to the locally available arrack sold by the Indian contractor. The Tibetan officials are not able to stop this business since it goes on quietly and in the dark. When caught by the Indian Police and Excise Officials they conveniently escape telling that *chãng* and arrack are their ritual requirements; and so nothing could be done about it. But the truth is that in Tibetan society *chãng* alone has its socio-religious function and not the arrack and every one is aware of the fact. They have not been able to stop this activity since it brings extra cash to the Tibetans and enjoyment to the Indians.

The Tibetan economic system here has undergone a drastic change - from the traditional barter system to cash transaction at all levels. In this way their contacts with the new economic system has brought radical changes in the sphere of economic relations among themselves and with local Indians.

## Credit, Savings and Capital Formation

Chen Hsi divides the Tibetan economy into three categories: agricultural, animal husbandry and the handi-crafts (loc. cit., Legal Inquiry Committee on Tibet, 1966:103). Main agricultural products include wheat, barley, maize etc. Herdsmen had large herds of cattle and sheep. Apart from this Tibet is rich in its natural deposits and forest products. Even though serfs formed the bulk of population in Tibet, all of them were self sufficient with their own type of economy, either from land, cattle or business etc. Richardson's account regarding Tibet taken from the Legal Inquiry Committee on Tibet (1966:103) gives the following picture. Tibetans though are in their homespun clothes and may not have given an impression of material prosperity, but the wants, destitution or starvation were very rare in Tibet. The people were sturdy and enduring and although a Tibetan peasant lacks the comforts he is claimed to be higher than several people of various parts of Asia. He concludes that the Tibetan economy is a more balanced one with its policy of imports and exports with the neighbouring countries.

The Dalai Lama (1966:104) in his answer to questions by the Legal Inquiry Committee on Tibet says that "It is unfair and untrue for the Chinese Communist Government to state that the majority of the Tibetans are serfs and that very few Tibetans possessed any property." However, Dalai Lama agrees that the poverty did exist in Tibet. He further says the number of destitutes in Tibet was not that large. He maintains that every Tibetan was engaged in an agricultural or some other occupation, however poor a man may be he possessed minimum of five to six cattle and about thirty sheep. The land possessed by each one gave him an yield of 100 to 150 khaes of barley. The well-to-do farmers obtained an annual yield of a few thousand khaes of barley plus each saving of about ten to thousand rupees in Indian currency. A nomad may possess one thousand yaks and ten thousand sheep. Thus the propaganda of the Chinese regarding the poverty of Tibetans is fake according to him.

No doubt Mundgod Tibetans are poor and they also have to spend a lot on rites and rituals. They are thrifty and cannot spend much on food, clothes and other basic necessities. Many have started saving from the day they came to rehabilitation camps. This has helped many of them to invest their money thus saved on land, in business etc.

Tibetans are not yet fully convinced about the benefits of banking and therefore most of them do not have a bank account. They either keep the money with themselves or put it into circulation. But it is noticed that very recently, a few of them have opened accounts in banks and they are found to be either of employees or of rich businessmen. In one of the banks, however, there are 430 savings deposits, 30 cash certificate deposits, Eight fixed deposits, One Akshaya deposit, Three gift coupons, 20 pigmy deposits, One prize deposit and Nine recurring deposits(1978). In another bank there are about 800 accounts but nearly 75% of them are not operated since long. The Tibetans feel that keeping money in a bank is not profitable. Instead they invest it on land and business or lend it for higher rate of interest.

Tibetans collect interest on their capital both in cash and kind. Under cash payment the agreed interest and the principal are paid in cash. Payment of interest in kind i.e., paddy or maize, is also practiced mostly by the farmers. They return the principal in cash and pay the interest in kind. Sometimes both the interest and the principal are paid in kind. For security purpose the money lender takes a bond from the borrower. In the bond however instead of the cash taken on loan, the sale of a bullock, cow or a cart is shown. Usually the amount lent will be lesser than the actual value of the animal or the thing. The animal or the thing mentioned on the bond paper will be safe with the borrower himself. When the principal and the interest are paid the Tibetan will return the security bond to the borrower. There is a lot of risk involved in money lending. When a borrower fails to return the money or the interest the Tibetans lose the money since the security bond he possesses is not legally valid. In contrast to this sometimes the gold and silver ornaments deposited by Indian borrowers as security will be taken by the Tibetans when they fail to take it back within the agreed period.

Like this some Tibetans have also earned lot of money and movable property.

It is noticed that usually Tibetans spend lot of money on rituals. They believe in the *Karma* - the wheel of life and the fortunes of good and bad luck. To earn merit (*Gewā*) they arrange for worships and invite Lamas to their homes. The number of Lamas they invite depends upon their economic status. The worships are performed throughout the day followed by recitation of holy syllables (*mantrā*) and reading of the sacred texts, and by feeding the Lamas and the invitees. All this requires lot of money. Almost all Tibetan families arrange for such worships at least once in a year. A few rich families may arrange for them once or twice in a month. Apart from this, all socio-economic activities of the Tibetans including a casual journey are preceded by a worship. The Tibetans say the number of such worships and expenditure on them has been cut down now-a-days because of their poor financial conditions. Moreover now their economy is based on cash and thus they have to buy every thing, paying cash. Whereas in Tibet the things needed for a worship were either produced at home or easily secured through the barter system.

It is also expected of a devout Buddhist to visit places of pilgrimage, at least once in a year. They are obliged to visit monasteries and make offerings of ghee, gold and also cash to the lamas and the deity. While in Tibet they walked the distance spending very little or nothing on the journey. Here in India they have to take a train or a bus or a taxi and thus spend a lot on transport.

The Tibetans who are in need of money receive loans from the two banks in the settlement. One of the banks issues loans to the Tibetan peasants directly and also through the Tibetan Co-operative Society. This year 29 Tibetans have taken loans from this bank directly, on individual basis (1978). The loans for the agricultural operations too are given through the Tibetan Co-operative Society. There are the short term credit loans given for agricultural operations at the time of sowing or harvesting; and also for purchasing of seeds and fertilizers. One should be a member of the Society to get this facility. The Society retains 10% of the loan issued by the bank of the individual as his share in the Society.

Another scheduled bank situated in Mundgod Settlement, also grants loans to the individuals directly and without the security of the Tibetan Co-operative Society. The bank offers loans for agricultural purposes and a special credit facility is provided exclusively for woolen garments business. During 1977, as many as 122 took loan, and every year Rs. 2,50,000 is given on loan to the Tibetans to undertake this particular business.

Tibetans also take loans on interest from their friends and relatives. The monks and Lamas who have saved money by hiring lands, lending on interest etc., also give loans to the lay. The interest charged varies from 25% to 40%. Most of the Tibetans claim they are illiterate and cannot follow the bank procedures easily and so prefer to take loan from private parties. However, the younger generation which has acquired modern education is making a good use of the banking facilities.

To sum up, in the present set up, the Tibetan refugees have lost their traditional occupations and are settled mainly as farmers with the cultivable land provided by the Settlement corporation. This sudden shift from their traditional occupation has affected them in the economic and other ways of life. Those Tibetans who were traditionally shepherds or traders find it very difficult to till the agricultural land as it needs a special skill and the knowledge of agricultural operations suitable to the local soil types, seasons, crops, etc., and they also incurred heavy losses in the initial stages. They thought that their stay in India is for a short period. This also hindered them taking extra pain to acclamatize to the new mode of living. However, things have changed a lot after 1974 when the lands were allotted on permanent basis. Local people of the surrounding villages helped them to learn the local agricultural methods. The Tibetans were also given training in dry as well as wet cultivation and local methods of agricultural practices under different schemes sponsored by State as well as Central Governments and some voluntary agencies abroad. Such trainings helped them to learn more about the agricultural practices. Effort is being made to irrigate the land from the nearby dam. The Tibetan Co-operative Society plays an important role by providing tractors for ploughing, improved variety of seeds, fertilisers, etc. All these have helped them to get higher yield and more profit leading a happy life. A few have taken land on lease from others.

While few other Tibetans especially those who were

traditionally shepherds and traders and could not learn the local methods of cultivation either depend on local labourers or leased out the land and taken to other pursuits such as woolen garment business, petty shopkeeping, service, etc. A few others migrated to places such as Simla, Dehradun, etc., which are comparatively cool and preferred to easy going and more remunerative occupations.

Their main complaint is that their leaders have failed to bring some more projects where they get employment and earn their living. The Tibetan economic system has undergone a drastic change from the traditional barter system to the regional level market and cash transactions.

# 7

# Leadership and Social Control

Though Tibet had lot of cultural links with her neighbouring countries, she maintained her own individuality in matters of religion and polity. The structure of the Tibetan political, and the social institutions was naturally based on the Buddhist philosophy. Religion also served as the base of social and cultural life of Tibetans and so Tibet was known as the land of Religion.

Puntsok Wamgyal (1975:78), says that Tibet, the land of religion, had its own polity and has always been governed by its own institutions and officials. Polity, the form and process of civil government in Tibet, was often termed as "*Cho-si nyi-dãn*" (*Cho-srid gnyis-ldãn*). In expression "*Bo-zhung Cho-si nyi-dãn*", "*Bo-zhung*" means "Government of Tibet" and *Cho-si nyi-dãn*" means religion and politics; totally meaning "The Tibetan Government of Religion and Politics".

We already know about the divine origin of Tibetan royalty. Their very first king Gnya-kri tsan-po (127 B.C.), was believed to have descended from heaven. His descendents upto VIIth generation, known as the heavenly thrones, are very much responsible in bringing the religion close to politics. Son-tsan Gyan-po, son of Nam-ri Sòn-tsan-po ascended the throne in 620-650 A.D. He was titled, Cho-srgyal (Religious King) by a lama historian of the period. The term "*Cho*" means the established religion and "*gyal-po*", the established political authority, the king. Hence it is understood both the religion and politics were reposed with the King. Thus Tibet maintained her dual character of religion and politics in the hands of *Saskya- pa* and then the *Geluk-pa* ecclesiastical order.

As we have already discussed the reign of the Glang Dar-ma (836 A.D.) was an anti Buddhist one. Without a central focus or authority, it laid foundation for the birth of local lords maintaining the kingship on the clan system. This led to a land owning nobility who never lost thier power and responsibility of Government with the ecclesiastical rulers. Long before Buddhism came to Tibet, the modern political system of dual nature was instituted. The initial founders of Government to retain their control with the help of force transformed obedience as duty. They found necessity of the religion and the legal basis of power (Phuntsog Wangyal, 1975:80). Thus the dual natured Government was formed by uniting the political authority along with the religious authority.

The Tibetan state organisation was land based. Ownership of land determined the past of the members of the public. They were expected to play certain roles for the Government. It was the duty of every noble man to keep his sons into public service, for which he owned land from the Government and rarely he was paid anything by way of salary. The basic principle of Tibetan political organisation was the obligation for a noble to serve the Government. This nobility claimed their origin to any of the three sources: to an ancestor who was ennobled for good work done for the country; the family in which the Dalai Lama or Tashi Lama took rebirth; and to their ancestry traced right back to the early kings of Tibet.

The Dalai Lama, the charismat of temporal and spiritual power, was the head of ecclesiastic and the secular state. He is the one now considered as the early presense of *Chenrezi* –patron of Tibet and embodiment of compassion. He was personally chosen by the early lama to carry out his mission of salvation. Thus he upholds the ancient tradition that affairms his periodical descent to the land of snows for the specific purposes of watching over the spiritual destinies of its inhabitants. As a *Changchup Sempa* (Bodhisatwa) and one of the most highly worshipped in Mahãyãna Buddhism, renounces the opportunity of vanishing into indefinable *nirvãna.* By taking human form and undergoing birth, death and all other vicissitudes mankind is subject to, he may illumine with words and example, the creatures he protects. By this he swiftly leads them to that state of spiritual perfection which provides them paradise or liberation within the bounds of their ability, keeness and *Karma.*

## I. Tibetan State Administration

The state administration of Tibet operated in four levels Central, Province, District and Village. Though each level had certain amount of administrative independence it was ultimately controlled by the next higher authortiy and finally the administration in Lhasa. Now owing to refugee situation and also adoption of new steps to democratise the administration, though certain changes have come, the administrative structure of the Dalai Lama's establishment in Dharmasala is almost the same and a few minor changes have been made here and there in the appointment and approval of the office and also its function.

The administrative structure of the erstwhile Tibetan government as shown by Richardson (1962:19) is presented in the chart on the next page.

(A) *His Holiness the Dalai Lama*

The practice of maintaining a spiritual lineage of Lamas through reincarnation entered in the Tibetan history in the fourteenth century, when for the first time black hat Karma-pa, the Rang-byang rdo-rje proclaimed that he would be reborn. Taking the clue the other sects also began to adopt this practice. Later Altan Khan (1502-81) Chief of the Mongole, in order to put an end to the powerful hierarchy of the Karmapa of the Kargyupa sect and its patrons who were supporting China, created the institution of Dalai Lama in 1578, by conferring this title on the third grand Lama of the Drepung Monastery, Sonam Gyatso. In 1642 Gushri Khan and his supporters of the Gelukpa sect killed the ruler of Tsang, the supporter of the Karmapa sect and conferred the sovereignty of Tibet to Ngawang Lobsong Gyatso –the Vth Dalai Lama. He unified the country under his leadership and succeeded in placing the institution of Dalai Lama on a firm footing. 'The institution of Dalai Lama', as Rahul (1969:496) says "being an instrument of social and political order has been a great directive force in the history of politics of central Asia in modern times and the tremendous force behind the institution lies not in its originality or novelty but in its lofty, moral character and the spiritual message it holds for the people".

After the VIII Dalai Lama (Jampel Gyatso), four successive Dalai Lamas died before they attained the age of maturity. Dalai Lama XIII, Thubten Gyatso, had to flee two times – first to Urga to escape a British military expedition under the Young-husband in 1904 and secondly to Darjeeling in India, to escape a Chinese military expedition on Lhasa, in 1910. Owing to her internal difficulties China lost her control over Tibet and in 1912 Dalai Lama XIII declared indepdendence of Tibet. In 1935 Dalai Lama the XIV, Lobzhong Tenzin Gyatso, came to power. When the Chinese army once again moved into Tibet in 1959, it made the

The Administrative Structure of the Erstwhile Tibetan Government

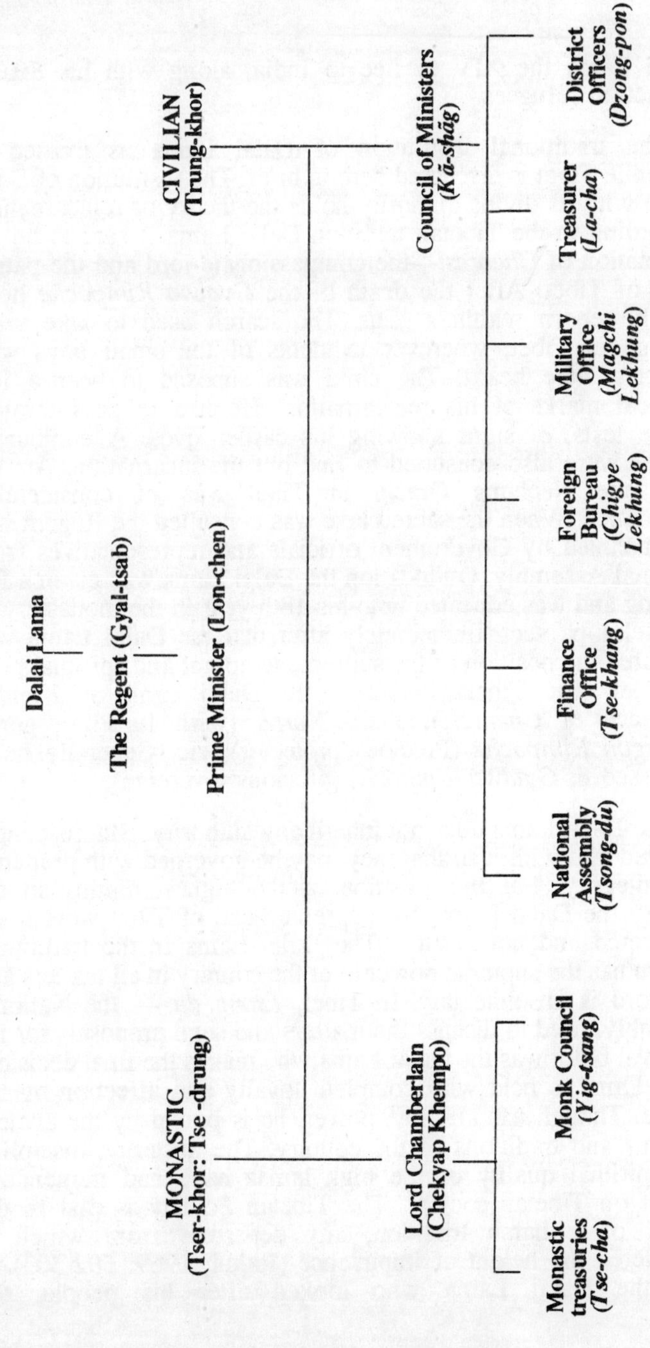

Dalai Lama the XIV to flee to India, along with his 80,000 subjects as refugees.

The traditional institution of Dalai Lama as existed in erstwhile Tibet is discussed here in brief. The institution of Dalai Lama with its divine authority holds the theory of reincarnation. According to the Tibetan tradition Dalai Lama is said to be the incarnation of *Chenresi*—the compassionate lord and the patron deity of Tibet. After the death of the *Gyalwa Rimpoche* he is usually reborn within a year. The search used to take place throughout Tibet; wherever incidents of the small boys with miracles were heard. The child was suposed to bear a few physical marks of his reincarnation. He had to pass through severe tests, of signs showing his eariler lives. A number of oracles were also consulted to find out the incarnation. Among them the Nechung Oracle in Tibet was of considerable importance. When the sacred lake was consulted the Regent was accompanied by Government officials and representatives from National Assembly. On location the Dalai Lama was given a full training and was educated upto his 18th year in the monastery of the Geluk-pa sect. Immediately after that the Dalai Lama was honoured the position as the supreme temporal and spiritual ruler of Tibet. The Tibetans address the Dalai Lama as *Kunden* (Presence of *Chenresi*), *Yishi Norbu* (wish fulfilling gem), *Chamgon Rimpoche* (Precious protector), etc. Generally he is addressed as *Gyalwa Rimpoche* (precious sovereign).

The Dalai Lama does not inherit any authority. But his people invested him with it so that they may be governed with prudence and integrity. For this position of the highest dignity in the country the Dalai Lama, the supreme head of Tibet were to be discovered and not elected. The Dalai Lama in the traditional custom has the supreme power over the country in all matters and his word is absolute law. In Tibet, *Tsong du* — the National Assembly, used to discuss the matters and send proposals for his approval but it was the Dalai Lama who makes the final decision. Dalai Lama is held with complete loyalty and affection by his people. Though has absolute power, he is bound by the ancient customs and traditions of the country. The austerity, discipline and spiritual quality of the high lamas have had tremendous impact on Tibetan society. The Tibetan Society is cast in the mould of a harsh tradition, any departure from which is considered the height of impudence (Rahul, 1969: 502-503). It was the Dalai Lama who looked after his people, the administration and the welfare measures like reducing heavy taxation, mediation in local feuds, establishing the monasteries, providing the facilities of education by building new monasteries and also training lay and monk officials, bringing in the apropriate law and social control in thier traditional society in Tibet, etc.

Traditional Tibet was a feudal state. The poeple remained faithful to the final authority, H.H. the Dalai Lama. There remained personal loyal relations between the lord and the commoners. Dalai Lama being the head of the spiritual and temporal power was the religious and the secular head of the state. Thus domain comprised, both the religion and the state.

The Tibetan refugees claim that Tibetan relgious and political supremacy rests even today with H.H. the Dalai Lama. On June 30, 1959 the Indian Foreign Officer said that the Government of India did not recognize any separate government of Tibet other than in Lhasa and there was therefore, no question of a Tibetan Government functioning in India under the Dalai Lama. Jawaharlal Nehru, late Prime Minister of India, had made it clear on more than one occasions that, the Governmnet of India is glad to give asylum to the Dalai Lama and show him the respect due to his position, it has no reason to believe, that he will do any thing that which is contrary to international usage and emberassing to the host country. It was confirmed by this statement that "The Government of India wants to make it clear that it does not recognize any separate government of Tibet and there is therefore no question of a Tibetan government under the Dalai Lama functioning in India." The Dalai Lama has expressed that as long as he was followed by the Tibetan Cabinet members (*Kã-Shag*) his government is in existence.

The structure of the Dalai Lama's establishment in Dharmasala resembles that of the traditional one, with the Dalai Lama as the head of the ecclesiastic as well as the temporal.

Dalai Lama after coming to India, promulgated a new draft constitution of Tibet in the year 1963. According to Chapter V, Article 29 (1) of the New Constitution, the executive power of the state shall be vested in His Holiness the Dalai Lama on his attaining the age of eighteen. Dalai Lama is expected to preside over the meetings of the *Kã-Shãg* (Article 31 (1)). Dalai Lama shall promulgate laws. And any disagreement with the National

Assembly leads him to submit the proposed legislation to a referendum (Article 32 and 33). Dalai Lama holds the authority to dissolve the National Assembly and order new elections but with due consultation with the members of the *Kā-Shāg* who are appointed by him, and the speaker of the National Assembly who is elected by the members of the Assembly.

H.H. the Dalai Lama may in his discretion or on the recommendation of the *Kā-Shāg*, refer any proposed legislation to a referendum and if the proposed legislation is approved by the majority, H.H. the Dalai Lama shall promulgate it within the period specified (Article 33). The Dalai Lama directs that an amendment should be submitted to a referendum and should be upheld by two thirds of the majority of the National Assembly.

The Dalai Lama though not elected by the people cannot bring his undue influence over the people or the National Assembly. The Tibetan refugees though claim that religious and political supremancy lies even today with H.H. the Dalai Lama, but the draft constituion promulgated by him in 1963 is highly democratic and brings freedom to commoners. Under this constitution the people have enough legislative authority to check the Dalai Lama's executive powers. The constituion will also reduce the Dalai Lama into a formal figure head may be of the future Tibetan State. In 1969 he declared that – "the system of governance by a line of Dalai Lamas may or may not continue, it is the will of the people that will ultimately determine the future of Tibet" (Editorial, Tibetan Review, 1976: 3-4). This statement has shocked many of the Tibetan refugees because they believe that Tibet cannot exist without the institution of Dalai Lama.

But few of them who are aiming and returning to a democratic Tibet say it is good for the Dalai Lama and also for the country to discontinue it. There are also those who say that the institution, at present has some vital functions to perform. So it should continue till an alternative institution is found or the present one itself may continue with some changes. Dawa Norbu (1976:4) in his editorial to the Tibetan Review commented - "it is not only the Dalai Lama's promise which will guarantee a democratic set up, but the objective condition in Tibet will not allow a return to the old order. If such be the case one cannot see much in the present Dalai Lama's statement. The Tibetans need the Dalai Lama most as a unifying force in their struggle for freedom. Or else if times are bad he may even turn out to be a manager of chaos and even of anarchy. Dalai Lama might prove useful in a figurehead symbolizing continuity in Tibet's history and culture. Indeed it is not necessary to abolish the institution of Dalai Lama altogether to usher democracy or socialism in Tibet. Dalai Lama for the good will of his own or for that of Tibetan peoples and also historically, it would not be incorrect for a Dalai Lama to abolish the institution or succession of Dalai Lamas. Being a national institution, it might require a national consensus, whether to abolish it or not".

The Dalai Lama's statement to end the institution may also mean something else. Ashok Chopra quoting Sinha (loc.cit. 1976:5) wrote "when an incarnate lama expresses his desires to enter Nirvana, that is when he does not like to be reborn, his followers petition him to change his mind. The incarnation desiring to stop his rebirth does not actually mean that he wants to end the institution of Dalai Lama. He may just want to lay down his political office". Further, Ashok Chopra interprets the decision of Dalai Lama to relinquish his office, as he may be thinking in terms of his own Nirvana. The Mahãyãna conception of Nirvana differs from that of Hinãyãna in the sense that in the latter it rests with one's individual self and the former for the welfare of the humanity. Dalai Lama's announcement of relinquishing his office thus would go against the fundamentals of the Mahayana system of Buddhism. Chopra (1976:5) further writes that *Mahãyãna* doctrine represents the *Karuna* aspect of the Buddha himself. Scholars believe that it is left to the deity - *Chejen drolma* and not to the Dalai Lama, to take the decision. In this connection what Elnor Reas (loc.cit. Chopra, 1976:5) says is also important. To him the only fate awaiting the future of Dalai Lamas is of "figurehead" with reduced power or none at all. In such a case the Dalai Lama should withdraw from public "activity" which goes at the cost of the spirit to dedicate his life to a worthier cause.

Tibetans in exile have also undergone drastic changes in their economic and social organization. These changes in turn have forced them to bring changes to some extent in their administration. However, the ultimate faith in Dalai Lama as the temporal and spiritual head of the State can never be wiped out from the mind of the people completely. It is certain that without him and his charismatic authority, the Tibetan Society cannot function properly or may not protect its traditional socio-cultural identities.

Now, a good lot of change has taken place in the Tibetan Society - from lord-serfdom type to the democratic one. This, however, may bring only the economic liberty and political freedom and not religious. The Tibetans believe that their culture, its values and concepts are based mainly on the religious values controlled by the charismatic authority. To break off from the religious fold means losing them permanently. They say that they need the utmost control of their charismatic leader H.H. the Dalai Lama. They strongly hold the Dalai Lama as their political and religious head. Side by side they also want to have the present systems of democratic practices but not at the cost of the tradition. The Tibetans can tolerate anything but not the disintegration of their religion and the religious head. This fact is evident from the history of Tibetan administration.

(B) *The Regent (gyal-tsab) and the Council of Regency*

In the absence of Dalai Lama or during his minority, the Regent (*gyal-tsãb*) ruled the country as the deputy of the Dalai Lama (Puntsog Wangyal, 1975:82). The title of *De-si* was conferred by the Vth Dalai Lama to Sonam Chopel in 1642 who performed the role of a *gyal-tsãb*. This title which is equivalent to that of Prime Minister, became the designation of the chief administrator who survived under the Fifth and Sixth Dalai Lamas (Shakabpa 1967:111). The term *De-si* may be rendered as political administrator of the country (Phuntsog Wangyal, 1975:83).

The first person to become the Regent (*gyal-tsãb*) was De-mo Nga- wang Jam-pal, in 1757. The first six Regents were appointed by the *Kã-Shãg*, the Council of Ministers in consultation with the Government officials. Since 1875 the Regents were appointed by the *Tsong-du*, the National Assembly. The Regent must be a high class incarnated Lama of one of the three Lamaseries - Dre-Pung, Se-Ra and Gan-Dan.

Before the promulgation of Constitution of Tibet, one of the three senior Abbots of the above mentioned monasteries used to be appointed by the National Assembly to work as a Regent. According to the Article 36(2) of the draft Constitution of Tibet the Council of Regency shall consist of three members elected by the National Assembly; one of whom shall be an ecclesiastical representative. The Council of the Regency exercises its executive powers during the absence of Dalai lama, or when he is still a minor, or in case of any disability which prevents Dalai Lama from exercising his executive functions, or in the absence of His Holiness the Dalai Lama from the State, or when it is decided by the National Assembly by its 2/3 majority that the executive functions of Dalai Lama shall be exercised by the Council of Regency (Article 36(1). The Council of Regency in consultation with the *Kã-Shag,* Ecclesiastical Council and the standing Commission of the National Assembly will conduct the search for the reincarnation of His Holiness the Dalai Lama (Article 36(9)). The Council of Regency shall have no power to alienate any part of the territory of the State or enter into any international agreement in relation to the independence of the State except it is approved by the majority of the members of the National Assembly (Article 36(10)). The duration of each Council of Regency will be of the same period as that of the National Assembly (Article 36 (8)).

(C) *The Prime Minister (Lon-chen)*

Next in the line of administration there might be one or more Prime Ministers. This position was always held by a senior lay official but it was not a necessary part of the system. This post was retained at the time of XIIIth Dalai Lama who ruled Tibet from 1805 to 1933 to serve as a link between himself and the lay council. Prime Ministers did not preside over the council but passed on its recommendations to Dalai Lama with note of their own opinion. But according to the draft constitution of Tibet His Holiness the Dalai Lama from time to time, appoints any number of Ministers as may be required. Out of these Ministers His Holiness the Dalai Lama shall nominate a Prime Minister and not less than five other Ministers to be members of the *Kã-Shãg* (Article 30(1)). No Minister shall be a member of the National Assembly (Article 30 (2)). In the absence of the Dalai Lama however the Prime Minister presides over the meetings of *Kã-Shãg* (Article 31 (1)).

Next to Dalai Lama or the Regent, on the civilian side, comes the Council of Ministers (*Kã-Shãg*). This is the principal executive body. It consists of three lay and one monk high ranking officials. The *Kã-Shãg* represents both the religious and the secular communities of the country. It shall aid and advise the Dalai Lama in the administration of the state (Article 30 (5)). This council functions as a Court of justice, also.

(D) *The National Assembly (Tsong-du)*

It came into existence in the year 1871. In the beginning it was called the "Small Assembly", consisting of the government officials and the Abbots of the three monasteries - Dre-Pung, Se-Ra and Gan-Dan. Puntsok Wangyal (1975:83-84) says presently there is a change in the composition of the National Assembly, also known as the "Great Assembly"; "*Tsong-du gya-dzom*", besides the government officials and the Abbots, included representatives of every group and occupation of Tibetan society: traders, shop keepers, farmers, workers, etc.

The present constitution promulgated by the Dalai Lama says "All legislative powers shall vest in the National Assembly subject to the assent of His Holiness the Dalai Lama" (Article 38). Article 39 provides the National Assembly to consist of 75 per cent of members directly elected by the people in the territorial constituencies, 10 per cent of members elected by the monasteries and other religious institutions, 10 per cent of members elected by the Regional and District Councils, 5 per cent are nominated directly by the Dalai Lama and they have the distinguished services for their credit in the field of art, science or literature etc. Each National Assembly unless dissolved shall continue for five years (Article 40 (1)). During the urgent situations the Dalai Lama may consult the standing committee of the National Assembly if the latter is not in session (Article 59 (1)). When a bill is passed by the National Assembly it shall be presented to the Dalai Lama for his consent. He either assents or withholds the bill. The Dalai Lama may return the bill to the National Assembly requesting it to reconsider the bill or introducing any such amendments (Article 60). Further, Article 61 (1) says the validity of any proceedings in the National Assembly shall not be called in question on the grounds of any alleged irregularity of procedure. And in exercising the powers, vested by or under the constitution by any member of the National Assembly shall not be juridically questioned (Article 61 (2)).

For the present among the Tibetans in exile, the representatives to the National Assembly are elected by the common people. The duration of their office is for three years. The number of representatives elected from various districts (their origin in Tibet )are as follows:

(i) **Lay:** Four representatives are elected from each one of the three main provinces of Tibet-Amdo, Khamba and U-Tsang, together they are called *Choga-Sum,* the three provinces.

(ii) **Ecclesiastic:** From the ecclesiastic side one member is elected from each of the four main sects of Buddhism - *Saskya-pa, Nyingma-pa, Geluk-pa* and *Kargyu-pa.* These sects together are called as *Chulu Sheiy* - meaning four sects. Elections will be held once in three years in all the Tibetan Settlements in India to elect their representatives. The Council of Ministers (*Kã- Shãg*) also functions as the National Working Committee.

The six Councils which are functioning are: (1) Council of Revenue Records (*Tse-khãng*), (2) Council of Religious and Cultural Affairs (Cho-thenyw), (3) Council of Home Affairs and Rehabilitation (*Nang-shēy*), (4) Council for Tibetan Education (*Te-tha*), (5) Office of the Publicity and Information, and (6) The Office of the Security and the Personnel (*Meg-chi*).

The Council for Revenue Records (Finance Office) and the Council for Religious and Cultural affairs are represented by four lay officials and the four monk officials each and ultimately are directly under the Dalai Lama. The other offices are headed by two to three members.

While in Tibet there were two schools *Tse-khor* and *Shor-khor* - the ecclesiastical and the secular, which prepared candidates to serve in the Government. *Tse-khor* composed of monk officials, *Tse- drung,* who must have been enrolled as members in any one of the three monasteries: *Dre-Pung, Se-Ra* and *Gan-Dan.* Anybody except those who belonged to the groups of untouchables - like the smiths, butchers, fishermen, hunters, etc., could become the monk officers. A candidate of 10-12 years, got admission in the training school, *Tse-lub-dra*; which was a part of the Secretariat. The Secretariat, under the Council of Ministers, was staffed purely by clergymen and maintained records and discipline of the monks and the restrictions of the lama dignitaries of all sects. It maintained records of the monastic organizations. A few *Tse-drung* however came from the noble families. They formed a special class within the ecclesiastical court and enjoyed higher prestige. This was the only way a serf was able to become a monk officer in the monastery.

*Shor-khor*, the Secular court, was a monopoly of the nobles. They had also a training school attached to the Finance Officer (*Tsi- khang*). The candidates were put to the school between the age of ten and twenty and given few preliminary lessons. Soon after his training a candidate was assigned with a position in all the public functions and became a probationary officer. A commoner may work for the Government but he could at best become a clerk but never a 'ruling man' (*pon-põ*).

Now under the draft constitution the situation has been completely changed. Any one can become an officer in the monk as well as the lay courts or offices irrespective of his social and ritual position in the society. What he needs to possess is the required modern education and capability to become a leader or an officer.

## II. Tibetan Provincial Level Administration

There were mainly four provinces in Tibet - Northern, Eastern, Western and the Central. These were administered by provincial heads - the Governors. They were the senior most officials staying outside the capital city of Lhasa. Each province was administered by a Governor (*Garpõn*) coming from an aristocratic family. He was helped by a monk colleague of equal rank. Each checked the other in the administration of the province. The government orders were issued to the Governor and he in turn issued the same to the district officers. His duty was to fix and collect the tax and later send the same to the central administrative body at Lhasa. The Governor was paid in kind, out of the taxes collected by him from the districts.

## III. District Level Administration

A district is jointly administered by an administrator who comes from an aristocratic family — *Thongar* or *Dzong-pon* of Lhasa, and a monk colleague. They functioned as magistrates also. The monk officer had an equal or even higher rank than the civil officer. One was expected to watch over the other so that the danger of autocracy and discrimination - the lay and the ecclesiastic is put to a minimum. As Dawa Norbu (1974:27) says apart from the political motive, this system of administration headed jointly by a lay aristocrat and a Lama was to keep the concept of ideal Tibetan government. Usually the district officials were posted for three years tenure.

*Dzong-pon* was the officer to whom the Government orders were addressed. He in turn transmitted them to the village leaders (*pom-bo*). *Dzong-pon* stood above all the village leaders (of his district) and had the full authority over them. He had authority to fine the guilty and the disobedient. He was consulted and his consent was necessary before a leadership could be transferred from one person to another. From time to time the leaders gathered in his office to discuss matters of public interest. Disputes between men and high authority were also settled by him.

The main duty of the district administrators was to collect taxes through their representatives - *Lechen-pa* and *Shapto-bã*, and maintain law and order through the courts of law. The revenue taxes were collected from the village heads by sending the representatives to all the villages. The tax was collected both in cash and kind. The nobles and the ecclesiastical groups paid tax of their own including that of their serfs. The serfs of state land, i.e., the *tre-bas* and the *du-jung* (bound) paid their taxes to their respective group leaders who were responsible for the collection of the tax. Thus the serf very rarely came in contact with other officials and so were less conscious about any other form of leadership. The tax payable by the serfs was fixed and levying of more taxes by any district officer was unauthorised and so such cases were reported to the higher authorities at Lhasa.

The Tibetan way of redistribution of tax was also fixed. The tax collected from the common man was always stored at Lhasa and used mainly for the maintenance of the monasteries and the armed forces. The commoners also got a portion of it during their needs like failure of crops, famines, drought, etc. Except the collection of the taxes the state government had no other direct administrative control on the villages.

In Tibet the state and the common people had their obligations to each other in running the administration smoothly. The head of the state the Dalai Lama, was responsible for protection of both the materialistic and spiritual life while the people in return owed him taxation in service, kind or cash at the need of his immediate master. Thus every Tibetan was a subject of the state or monastery directly or indirectly.

## IV. Village Level Administration

Tibetan villages were administered by village headmen. In all the cases they were nobles. The nobles with higher economic and social status had many privileges and one among them was the right to village leadership. Their economic position helped them to spend much of their time on the official matters like maintenance of law and order in the community, while the serfs who attached to their land; had very little free time for community matters. However, the nobles and the commoners co-operated in fulfilling their obligations towards each other and were self- contented.

A Tibetan village was a territorial as well as a social, political and a ritual unit. They were structured in such a way the members undertook mutually depended activities combined in an organized way, for a concerted action. The village was a community of families, many of these were interrelated by ties of kinship and affinity or interwoven by lord and serfdom relationship. This proved their capacity for acting in common for the preservation of traditional customs, the maintenance of public peace and harmony, keeping up of the economic stability and for the performance of ritual activities essential for material and spiritual spheres of the village as a whole.

The following were the village leaders and their status and roles:

## (1) The Headman

The headman was known by different names such as *Gon-po, Ding-pyun* and *Pom-bo*, depending upon the dialect of the region. The post was always held by the nobles and richest persons. Richer a person was higher the status he had in the Tibetan society. Most of the time the village leadership used to be hereditory. Because, once elected a person became rich, honest and dominant and he continued as a leader forever. This position was inherited only by his sons preferably the eldest. Usually such persons were supposed to possess all the qualities of a leader and then only they were allowed to inherit the office. Or else it was given to another person belonging to the same clan or any other person of the village who had a high status. In a few cases a leader was persuaded by his followers to withdraw from his position if he was found unfit to lead them. Thus succession to leadership was partly hereditory and partly on the basis of personal ability.

Leaders got some amount of land and the serfs attached to it, in return to their duties. One had to relinquish the land and the serfs when the leadership was transferred to another person; and this happened very rarely. Thus the Tibetan village administration was based on clan system and was always in the hands of the nobles or aristocrats. The headman being away from the centres of the state and the district headquarters, enjoyed a very high status in his village.

Functions of a village leader were to provide military personnel from his village as and when required by the Central Government and feed them when they visit the village. It was also his duty to replace old or dead soldiers. He was also a host to the officers coming from the district places. He maintained law and order in the village and in the course of this he used physical force. He helped the villagers in all their needs and necessities. To become a popular figure among the other nobles of the society generally he gave huge amount as charity. *Pom-bo* held a very important position in various ceremonies arranged in the village like marriages, community rituals, etc., as a social father or the leading ritual head; and he even bore some of the expenses, incurred. Similarly he used to bear the expenses or he used to arrange for the funeral rites of an individual if he had no heirs or kinsmen in the village.

As the judicial head of the village, headman seldom allowed a divorce. The parties were brought to peace through persuasion. Family solidarity was valued. He could fine and or give heavy punishment whoever acted against the rules. Guilty ones were made to offer the leaders with *chãng* and *khãtã* (sacred scarf) sometimes cash also, after making them accept their fault in public. Criminal cases like murders and those disputes which the headman could not settle, were refered to the court of law, the *Dzong-pon*, at the district place.

Another duty of the village leader was to see that all the serfs in his village were fed well by their nobles. If not, it was feared that·the serfs may run away to other districts and affect the territorial solidarity and prestige of the leaders and the officers concerned.

The guiding principle in a village for its administration lies in the authority in the totality of its inhabitants. The authority of the leaders was always used in its legitimacy. The village community as a whole may not correct the action of a *pom-bo* if he himself was guilty. But they could express their disapproval by petitioning the case to the higher authorities and/or by reelection or by blocking any future appointment. It was not only the leader who maintained or effected the common good, but all the people in the community were responsible for the well being of the community. Bound by such duties the people were guided by the social and religious sanctions. It brought a civic responsibility and a remarkable degree of discipline also in the matters of community and its welfare. In all these cases it was the village leaders who had an important role to play. They were also the links between the people and the Government. The village leaders were assisted by two or three assistants (*Tse-mey*) depending on the size of the village in the administration. They helped him as the personal assistant, as accountant and as store keeper of food, etc.

## 2) Assistant Headman (*Genjung*)

*Gunjung* acted as the mediator between the headman and the common people. He transmitted official information to both groups. Depending on the size of the village four to five such leaders were appointed in a village. This position was shared by all residents of a village in turn. Sometimes such a leader was selected after an informal discussion by the elders of the community. His main duties were concerned with agriculture. He acted as a leading man for his group to arrange for the rites performed for the crop gods.

Accompanied by all his people, carrying sacred books and images of the gods, he goes round all the village fields to protect the crop against evil spirits and thereby bring more fertility to the land. He also collected contributions from his people to arrange community rituals and common festivals at the village temple (*Gomba*).

The nomads also had a leader of their own. He used to be the richest person of the group and had a high socio- economic status. He was directly linked to the leader of the village to which his group belonged. The village leader had all duties and responsibilities towards these nomads also.

## Administration and Leadership in the Present Settlement:

The Tibetan form of state administration seems to continue here at the settlements also. But, since the refugees are rehabilitated in different packets and in mixed manner irrespective of provincial and district background the administration of these levels has changed, a good deal. At the top is the Dalai Lama and his cabinet with its establishment in Dharmasala. Each settlement is directly administered by the Dalai Lama through his representatives. Each settlement is divided into several villages which are administered by elected village leaders. There are nine villages in Mundgod settlement each administrered by an elected leader. Villages VIII and IX which are too small and very close to each other are clubbed together and are put under a single village leader.

### A) The Representative of H.H. the Dalai Lama (*Thon-Jeyw*)

All the villages of the Settlement are administered by the representative of H.H. the Dalai Lama (*Thon-Jeyw*) who is appointed by the H.H. the Dalai Lama's office to officiate as the local administrator of the settlement for a tenure of three years. Along with his office staff he lives in the official quarters provided in the Settlement. He is paid directly by the Dalai Lama's office. He forms a link between the Dalai Lama, the common people and other agencies within and outside India. In running the general administration of the Settlement, he takes the help of the village leaders. He often conducts meetings with them. Occasionally, public meetings are also held to collect the opinion of the common people for a certain project etc., to be started. The representaitve of H.H. the Dalai Lama is honoured and respected as a lord of the Settlement by the commoners. He undertakes the community level administration for the Tibetan Settlement, and all transactions with the Ministry of Supply and Rehabilitation, Government of India, through the Administrator II. T.R.R.S. Scheme at Hubli, and with many other inland and foreign agencies that aid Tibetans in one or the other way, are handled by him.

Another duty of the *Thon-jeyw* is to collect the levy of food grains on behalf of the Government of Karnataka. As per the communications issued to him by the revenue authorities of

Mundgod, the tahsil or the local revenue headquarters the *Thon-jeyw* asks the village leaders to collect levy from their villages. The account of the same is maintained by a village accountant who is temporarily appointed by the village leaders and works honorarily. This in turn is submitted to the office of the Tahasildar, Mundgod Ṭaluka.

The *Thon-jeyw* as Chairman of the Tibetan Co-operative Society and an administrator of the Settlement plays a dual role in the administration, becuase as a representaitve of H.H. the Dalai Lama, he rules the Settlement as the local administrator and undertakes programmes for the welfare of the Tibetan refugees. As an administrator he also holds his supreme position and authority over his people. The Chairman's position is a formal one, and holds a strategic position in the settlement. His office is open for supervision by two senior officials–one monk and another a lay official from the Dharmasala.

## B. Village Leader or Headman (*Pom-bo*)

The traditional method of Tibetan village administration was based on the clan system and leadership was passed on clan basis. Here in India, clan organization has lost its significance. The change in the social orgnization from lord-serf relation to a more democratic one has brought much structural changes in the leadership and political organization among Tibetans.

At the Settlement here a village leader is elected by all the heads of the families. It is not necessary for a leader to own property or to occupy higher economic position as it was the case in Tibet. Every Tibetan irrespective of his background gets the voting right. They vote and elect a person who is educated and not necessarily coming from a noble or rich family, and they are accepted as leaders by most of the commoners. However, it was noticed that most of the past and present village leaders thus elected in the Settlement belong to some or the other high status group in Tibet.

In a few cases elected persons may not agree to take up the responsibility, because now they have to work in the fields to make a living. Further leadership position also takes away one's time in visiting officials and conducting public meetings. In Tibet the village leaders had lot of property and other economic gains. Therefore there was no need for them to work on the farm. Now the situation has changed and the leadership never brings any additional income to him.

Secondly, here there is very little competition in the field of leadership. Because the present situation needs an educated person to hold the office and the majority of the Tibetans are illiterate. A few persons reject the leadership offer owing to their low status and a feeling of no authority. Therefore usually when an elected person refuses, the person who gets the next winning votes gets the leadership position. The office of a village leader is for one year. In a few cases a leader who is liked by his village people is retained for several years.

## C. Sub-leader (*Chok-penyw*)

The sub-leaders are elected or nominated by the village leader. One may also get this chance when the appointment is made on rotation basis. A sub-leader has a few formal roles to perform and also some authority, as well. He acts as a mediator between the village leader and the people. Once appointed he works for six months and in some cases for one year. Since he has a few offical roles to perform he is classed as a formal leader.

There are few leaders among Tibetan refugees who do not come under any of the categories we have discussed so far. These leaders by nature are constructive and innovative. There are a few situational leaders also. Some of them take interest to collect funds to build community halls and to conduct meetings. They teach people about the importance of modern education and the need to change the traditional outlook. They also maintain contacts with a few local officials namely the health, police, agricultural officials and teachers and use these contacts for the good of their people.

The qualities of leadership have also changed owing to the changes which have taken place in the basic structure of the society. A leader's position varies according to the situations and duties which he undertakes. Even when the goals are set, the methods employed by a leader to consolidate his following differ according to the circumstances, by which the community is influenced by. There are many methods of acquiring leadership positions. Some may inherit by descent and others may achieve by legal acceptance of the people through election and nomination. Still others may get it by the character or traits possessed by them namely, the charismatic, political status, education, etc. In other cases one may be forced to subordinate his main purpose in propaganda and to encourage the tempting of his followers by the prospect of some one or the other advantages. A leader can arouse the faith of his followers by this impressive personality. The traits of personality may vary with the programmes in view. These qualities of leadership however may vary from leader to leader.

Tibetans consider the hereditory (*Rugo*) type of leadership as the most appropriate one to hold the administrative power. Persons tracing their origin to the early kings, families rewarded by government for rendering a service of high quality are considered more appropriate for leadership.

Now in Mundgod, the situation has changed much. In Tibet an aristocrat who held lot of land along with the serfts attached to him, used to be more interested to attain a high status in his society. Here as the land holding pattern is different, every one enjoys equal right and freedom. At the same time like the leaders in the traditional society have no problem of bearing heavy expenses to maintain their status in the society. They need not spend for the high officials who visit them. Higher economic status as a leadership trait has, therefore, lost its significance. However, values attached to the high classes, still continue and the people seem to prefer their leaders to be of a high social rank.

Education is also an important trait of leadership. In Tibet only the rich were either able to send their children for education to district places or train them privately at home. People of the middle and the poor classes could not afford this. In Tibet every headman had to have the education to deal with the official and village administration. Therefore every working leader in the traditional Tibetan society, used to educate his children to retain the leadership position within his own family. Today also literacy is one of the important traits required to be possessed by a leader in the Mundgod Tibetan society. A literate leader can read magazines and news and aquire knowledge of the outside world. Thereby he can guide his people in their political, social, economic and religious life. The leader is the representative and the authority of his community. He comes in contact with the leaders and commoners in other Tibetan as well as Indian villages. If he is educated it helps him to know the socio-economic and other aspects and the institutions.

To maintain good contacts with people outside the community one has to speak Kannada and/or Hindi fluently. So a leader is supposed to know the local languages at least better than his followers. A leader is supposed to introduce many new things into the traditional Tibetan society. To do this effectively he has to accept new things first and set an example to others. Thus we see innovation of some kind has also taken as an important trait of leadership, here at the settlement.

Sympathy is another trait of leadership. A sympathetic and kind leader is liked by one and all. Most of the Tibetans have lost their own kin and property and depend on the government help and the allotted land. A few are very poor, handicapped or too old to work. They need material help and sympathy from others. Only a kind and sympathetic leader can cater to this need. Similarly the children of poor and handicapped, also need a sympathetic leader. An unsympathetic and selfish leader is publicly condemned by one and all.

Boldness is also a trait for leadership. Tibetans who come from different provinces of Tibet differ very much in their socio-cultural background. To control them, to passify them, and to lead them in a foreign situation, one needs courage. When others are demoralised by their own problems the one who leads them should be morally and mentally strong. So a bold person is always preferred as a leader by the Tibetans. In addition to this morality, honesty and ideal characters are also the traits for leaderhip. Without these one cannot face and control his followers properly. Owing to the weakening of traditional socio-cultural values, morality among the Tibetans seems to be weakening. Under these circumstances a person who continues to uphold them and care for them is considered a good person and fit for leadership position.

Self sacrifice is another trait for leadership. A leader interested in the community welfare should sacrifice his personal comforts, gains, etc., and help his followers. While selecting or electing a leader the settlers take into consideration another factor—his official place and residence in Tibet. Those who come from one village or district or even the same province think they are nearer. This regional feeling is important from the point of settlers since they believe a person close to them will help them better.

## Law and Social Control

Every society has a set of ideals according to which it trains its people. In all societies either the traditional or modern, there exists a type of social control brought about by the customs and convention, but not necessarily by law; while in some the legal law is continued to be enforced by some authority. The Tibetan law is contained in a book – *Trim Yig Shelche Chusum* – which means 'the thirteen decrees'. This is believed to have been promulgated by King Songtsen Gompo in the seventh century A.D. The thirteen decrees are in fact thirteen laws dealing with various types of offences, punishments and sanctions. According to Dawa Norbu (1974: 77) the Tibetan laws include a few primitive methods of mutilations like plucking out the eye balls, amputation of tongue or hand, throwing the criminal alive into water or from a precipice. However, with the influence of Buddhism these severe modes of punishments have decreased considerably. It is also on record that the thirteenth Dalai Lama officially banned such un-Buddhist punishments.

The book 'the thirteen decrees' also contains fines to be imposed. The laws deal with the duties of officials, which expect them to be selfless and honest. They also deal with the holding of investigations. The eighth clause strictly forbids abortion. The ninth deals with methods with which disputes are resolved when evidences are lacking. Under such circumstances disputes are resolved by an oath and by playing dice or picking out black and white pebbles from the boiling oil. Swearing is more effective because of their profound belief in their faith. The tenth clause deals with matters on thieves and robbers (*chakpa*). A reward will be given to the one who kills a robber. For stealing even small items, the thief was beaten 50 to 100 times with a leather whip (*chakchey*) . Stealing during the night is considered bad compared to stealing by day. If, the owner of the robbed things was beaten by the thieves it is not considered bad, as it indicates the strength of the robbers. It was also considered that the things were taken away directly.

The eleventh clause which deals with divorce, provides that in case of divorce the dowry should be repaid and sons of the union in marriage should go with the father (*phu phãtõp*) and the daughters with the mother (*Phõmõ matõb*). When a son or daughter desires to live separately, a daughter gets a quarter of the amount given to a son. If one of them was in the ecclesiastic group, as a monk or a nun, the family bore the expenses of his or her food and clothing.

The twelfth decree deals with adultery. In the traditional order punishment was considered on three factors. First, invitation for sexual intercourse, second the verge of sexual intercourse and third, the act of intercourse. One or two intercourses were condoned. But if there have been more than sixty occasions, the adulterers were fined sixty *khels* of grain. A married woman when caught at extramarital unions, her nose was cut off.

A man who seduces another's wife, was fined three gold coins, which in turn were paid to her husband. He was also asked to give a written pledge stating that in future he will not do this blunder. A commoner if committed the offence of adultery with the wife of an authority, his limbs were cut off.

The last decree the thirteenth law, deals with the general laws of the human relations.

There was no separate judicial power as such in Tibetan administration. The Governor of the local government appointed two senior officials to investigate and act as judges. Regardiing the judicial procedure Dawa Norbu (1974:83) says, after placing a *Khā-dar* (sacred scarf) before a judge a disputant retreats a few steps, and with bowed head and bent knees reveals his case in the most dignified and honourable language. In the course of narration the original statements should be neither altered nor added to. He further says the people in judiciary should not accept bribes.

It should however be noticed that though there is a lack of efficient police force in Tibet the number of crimes committed were less. This was because of religious stigma on the bad things or the suffering in the wheel of life–the *Karma* of bad deeds, have played their role in this. During the researcher's stay of about a year and a half with the Mundgod Tibetans, cases, of theft, quarrel and sinful act committed by the Tibetans were very rare. The informants also told that even in Tibet, the severe punishments suggested in the Tibetan law are for exceptional cases. They also confess that they have never seen a person so severely punished as mentioned in the decree. It is said the thirteenth Dalai Lama rooted out such un-Buddhist punishments.

When a thief is tried for a minor theft by the village leaders, he is asked to repent for it and also asked to return the articles to the owner. He is also made to pay one hundred to five hundred *tsaks* (bow from foot to head) depending upon the nature of crime, and also to offer a scarf and oil lamps to the god. Here at the Settlement in case a local Indian is involved both the Indian as well as the Tibetan leaders have to intervene. Here, mention may be made of the case of a Tibetan from village No.5 who bought a stolen roller from an Indian. After a few days the owner of the roller traced it and asked the Tibetan to return it. The Tibetan asked for the return of his money first. Ultimately the matter came before the headman of the Koppa–a nearby village. During the negotiations, however, it was found that when the Tibetan bought it he knew that it was a stolen one. The headman told the Tibetan that he has committed an offence by encouraging a thief and so asked him to return the roller to its original owner and the thief was made to pay the money to the Tibetan.

There are also cases where Indians, who work as labourers to Tibetans, stealing paddy and corn from the fields owned by the Tibetans. But when this was brought to the notice of the headman of the culprit's village the headman has invariably taken suitable action. As aliens the Tibetans are not supposed to approach the Indians directly for such matters but only through their village leaders. However, some of the Tibetans do not involve their leaders in these matters because of the fear that they themselves have violated the rules of the Settlement and the same shall be disclosed. Thus the aggreived party directly takes up the matter with the concerned person and this leads to further complications. On the other hand even the village leaders sometimes keep aloof and pretend ignorance. For example, during 1976, owing to abolition of rural indebtedness, a few Tibetans who had lent money to the Indians and had taken their land on long term lease, for eight to ten years, had a few disputes. The Indian borrowers belonging to poor and low castes had received this land as a grant from the government. Sometimes the owners of these lands lived away in far off villages or were employed somewhere else. They had found it profitable to lease it to some one and the enterprising Tibetans took it. When the law to abolish rural indebtedness was implemented the Indians claimed the land back. Here again the village and settlement officials wisely stayed away and asked the parties involved to settle the matter as quietly as possible. Because of this a few Tibetans lost their money totally or a portion of it. Knowing this check on the Tibetans a few Indians took advantage of the situation. Here too the Tibetan leaders kept away from the problem. When the aggrieved Tibetans protested against this they were reminded of the instruction of the Dalai Lama that they should maintain at any cost peaceful and good relationship with the hosts.

There are many sex offences committed among the Tibetans at Mundgod. A few had premarital and extramarital sex and this resulted in illegitimate births. Had it been in Tibet these would have created a more serious situation. But here such cases are secretly settled among themselves and are not reported to the leaders. However, we find that a few such cases have ended in the informal dissolution of marriage. In a few cases the village leaders have remained aloof to avoid legal complications. In Tibet there were ways and means to deal with such sex offences. In one case of premarital sex the offender was given a very simple punishment i.e., he was asked to marry the girl and accept the fatherhood of the child, after performing a ritual. In another case of extra marital sex, the offender was accepted as another husband for the woman, thus establishing a non-fraternal polyandrous marriage, instead of giving a divorce.

Regarding serious offences like murder, in Tibet, an offender was punished by making him to move about wearing an iron ring weighing five kilograms, around his ankles. Sometimes he was also made to carry a heavy and long wooden plank around his neck (*Tsejak*). In India such cases are dealt directly by the local courts of law and the punishment sanctioned is given. A few elderly informants said that it is because of their sins in previous birth that they are suffering as refugees. Now they say one cannot afford to commit any more sins, but should lead a religious life and see that they will earn merit and go back to their homeland.

## Tibetan Public Welfare Agencies

The Tibetans in Mundgod settlement maintain a Co-operative Society of their own and the representative of H.H. Dalai Lama is its Chairman. Each Tibetan village elects a representative to work as the director for the Society. There are eight directors-one each from the eight villages. This position sometimes becomes dual since most of the village headmen are elected as the directors. A monk official and another a lay official, from the Dharmashala visit the society for auditing and discuss administrative matters with the officials in the Settlement. Finally the accounts are placed before the general body in a public meeting. The Tibetans receive fertilizers, seeds and tractor services from the Co-operative Society, on credit basis. As a rule they sell their agricultural products through the society. This makes it easy for the officials to collect the loans given to them.

The society also owns two trucks and maintains a workshop for the use of the members. It also runs flour mills, hotels and grocery shops in different villages for the convenience of its members.

In 1976, the Society started a handicraft section to prepare Tibetan carpets. Here about fifty men and women are working on daily wages. From time to time, they admit trainees so that after training they can get employed in the handicraft section in the Settlement. This has brought a secondary source of income for a few persons in the Settlement.

During 1973-74 the Tibetan Co-operative Society earned a net profit of Rs. 2,14,828.83. During 1974-75 it underwent loss to the tune of Rs. 72,798.30. Again in the year 1975-76, it suffered a heavy loss of Rs. 1,09,286.12. The members say that this loss was due to the mismanagement and misappropriation of funds by the Society officials. It is also true that owing to the lack of proper leadership and inefficiency, the management was unable to recover loans from members; in some cases even the arrears of past 6-7 years. Members of the Society also feel that a few persons are in office almost permanently and there are every possibilites of misappropriation, and that their long association with the Society has also taken away their efficiency. Some members are of the opinion that the Chairman of the Society is too young to understand their problems and that he seldom mixes with the village leaders and other members. They are also of the view that he lacks the leadership quality. But still no one dares to complain against him to the higher authorities in Dharmasala because he is an influential person.

The Society is a registered body under Karnataka State Co-operative Societies Act. The Chairman of this Society becomes an ex-officio member to all the co-operative socieites in the Taluka. In this capacity he gets a voting right to elect directors of all the co-operative societies in Mundgod Taluka.

A District Co-operative Credit Bank Ltd., and scheduled bank have their branches in the Settlement. The credit bank is attached to the Tibetan Co-operative Society and provides loan and credit facilities to the farmers. It is found that only the village leaders, as innovators, have taken maximum use of these banks by opening Savings accounts and fixed deposits. Large number of Tibetans are yet to develop faith in the banking system. Normally they borrow money from the banks and spend on unproductive items. A few Tibetans have also taken loan from the scheduled bank, on personal security, for the business of woolen garments. The amount comes to approximately Rs. 2,50,000 every year. The loan is returned with interest and borrowed again. A few Tibetans have taken loans from credit bank using the good contacts of their village leaders. It is required that those who borrow for agricultural purposes from the credit bank should produce a 'no dues' or 'no objection' certificate from the Tibetan Co-operative Society. Those who are very poor and have not returned the loan to the Co-operative Society cannot get this certificate and so cannot get fresh loan from any of the banks. This makes it difficult for the poor and they will have to stop their agricultural operations or have to take loan from private money lenders in the Settlement, paying a very high rate of interest. This has made a few poor farmers to lease their lands and get a very low return out of it. This in a way had made the poor poorer and the rich the richer. It is observed that the leaders of all levels have not yet taken note of this situation.

It is a must for all the Tibetans to keep their villages clean. It was found that the people have not cared for this. A few have taken interest in cleaning the space around their houses as a precaution against fire accidents. Except this no community level health and hygienic programme is undertaken in the villages. It is also the duty of the leaders to see that the nursery school in their village works properly. Tibetan mothers leave their children (between three to five years of age,) here, when they go for work, and they stay throughout the day here under the care of two maid mothers of the school. It is noticed that the arrangements are not satisfactory. Children get mid-day meal with the aid from Swiss Government. The parents also contribute, a certain amount per child per month. This amount is used towards the payment for the house maids, the cook and for buying other things needed for the mid-day meal. In all the villages except the IIIrd and IVth the villagers have constructed separate buildings to house the nursery schools. These buildings are also used for conducting community meetings. Recently a few active and young men in the Settlement have taken initiative and organized the people in the villages III and IV to collect funds both in cash and kind including free labour for constructing buildings for Nursery School. Extra money needed for this is obtained as a loan from the credit bank.

Those Tibetans who do not have any secondary occupations complain that their leaders are not taking any initiative to bring small scale industries to their village. The leaders in turn put the blame on the higher authorities. The representative of H.H. the Dalai Lama however says that he has no funds with him for this purpose. The Society officials are also unable to get a loan from the banks as the Society itself is in loss.

We cannot but fail to mention another area where the leaders have failed. It is in preventing the Tibetans from manufacuring arrack and the Tibetan beer (*chãng*) which is sold both to Tibetans and Indians alike. Some Tibetans have resorted to this illicit trade because they are poor and helpless and there is a lucrative demand for liquor.

The village leaders have also failed in settling a number of familial disputes and as a result there are a number of divorces, breaking of joint families, cases of premarital sex and unwed mothers. Cases of extra-marital sex, are also reported.

But in general the Tibetans say that their stay in India is happier and more democratic because compared with their native land here they are not very much bound by traditional laws and regulations. In Tibet the powers and authority of a leader were absolute. Here owing to changed situations the authority and the powers of both the leaders and the law have completely changed.

## The Youth Leadership (*Shunu*)

The Tibetan youth are very different compared to their elders. They are now living in a society which is changing fast and upholds equality and democracy. They have attached to the new values instead of traditional values of the Tibetan society. As they are now put in a different world of culture, they are able to adopt to many new things. They work for the welfare of their community as a whole, and feel that the fundamentals of their traditional culture and society with its religion should not be disintegrated irrespective of the adoption of a few useful innovations. The Tibetan youth are also interested in learning from the outside world. A few old persons and persons of higher social strata in Tibet did not like the youth leadership, a few think it creates a sort of groupism among the Tibetans. Others think that it is against the traditional order and system of administration. Still others think it is not of any use to them when they return to Tibet. Most of them uphold the traditional ways of life with their traditional administration with minimum innovations like education which are only useful to their society. A few informants who appreciated the youth leadership had all the regrets that only a few youth leaders came to the front and many others are busy with their day to day affairs.

In the Settlement the Tibetan youth have started a Tibetan Youth Society (*Shunu*) in October 1970. The Society has five official positions, viz., President, Vice-President, Secretary, Cashier and Sports-in-charge. They are elected by the members once in three years. It should be mentioned here that the Tibetan youth all over India, have a union with its headquarters in Gangtok (Sikkim). Every year the youth meet and discuss about their problems and the possible ways and means to achieve independence of Tibet.

The Tibetan Youth Society at the Mundgod Tibetan Settlement, has many plans and programmes like sanitation, teaching the Tibetans the practices of health and hygiene, providing the poor with financial assistance, educating people against alcoholism and gambling, controlling and protecting the youngsters from falling into bad habits, conducting adult education programmes, making Tibetans to understand the local situations, starting small scale economic projects, and teaching the values of legitimate and illegitimate sex and the new and modern methods of agriculture. They also arrange for the staging of Tibetan traditional dramas, dances and songs so that the people will be in touch with the traditional culture and values of their society. The members visit every village and conduct meetings to educate the people about the freedom of their country. They also arrange for the show of a few films which give knowledge of the outside world, types of foreign games and the modernized methods of agriculture, etc. However, the achievements of the youths in the Settlement are not upto the mark. The officials of the Youth Society said that they lack the necessary funds and also the time because most of them are employed in different capacities. They also realised that without the help of their village leaders they alone can not bring these developments. The youth leaders also told that many factors have made their leaders ineffective.

The foregone pages show that the leaders do not take much interest in the leadership activities since they are of the opinion that their stay in India is temporary. Leaders also think that they have no economic or social status to hold the leadership positions as in Tibet. The leaders here seem to only play the roles of a mediator between the people and officials and nothing more than that.

We should notice the fact that in Tibet the abrupt end of autocracy has freed the commoners from the economic dependence on the nobles. Here in the Settlement however the Co-operative Society has provided the common man with an alternative to money lenders. Now all the Tibetans are treated as equals and this change in the social organization has made each one of them independent in thought and ways of life, etc. Now a commoner can also become a leader, if he possesses qualities of leadership. Under these forces of change the old power structure is gradually giving way to a new structure of power in the Tibetan society. The people here have now assigned the leadership to the active and mature men instead of the dominant people as was done in Tibet. This is due to their shifting from the traditional world of culture to the modern world with modern trends of democratic views, and perceptions. But along with all this they have great attachment to the traditional values and culture. They say they need a leader who brings new changes within the traditional values, so as to adjust themelves to the present situation of the change. But it should be noticed that to some extent the leadership of the community continues to be in the hands of dominant people.

However there has been a lot of change in the leadership of the present times. We notice that there was enough competition for leadership in Tibet. Because leadership meant prestige and high social and economic status. It also encouraged joint families necessary for leadership. But now at the Settlement conditions have changed, leading to independent families with their own pieces of land and with their own family members. The traditional values of high and the low class distinctions are almost vanishing. As the leadership is not hereditory and is temporary, the people have developed new values. The competition for leadership has almost died out and sometimes inactive persons are compelled to accept the leadership positions.

# 8

# Tibetan Buddhism

Religion is the most important aspect of the cultural system of a society. It significantly interacts with many other cultural and social institutions of a society, such as material culture, behaviour, morals, ethics, systems of family organization, marriage, law, economics, politics, medicine, science and technology (Malefijt, 1968:1). Religion is acquired by a person as a member of his society through socialization or enculturation.

The essential function of the religion lies in the regulation, maintenance and transmission of sentiments on which the society depends. Religious rites unite the members of a society in common group and enforces the social interaction. It thus promotes the establishment and maintenance of social patterns outside its own immediate field. Religion also has provision of authority for the belief and action. It has one of its most important functions in the provision of meaning for social action. It gives pattern and order and also interprets them in terms of ultimate ends.

Emile Durkheim (1961:62) defines religion as “a system of belief and practices pertaining to the sacred”. Religious beliefs are always group beliefs, shared by members of a society and preserving their unity. Everywhere religion has a "church", a place where people come together for shared social action; while there is no church of magic (Ibid: 60).

Radcliffe Brown (1952) who draws heavily upon analogies between social life and organic life says religious ritual is an expression of the unity of society and that its function is to affirm and strengthen the sentiments upon which social solidarity and therefore the social order itself depends. In his study on the Andaman Islanders, Radcliffe Brown (1964:404) observes, ‘through regular expression in ritual, these important principles are kept alive and passed from generation to generation’.

Malinowski considered society as something that can survive only if its basic needs are fulfilled. In his view the religious rituals such as the magical ones, are carried out in situations of emotional stress. Among the Trobrianders the death of a member breaks the normal course of life and shakes the moral foundations of a society (1960:53). However, the society steps in to lead the striken individuals through the comforting experiences of religious ceremony (Ibid: 62-63). Thus the religious dogma contains the value structure upon which the proper functioning of society depends, and the society's doctrines are regularly acted may be safeguarded and transmitted to succeeding generations (Ibid: 67- 68).

The religion thus forms an important aspect in the cultural system of a society. It holds the individuals in the social, cultural and the physical relations. It maintains the individuals in the moral characters and binds one into the right path giving the ideas of good and the evil and thus helps to run the society smoothly. The religious rituals unite the family as well as the community members by binding them into a group holding the obligations of the rituals and the socio-ritual functions towards one another. The magic is said to be the part of the religious activity which fulfills the personal problems and is unable to serve the ends on the social system as a whole. Thus magic cannot bring the social solidarity. But the religious beliefs are the common beliefs held by the entire community as a whole and serve to fulfill their ends. Lobsong Lalungpa (1976:10) views religion, mainly considering Buddhism as 'a belief in psychological realignment with sets of principles and practices which lead to the realization of the ultimate truth'.

Buddhism came to Tibet in the seventh and eighth centuries and found flourishing system of popular beliefs and practices loosely identified with *Bon*, the pre-Buddhist religion. Certain aspects of this early religion were absorbed, facilitating the change of faith. This successful blending, as Lobsong Lhalungpa (1976:10) says, was an indication of Buddhism's ability to adapt to local conditions while retaining its innate doctrinal purity. Even today the pre-Buddhist customs and their symbolism have remained in Tibetan society. It can be observed in the belief of the Tibetans that the rooff top and the hearth are considered sacred and incense sticks are offered regularly. The walls of the houses are decorated with auspicious figures and signs representing the deities of old religion. The symbols of four elements, the tiger, lion, eagle and dragon, are still used in the Buddhist philosophy. The practice of selecting high places or hills (*rēy*) to perform worship to spirits is also an age-old practice

pso Festiv

(ii) A Meeting of Village Leaders

Interior Arrangements in a Monastery

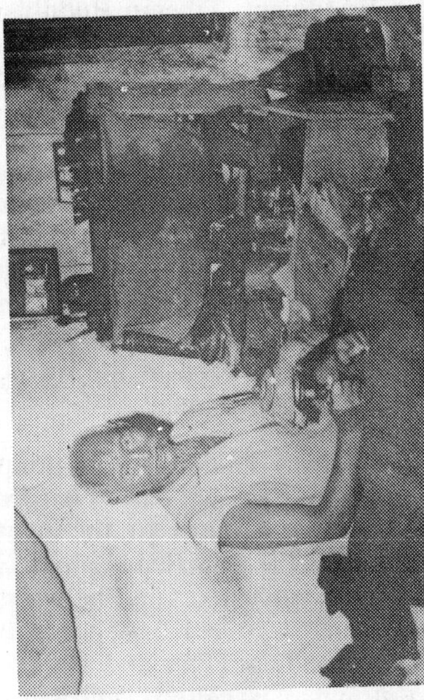

**(iv) An Inmate of the Old and Infirm Peoples' Home with His Belongings.**

belonging to *Bon* religion. Erecting the prayer flags on the roof tops etc., also indicate the elements of *Bon* religion incorporated in Buddhism. Tibetan Buddhism has many more practices from the *Bon* religion, namely oracular priests, local divinities and a notion of divine kingship (Giuseppe Tucci, 1974:402)].

Buddhism originated in India in the 5th century B.C. in an area that extended roughly from Varanasi to Gaya, Rajagarh and Pataliputra. Buddhism developed in two directions. One usually called *Theravāda* the true tradition of the Buddha's teachings, is also called as the *Hināyāna.* The other called as *Mahāyāna,* "the means of salvation adapted to a larger number of people". Both lead to *Nirvāna* the salvation. Currently still one more branch the Tantrism is added to the former two. Each branch however has several sub groups.

Tibetan Buddhism is unique in that it contains both the traditions known as *Theravāda* and *Mahāyāna.* Its other distinctive features are the institution of the incarnate Lamas, the presence of married Lamas, and the spiritual and temporal powers invested in the person of Dalai Lama (Lobsong Lhalungpa 1976:12). The distinctive form of Tibetan Buddhism developed in Tibet and it also includes the *Vajrāyāna* thought. *Vajrāyāna* is called Tantrism or the *Mantrāyana.* It holds the *Mahāyāna* concept of *Nirvāna* as the base. *Nirvāna* or the Voidness is seen as the passive wisdom which is like a diamond beyond all duality.

Tantrism believes in attaining enlightenment through one's own body. To achieve the goal of enlightenment one must follow the instructions of his master or the teacher who guides him in controlling his physical and the mental processes. Hence every monk whose aim is to attain *Nirvāna* or the Voidness, should be initiated by a recognized teacher - *Khen-po,* the Abbot of the monastery.

The pre-Buddhist *Bon* religion was largely magical, a defence against the invisible powers present at every place and every mountain, the spirit at every place and every mountain, the spirit *Klu* - dwelling in water, the *Sa-bdag* - dwelling in the ground, and the *Lha* in the sacred mountain etc. Bon religion also had many animistic magical rites of sacrificing animals and even humans in the ancient times, and the practices of black magic to bring the bad effects on enemies. Yet the Tibetans without a cultural heritage, slaves of century - old superstition, suddenly awake and also translated, comprehended and explicated the most difficult works of *Mahãyãna* speculation, carrying on the tradition of the most famous monasteries of India (Giuseppe Tucci, 1974:399). Mahãyãnists have two choices - the *Sūtra*, the exoteric course; and the other *Tantra*, the esoteric course. Both the courses are contained in the *Tripitaka*, which in Tibet is classified into two collections, the words of Buddha (*Kan-Gyur*) and the commentaries of others (*Ten-Gyur*). Tibetans as Mahãyãnists follow the esoteric course rather than the exoteric course.

Buddhism was given recognition in Tibet during the reign of Srong-brtsan-Sgam-po from 620 to 649 A.D. The Warlike king was able to establish his authority over the other wild clans of Central Tibet and whose son the Srong-brtsan-Sgam-po, harassed the western borders of China; so the Chinese Emperor Taitsung of the Tang dynasty gave this young prince the princess Wencheng of the imperial house, in marriage. Two years earlier to this Srong-brtsan-Sgam-po had also married Bhrikuti Dēvi a daughter of the King of Nepal, Amsuvarman. Both these queens were effective in turning their husband to the Buddhistic principles, and sent people to India, Nepal and China for Buddhist books and teachers. The religion received active encouragement from Khri-Srong-lde- btsan and during his reign (775-797 A.D.) the first monastery was built at Samye and the Tantric master - the Padmasambhava, was invited from India. There was another Indian monk Santirakshita, whose disciple Kamalasila, represented the Indian point of view in the debate at the council of Samye(792-794 A.D.), as to decide whether the Indian or the Chinese forms of Buddhism, should be followed in Tibet. The Indian side emerged the winner. Buddhism also received the encouragement from Ral-pa-can's reign (815-838 A.D.), the third of the religious kings, but after his assassination in 838 A.D., it suffered a period of suppression. Again at the time of king Srong-Tsan Gam-po, Tho-mi Sa-mbho-ta was sent to India. After a stay for several years in India, he studied under Lipidatta, and returned to Tibet, carrying several books on Buddhism and the so called "Tibetan" alphabet. Later it was he who gave a script to the Tibetan language and composed grammer for this purpose.

The founder of Lamaism, saint Padmasambhava (the "Lotus born one"), is usually called by the Tibetans as *Guru Rim-po-che* or the precious *Guru* or simply the *Lo-pon*, the Tibetan equivalent of the Sanskrit term "Guru". With the help of learned lamas Buddhism was again revived in the 10th to the 11th century and the ruling noblemen in western Tibet helped them in their struggle. Many travelled to India in search of books and masters. A great many books were also translated into Tibetan language. Atisa, the *Mahāyāna* master enabled the Buddhism to strike the deep roots in Tibet. By 14th century the Tibetans had translated all of the Buddhist literature and they produced their own canon, the Bka-gyur (*kanjur* or Kagyur - Translation of the Buddhist world and the *Btsan-gyur Tangyur* - Translation of teachings). Slowly it led to the formation of separate orders of monks developed around particular masters. The head of the Dge-lugs-pa sect, who is believed to be a reincarnated Abbot, known by the honorific title of Dalai Lama - appealed to the Mongol chieftain Gushrikhan, for help in the struggle against the rival Karma-pa sect. The Gushrikhan after conquering Karma-pa forces awarded Tibet as religious gift to the heads of the Dge-lugs-pa sect. From 1642 A.D. until the advent of communists in the year 1959 the Dge-lugs-pa had been the dominant sect in Tibet and the Dalai Lama the effective ruler.

There are four main sects in Tibet - Sa-Skya-pa (named after a place, 1034 A.D.), Bka-brg-yud-pa (black hat sect, 1012 A.D.), Rnying-ma-pa (red hat sect, 810 A.D.) and Dge-lugs-pa (Yellow hat sect, 1357 A.D.). The Dge-lugs-pa (Gelugpa - the virtuous), constitute the reformed sect in Tibet; the members of this sect are called Yellow Hats; from the colour of their head cover. The sect was founded by Tsong-kha-pa, who attended the most important schools in 14th century - the Sa-skya-pa and Ka-dam-pa. He was the first to invite the reform of monastic discipline by the general laxity of morals, less rigorous observance of monastic rules and so on. Tsong-kha-pa attached great importance to the study of the logic and instituted the regular holdings of debate at the monasteries. Various ranks of monks were established on the basis of examinations, the highest being that of Ge-she. Tibet enjoyed its independence with the head from the Geluk-pa, H.H. the Dalai Lama.

The Geluk-pa sect has three monasteries - Dre-Pung, Se-Ra and Gan-Dan and all the three are in Central Tibet. These three sub-sects are further subdivided as follows:

1. Dre-Pung:
   1. Loseling
   2. Gomang
2. Se-Ra:
   1. Serji
   2. Sermai
3. Gan-Dan:
   1. Shartse
   2. Shangtse

The other sect Nyingma-pa, the "ancients", trace their origin to Guru Rim-po-che - the Padmasambhava of the eighth century A.D. They favour the deeper practices of *Yõga* and believe that the *Yõga* and meditations lead to the purity of man. The Milarepa school took its birth in 11th century and practices the *Hathayõga* exercises - called as Kargyu-pa. Lamaism, therefore, cannot be seen as a single religious current. It contains many trends. They are set out from the same premises and have sprung from the same concern with salvation. "The Tibetans recognize the plurality of schools but rightly insist on the fundamental unity of inspiration and aims, wherein different methods are used to reach the same end-salvation, by rebirth in some paradise or final escape from rebirth with the attainment of nirvana" (Giuseppe Tucci, 1967:67).

Despite many differences on the points of doctrine, all Tibetans accept the law of the Buddha and describe themselves as *Nangpã*, those who are all within the laws of Buddha. And the word Lama refers to the teacher who is well educated and can guide the pupils in the spiritualistic way. Tibetans have been able to retain their most traditional religion with its own traditional fundamental concepts, laws, beliefs and practices. Monastic life of the Tibetans is hard with strict discipline and demands the sacrifice of life, learning thousands of ecclesiastical pages by heart, and cultivating a better mind by meditation for attaining the *Nirvãna*.

There is a great emphasis on discipline in monastic life. The Geluk-pas are not allowed to marry and indulge in enjoyments like drinking and smoking. They were prohibited to live in layman's settlements. But as compared with other sects the Sakya-pa in particular is liberal and their monks can even marry and stay with commoners in their settlements.

Monasteries, each headed by an Abbot, the authority on religious matters, played an important role in the life of the Tibetans. The lamas and monks lived permanently in monasteries. The monks were sponsored by their respective families and all their necessities would be provided by them.

In 1953 a Buddhist association was set up under the presidentship of Shes-rab rgya-mtsho who affirmed that Buddhism was a doctrine of revolutionary character and hence not opposed to the new democracy. Thus monks were directed to participate in reforms, to become reactionaries and help to adopt their religion to the new situation (Giuseppe Tucci, 1974:401).

In 1959 it is alleged that the Chinese authorities in Tibet proclaimed to weaken the Buddhism gradually and ultimately suppress it. In the same year the Dalai Lama fled to India. Followed by this it is alleged that many temples were destroyed, monks were forced to work with secular persons and also teach them.

Presently at Mundgod Settlement there are two lama villages. In one of them monasteries for Shartse and Shangtse (of Gan-Dan sect) and Nying-mã-pã sects are located. In the other the monasteries for Loseling and Gomang (of Dre-pung sect) and Saskya-pa sect are located. Devotees belonging to Se-Ra sect do not have their monastery in this Settlement and they go to Byalakoppe settlement in Mysore District, for their religious activities.

There are 908 monks and lamas including, child monks and lamas settled in the two Lama villages in the Mundgod settlement (1978). Of them 393 are child monks and remaining 515 are adults. Their rehabilitation is financed by the United Nations Refugee Rehabilitation Organization, Geneva. They have been provided with 400 acres of cultivable land for their subsistence. The land is given to a group of monks and lamas in common who belong to one sect or sub-sect. All the members of a group work, eat and live in common. Now more and more younger monks from other Settlements in India, are joining the monasteries, there is a derth of agricultural land to them. Since the parents of these young monks are poor and cannot contribute towards their food and clothing, the monastery itself has to provide all these to them. Further there is a competition among the different monasteries to develop their sects and sub- sects well and they also want to have more and more number of monks with them. This means need of more money and to earn this extra money they have taken-up measures like leasing-in of land and extended loans on interest and so on. Each group also sends its selected monks on woolen garment business to distant towns and cities in India. The money earned so is utilized for the improvement of living conditions of the monks and lamas and building of new and big monasteries, and conducting more and more rituals for the welfare of their people, their God-King and their traditional homeland-Tibet.

It was, also observed that a few monks have taken lands on lease individually, from the local Indian farmers and, have earned additional money. They also lend money to needy Tibetans and Indians, on interest which has helped them to increase their capital. The money thus earned is said to be donated to different monasteries to get merit (*Gewa*). A part of it is also kept aside to meet the expenditure of their funeral rituals. With all the stresses and strains the monks and lamas are successful in reestablishing their religious order. They have taken pains to construct monasteries, prayer halls, and schools in both the lama villages.

In Tibet the monasteries were exempted from paying taxes and services to the Government. They were independent lords of their lands with serfs attached to them. These yielded them wealth and services in plenty. The monasteries also supplied officials to Government and for this they received titles in accordance with the hierarchical order. Social hierarchy was maintained within the monasteries. Monks coming from one family, village or district shared houses in common in the monasterial village. In the non-reformed orders that allowed marriage, the married monks lived in their native villages and tilled the family farm. The lower clergy who could not finish a lengthy course of studies and reach the highest monastic position and often remained illiterate, served the monastery in cooking food for the monks, helped in playing music and in preparing offerings, etc. A few of them also served as warrior monks (Stein, 1972:140-141).

On initiation to monkhood candidates had to take vows from the Abbot, regarding the rules of discipline. They were allowed to drink only tea, milk and eat grain and butter. They were allowed to wear an under-robe and a red-robe. It is strictly obligatory for them to stay always in monasteries. They were prohibited from drinking *chãng*, eating meat and excessive food. Those who act beyond the bounds of the religious law were punished heavily by the Royal Law.

The monks in the Settlement have now changed considerably and have now also adopted many new ideas and customs. It is observed among the monks of younger generation that though they lead a religious life and lived in a holy environment a few of them do not follow the religious laws strictly. They are even attracted by profitable ways of earning money such as taking land on lease and lending money on high rate of interest and have bought worldly and luxury articles such as radios, bicycles and watches. A few youngsters go to see cinemas and dramas for recreation. All these were strictly prohibited while they were in Tibet. In Tibet monasteries were far away from the villages of common men, were situated on hills and had minimum contacts with them, and the possibilities of violating the Royal Laws were very remote. The senior monks expressed that at Mundgod as the monasterial villages and buildings are surrounded by the villages of commoners, the monks always come in contact with the lay people and their womenfolk.

The candidates who are intended to be initiated into monkhood are sent to the monasteries at a very young age of five or six. In the monasteries at the Settlement it is observed that the candidates also have come from distant places in India. Parents send their children to any monastery they like and no discrimination of sect is made at this level. Candidates are left to the care of a teacher (Lama) who gives them spiritual education and their maintenance is paid for by their parents. The poor and orphan candidates are looked after by the monastery, and the teacher. In rare cases the grown-up monk students have left the monasteries to accept the life of householder and to help their parents in maintaining the family. The Tibetans say now-a-days the student monks are drawn more towards the worldly matters than spiritual ones and they tend to leave monkhood.

Life in a monastery is very rigid and disciplined. The first prayer starts at 5.00 a.m. and lasts for an hour. After the prayer they take tea and *tsampa* or the fried bread. The higher lamas engage classes to students and the lower order may go for farm work or to attend their assigned duties such as working in kitchen, cleaning monastery, prayer hall and so on. In Tibet there was no need for the monks and lamas to work in the fields. The serfs attached to the monasterial land worked for them. The monks have been now assigned with secular duties as said above in addition to their religious duties.

Debates on religion, philosophy, etc., also take place between the monks who belong to different sects in the Settlement. These debates usually take place at the time of major festivals and are presided over by the senior most lama, the Abbot. Commoners and monks from the Settlement attend the debates to enrich their knowledge. Such debates are also arranged for lamas coming from other settlements in India. On such occasions the lamas of both the Dre-Pung and Gan-Dan monasteries jointly face such debates. Some times both the senior tutor (Yong-tzen Ling Rim-Po-che) and the junior tutor (Yong-tzen Trijang Rim-po-che) of H.H. the Dalai Lama arrive in the Settlement, between December and February, and arrange for common prayers and teachings. Monks will have to appear for their religious examinations at the time of New Year festival. A monk normally takes 25 to 30 years to pass the highest degree-*Geshey*. The commoners who will have finished their harvest work by now, will also conveniently attend these sessions.

Monastries play important roles in the life of Tibetans. Being the seats of religious activity, they attract commoners at the time of major festivals and celebrations. The worships conducted by the Abbots and the senior lamas provide them with an opportunity to visit the monastery and receive blessings from the lamas. Commoners visit monasteries on their own also to offer food, money, prayers, etc., when their vows are fulfilled. The monks from the monasteries attend to the life cycle rituals performed by the householders. They are invited to conduct worships before they start any socio-economic activity. Their services are also taken in conducting rituals for curing diseases.

There is a belief among the Tibetans that if they contribute their self earned money to the monasteries they get merit in life. So old people at the end of their life give away their savings to their eldest son or to a village leader, to distribute it to different monasteries throughout India. In two cases it was noticed that an old man and an old woman from the Old and Infirm village gave a lumpsum amount which they had saved over years to be spent on their funeral rituals and to donate the remaining amount to different monasteries. Likewise after their death, their wish was fulfilled by the village leader.

Monasteries and the rituals conducted in them also provide an opportunity for the lay Tibetans to come together. The differences of sects which prevailed in Tibet is now gone and the Tibetans feel that they are one people. H.H. the Dalai Lama also advises his people to forget the old order and adopt to the new situations. In Tibet the different areas had different sects. A lama or a scholar who was effective introduced his own philosophy and influenced people to follow him, thus founding a new sect. These sects had their own traditions, beliefs and practices which were made to be followed by their following. Owing to lack of easy means of communication and transport in Tibet, the society was much isolated and the people also readily accepted the ideas preached by a lama. In a way it is only after coming over to India that the commoners belonging to the different Tibetan sectarian groups have come in contact with one another. For example the Settlement has monasteries of all sects and they are open for all Tibetans. The Geluk-pa, the dominant religious sect under the headship of the temporal head of the Tibetans - H.H. the Dalai Lama, is the sole authority of all the Tibetans at their present refugee situation. This has made the Tibetans to focus their attention on him for their protection in India and to plan their future in India or in Tibet. This has made the Tibetans to think, that they are one and belong to one religion — Buddhism. However, the monks and lamas in the monasteries strictly follow the rules of the sectarian division. The common men who are just concerned with the good life, the life away from committing any sins and meditate only to purify one's soul (*Tsō-sayā*), are not much concerned by the sectarian division.

H.H. the Dalai Lama has written a few verses which are compiled in the form of a book (*Nga-ring Chemo*) and these are read by all the Tibetans. These verses are also sung by the children regularly in the schools. All these have made them to understand and believe in the ultimate end - the Buddhism. Though they possess the photos of the heads of their own sects in their homes and regularly worship them and they may not exhibit it in public. So it was real problem to collect the names of sects to which they actually belonged. The Table 24 shows the distribution of Mundgod Tibetan families according to their affiliation to different sects.

### Table 24: Distribution of Tibetan Families in Different Sects.

| Sr.No | Villages | Geluk-Pa | Nyingma-Pa | Saskya-Pa | Kargyu-Pa | No Specific | Not mentioned | Total |
|---|---|---|---|---|---|---|---|---|
| 1 | I | 106 | 17 | 8 | 6 | 3 | - | 140 |
| 2 | II | 45 | 6 | 5 | 7 | 3 | - | 66 |
| 3 | III | 87 | 18 | 10 | 8 | 9 | 4 | 136 |
| 4 | IV | 108 | 28 | 6 | 50 | 12 | 4 | 208 |
| 5 | V | 48 | 5 | 2 | 3 | 1 | - | 59 |
| 6 | VI | 58 | 15 | 26 | 13 | 11 | 9 | 132 |
| 7 | VII | 80 | 14 | 6 | 50 | 11 | - | 161 |
| 8 | VIII | 37 | 7 | 10 | 24 | - | - | 78 |
| 9 | IX | 22 | 2 | 5 | 6 | - | - | 35 |
| | Total | 591 | 112 | 78 | 167 | 50 | 17 | 1015 |
| | Percentage | 58.14 | 11.08 | 7.69 | 16.48 | 4.93 | 1.67 | 100.00 |

## Sacred Objects and deities

### *Flags*

As one enters a Tibetan settlement or village, he first comes across sacred flags tied to long poles and fixed at the entrance. He also comes across lines of thread with small paper flags stuck to them, on these are printed the pious sentences, charms and prayers and tied across the road overhead. Individual families also hoist such flags infront of their house. The paper prayer flags are printed on unglazed paper brought from Banaras and available with the lamas. In general the Tibetans use the following four kinds of flags:

(1) **Lung-tã** is a six inches, square shaped flag. In the centre the figure of the sacred horse is printed on it with the mystic jewel - *Norbu*, in the background. It is usually hung on the ridges of the houses, (2) The second type is a luck-flag called *Cho-pen.* It is long, narrow and oblong shaped and is about ten inches in length and six inches in breadth. These flags are tied to branches of trees, and bridges. Sometimes they are planked on top of hills. When a person is in trouble, he is advised by a tantric lama to put a number of such flags on bridges, near water pools, on hills or on the branches of trees near a spring. The Tibetans offer these flags usually on the third day of the lunar month, along with incense sticks. A small quantity of maize flour and *chãng* are also offered to the spirits by sprinkling them towards sky. While offering the flour and *chãng* they utter *Sõ Sõ,* meaning relieve us from the troubles brought by the evil spirits and also drive them away.

A much wider form of this luck-flag (*Gyal-tsãn dse-mo*) contains larger number of holy texts and also the eight glorious symbols - the golden fish (*gser-tã*), the umbrella (*gdugs*), conch shell trumpet (*dun*), symbol for good luck (*dpal-be*), victorious banner (*rgyãl-mtsen*), vase (*bum-pã*), wheel (*K'or-lo*) and finally the lotus (*padma*), at the base. It is supposed to bring good luck to a person in all aspects — health, wealth and power.

There are also other type of wider flags known as *glãn-põ stob-rgyãs*. These flags are made by drawing pictures on pieces of wide plain cloth using oil paints. They are hung from the walls of houses and covered with a thin sheet of cloth so as to protect them against dust and smoke. There are many varieties of flags with different designs of paints, showing the family deities, divine emblems, and the symbols. They are arranged to be drawn by a Tibetan artist in the memory of a dead family member. It is also believed that by offering these flags, the gods and goddesses will be satisfied and lift the soul to heaven. These flags are also drawn to raise the wealth and also to protect oneself from the harmful spirits. A few Tibetans, in order to fulfil their wishes during their life time or after their death, arrange for engraving a few sacred syllables such as *Om Mani Padme Hum*, or the sacred texts on stone slabs and put them on hill tops, which are considered to be auspicious places by the Tibetans.

In every home a well cleaned room is reserved for the family altar. There we can find many pictures of gods, and goddesses and the senior lamas of the different sects, arranged.

The three popular deities are the Bodhisattvas - *Chenresi, Jampeyang* and *Chandorje.* The white coloured *Chenresi* is the embodiment of compassion. He is expressed with six syllable formula - *Om Mani Padme Hum*. He is also a means of compassion and higher knowledge — the Voidness. The symbols '*mani*', the jewel, he possesses indicates that he is male (*dorje*), the symbol for means of light; and *Padme*, 'lotus' with the bell (female) standing for emptiness. He is the great protector of Tibetans in the spiritual and physical dangers.

*Chenresi* is shown with four arms. Two of them are joined, with right palm placed in the left. Of the other two hands, in the right one he holds a rosary and a lotus flower in the fourth. This form is sometimes replaced by another in which he has eleven heads. The upper half of the body is shown dark blue and the face with an expression of anger - a symbol of disapproval to evil doers. The Tibetans say that his eyes and hands are so many and also so quick that no evil doer can escape and so also no merited person is allowed to suffer. The Tibetans also say that the image of Avalokitesvara, the *Chenresi*, is modelled after the Hindu God Brahma.

The *Jampeyang* is red in colour and is the symbol of knowledge. The book in his hand is the indication of knowledge, and he is expressed by the syllable - '*Om Arã Pacho Nadi*'.

The *Chandorje* is the god of battles. He holds a sword in his right hand. He protects the religion from the spiritual foes. He is expressed by the syllable — *'Om Benzar pani Hum'*.

The female Bodhisatwas, the energies, are the *Tārā* and *Marichi*. Tārā, *Drol-ma* in Tibetan, is the most popular deity. She is the goddess of mercy. She is shown in two forms — the white and the green Tārā. It is said the two wives of Song-tsen Gam-po, the King who introduced Buddhism in Tibet; are the incarnations of the *Drol-ma* in white and green forms. The deity holds a lotus in her left hand. The right hand is held in the giving position.

The other deity *Marichi*, has three faces and eight hands. Various weapons, including an axe and snare, are held in her hands. She sits in an enchanting pose upon a lotus which will be on the back of seven pigs.

The Guru *Rim-po-che* is the great teacher of the 'ancients', the Nyingma-pa sect. But everyone regards him as one of the most authoritative manifestation of the law regarding the miracles. He is the strongest propagator of Buddhism in Tibet, defeating the power of the old Bon-po religion.

Though most of the Buddhas and the Bodhisats are the protecting gods, *Vajra Bhairava* or the *rDo-rJe* (*Jigs-byed*) -a form of Siva, the Hindu God of destruction, is conceived to carry the same function in the Tibetan religious belief.

The other defender gods of the faith are the *Tam-din* and *Pal-lden Lha-mo*. Tam-din's picture depicts him with horse's head and neck and with bow and arrow in his hand. The Goddess *pal-lden Lha-mo* is equated to the Kālidēvi or Durga of Hinduism. She is surrounded by flames and also splitting the flames and riding on a white faced mule, upon a saddle of her own son's skin. She is covered on all sides by the human skulls and she weilds in her right hand a trident rod. She is considered the most important deity and is accepted by all the Tibetans as the favourite protective deity. She protects the Tibetans from all the evil spirits. The Tibetans, therefore, worship the deity for seven days during the New Year festival. The cake offered to her was having ingredients such as the fat of a black goat, blood, wine, dough and butter. All these were placed in a bowl made of human skull. After the spread of Buddhism these *Bon-po* practices of offering animal and blood is replaced by the offerings of products prepared out of grain in the forms symbolizing the animals and their flesh. A red liquid is also put on the offerings prepared out of *tsampa* to signify the blood.

The Tibetans in Tibet had domestic Gods whose head resembled the head of a pig and wearing flowing robes. They were believed to occupy different positions at different seasons or months in a year. When these Gods were disturbed or angered, to appease them, worship and offer them with their necessities, lamas were called. It was said, after the introduction of the Buddhism and establishment of monasteries, in all the places the conception towards the old deities was changed and they were accepted as favourite family deities. After coming to India as refugees it is observed, most of the Tibetans have lost their ties and affinity with their family deities who are now left in Tibet. In their place, they have now taken the protective deities like *Pal-lden Lha-mo, Shungden, Chenresi, Gombo* as their family deities. In all 81 family deities were listed among the Mundgod Tibetans. *Pal-lden Lha-mo* the protective deity is being accepted as the family deity by 638 (63.94%) families. Next comes the *Gombo* who is claimed as the family deity by 41 (4.05%) families and another 40 (3.95%) families claimed the *Shungden* as their family deity. The remaining 296 families claimed as many as 78 deities as their family deity.

While in Tibet the Tibetans considered that each and every place was considered to have housed a spirit or a deity. Owing to their deep religious belief the Tibetans believed that all good and bad things in life occurred because of their family deities. To perform any tantric or the magico-religious practice, preference or involvement of traditional family deity was most essential. Now the change of their residence has brought changes in this belief system also. Gradually the old Tibetan deities and beliefs connected with them have been slowly disappearing. Only the older people are able to tell the names of their family deities and others have totally lost them since no elderly person belonging to these groups of families is present here.

## Rites, Rituals and Festivals

A Tibetan morning starts at about 5.30 a.m. with a homage offered to the family gods. The holy cups (*ting*) filled with holy water which number seven or eleven are arranged in a line on the altar. In the middle of which is kept a holy lamp, a short pedastalled bowl, with a socket in the centre and with a cotton wick. It is fed by butter. On the altar a silken or cotton parasol painted in five colours — yellow, red, green, blue and white is hung in the centre. This is the symbol of royalty. On the altar the pictures of all household deities and lamas are arranged in an hierarchy. The images and pictures of lamas are kept in the centre since the Tibetans view lamas as the actually existing reincarnations of god. Next to them. come the protecting deities (*Yidam*), the gods of wealth (*Khāndo*), the god of the defenders of faith or the Dharma-pāla (*Chokyonw*) and lastly the *Sungmā* the family deities. All these deities protect the people from the attack of evil spirits and also uplift the householder to heaven.

The pictures of deities arranged on the altar of a house in the Settlement are as follows: (1) *Jamyang Chenresi* - the God of mercy, (2) *Yongjema* - deity which may be equalled to the Hindu deity - Saraswati - the deity of knowledge, (3) *Chotā Lāngnā* considered by Tibetans as equivalent to the Hindu deity Ganapati - remover of obstacles, (4) *Chejun Drolmā* equalled with the Hindu deity - Laxmi - the goddess of prosperity and wealth, (5) *Sēmō trāksing* - the incarnation of *Chenresi* in the form of monkey, (6) *Palden Lhamo* - the protective deity, (7) *Gyalwa Gendhun Drolba* - the disciple and the nephew of the Tsong-kha-pa (reorganizer of the Atisa's reformed sect and altered the title to the virtuous order - the Gelug-pa) who was the first reincarnated Dalai Lama, (8) *Nejung Chokey* - the oracle god of Tibet, (9) *Chongo gye Lamjo* - an oracle lake which indicates the birth place of Dalai Lama and other reincarnated lamas, (10) *Nyanjorma* - female deity, the worship of whom brings good luck, (11) *Tārā Rim-po-che* - the female reincarnate showing the path of salvation, (12) *Tsona Trulku* - 13th reincarnation of Drepung, (13) *Kyapto ling Rim-po-che* - senior teacher of Dalai Lama, (14) *Kyapto Tejang Rim-po-che* - the junior teacher of Dalai Lama, (15) *Dogyor* - god of war, and (16) *Tsephemy* - god of long life.

Apart from these the Tibetans also place the pictures of many Hindu deities such as the Ganapati, Laxmi, Saraswati, Krishna, Shiva and the Hanuman. On enquiry they said that they were not aware of these deities while in Tibet. They came to know about them through their youngsters who have more contact with outsiders. Others said that they learnt about them through the Hindu religious books which are available to them now. A few of them witness movies and dramas which are mythological in nature and also listen to the radio and learn about them in the form of songs and stories. A few Tibetans can repeat stories about the Hindu gods and goddesses. The pictures of Mahatma Gandhi, Vivekananda, and others, are also found and are worshipped as the incarnations of Hindu gods.

## Holy Scripts

The five sacred books of Tibet known as *Shungchen Kãpungã* are placed on the domestic altar and worshipped. These books are believed to be very tough to understand and only the teachers of the Dalai Lama - the men of wisdom and knowledge, can do that. The other books commonly read by the commoners are: (1) *Ngãring Chemõ* - which professes the oneness of all the five sects (*chulu* - the four Buddhist sects and the Bon-po religion) and also states that these sects are only the different paths to attain *Nirvãna.* The book, irrespective of the sects followed by them also states the first means to achieve *Nirvãna* are the reading of sacred books *(Duwã)* and the second means being the meditation (*Ngã*). (2) *Lãmring Chomõ-* gives the people the rules of meditation, good qualities and the moral character. (3) *Kyapto Tejang Rim-po-che Namdãr* — Autobiography of junior teacher of H.H. the Dalai lama. (4) *Khãtãng Tengã* — the book written by Lobeng Rimpoche, in which everyting about the Tibet's future is written. (5) *Sãgyen Pejã* - The book containing the rituals to be performed for the family deities and spirits which help to bring fertility to the householder. The family deity is always kept decorated with flowers, maize and paddy stocks and the fruits, to get goodluck and fertility to the family. On both the sides of altar are placed the flower pots.

Every day early in the morning, the womenfolk of the family after lighting the sacred lamp, filled the holy cups (*ting*) with fresh holy water, and chanted mantras '*Om Mani Padme Hum*'. She also sprinkled holy water throughout the house. Then men and women in the house start reading the sacred books. After this, the ritual food — a mixture of five varieties of foods like *tsampa, chãng*, milk, ghee and food grains is mixed and put on the oven fire, kept outside the house, as an offering to the god. The smoke which raises from this is believed to go as food to the deities and also the evil spirits. It is only after these activities the fast for the day was broken with the tea. Now this routine is disturbed owing to the new environment and new occupations followed by them. Now the Tibetans also get much less free time. So they simply repeat the sacred mantra for some time and start their day.

It is observed that a few older Tibetans read the sacred books for about two hours in the morning and again for another two hours in the evening. Rest of the time though they will be busy with their household duties, they will be chanting the sacred mantras. Very old men and women who cannot read and write, count the beads from the rosary and recite mantras in a low tone. It is observed that the middle aged and the younger generation are devoting comparatively less time to religious affairs and that they did not have much free time to spend on worshipping. Unlike in Tibet here they have to struggle hard to earn a comfortable living and also many aspire for more materialistic wealth. Whereas while in Tibet by working for a few hours they got enough income to make a comforatable living and so rest of their time was devoted for religious activities.

## Rosaries

Rosaries are not only used by all the monks but also by every Tibetan layman and woman. The Tibetan name for rosary is *ten-wa*, and commonly it is known as *mani* since it contains beads in it. Customarily the rosary should have only hundred beads. But actually there will be one hundred and eight beads in a rosary. The extra eight beads are added to make up any omission of beads while counting the *mantras* uttered. The two ends of the strings of beads are knotted in such a way each passes through three of the extra beads. The middle one will be larger than other beads. These extra beads are called *mdo-dsin*, which means the "union holders", and they indicate the completion of one cycle of the rosary while counting and chanting *mantras*.

Attached to the rosary is a pair of strings of ten small pendant metallic rings which serve as counters. These rings help to count the cycles of the beads. Regarding the material used for the beads, in Tibet, Waddell (1974:205) says, it varies according to the wealth of the wearer. The Abbot of the large and wealthy monastery may have rosaries of pearl and other precious stones and even of gold. Turner (1800:261) in his book - "Embassy to Tibet" writes that 'the Grand Tashi Lama possessed rosaries of pearls, emeralds, rubies, sapphires, coral, amber, crystal and lapislazuli'. It is also noticed that different sects use beads of different colours and materials. Waddell (Ibid:207) says Tibetans of Geluck-pa sect used yellow beads (*Ser-ten*) prepared from the deep yellow wood of the Bodhi tree. The rough brown seeds of a tree which grows in the outer Himalayas is used for preparing the rosaries by the Nying-ma-pa sects. The white conch shell rosary - *Tun-ten*, which consists of cylindrical perforated discs of the conch shell and is specially used in the worship of Avalokita, is a special rosary used only by the nuns. There were also rosaries with beads made of plain crystal or uncoloured glass, red sandal wood, used in worshipping the protective deity — *Tam-din.* In a few cases discs of human skull were used as beads in a rosary and this was used only while worshipping the fearful deities like *Vajra Bhairawa.*

## Prayer Wheels

Tibetans also turn prayer wheels and prayer cylinders while meditating. In a Tibetan settlement, it is a common sight to see old men and women roaming around rotating their prayer wheels with the right hand and counting the beads in the rosary by the left. The prayer wheels are made of wood and lined with silver or copper and fixed with a wooden handle. They are tied with a weight so that when rotated it turns on the axil in hand. In the inner space of these prayer wheels are put the sacred syllables — *Om Mani Padme Hum.* Heavy sacred cylinders fixed to table or cots in the houses, are also turned by very old and disabled Tibetans who stay in one place. Tsung-Lien Shen and Shen-Chi Liu (1953:141- 142) describe the prayer wheel (*Khor*) as follows: "The world rotates in a *Khor* around Mount Sumeru; the sun and the moon around the earth; all living beings around the wheel of transmigration. Life rotates around some holy object like a lake, holy pagoda, a holy wall or a holy man. The beads whirl around the fingers, and the prayer wheels around the sacred formula. Like this there are wheels turned around by fingers, by hand, by winds, by the hydraulic power, etc. Tibetans, muttering scriptures, counting beads and turning prayer wheels continually walk around the monasteries. This scene is common in all parts of Tibet". A much similar picture will be seen by any one who visits Mundgod Settlement and especially the old and infirm peoples' village.

## Sacrificial Objects and Offerings

The form of offering depends on the nature of the god or the spiritual deity who receives them. Nebesky-Wojkowitz

(1956:343) says "a wrathful deity is given a *gtõr-mã* consisting of meat and bone, a libation of blood and bile, skull drums and high bone trumpets are played for its entertainment, etc., while a peaceful protector of religion is presented with such gifts as medicines, sweet and tasty food, fragrant incense and pieces of silk. The deities of both groups are further symbolically presented with arms they carry, and dresses they wear and the animals to ride, etc." He (Ibid:343-345) further says that in the magical processes, the Tibetans consulted texts. According to these texts blood was used in magico-religious practices of Bon-po. The blood may be taken out from a dead body suffered from dangerous diseases, the menstruation blood of a widow or a prostitute, or the blood of a young healthy man killed in a fight or the blood of an eight year old child of an incestuous union, etc. Also the blood of animals like that of black horses, or greyish dogs, mad dogs, black bears, blood of cows died of cattle disease, sheep, yaks, wolves, goats, and pigs was used. When Tibet came under the spell of Buddhism these practices were replaced with liquids signifying blood were used in rituals. They are the ordinary water added with red colour or the water from 108 different springs, water from a glacier (*gangs chu*) or from a state mountain (*g-ya chu*), milk (*O-ma*), Tibetan beer (*chãng*) or the alcoholic drinks.

With the total introduction of the Buddhistic principles in Tibet these Bon-po practices were left over. Their values and concepts however remined in the traditional Tibetan society. Though the Tibetans discorded the offerings of animals and human beings, they replaced them with vegetarian materials and these objects were sacrificed in the same old fashion. Under the vegetarian practices the three sweet substances - sugar (*Kã-rã*), honey (*sbrang-rtsi*) and treacle were offered. Milk, butter and curds are also offered to the peaceful deities. The typical gifts which are presented to the wrathful deities are the blackpeas, radishes, onions, garlic and the yeast for making beer. All these are called as *mi-dga-rdzas*, the unpleasant eatables. The *gtor-ma* are prepared with the help of wooden moulds (*Zan-par*). Most frequently the barley flour was mixed with water, milk, blood or alcohol to make the dough. Today, in Mundgod, they use water and also put red colour over the *gtor-ma* to symbolise blood. There are also some weapon like structures made of the dough, butter and sugar and are placed around *gtor-ma*. They are known as zor and are thrown away after the ritual; and thus the evil spirits are made to move away.

## Sacred Objects

Another important item used in all the ceremonies is the divine arrow (*dã'dar*), the symbol of male element. The presence of a divine arrow is a must to secure divine rites. The application of the *dã'dar* in the rites of the Tibetan Buddhist clergy has been accepted from the usage of the Bon-pos' (Nebesky- Wojkowitz, 1956:365). In Tibet a variety of *dã'dar* were used in the rituals in honour of deities. The important ones are: (1) *Tshe-sgrub -mdã'dar* - the point of this arrow is made of iron and its shaft has five ends; each bearing three vulture feathers, painted in five different colours - white, yellow, blue, red and green. A silk cloth is attached to these five ends of the respective colours. These arrows are used in ceremonies performed in honour of *Tse-pag-me* (Amitayas) (2) *g,yang Sgrub mdã'dar* — is a simple arrow with an iron point and a single shaft bearing three feathers. A conch shell and three or five pieces of silk cloth are suspended from its shaft and all of them will be of only one colour. This type of *dã'dar* is used in the ceremonies performed for ensuring luck and prosperity. This is also used in the Tibetan marriage ceremony, when it is put into the collar of the bride. The third variety is same as that of second *dã'dar* except the silken streamers here are of five different colours — white, yellow, red, blue and green. In Mundgod the third variety of *dã'dar* is more commonly used. The present day *da'dar* are more simplified and wooden shafts are used instead of iron shafts and cotton streamers are used instead of silk. It is observed that many families do not even possess any of them though it was considered to be a most essential and auspicious object for Tibetans. Now when they need it at the time of rites such as marriage, it is borrowed from others.

Waddell (1974:424) says there are seven recognized stages in any Tibetan rite. They are: (1) the invocation — calling to the feast or sacrifice; (2) inviting the deity to be stead; (3) presentation of offerings— sacred cake, rice, water, incense, flowers, lamps, music; (4) hymns in praise; (5) repetition of the special spell or the *mantra*; (6) prayers for benefits already present, and to come and (7) benediction. All these steps are carefully observed to get the desired ends.

On special or festival occasions sacred food (*tsemã'r*) is prepared by mixing *tsampã'* - the roasted flour with sugar and ghee. This offering for the gods is specially placed in a wooden box - *throsho-Chemol.* Over this are put variety of sweets. During New Year Festival, friends and relatives who visit the family take pinch of *tsemãr* and throw it towards the altar. This is repeated three times as an offering to the gods (*Tsophã byuwã*). Lastly a pinch of it is put into their own mouth and utter *Tãshi Deleigh* - meaning good luck to all family members. This is an act to show their affinity towards the family members whom they have visited. The fried *tormas* - the offerings made to the gods and goddesses, called *Kãpse.* are distributed to all the visitors for eating.

Apart from the worships conducted at home and monasteries the Tibetans also go round *Chõrtens.* Waddell (1974:262) describes a *Chõrten* as 'receptacle for offerings'. Tibetans attend them daily — both in the morning and evening and turn the prayer wheel and also go around the *Chõrten*, as many times as possible. They count the rounds they finish by keeping a piece of stone in a place and finally count the rounds for the day. The *Chõrtens* are solid domelike structures, convex shaped upwards and crowned by a square capital surmounted by umbrella, the symbols of royalty. *Chõrtens* contain more plinths and are considerably elongated. Above the square capital are the bluntly conical or pyramidal spire of thirteen step like segments representing the thirteen Bodhisat heavens of Budhists. over this is placed a tapering pinnacle. They are mostly built as *Cenotaphs* in memory of Buddha or a high lama. A few *Chõrtens* in Tibet were tombs built for high lamas. The bodies of high lamas were first buried in the earth and salt was put around the body and left for some days. After one or two months, when all the organic matters were dissolved the skeletal remainings were collected and pasted with clay and painted to give live appearance of the lama. This effigy was then placed in the *Chõrten* built for him and the door was closed.

Waddell (1974:263) says the shape of the Tibetan *Chõrten* is like those of the Japanese symbolic of five elements into which a body is resolved upon death. The lowest section, a solid rectangular block, typifies the solidarity of the earth, above it is the globe representing the water; fire by triangular tongue; air by a crescent the inverted vault of the sky, and ether by an acuminated circle, the tapering into space. Near these *Chõrtens* are built rooms to deposit the small clay structures (*tsãdi*) prepared as offering after the death of a person. Tibetans in difficulty, pray to the god to relieve them from it and in return they take a vow to donate stone slabs carved with sacred syllables, which are placed around the Chorten or on the hill (*Norbu rey*). In Mundgod this hill is known as *Norbu rey*, named after H.H. the Dalai Lama. The *Norbu rey* is a high sacred place where important rituals such as *Lhapso* - spirit controlling rituals, are performed by senior monks; and all the people of the Settlement assemble here during the rituals.

## Tibetan Festivals

The Tibetan years are cyclic in nature and are named after the twelve animals and five elements. The name of a year changes every year. The twelve animals are: (1) Mouse (*Tsewa*), (2) Ox (*Lang*), (3) Tiger (*Tak*), (4) Hare (*Yõ*), (5) Dragon (*Druk*), (6) Serpent (*Dull*) (7) Horse (*Ta*), (8) Sheep (*Luk*), (9) Monkey (*Tee*), (10) Bird (*Cha*), (11) Dog (*Khey*), and (12) Pig (*Fukphã*). The five elements are (1) Wood (*shing*), (2) Fire (*mey*), (3) Earth (*Sã*) (4) Iron (*Chãk*), and (5) Water (*chū*).

The Tibetan year begins in the English month of February. The Tibetan months (*Dãwã*) are named as first month (*Dãwa Thãngo-bo*), second month (*Dãwã Ne-wã*) and so on upto twelfth month (*Dãwã Chu-ne-wã*). Similarly a week is divided into seven days (*za*), the name of each day is adapted from the Indian system. They are *Nyimã* (Sunday - after the celestial body - the Sun), *Dãwã* (Monday - after the Moon), *Mig-mãr* (Tuesday - after the Mars), *Lãg-pã* (Wednesday - after the Mercury), *Pur-bu* (Thursday - after the Jupiter), *Pã-sõn* (Friday - after Venus) *Pen-bã* (Saturday after the Saturn).

The change of place made the Tibetans to include a few more and new festivals into their traditional list. These festivals are celebrated according to the Tibetan calendar and the dates are not fixed and so cannot be exactly correlated with Christian Calendar. The list of a few such important festivals is as follows:

| Month | Day | Festivals |
|---|---|---|
| 1st | 1st day | New Year's festival |
| | 15th day | Buddha's incarnation (*Tsongã chopa*). |
| 2nd | 29th day | Expulsion of the demon of bad luck and the up- |

| | | |
|---|---|---|
| | | rising day of Tibet (*pondā Shive-tse*). |
| 4th | 8th day | Attainment of Buddha-hood (*Sukhandhne Thucheyn*). |
| | 15th day | Buddha's death. |
| 5th | 10th day | Birth of Saint Padma Sambhava (*Jamling Cheesāng*). |
| | 16 day | Dalai Lama's birth day. |
| 6th | 4th day | Buddha's birth and his first preaching. |
| 7th | 20th day | Republic Day of Tibet |
| 9th | 22nd day | Buddha coming from heaven (*Lhabhap Thucheny*). |
| 10th | 24th day | The festival for the founder (Tsongkha-pa) of Geluk-pa sect. |
| 11th | 6th and 7th days | Navagraha rite (*Ngye-mba Gunjum*). |
| | 22nd day | Starting of the English New Year. |
| 12th | 17th day | Indian Republic Day. |
| | 29th day | Ending of the Old Tibetan Year. |

The New Year festival is celebrated in the month of February, the 1st Tibetan month, which comes after the harvest. This festival is mainly a merry making one and people pass the time in eating, drinking, singing, dancing and playing games. In Tibet this festival was celebrated for one full month and now it is limited to only three days. This festival promotes closer affinity and friendship among the Tibetans and the people have an obligation to visit each other to exchange greetings and share *chãng*. Friends, relatives and even people belonging to a common tribe or ethnic group assemble in one place - a house, prayer hall or a monastery and sing and dance. During this period the lamas at the monastery arrange for special worships and rituals. All the people irrespective of their class, sect and status mingle and perform worship and listen to the preaching of the lamas.

For the New Year festival the houses are cleaned and white washed. The household materials like bedding and furnitures are also cleaned. New prayer flags are hoisted. The womenfolk fry cakes (*Kãpse*) in plenty, in butter or vegetable oil and exchange them with friends and relatives. While in Tibet a community meal was arranged by each and every family on rotation. In this Settlement people belonging to an ethnic group or a district meet at one place to drink *chãng*, sing, dance and enjoy; this goes on for three to fifteen days.

The New Year festival celebration lasts for three days. On the day previous to the New Year day, all men and women take oil bath. On the first day of the festival they put on new clothes and traditional ornaments, which are not usually worn on other days. Later all the family members visit the monasteries to offer presentations to the deities and to receive blessings from the senior lama. They also request them to excuse for the sins they might have committed during the year and to get their souls purified (*Tsosãyã*). Token gifts of cash and kind are also made to the monasteries. The gifts in the form of materials will be the idols of the deities and oil lamps (*Tseugung*) and copper cups to fill holy water (*Chu-ting*). These cups will be made of silver or even gold, if the family can afford. Along with these gifts they carry the incense sticks, flowers, and ghee - to offer to the burning lamps at the monastery; and the sacred scarf *(Khã-tã)*. They bow to the deities lying flat (*Tsãk*). Those who have taken a vow to the deity will prostrate around the monasteries. The Tibetans said that in Tibet they had plenty of resources and so they made costly offerings to the deity both in cash and kind. Now they are not in a position to offer much since they themselves do not have in plenty.

The second day of the New Year festival starts with a meeting with their friends and relatives and exchange of *Khã-tã* and sharing of *chãng* and arrack. It is an obligation for every man to visit their kin to maintain good relation with them. In Mundgod Settlement apart from their friends and relatives they visit all those who belong to their district in Tibet, to maintain the bondage of unity. During night these people with such common background, come together to sing and dance. It is common that those who are in sectarian or regional minority will join the major groups in their villages in celebrating this festival.

The third day festival activity starts with a worship to the family deities, spirits in nature and offering of foods to them. All the Tibetans in the Settlement assemble on the top of the hill (*Norbu rēy*) where the worship for the gods (*Lhãpso*)are offered. This hill is away from the village site. At the officially announced hour, in the morning, the monks, lamas and lay from all the villages assemble here. First they offer *chãng* and tea to the spirits which control the nature. They also chant *mantras* in honour of benevolent deities from the sacred book *Gãbo Kunga Dokham Thãngmo Mãchik Pelã* and a sacred book for worshiping the pal-lden Lhã-mo is read. The rectangular or square shaped flags (*thãrjok*) - of thin cloth of 10" - 12" size, printed with the sacred syllables, are tied to the poles erected on the hill. Tibetans believe that these holy flags will even flow through the wind and take away the bad spirits which troubled them. They also offer *tsampã* (flour of the roasted maize or wheat) food to the god of fire. At the completion of the long recitation of the syllables all the people assemble and stand in a circle and throw *tsampã* towards the sky so that the spirits in nature who control it, will receive them. By dawn the old flags from the poles infront of their houses, are replaced with new ones and a worship is performed for it.

On the Fifteenth day all the monks and lamas assemble in the monastery of Lama Village No. II and observe the Great Prayer of *Mon-lam* festival. Regarding the celebration of this festival the Tibetans tell a story, of the deity *Ka-Ma-Sha*, the oracle deity of *Se-Ra* monastery. *Ka-Ma-Sha*, was holding his position as the oracle deity of *Se-Ra* monastery at the time of Fifth Dalai Lama. It is said with the increase of importance to Dre-Pung, the *Ka-Ma-Sha* became jealous. So he mixed some poison to the tea used by Dre-Pung congregation. But the Nai-Chung - the oracle of the Dre-Pung monastery, hurled a knife from Dre-Pung monastery to Lhasa and wounded the deity *Ka-Ma-Sha* in his leg. From that day the Dre-Pung monastery started celebrating the occasion of expelling the *Ka-Ma-Sha* from the monastery as the Great Prayer festival.

Rituals also take place for the chastisement of devils. After the end of the services the lamas and monks followed by their *Khen-Po* - the Abbot, go round the monastery. In Tibet this function was celebrated as follows: The column of men behind; the Abbot, carried a huge effigy of skull, raised on a stand painted with designs. The *Khen-Po* executes a mystic dance. Then the monks and lamas came to the southern suburb. After them enters the oracle Nai-Cung, in a trance, with his attendants. On coming within the sight of the suburb, where two pyres are standing, *Nai-Chung* shoots an arrow in the direction of the pyres. The pyres are then immediately lighted and the skull effigy was thrown into the fire amid volley of shots by the foot soldiers. Across the river, towards a hill, a black tent stands with a black sheep - symbol of a demon, chained inside. Burning of the effigy conveys to the public the news of the defeat of the demon Buddha's enemies (Tsung-Lien Shen and Shen-Chi Liu, 1952:185-186). Over here these rituals have been considerably simplified. The Abbots accompanied with the lamas and monks simply go round the monastery carrying burning lamps in their hands. This is followed by competitions in weight lifting, running, cycling, foot races, etc. After the celebrations are over all the monks return to their respective monasteries.

Tibetans have still maintained the practice of staging traditional Tibetan theotricles (*Temõ*). For staging these the artists use masks. The dramas are mostly historical and mythological depicting the life of a king or a senior lama or the gods and the goddesses. Both men and women take part in the dramas. Dramas contain for the most part songs and dialogues accompanied with music and action. Singing will be of very high and very low tunes. Usually most of the people of the Settlement assemble to watch these. They also stage small plays depicting the life of nomads in the Tibetan mountains, Tibetan animals, etc. After the show is over the participants are honoured by the village leaders by presenting them with *Khã-tã*.

While in Tibet festivals were also observed to mark the change of seasons. Tibetans recognized only two seasons – winter and summer. They celebrated rites to mark the change in their dresses according to these seasons. The Dalai Lama also changed his living quarters from *Potala* to *Norbu Ling-ka* in summer. This change of residence by the god king was observed as a festival.

The Tibetan fourth month is an auspicious month, for the Buddha was born and attained *Nirvāna* or Buddhahood in this month. Tsung-Lien Shen and Shen-Chi Liu (1952:159) says this whole month was considered as a meatless month and people also observe penance. A few observe fast from sunrise to sunset, and a few others observe silence, for eight to fifteen days. Tsung-Lien Shen and Shen-Chi Liu (Ibid, 160), said further that a few sat quietly beside the monasteries turning their prayer wheels and muttering scriptures. While others sat beside a running stream, dipping their water prayer wheels into the current. Still others went around the monastery prostrating.

In Mundgod, the fourth month is a very busy one in terms of agricultural operations such as sowing and weeding. So the Tibetans do not devote much time for festive activities except lighting oil lamps at the family altar, attend only the important rituals arranged in monasteries and invite monks to perform rituals at their homes.

Water festival is another important festival. Waddell (1974:509) says it is a thanks giving festival. On the festival day, after the pooja (*Lāpsō*) on the Norbu rey, the devotees run to the nearby streams and canals and take a bath. Tibetans are not habituated to taking bath regularly. But on that day they take a cold water bath and request the water spirits to give them the sacred water. On the last day of the festival one member from each family assembles near the village gate. Under the leadership of the village headman they go around the village fields carrying sacred books, photos of reincarnated lamas, etc. It is believed that these sacred objects drive away evil spirits and the lands are blessed by the lamas for a good yield of crops.

The Tibetans in India have added a few more festivals to their traditional list. For example they celebrate the 10th March as the Uprising Day. On that day all the Tibetans - monks and lay, young and old, men and women assemble and start their meeting with prayers for the freedom of Tibet and for the protection of H.H. the Dalai Lama. August 15th - the Independence Day of India, 26th of January - the Republic Day of India and 2nd October - the birth day of Mahatma Gandhi are also celebrated by them. On the occasions of national festivals the important leaders– both ecclesiastic and lay, are invited for a feast by individual families or the community as a whole. During a few other festivals the villagers contributed both in cash and kind and also actively participate in it. Feasts given to benovalent spirits are the other celebrations. Tibetans never miss these occasions to give a feast and earn the good will of the community members and also gods and spirits.

Today many of the community level festivals are not celebrated since they have lost their significance here. Above all the people coming from different districts and regions may not consider a particular rite essential and so no unanimity is found with them. A few families who still believe in these rites observe them at only family level.

## Life Cycle Rituals

All human beings have to pass through certain stages of life prescribed by their society. At every stage of social recognition certain rituals are performed. They are called the life cycle rituals or the Rites of Passage as termed by Van Gennep. The individual thus is recognised by the society and is accepted by the members in it. For example an individual does not become a member of his society merely by being born. As an infant he is given a name publicly and presented to his kins and the members of his society. With this the individual enters into a new relationship with his community and the world with new responsibilities by passing through these life cycle rituals at certain stages of his life. Birth, marriage and death bring adjustments and readjustments in the social structure of a society. For example after his marriage a person passes from his childhood to adulthood and this brings him a new status and new roles to perform not only in his family but also as a member of his society. This also brings change in the status and roles of other members of his family. The individual is not only elevated in his social but also in his ritual status. The rituals generally include religious purificatory rites, and ceremonies for sanctifying the body, mind and intellect of an individual. These rituals are significant throughout the life of an individual.

Tibetans with their Buddhist influence, view life in two separate ways - the life of a householder and a monk. Among these the latter status is more important, where societal good is stressed. So social recognition rather than the ritual process is important in Tibetan life cycle rituals. At the time of the celebration of these rites, role of a lama or a monk, the priestly group, is not significant. But, a few families who can afford costly rituals, invite one or more monks and conduct rituals for the wordly benefits of that individual in future. But these rituals do not have any importance in the social acceptance of the individual.

It is noticed that death has ritual significance among the Tibetans and monks are invited to conduct rituals for the benefit of the soul. In this way the religious rituals performed by the monks can be distinguished from those performed for social gains and so they differ in their aims and values. Social rituals are performed for one's acceptance in the society and the religious rituals are celebrated to get spiritualistic path which ultimately ends in *Nirvãna*. So every individual to get himself into the ecclesiastic group has to undergo an initiation ceremony, consisting of series of rituals and taking of certain oaths to keep himself away from the wordly life. Thus the religious rituals such as taking oaths, etc., observed in the marriage ceremony of the Hindus are not found among the Tibetans. They perform certain ceremonies for the individual to make him socially accepted; this also includes certain rituals. But they need not bring a priest to perform the rituals.

## Birth Ceremony

Child birth always takes place in the conjugal home of the woman. Child birth is viewed as a polluting incident and so it always takes place in a tent erected away from the living quarters. Child birth also defies both the mother and the child and so for three days in case of the birth of a male child and four days in case of a female child, they are segregated from the group. On the third or the fourth day as the case may be, the mother and child are given a holy bath and brought inside the house. Certain rituals are performed to the family deity seeking blessings to the mother and the child and also to protect them from evil spirits. Now due to lack of space and facilities, these customs are rarely observed. The only room available for child birth in the house is the room where the family altar is put. Due to pollution involved in birth, ideally this room cannot be used. But a curtain is put to separate symbolically, the altar from the area where birth takes place. The mother, who will be in the state of ritual impurity will be provided with a separate bed and other things for personal use. She is also prohibited from entering the kitchen and touch the hearth.

On the day of purification of the family from birth pollution a rite is observed for which kinsmen and friends come with gifts, three sacred scarfs, one each to the father, mother and the newly born child, together with *Chāng*, and some amount of cash or a piece of new cloth to the child. Those who held a very close relationship bring valuable gifts such as gold ornaments to the child. A few may even bring new clothes for the parents of the child. The maternal grand parents of the child are to bring not only the golden ring (or any other ornament) to the child but also new clothes to the parents and the child. Community members present tea, ghee, eggs, mutton, fruits and *tsampa.* This ceremony of presenting gifts is locally known as *Tam-dil.* On the same day the naming ceremony (*Phā-ng Sā-ng*) is arranged in which the parents give a temporary name to the child. After one month a lama is consulted to choose a permanent name to the child, considering the day and time of child birth. The guests are treated for a feast and *chāng.*

No puberty rites are performed for girls among the Tibetans. Women in their menstruation period are considered polluted and so for three days they are prohibited to go near the family altar and to enter a monastery. After three days and after taking a ritual bath they are considered ritually purified. However, a woman who stays alone in her house is exempted from these ritual observations because without anybody to assist her in the house she will have to miss her daily worships and food.

## Marriage Ceremony

Dawa Norbu (1974:94) quoting his mother's words says - "The duty of the good parents is to prepare their children for the journey through life". He (Ibid:92) quotes a Tibetan proverb which says "Girls and garlic should be sold before their scent dies". That means, girls will be given in marriage at an early age. Wedding rites are usually arranged after the harvest season, during the months of December and February. A Tibetan marriage has no legal or religious implications. The Tibetans being luck addicts an animistic rite would be performed on the roof of the world, on the wedding morning.

In the selection of spouse, usually the groom's party approaches the bride's family to ask the girl in marriage (*nā-mā*). The procedure will be a reverse one in case of a *mag-pa* marriage. In other words it can be said whoever wants a spouse approaches the other party. As a rule matrilocal marriages take place at the bride's residence and patrilocal marriages at the groom's residence. To understand a Tibetan marriage, the *na-ma* marriage is discussed here in detail. The groom's mother's brother or any other close relative standing in the same kinship relation or a friend (*trokh-po*) of the groom's father, at the former's absence, approaches the bride's family asking for the hand of the girl. If the bride's party accepts the alliance, on an auspicious day selected consulting a lama, the groom's father along with the above mentioned members, approach the bride's father and present him with new clothes, *chāng*, and the *Khā-tā*, as gifts. During this visit the quality and the quantity of marriage gifts (*Ne-to*) to be exchanged are negotiated. Later the guests are treated for a feast and *chāng*.

Depending upon the case - *nā-mā* or the *māg-pā* marriage, bride or groom price is paid to the parents as breast milk price. It varies from one rupee, in case of poor families to one thousand rupees or even more in case of rich families. In Tibet a number of livestocks of much more value were given as bridegroom price. Though its importance is lessened here in India it is still followed as an important custom. At the same time, as we have already discussed, women have equal status with men here. She is entitled for a share in her parental property. Among Tibetan nomads it was a practice to give a number of livestocks - sheep, yak, horse, etc., to their daughters during the marriage. Valuable dresses and ornaments and some amount of cash, were given in case of peasants and traders; and the nobles paid her both. The things given to a girl in her marriage are listed on a piece of paper (*nye-nyik*). In future if the marriage breaks, the husband has to return all these things enlisted to his divorced wife.

The auspicious day and the time for marriage is fixed by consulting a lama. Dawn is considered the most auspicious time for celebrating a marriage. People who arranged for the marriage and attended the betrothal ceremony come to the bride's family one day prior to the marriage day, to make arrangements for the rite. The kinsmen and family friends are informed of the marriage day, well in advance. Close relatives come well in advance to the wedding family to prepare food, drink and dress for the marriage. They erect tents and arrange for beds for the members of the visiting bridal party.

The people from U-Tsang province brought many types of ornaments, clothes, etc., to present for their brides. Customarily the groom's father's brother presents those gifts to the bride. The Tibetans of *Kham-ba* province do not give any thing to a bride, except the bride price (*nu-ri-ng*). Bride's parents depending upon their financial status, give her 3,5 or 9 types of ornaments. Among these the head ornament (*Thã-khch-ãr-bãta*), which is U shaped and made of gold, pearls, and beads, is considered the most important one. As a custom this is given only by the groom's parents.

It is customary that the mother's brothers (real or classificatory) of the groom to be present at the bride's residence one day earlier to the marriage day to bring the bride to the groom's family. Male kin get busy entertaining the men from the groom's party, with *chãng,* glasses after glasses and singing songs. On the other side the female kins prepare the bride for the rite with her new clothes and ornaments. Exchange of *Khã-tã* and good wishes take place between the kinsmen - each saying *Tha-shi De- leigh* to the other. A sacred divine dagger (*dã' dar*) and a stick covered with five coloured (red, green, yellow, blue and white) silk strips or ribbons is put around the neck of the bride to bring her good luck. This also helps to keep evils and demons away from her way to her conjugal home. In her first journey to her conjugal home the bride is accompanied by one of her closest girl friends (*pho-gyu*), who consoles and gives moral support to her and her mother's brothers. It is customary for the bride and her parents to weep and even loudly at this time of parting.

At the scheduled time the five married women, who are the actual or the classificatory sisters of the groom and his mother wait at the door of their house holding kettles full of Tibetan tea and *chãng;* to welcome the bride. The groom's mother welcomes the bride wishing her good luck (*Tã-shi De-leigh*). Now the bride takes the *chãng* with her fourth finger of right hand and sprinkles it thrice towards the sky as an offering to the family deity. She is now asked to enter the house putting her right leg first. In the house she is made to sit on the left side of the groom. The *Pho-gyu* also sits by the side of the bride. Similarly the bride's mother's brothers sit in a line, to the right of the bridal couple and the groom's mother's brothers sit in a line to the left. At first the groom's parents garland the newly weds and then the maternal uncles of the bridal couple. The nearest kin are served with a full bowl of sweet rice (*Dē-See*), prepared mixing sugar, rice and ghee. Later they are served generously with *chãng* till they get drunk. Meanwhile ceremonial songs are also sung. The close kins, both the cognatic and affinals, visit the bridal couple and present them with many types of new clothes. The distant relatives and friends (*trokh-põ*) present only cash and *chãng*, and also honour the bridal couple, their parents and their mother's brothers and the *phõ-gyu* with *Khã-tã*. One *Kha-ta* is also put over the *throshõ-chemõl* - a box divided into two equal halves and filled with sweets and corns in one and *tsampa* in the other and over these the sugar lumps or chocolates are put. Invitees on their arrival, throw little *tsampa* towards the altar thrice and then put a pinch of it into their mouth also. Of the ten *Khã-ãs* brought by them one is offered to the family altar and one each to the bride, groom, groom's parents, the kin who brought the girl, bride's mother's brothers accompanying the girl and the *phõ-gyu*. *Khã-tãs* are also presented to other members of the groom's party such as the kins helping the family in conducting the marriage. In a few cases cash is individually presented to all the above mentioned persons.

A Tibetan marriage lasts for three days. All these three days friends and kinsmen who have come together for the occasion eat, drink, sing, dance and enjoy the stay. If it is an inter-district marriage the two bridal parties cannot sing and dance together since they differ much in their culture. So one will watch as the other perform a dance. Since they all belong to one ritual group they drink *chãng* using a common glass and taking from a common kettle placed at the centre of the hall. When a low caste guest is partaking in the marriage feast, he is provided with a separate glass to drink.

A lavish three day marriage is not the order today. A poor man's marriage ends in a day since he cannot afford all the luxury. The informants told that here in Mundgod, marriage ceremonies have become very simple and economical. In Tibet rich families celebrated marriages spending lavishly and invited relatives and friends well in advance and also retained them entertaining for weeks and months. A large number of monks and lamas, even higher ones were invited to conduct rituals and bless the bridal couple. The family also spent more on the costly gifts exchanged such as the gold and silver ornaments and clothing. Now all these have disappeared and only essential things are brought and essential persons are invited for the rite.

## Death Rituals

For Tibetans death is not a sorrowful act. They consider it another chance given to the soul to take rebirth. The Tibetans believe that rebirth is based on the good and bad deeds done in one's previous existences. Depending upon the merits a system of rewards and punishments such as sinking down the soul with bad deeds (*Dig-pã*) through the lower stages of human and animal existence, and lifting the good (*Ge-wã*) soul to the level of higher birth are given.

A dying person should forget his family, property and followers and concentrate on the lama who leads his soul. It is believed those who die with desires will take a rebirth and his soul rotates through the cycle of birth and death - the 'Wheel of life'. As Wadell (1974:101) records the wheel of life has six forms arranged in the following form and order:

| | | |
|---|---|---|
| I | The Gods | (*Lhã*) |
| II | Titans | (*Lhã-mã-yin*) |
| III | Man | (*Mi*) |
| IV | Beasts | (*Du-do*) |
| V | Tantalized Ghosts | (*Yi-dvag*) and |
| VI | Sent to Hell | (*Nal-K'am*) |

After death each soul is sent to these worlds depending upon the merit he possesses in his previous life. According to the Tibetans the first three worlds are considered good and are known as heaven. The last three are termed as hell. 'There are eight types of miseries under Buddhism. They are the miseries of: (1) birth; (2) old age, (3) sickness, (4) death, (5) existence, (6) misfortunes and punishments for law breaking, (7) separation from relatives and cherished objects, (8) offensive objects and sensations' (Waddel, 1974:101).

It is believed necessary to conduct worships after the death, to relieve the soul from the worldly attachment and to wish him a better life than one in any lower animal groups. Worships continue for seven weeks and many relatives and friends work hard for their success. Usually a large number of guests are invited to the first and the last day rites. Close relatives bring food and *chãng* in large quantity. It is believed that for forty-nine days the soul of the departed suspends in a state of "middle being", i.e. intervening between this life and the next. Finally it reaches its destiny - hell or heaven, depending upon its good and bad deeds in life.

When a Tibetan is seriously ill his family members consult a monk-astrologer, to find out the reason and remedies for it. If the suggested remedies prove fruitless they may commission lamas and monks to conduct rites to remove malignant spirits from the house and to recite sacred books for the patient's benefit.

On death the corpse is covered with a sheet of white cloth and immediately words are sent for a lama since others cannot touch it. On his arrival the lama inspects the corpse to determine through which part of the body the soul has emerged. It is believed that a saint's soul escapes through his head and a relatively good man's through his eyes. Escaping through the nose is an indication of the soul's rebirth in the titans and that which goes out through the mouth will take its rebirth in an animal. The soul which goes out through the lower hole is believed to get rebirth in hell. It is only those souls which go out through the heart and with pain, will take rebirth as human beings.

After his inspection the lama starts reciting a prayer (*Pho-giau*). He consults an astrological manual (*tsi-pi*) and a calendar (*da-du*), to know where, in which manner and by whom the corpse should be disposed off. In considering it the factors like the year in which the person was born, the day, month and week and the time of death, the constellation of stars at the time of death, the position of *Pum-dung* - a bird like structure with a human body, are taken into account.

In preparing the corpse for funeral rites no assistance is taken from any member of the mourning family. Fellow villagers who are experienced in this work do it. The corpse is then tied up in a sitting position with the help of a rope and is covered in a white sheet of cloth and placed, with its back to the wall, near the main entrance to the house. Over its head is put a printed paper containing many auspicious symbols and syllables to protect the corpse against evil spirits. The *torma* (the idols made in *tsampã*) are prepared in accordance with the astrological book – *Drowa Kundrol*, to represent the deities to be worshiped.

The lamas recite the *mantras* for the whole day and night, till the corpse is carried for disposal. While in Tibet the corpse was disposed off only after three, seven or more days, till the auspicious day was found. The cold weather in Tibet slowed down the decomposition of the body and so they could keep the corpse that long. But in Mundgod Settlement a corpse is disposed off within one day and that too by cremation and not by any other means. So the act of consulting the astrological book has become redundant in this respect. Now immediately after the death a few rites are performed and the body is removed to the cremation ground lest it decomposes.

Now only a few lamas are invited to the death rites, depending upon the economic status of the family. While in Tibet many lamas and monks were invited to chant syllables, and to read sacred books. A senior lama guided them in their activities. Now the funeral rites have become short, simple and also less expensive.

Kinsmen and friends of the deceased person and the family as a sort of consolation bring *Khã-tã* to put on the corpse. They also bring *chãng* for the members of the mourning family and also contribute in cash, for the funeral rite. The mourning family on its part entertained them with food, *chãng* and tea for the days till the disposal of the corpse. Whenever the invitees eat and drink some food is also offered to the corpse (later this is thrown away). Even after its disposal the corpse is given food three times a day, for forty nine days. This is because of the belief that the soul of the dead roams around the house during this period to accept food. In a few cases food is offered to the soul through smoke by putting a mixture of butter, barley, sugar, milk and sandal wood, on fire.

Conducting rituals for the benefit of the spirit of the dead is a costly affair since a large number of lamas, kinsmen and friends are invited and fed. To lessen the burden on the mourning family welwishers and kinsmen come forward with help - both in cash and kind. In Mundgod the funeral rites of Tibetans who are destitutes, is performed by friends and village members. By doing this ritual act they believe that they earn merit (*Ge-wã*) in life. A few such destitute persons save enough money for their funeral rites and leave it with a favourite lama or a friend, with instructions to conduct their funeral rites properly. A few also leave some amount of money to be donated to different monasteries in the settlement and throughout India. There are cases of two persons from the old and infirm blocks who saved Rs.650/- and Rs.525/- each towards their death rites. After their death, as per their last wish, their savings were utilized for their death rites and a part of it was also sent to all the monasteries in India. Tibetans believe that their death rituals should be performed using the money saved by themselves and not from the contributions of others; or else their soul will not get peace.

Tibetans believe that human body is made up of four elements - fire, water, earth and wind and use one of these elements to dispose off the body. Thus the Tibetans follow four means to disposed the body - cremation, burial, floating in water and exposure to wind i.e. feeding to vultures, so that it mixes with one of the four elements. In Tibet those who died of infectious diseases were buried in the earth. For this a deep pit with a cave inside in one of its walls was dug so that the body was placed in it in the sitting posture. Later it was covered with mud. The second mode was cremation which was adopted mostly for high lamas. The funeral ash was later collected and mixed with clay and this was moulded into hundreds of tiny symbols of *pagoda* and were finally put into *chõrten.* The other mode was the *Ja-tõr*, feeding the vultures. A community of people known as *Ru-ba*, took away the corpse along with the belongings of the dead such as his clothing, beds, etc., which served as their fee, and cut the body into pieces. In villages where these people were not present, any body, kin or friends, except those who were prohibited to touch the body, carried away the corpse to a nearby hillock (*To-ryõ*) and cut the body into pieces. The hairs on the corpse were burnt. The pieces were then left to vultures (*pro*) to feed on. Sometimes it also happened that the vultures did not come readily to eat. In such cases it was believed that the dead person had committed lot of sin in life and so a lama was requested to perform some more rituals at that spot, chant some more syllables and ring the holy bells louder. It was believed it made the vultures to come and feed on. After everything soft was eaten by the vultures, the bones and the skull were powdered and mixed with *tsãmpã*, and this was again fed to the vultures. In this way everything which belonged to the dead person was removed from the sight and this was done with the belief that the body without soul has no significance and should be removed completely.

The last mode of the disposal of dead was to throw the corpse into water, by tying stones to it. By this the corpse was allowed to be eaten by fish.

On their arrival in Mundgod settlement the Tibetans faced some problems in disposing their dead in the traditional modes. Feeding to vultures horrified the local people and a few nearby Indian villagers who saw them cutting the corpse into pieces and pounding the bones complained to the local police and health officials to intervene and stop it. On realizing that these Tibetan methods of disposal of dead are hazardous to health, now they are strictly prohibited. In this connection the higher authorities of the Tibetan settlement are taken into confidence to see that the cutting and exposing methods are stopped and the settlers adopt local methods.

Now the Tibetans cremate their dead and this is the only mode of disposal of the dead adopted by Tibetans in Mundgod. This brought a few psychological and value problems to the people. Especially the old and the traditional minded and those who had already expressed their desire to dispose their corpse in one of the traditional methods, got upset when they heard about the prohibition. Even in cremating their dead the Tibetans face a few problems. As of now there is only one cremation ground in the Settlement and the dead from all the villages have to be carried here. The distance and other factors have made it difficult for them to adhere to the auspicious time and place, directions of disposal and so on which all have some ritual and religious relevance. To overcome this problem the Tibetans are forced to perform a few special rites to please the gods, souls and also to secure mental peace for themselves.

Now when a death takes place it is the duty of the headman (*Po-mbo*) and the sub-leader (*Chok-penyw*) of the village to arrange for the cremation. Immediately after the death, the sub-leader consults a monk-astrologer and arranges for further activities. The kinsmen and friends of the dead follow the suggestions and directions given by this leader. This is untraditional since in Tibet it was an elderly person who guided them. The corpse is bent to an embryonic shape and later tied in a sheet of white cloth. The eldest son of the deceased, as his last obligation towards his father, carries the corpse for a short distance from the house. Here he hands it over to others who carry it to the cremating place and as a custom the members of the mourning family will not be present at the cremation.

The funeral procession is preceded by a lama who tinkles a bell as he walks. After reaching the cremation ground the body will be covered with wood. A distant relative lights pyre and never a close relative like the son, father, brother, husband, sister or wife. The lama present at the funeral, chants spells and also sprinkles the eight different offerings such as - wheat, barley, rice, linseed, buckwheat, grass and mustard seed to the fire. As a custom the funeral party waits there till the whole thing burns down to ashes. Later the ash will be collected and mixed with mud and colour. Out of this mixture a number of small idols of their family deity or that of their favourite deity, are moulded. They are known as *tsa-di* and later they are placed in a holy place *(chõrten)*, a pagoda like structure.

The funeral rites for an adult will be more elaborate since he is believed to have committed more sins during his equally longer span of life, and children need only a few and short rituals.

## Shrines and Pilgrimages

Going on pilgrimages to holy places were most common among Tibetans while in Tibet. Tibet had a great number of sacred centres such as places of reputed reincarnated or supernatural lamas, self created images, relics of the Buddhas, holy foot prints, sanctified trees etc. The pious persons throng them with gifts of gold and other precious offerings. The Tibetan Buddhists also had many places of pilgrimage outside Tibet, in India, China, Bhutan, Sikkim and Nepal. The rich and religious minded ones regularly made trips to these places though they used to cost them time, money and sometimes their life.

The pilgrims in Tibet, were restricted by the lack of transportation facilities. The rich people, who could afford moved with transportation animals, servants and food and money, to distant places of pilgrimage and often. The poor visited only the nearer ones and that too rarely.

There are two holy lakes in Tibet — Khãng Rimpoche and Tso Rim-po-che, which are very big and situated on the top of hills. Going round these lakes is considered a religious act and it took one and a half to two days to complete a round. A few Tibetans said that they have gone around the lakes many times. The most revered place is Lhasa - the seat of H.H. the Dalai Lama. It was the desire of every Tibetan to visit this holy place as many times as possible, especially at the time of New Year festival, to receive blessings from H.H. the Dalai Lama.

There are also many tombs of the departed grand lamas (*Stupa*) which are considered the holy places of pilgrimage. The famous tomb of Jā-run Kā-sor Cho-rten lying about two miles to the north-east of Kathmandu, was also visited by the Tibetans. The sacred mountain *wu-tai*, in Northern China, believed to be the birth place of Manjusri - the God of knowledge, also served as a place of pilgrimage. A few monasteries are also visited on pilgrimage. Among them the famous monastery of the Panchen Lama at Thashi Lunpo, is important.

Situations at present have changed a lot and one cannot dream of visiting the shrines in Tibet. The Paradox of their life is those shrines which were dearer and nearer have been lost to them and those which were once beyond their reach such as Buddha Gaya have become nearer. Many Tibetans said when they were in transit camps in northern Himalayan regions, they were able to visit many Buddhist temples and monasteries which are considered most sacred by the Buddhists. They also told that they were very happy for getting a chance to see these sacred places where the founder of their religion - the Gautama Buddha, took his birth, attained *Nirvana* and preached his disciples. Tibetans who can afford to visit sacred places such as Sārnāth, Buddha Gaya, Nālanda, Lumbini, etc., do so once a year. Whenever they go to north India they also make it a point to visit Dharmasāla, the place where H.H. the Dalai Lama resides. A few Tibetans told that by visiting these places they get peace of mind. Others are of the opinion that to some extent, they can even forget their stresses and strains by visiting these holy places.

# 9

# Conclusions

In the foregone chapters we have seen how the traditional and the Mundgod Tibetan societies function. The geographical situation of Tibet is mountainous, and pose problems in providing good transport and communication facilities and the cultivation is adopted to terrian type. The Tibetan weather is cooler and accordingly the house design and dress types are made. There is less or moderate rain and so river water was used for cultivation. The less fertile and rugged land, and the traditional methods of cultivation were not able to feed the population. So Tibet had its own ways and means to control its population. To see that its population will remain at optimum level the society had adopted the institution of polyandry and lamaism. To support the subsistent state economy the land was shared only by the nobles and the commoners depended on them for every thing in life. In order to obtain adequate supply of labour force the serfs were attached to the land which they cultivated and their welfare was the obligation of the lords. With this security of land and serfs the lords not only paid their taxes to the government properly but also took care of the visiting officials to their villages and also contributed towards the rites and rituals celebrated in monasteries. To maintain their status the lords collected taxes regularly and this made the commoners to work hard on the farm, rear cattle and go on trade.

Tibetans have a few remnance of *Bon* religion even today. They offer worships and food to supernatural beings believing that they guide all the natural phenomena. In order to meet the heavy cost of ritual celebrations and festivals, these were arranged according to the ecological changes in a year. At times of need like drought, famine etc., they had ways and means to provide alternate means to the existing conditions. With their socio-economic and religious institutions and practices structured in the local manner, the Tibetans had lesser stresses and strains in making their living. Above all they had their own rationale explanations to offer for their problems. Now, as refugees all these have changed and this disturbed situation has brought lot of stress and strains in their life.

When the Tibetans fled to India, they thought that their stay in India was going to be short. They choose India as a place of refuge because they always held India to be closer to them in terms of culture and religion, as the land of Buddha and expected a friendly treatment here without any threat to their life, culture and religion. History shows that the two countries had cordial relations and many religious leaders and scholars exchanged visits. Further with communist China taking over complete administrative control of Tibet there was no other neigbour who could give them a place of refuge except free India. Moreover the Dalai Lama had also fled to India and the traditional minded Tibetans were happy to be with him here. When it was realised that their stay in India is going to be much longer the Tibetans began to face difficulties. Till the national and international relief agencies came forward to help them the Tibetans had a hard time in supporting themselves. When the Government of India decided to accept them as refugees and help them, they were shifted from Himalayan border area to the much permanent rehabilitation camps in different states of India. Though adequate care was taken to select suitable places for them, the first problems they faced were with regard to weather, food, language and so on. So the rehabilitating agencies took all possible steps to see that the refugees should adjust better within the given conditions. In the course of this the refugees faced a few new problems which were both socio-cultural and psychological in nature. The warm and uncomfortable weather of their new home prevented them from going out, and earn, though they were willing to work. The rehabilitating officials and Indian neighbours thought that Tibetans were lazy and the generous gifts and grants given have spoiled them. The Tibetans are hurt by such criticisms because they are not true.

Tibet owing to her unique geographical conditions had developed customs, institutions and behaviour which were suitable to her society and culture. Thus a few traditional Tibetan customs have created problems to the refugees. For example, while in Tibet the corpse of the dead were disposed-off as per the traditional beliefs; and in the way the deceased opted burial, cremation or to be fed to animals. By becoming food to hungry animals they wanted to be of some help to others even after their death. Further by not leaving anything behind in this world the Tibetans got satisfaction that they will attain *Nirvāna*. After coming to Mundgod the Tibetans faced lot of humiliation and problems in disposing-off the dead. The local people condemned the traditional practice of cutting the corpse and feeding to birds, as a barbarious act. They even succeeded in stopping this practice through the intervention of the public health and police officals. As a result, a few traditional minded Tibetans who had already expressed their wish to dispose-off the body through feeding to the birds and animals are facing psychological problem, fearing that they will not attain *Nirvāna.*

There are also problems regarding the celebration of Tibetan fairs and festivals. Change of seasons, and of the harvest activity, change of residence by the Dalai Lama, etc., were marked with rituals and festivals while in Tibet. These were again arranged in the ritual calendar in such a way that they came when the people had plenty of leisure time and money to go on pilgrimage, drink, dance and enjoy. Over here the Tibetan festivals and the local ecological conditions do not coincide well. The Dalai Lama now never changes his residence according to changing seasons. The Tibetans also do not change their dress when summer or winter sets in since the changes in weather are minimal. Most of them still adhere to their traditional dress pattern which is not suitable to climatic conditions in summer here and many of them suffer from a number of skin ailments. The traditional method of preservation of food such as hanging the meat pieces from a line of rope and allowing it to dry in Tibet, is still continued here. But because of the warm weather here the meat starts rotting early and is easily infested with disease causing bectaria. The consumption of such meat has made them to suffer from a number of diseases relating to digestive system.

In Tibet people cared more for ritual purity and pollution. To guard ritual privacy they constructed their houses with separate altar rooms and kept it closed for outsiders, who may pollute the objects and persons. The houses in Mundgod settlement are planned by Indian engineers and they have failed to take into account the dwellers' traditions and customs. Originally it was planned to allot a house to each refugee family. The houses are big enough to house ten members. Later it was found that the Tibetan families were smaller in size since many of their members were lost in the flight. Owing to this and also due to lack of sufficient number of houses, it was finally decided to group two to three families and put them in one house to make the total of persons in a house to ten. This type of indiscriminate clubbing of Tibetans coming from different background, lead to several problems. Because of this arrangement if one family got the kitchen room the other got the bath room and so on. As a result a few started cooking food in the verandah and other took bath in open; thus leaving everyone in trouble.

The deeply religious Tibetans have now kept aside the biggest room in the house for the altar and use the remaining space for other activities. Later, owing to scarcity of space they started using the altar room also for other activities. Now it is used for sleeping purposes even by the married couple. Traditionally it is forbidden to use this room for non-religious purposes and more particularly to have sex. The kitchen was also not properly planned and so now the varandah is used for the cooking purpose. As a result visitors to the family pass through the cooking place and pollute the place and also the food, and thereby embarrass the housewives. While in Tibet the Tibetans had separate and safer store rooms and stored large quantity of food grains and dried meat, for winter months. Now they have to store these in the altar room or varandah. The lavatories constructed in the house did not serve the purpose due to lack of water and also due to their traditional practice of not cleaning their bottom. All these have made Tibetans feel guilty, helpless and insecure.

Tibetans also had problems in learning local methods of cultivation. Many crops they had to produce were new and so were the local agricultural tools. Since they could not grow barley they were forced to eat maize, rice and wheat. In the beginning the local labourers and merchants were also not cooperative with them. Tibetans who could not work on their farms in the hot Sun were forced to hire Indian labourers. This was not only an additional burden on their economy but also lead to false notions about them that they are lazy, easy going, etc.

The local labourers hired by the Tibetans sometimes cheated the latter and also blackmailed them for higher wages. Living in neighbgouring villages few of them also stole food grains from the Tibetan fields and threshing grounds. This was done out of jealousy towards the Tibetans, who are outsiders and doing better in life which some of the local labourers thought was at their cost.

When the 20-points programme brought by the Karnataka Government was strictly implemented during the 1976 State of emergency period in the nation, a few Tibetans were duped further by the local population who took loan from them.

In Tibet common people were not entitled to education and only the nobles arranged private tution for their children. On the other hand the monks got the religious education in the monasteries. But now as refugees they get education free and compulsory. This naturally was not welcomed by a few traditional minded Tibetans, who think that the education will take children away from their traditional culture, values, beliefs and practices. However, now the Tibetans are not only sending their children to school but they also want them to have technical education. They also make every effort to get some education sponsorship for their children.

Today one can see the Tibetans possessing many modern gadgets such as radios, watches, bicycles, tape records and so on. One can also see them especially the youngsters wearing modern dresses and hair styles. The furniture they have at home, the food they eat, are all of modern type. However, it was noticed that the change accepted was only at the material culture level. At deeper level such as of religion, values etc., they have remained unaffected. Above all, as their financial position gradually improved several Tibetan customs and traditions were revived. As a result, except the youth, others are found to wear traditional Tibetan dresses. Many Tibetans have also started arranging domestic altars more in the traditional style.

Tibetans move freely in and around the Settlement and also visit other settlements. Most of them go on business tour to different towns of India and also on pilgrimages. The type of spatial mobility and mixing with people from different backgrounds has brought a greater understanding and unity among the Tibetans. They think that they are one group and have to be united to fight for their common causes.

While in Tibet a good number of lamas and monks were invited for familial rites and rituals. They were fed with a variety of traditional foods and also given with costly gifts. Now owing to scarcity of resources only one or at the most two lamas are invited for such functions and cheaper gifts are given. The food items prepared are also few. The length of time and the expenditure on the rituals have been curtailed considerably. By this the god fearing Tibetans are very much disturbed.

Now the lamas come in contact with the commoners very often since they live in the nearby villages. Owing to this contact the lamas get more attracted towards worldly comforts here and therefore a few of them are even dropping out of the monastic life. Owing to this the high lamas and a few religious minded persons are worried that their religion is degenerating and are of the view this is due to the changed situations and circumstances here.

The authority of the Tibetan village leaders and family heads has changed much. While in Tibet only the nobles could become village heads and they were respected and obeyed because of their high birth and financial status. Here in the Settlement all are almost equal in terms of financial status except a few who have either brought some movable property from Tibet or have been able to earn here through their hard efforts. The village leaders are elected on the basis of their educational qualifications and other leadership qualities and in the democratic manner. Family heads in Tibet were, always the eldest brothers and they enjoyed respect and obedience from their younger brothers. Now they have lost their status and powers. While in Tibet the polyandrous wife was met by other brothers with elder brother's consent who had priority over sex. But now the presence of the eldest brother in the house, will not bar other brothers to have sex with the wife. Now all are entitled for an equal quota of land and enjoy enough finanical freedom here.

In the Tibetan society, *chãng* has a ritual significance and it is offered to the deities and guests of hour. Now it has been brewed commercially by some Tibetan families and sold along with the Tibetan arrack. This is because of the uncertain financial and social conditions. The new situations have made the Tibetans earn more and more money which they think is the only means to get security in life. The demand for arrack inside and outside the Settlement has made them engaged in this trade. Another means used by the Tibetans, both a few lamas and the commoners, to earn extra money is by lending money or taking land on lease basis. Those who could not cultivate their quota of land owing to lack of funds, interest or man power, found it profitable to lease it to the Tibetans who were interested in it. These persons were mostly peasants who even took lands on lease from the local people from neighbouring villages. By investing lot of money and working hard they have earned lot of profit. Money lending is another profitable means to make extra money. By charging high rate of interest and mortgaging and leasing the borrowers' land and property, these money lenders have made lot of money.

Though money lending and land leasing by both the commoners and the lamas were found even in Tibet we learn that the people were not this money minded. This change in them has come due to refugee situation without kin and community ties they think money is their only means of security now.

Now let us view the situation from the anthropological approach. As it has been stated in the introductory chapter the study has three broader aims to achieve: to understand the cultural background of the Tibetans, to know how the adjustment of refugees has taken place at individual and group level and the progress of rehabilitation of Tibetan refugees. To achieve these aims we had proposed five research question or hypothesis.

We know the calm Tibetan culture was disturbed and those who could not bear the new impact and interested in traditional order, fled to India. The problems they faced during their transit situation and later in rehabilitation settlements were many and painful. The Tibetans no doubt have shown tremendous capacity to adopt to the new situation. Within a year or two of their coming to Mundgod, most of the rehabilitation programmes such as new methods of cultivation, modern medicine, education, food, housing etc., were accepted by them and new monasteries and other religious places were built. Through these as far as possible Tibetan way of life was restored. Now one can see the Tibetans well settled. But we are of the opinion that the adjustment took place only in the material cultural level and the more deeper aspects have remained untouched. Therefore as their financial position improved it is observed that the Tibetans begin to restore the old order. As a result now the dress pattern, food habits, etc., of the traditional Tibetan culture have been revived. Owing to this, today, we can see the Tibetans becoming more and more traditional in their outlook on life.

The Tibetans who left every thing they owned behind in Tibet and fled to India to protect themselves and their religion, are keeping a high morale and are well organized. They hope to go back one day when the evil is over. Their only hope is the Dalai Lama in whom they have deep faith. This faith has made the refugees to retain their religion and religious practices intact. They also contribute money for the maintenance of the Dalai Lama and his establishment at Dharmashala and pray for his well being. They always look forward to receive him in their settlement and listen to his advice. He is their only hope and under whose leadership they hope to unite and organize their liberation movement and one day return to their holy land with him. So they are ready to sacrifice any thing for him. Tibetans are again happy because the Dalai Lama is the head of both their religion as well as of the state. Now the Dalai Lama and their religion are keeping their hope alive and with this hope they are living here. To some extent this has helped them to forget their stress and strain. Thus the refugees have some one or some purpose to organize and raise their hope.

The temporary nature of the Tibetans' stay in India and their strong belief of going back to Tibet soon has made a few rehabilitation programmes incomplete. The Tibetans say the houses in which they live now in Mundgod are not properly planned. Though everyone complain about the lack of space but only a few of them who can afford, have attempted to build or renovate the houses according to their taste and many others do not like to invest in this as they stay on hoping to leave the place soon. They select spouses for marriage mainly from the district and the province they belonged to in Tibet having the same dialect and culture. This shows they want to build up their socio-economic and cultural contacts in case they go back to Tibet. But these were distorted when they were staying in transit camps.

Thinking in similar line the Tibetans have not invested their money on any of the stable properties and on such property which cannot be taken back with them if they go back to Tibet. So we see them buying only the portable and more easily convertable goods such as watches, transistor radios, clothing, ornaments and so on. But at times more settled type of trends are also exhibited by the refugees through constructing big monastries, which are not however, the individual activities.

Polyandry which was a necessity in Tibet is losing its importance now. While in Tibet except the elder brother other brothers in the polyandrous union, used to go out on trade and grazing cattle. Now each one has his land and no need to go out leaving his wife and children for a longer period of time. This type of a permanent stay of all brothers in the family has brought practical problems in having sex with the polyandrous wife. All these factors have made them marry independently and have an independent family of their own. This has given rise to the concept of nuclear family which is new to the commoners among the Tibetans. On the other hand, the concept of joint family has also lost its importance. In a polyandrous family the eldest brother who held a high status and authority, dominated over his other brothers in all familial matters; including the right to have sex with the polyandrous wife. In an elementary family the husband is the prime and sole owner and authority on all men and material in the family. This situation brought a drastic change in the Tibetan way of life. In Tibet only the elder brother could inherit the family property, while over here all brothers equally share the movable property of the family.

The refugees think that their stay is temporary and so they try to live for the present. They calculate the gains and losses before they undertake any activity and always decide in favour of the things which bring them profit and quick results. As a result we can see that no coconut trees and other fruit yielding trees which takes years to yield are planted. Though they earn a living by cultivating land they prefer such occupations like carpet making, woolen garments business, etc., to earn quick money and avoid the hot sun. Though every effort is made by the concerned officials to make their stay a comfortable one and to minimise their stresses and strains, they feel that their life here is temporary and incomplete. The rehabilitating agencies are helpless to do anything to remove the feeling nourished by the refugees. They also think that one day the Tibetans may have to go back to their country and their job is only to make their stay as comfortable as possible. To settle them well the refugees have to be first made to accept the host society as their permanent residence. As long as they are treated as refugees and guests we cannot expect them to settle well.

It is only after coming to India that the Tibetans have become more mobile and have come to know of other Tibetans coming from different districts and provinces of Tibet and have learnt each other's socio-cultural life dialect, etc. Now irrespective of their background noble or serfs, they have been settled in rows of houses and in a way this has brought greater understanding and unity among them. They also feel they are one group and have to fight together to meet the common problems they are facing. On the contrary we can also see the Tibetans establishing social, marital and financial relations with people coming from their own village or district in Tibet so that when they go back to Tibet they will be of some help. This shows that the Tibetans have made adjustments keeping an eye on their future.

The temporary nature of stay of refugees leaves a few rehabilitation programmes incomplete. Our findings show that the adjustment between the Tibetans and local communities is not very cordial. Adjustment between the two groups appears to be friendly and better. Our investigations show that inner and deeper opinions are not encouraging. First the Tibetans are not happy with the physical environmental conditions of Mundgod. Owing to its distance from Dharmasala and the Tibetan border, they never wanted to come to Mundgod and now never wish to continue to stay here. They make use of every opportunity to move towards North, either on employment or woolen garment business.

Secondly, the Tibetans earned the illwill of the local people from the day they were settled here sharing the already limited resources such as cultivable land, village sites, and so on. When the refugees were given the deforested land and many other privileges and facilities like borewells, tractors, roads, hospitals, school, electricity, etc., the local people who were land hungry and lacked many of these facilities, became jealous of the Tibetans. Sensing this attitude of the local population and also to develop friendly relation between the two groups, the Karnataka Government released some amount of land to the local people also. Unfortunately most of the Indian beneficiaries were either petty government officials or landless backward and depressed caste people, and came from far-off villages. Since they lived away from the land which was allocated to them, either they left the land fallow or gave it to the Tibetans on lease basis. This made both the landless and well-off in the villages around the Settlement to hate the Tibetans further and thus the aim of the governmnet also remained not fulfilled.

Further the Tibetan customs such as polyandry, feedings the dead to vultures, eating stale beaf, etc., made the local people to develop a very bad opinion about them. The Tibetans, who could not work in the hot sun and were also ignorant of local agricultural methods and ecological conditions, when hired local people to work in their farm and threshing ground, were thought to be lazy. The local labourers who were hired by the Tibetans, not only blackmailed the Tibetans for higher wages but also cheated them in the work, a few stole paddy, maize, etc., from the Tibetan fields and threshing grounds. In general, the local population were very much jealous of the Tibetans for taking so much benefit from their government and they thought it is at their cost. When the governmnet brought 20 points programme and later during the emmergency period in 1976, the local people got an opportunity to express their anger openly towards the Tibetans. Using the new laws in force the loans taken from the Tibetans were not returned and the lands leased on long term were also taken back. It was roughly estimated that the Tibetans lost about two lakhs of rupees during the year 1978.

During 1978 arrangements were going on to settle another thousand refugees in the Settlement. The Karnataka Government which cannot give any more land to Tibetans, had asked the settlement authorities to reallocate the already given land and give a portion of it to the incoming refugees. To see the refugees were not hit by this land reduction a new and intensive cultivation programme was proposed by the government to irrigate their land from a dam to facilitate them to grow two to three crops in a year. To train the Tibetans in the intensive wet cultivation a programme was started by the officials of the Settlement. But the Tibetans were worried because they had to share water of a small dam with the local people and this may spark some more conflicts. Therefore many of them were not happy with this new programme and some were openly skeptical about it. There were also some persons who felt that this was a plan to deprive them of the land already given to them.

Lack of restrictions on the movement of Tibetans and the local people also has created a few more problems, here at the Settlement. Local labourers and annual servants, businessmen, fruit and milk vendors freely move about in the settlement. Local people from neighbouring villages frequently visit the Settlement for *chãng* and Tibetan made arrack. All these had created problems since many of these transactions were unofficial and also illegal. There were a few formal or official relations between the local people and the Tibetans. Indian patients were allowed to be x-rayed and use the ambulance van from the Tibetan settlement hospital for which they had to pay. Further a number of local people work in government and semi-government agencies in the settlement. Our enquiries with these persons have revealed that they did not have any speical training to work among the refugees. So like any other local persons, they too do not carry a good opinion about the Tibetans. The employees had misunderstood the Tibetan attitude towards savings and said the Tibetans were more interested in borrowing money from the banks than depositing.

There was very little approved informal relation between the Tibetans and the local people. The limited number of relations they had such as lending and borrowing of money, selling paddy and maize, selling arrack, bribing the officials and so on were illegal. There were also restrictions to establish closer ties between the two groups since officially the two groups are supposed to transact through the Society or the banks and not directly. So what little informal relations they had, had made them feel guilty rather than friendly and happy.

The Tibetans and Indians do not have anything in common such as rites, rituals, celebrations, beliefs, customs and manners. So inviting each other to part-take in socio-religious activities in their families was practically absent.

On the contrary, a few customs and beliefs have led to misunderstanding between the two groups. The Tibetans observe ritual purity of action and thought, whereas the local Indian customes give more importance to the ritual purity of body, mind, place and also touch. A lack of importance to these aspects in Tibetan culture has made the local people to consider them to be low. Moreover on the basis of purity and pollution the Indian society is stratified into several endogamous castes and the division is more rigid. Whereas the Tibetan social stratification is based on economic classes, which are also hereditory in terms of pure and impure bones and of nobles and commoners. The local Indians just cannot accept the Tibetans who maintain that they belong to pure bone and at the same time eat non-vegetarian food and marry among the lower groups next to them. All these have puzzled the local Indians who follow the caste rules very rigidly.

A few informal social ties have been established by the Tibetan youth, who go with the local youth to see cinema, to hotels and in a few cases to have alcoholic drinks. Rarely they visit each other's houses to eat food on festivals and such other special occasions. A few exchange magazines and story books. Even here only the young men are involved and girls and older age sets very rarely come together. Exhibiting the photos of cinema stars in the house, listening to Indian film songs, imitating the Indian and Western dress and hair style by their youth has disturbed the Tibetans. The Tibetans are much conscious of their cultural identity and want to maintain it. They think that the local Indian customs, practices and values are 'spoiling' their youth and are worried that it may lead to loss of their culture. Therefore the aged refugees do not approve this land of a social intercourse and this had led to conflict between the two age groups.

The type of adjustment which has now taken place between the Indians and the Tibetans has been termed a progressive one by Palakshappa (1978:111). But our contention is that the present adjustment has taken place only on the material side. The settlement had a tremendous contributions to make towards the innovation of a variety of food crops, tools, use of machines in agriculture, use of co-operative movement for rural development and rural banking, bore wells, water pumps and a variety of new food items in the area. In turn the Tibetans also have learnt the local language, local crop pattern, knowledge of local tools and implements, and have accepted clothing, education, banking, postal facilities and so on. In a way all this can be viewed as a contribution of the settlement to the surrounding areas of Mundgod.

These are no doubt the indications of a progressive adjustment; in material aspects. In terms of more deeper and permanent aspects this adjustment is lacking. This, as we have already stated is due to the reluctant nature of the Tibetans themselves. One cannot blame them for this because the Tibetans try to maintain their identity so that when they go back to Tibet they may not be misfits in their mother land. Moreover they have fled from Tibet to guard and retain their tradition and religion of which they are proud of even in Mundgod.

To conclude we may mention that this is precisely happening because the stay of the Tibetans in India is temporary, and whatever little adjustment they have made in their culture is just to survive till they achieve their final goal i.e., freedom of Tibet. From this point of view the transplantation of Tibetans into Indian culture, with traditional ties is cordial, and has provided them proper environment to adjust and has also helped them to continue to survive. If the Tibetans intend to transplant themselves completely they can establish more deeper relations with the host society and flow into the national stream.

# Bibliography

## Reports

Legal Inquiry Committee on Tibet.

1966 *Tibet* and the Chinese People's Republic. A Report on the International Commission of Jurists 1959 and 1960. NewDelhi: Sterling Publishers Pvt.Ltd.

## Encyclopaedia

Kitagawa, Joseph M.

1974 *History of Buddhism*. In Encyclopaedia Britannica. Vol. 3. pp. 403-414. Chicago: The University of Chicago Press.

Lowell, Thomas, JR.

1962 *Tibet.* In the Encyclopaedia America. The Inter-national reference work, Vol. 26, pp. 606-609. New York: Américan Corporation.

Richardson, H.E.

1974 *History of Tibet.* In the Encyclopaedia Britannica, Vol. 18, pp. 378-382, Chicago: The University of Chicago Press.

Schechtman, Joseph B.

1974 *Refugees*. In Encyclopaedia Britannica, Vol. 15, pp. 568-573. Chicago: The University of Chicago Press.

Shakabpa, Tsepon W.D. an Turrel V. Wylie

1974. *Tibet.* In Encyclopaedia Britannica, Vol. 18,pp. 372-378. Chicago: The University of Chicago Press.

Singer, Milton.

1968 *The concept of culture.* In International Encyclopaedia of Social Sciences, Vol. 3, pp. 527-543.Macmillan Company and the Free Press.

Troy Adrian, G.B. De H.

1956 *Tibet.* In the American Peoples Encyclopaedia. Chicago: The Spencer Press, Vol. 18, pp. 811-812.

Tucci, Giuseppe.

1974 *Buddhism.* In Encyclopaedia Britannica, Vol. 3, pp. 374-403. Chicago: The University of Chicago Press.

Turrel, V. Wylie.

1969 *Tibet.* In Encyclopaedia Britannica, Vol. 21, pp. 1106-1116.Chicago: The University of Chicago Press.

Vogt, Evon Z.

1968 *Culture Change.* In International Encyclopaedia of Social Sciences, Vol. 3. pp. 555-558. The Macmillan Company and the Free Press.

## Books

Bailey, F.C.

1958 *Caste and The Economic Frontier: A Village in highland Orissa.* London: Oxford University Press.

Barnett. H.G.

1953 *Basis of Cultural Change.* New York: McGraw Hill.

1956 *Anthropology in Administration.* Evanston: Row Peterson and Company.

Beals, Ralph.

1959 *"Acculturation".* In A.L. Kroeber (Ed). Anthropology Today. Chicago: University of Chicago Press.

Beals, Ralph L. and Hoijer, Harry;

1953 *Introduction to Anthropology*. New York:Macmillan and Co.

Beijer, G.

1996 *"Modern Patterns of International Migratory Movements"*. In J.A. Jackson (ed). Migration (Sociological Studies-2). Cambridge: Cambridge University Press.

Bell, Charles.

1924 *Tibet: Past and Present*. London: Oxford Clarendon Press.

1928 *The People of Tibet*. London: Oxford Clarendon Press.

1931 *The Religion of Tibet*. London: Oxford Clarendon Press.

1946 *The Potrait of the Dalai Lama*. London: Oxford Clarendon Press

Benedict, Ruth.

1951 *Patterns of Culture*. New York: New American Library. Cook, Georgewood.

1971 *Into Tibet, the early British explorers*. London: Faberand Faber.

Benyie, L.

1960 "*Greek and South Slave Immigrants in Melbourne*". In Price, C.A.(Ed.) The Study of Immigrants in Australia, Canberra.

Dalai Lama, H.H.

1962 *My land and my People*. London: McGraw Hill Book Company.

1963 *Constitution of Tibet*. New Delhi: Bureau of his Holiness the Dalai Lama.

Dalton, George.

1971 *Economic Development and Social Change: The*

*Modernization of Village Communities*. New York: Natural History Press.

Dawa, Norbu.

1974 *Red Star Over Tibet.* London: William Collins & Sons.and Co. Ltd.,St. James Place.

Djamour, Judith.

1959 *Malay Kinship and marriage in Singapore.* London: The Athlone Press, University of London.

Durkheim, Emile.

1961 *The Elementary Forms of the Religious Life*. Joseph ward Swain (trans). New York: Collier books.

Eisenstadt, Shamuel N.

1954 *The Absorption of Immigrants. Comparative Study based mainly on the Jewish Community in Palestine and the State of Israel.* London: Routledge & Kegan Paul Ltd.

Ekvall, R.

1964 *Religious Observances in Tibet, Patterns and Functions.* Chicago: University of Chicago Press.

Evans - Pritchard, E.E.

1951 Social Anthropology. London: Cohen and West Ltd.

1965 *Theories of Primitive Religion.* Lond Oxford University Press.

Evans-Wentz, W.Y.

1957 *The Tibetan Book of the Dead* (translated from the Tibetan). London: Oxford University Press.

Firth, Raymond.

1951 *Elements of Social Organization*. London: Watts & Co.

Fortes, M., and Evans, Pritchard.

1958 *African Political Systems.* London: Oxford University Press.

Frazer, James George.

1959 *The New Golden Bough.* Theodon H. Gaster (ed.). New York: Criterion books.

Furrer, Heimendorf.

1964 *Sherpas of Nepal: Buddhist highlanders.* London: Murray.

Gennep, Arnold Van.

1960 *The Rites of Passage. Chicago:* The University of Chicago Press.

George, Wood Cook

1971 *Into Tibet, the Early British Explorers.* London: Faber and Faber.

Gordon, Milton M.

1964 *Assimilation in American Life, The Role of Race, Religion and National Origins.* New York: Oxford University Press.

Harrer, Heinrich.

1957 *Seven Years in Tibet.* (Translated from German by Richard Graves). London: Rupert Hart Davis.

Hutheesing, Raja. (Ed.)

1960 *Tibet fights for freedom:Story of the March 1959 Uprising as Recorded in Documents, etc.* Bombay: Orient Longmans.

Jackson, J.A.

1969 "Editorial Introduction" to J.A. Jackson (ed). Migration (Sociological studies-2). London: Cambridge University Press.

Jansen, Clifford.

1969 *"Some Sociological aspects of migration"*. In J.A. Jackson (ed.) Migration (Sociological Studies-2). London: Cambridge University Press.

Kapadia, K.M.

1958 *Marriage and Family in India.* London: Oxford University Press.

Karve, Iravati.

1965 *Kinship Organization in India.* Bombay: Asia Publishing House.

Keesing, Roger M., and Kessing, Felix M.

1971 *New Perspectives in Cultural Anthropology*. New York: Holt Renehard & Winston Inc.

Krober, A.L.

1944 *Configurations of Culture Growth.* California: University of California Press.

1952 Nature of Culture. Chicago: Chicago University Press.

Leach, E.R.

1967 *Polyandry, Inheritance and The Definition of Marriage.* In Rethinking Anthropology London: University of London Press.

Lowie, Robert H.

1950 *Social Organization.* London: Routledge & Co.

1960 *Primitive Society*, New York. Harper Torch Books

MaClver, R.M., and Page, C.H.

1971 *Society, An Introductory Analysis.* London: The Macmillan Co.

Mair, L.P.

1957 *Studies in Applied Anthropology*. London: London University Press.

1965 *An Introduction to Social Anthropology*. Oxford: Clarendon Press.

Malefijt, Annemarie De Waal.

1968 *Religion and Culture: An Introduction to Anthropology of Religion*. New York: The Macmillan Co.

Majumdar, D.N.

1960 *Himalayan Polyandry*. London: Asia Publishing House.

Majumdar, D.N. and Madan, T.N.

1967 *Introduction to Social Anthropology*. Bombay: Asia Publishing House.

Malinowski, Brinslaw.

1944 *Scientific theory of culture and other essays*. Chapel Hill: North Carolina University.

1954 *Magic, Science and Religion and Other Essays*. New York: Doubleday Anchor books.

1960 *The Sexual Life of Savages in North Western Melanesia*. London: Routledge and Kegan Paul Ltd.

1962 *Crime and Custom in Savage Society*. New Jersey: Adams & Co.

Medding, P.Y.

1968 *From Assimilation to Group Survival*. Melbourne.

Max, Weber.

1949 *Theory of Social and Economic Organization*. New York: Macmillan & Co.

1957 From Max Weber: Essays in Sociology (tr. & ed. with Introduction by H.H. Gerth and C. Wright Mills). London: Routledge & Co.

Metraux, Alfred.

1953 *"Applied Anthropology in Government–United Nations"*. In A.L. Kroeber (ed.) Anthropology Today. Chicago: The University of Chicago Press.

Mitter, J.P.

1964 Betrayal of Tibet. Bombay: Allied Publishers Pvt. Ltd.

Moraes, Frank.

1960 *The Revolt in Tibet.* New York: Macmillan Company.

Murdock, G.P.

1965 *Social Structure.* New York: Macmillan & Co.

Murphy, Dervla.

1966 *Tibetan Foot Hold.* London: John Murray.

Murphy, H.B.M.

1955 *Flight and Resettlement.* Paris: United Nations Educational Scientific and Cultural Organization.

Mustang, Michel Peissel.

1968 *A Lost Tibetan Kingdom.* London: Collins & Harvill Press.

Nadel, S.F.

1957 *The Theory of Social Structure.* London: Cohen and West.

Nebesky Wojkowitz, R.

1956 *Oracles and Demons of Tibet.* The Hague: Mouton and Co.

Norbu, T.J., and Turnbull, Colin, M.

1968 *Tibet.* New York: Simon and Schuster.

Palakshappa, T.C.

1978 *Tibetans in India: A case study of Mundgod Tibetans.* New Delhi: Sterling Publishers Pvt. Ltd.

Prince, Charles;

1969*"The study of assimilation".* In Jackson J.A. (ed.) Migration (Sociological Studies 2). London: Cambridge University Press.

Prince Peter, H.R.H.

1963 *A Study of Polyandry.* The Hague : Mouton and Co.

1965 *The Tibetan Family System* in Nimkoff M.N. (Ed.) Comparative Family System. New York: Houghton Mifflin Company.

Radcliffe-Brown, A.R.

1952 *Structure and Function in Primitive Society.* London: The English Language Book Society and Cohen & West Ltd. Glencoe Ill, Free Press.

Radcliff-Brown, A.R. and Forde, Daryll.

1950 *African Systems of Kinship and Marriage.* London: Oxford University Press.

Redfield, R.

1968 *The Primitive World and its Transformations.* New York: Cornell University Press.

Richardson, H.E.

1962 *Tibet and its History.* London: Oxford University Press.

Rogers, Everett M.

1969 *Modernization Among Peasants: The Impact of Communication.* New York: Holt Rinehart and Winston, INC.

Sahni, Bhisham.

1970 *Cultural Contacts Across the Himalayas.* Jullundur: Punjabi Publishers.

Saxena, R.N.

1961 *Refugees: A Study in Changing Attitudes*. Bombay: Asia Publishing House.

Scott, Franklin D.

1968 *World migration in modern times*. New Jersey: Prentice Hall.

Sen Chanakya (Ed.)

1960 *Tibet Disappears*. A Documentary of History of Tibet's International status. Bombay: Asia Publishing House.

Shakabpa, Tsepon W.D.

1967 *Tibet: A political History*. New Haven: Yale University Press.

Shen, Tsung -Lien., and Shen, Chi-Liu.

1953 *Tibet and the Tibetans*. California: Stanford University Press.

Shuval, Judith T.

1963 *Immigrants on the threshold*. New York: Atherton Press.

Snellgrove David and Richardson, Hugh

1968 *A Cultural History of Tibet*. New York: Fredrick A Praeger

Spencer, Herbert.

1885 *Principles of Sociology*. 3 Volumes. London: Williams & Norgate.

Stein, R. A.

1972 *Tibetan Civilization*. London: Faber and Faber Ltd.

Steward, Jullian H.

1955 *Theory of Culture Change*. Urbana: IIlinois University Press.

Tucci, Guiseppe,

1967 *Tibet: Land of Snows*. Translated by J.E. Stapleton Driver. Calcutta: Oxford & IBH Publishing Co.

Tylor, Edward B.

1971 *"The Science of Culture"*. In Walter Goldschmidt (ed). Exploring the ways of mankind. New York: Holt Rinchard and Winston, INC.

Tylor, E.B.

1958 *Religion in Primitive Culture*. New York: Harper Torch books.

Van Gennep (Arnold)

1960 *The Rites of Passage* (Translated by Monika B. Vizedom and Gabrielle L Caffee). Chicago: The University of Chicago Press.

Vayda, A., and Rappaport, R.A.

1968 *"Ecology, Cultural and noncultural"*. In J. Clifton (ed). Introduction to Cultural Anthropology. New York: Houghton Mifflin.

Waddell L.A.

1959 *Lamaism:The Buddhism of Tibet*. Cambridge: Heffer & Sons Ltd.

Waddell, Austine L.M.B.

1975 *Buddhism and Lamaism of Tibet with its mystic cults, symbolism and mythology and its relation to Indian Buddhism*. New Delhi: Heritage Publishers.

Woodcock George

1971 *Into Tibet: Early British Explorers*. London: Faber and Faber.

## Periodicals

Anand, R.P.

1969 "The Status of Tibet in International Law". *International Studies:* The Quarterly Journal of the Indian School of International Studies, Vol. 10, No. 4. pp. 401-445. New Delhi

Chandra Anjali

1970 "Where Tibetans Learn to Live Again: *The Sunday Standard,* January 11, 1970.

Chopra, Ashok.

1976 "The Dalai Lama to be or not to be". *Indian Express,* Vol. 44, No. 316. October 11, 1976, p.5.

1979 "Hopes, Dilemma after 20 years of Exile*Indian Express,* Vol.47, February 12, 1979. p.7

Clarke, J.J.

1970 "On the unity and the diversity of cultures". *American Anthropologist,* Vol. 72, No. 3, pp. 545-554.

Dastur, Aloo J.

1964 "The Tibetan Ordeal and India". *National Integration,* Independence Number, *Tibet Issue.* New Delhi. pp. 62-65.

Dawa, Norbu,

1976 "Is He the Last Dalai Lama. Editorial to *Tibetan Review,* Vol. XI, No.3. p.3-4.

Ekvall, Robert B.

1961 "The nomadic pattern of living among the Tibetans as preparation for war". *American Anthropologist,* Vol. 63, No.6. pp. 1250-1263.

1961 Nomads of Tibet: A Chinese Dilemma. *Current Science,* Vol. 1, No. 13.

1963 "Some aspects of divination in Tibetan Society". *Ethnoloy*, Vol. 2, No.1. pp. 31-39.

Gillan, John P.

1971 "Some principles of Socio cultural integration". *Current Anthropology*, Vol. 12, No. 1. pp. 63-71.

Goldstein, Melvyn C.

1971 "Serfdom and mobility: An examination of the institution of 'Human lease' in traditional Tibetan Society". *The Journal of Asian Studies*, Vol. XXX, No. 3. pp. 521-534.

1971 "Stratification, Polyandry and Family Structure in Central Tibet". *South Western Journal of Anthropology*, Vol. 27, No.1. pp. 64-74.

Jamkhandi, R.S.

1977 "Mari Tibet: Mayalok" (In Kannada) *Samyukta Karnataka* (Kannada Daily) Vol. 45, No. 96, 29th July 1977, pp 1 & 8.

Kroeber, Alfred L. & Kluckhonn Clyde

1952 "Culture: A Critical Review of Concepts and Definition". *American Archaeology and Ethnology Papers,* Vol. 47. No. 1

Leach, E.R.

1955 "Polyandry, Inheritance and the Definition of Marriage". *Man,* Vol. 55. pp. 182-185.

Lobsong Lhalungpa

1976 "The Religious Culture of Tibet". *The Tibet Journal,* Vol. 1, No. 3 & 4. pp. 9-16.

McGirk, Tim.

1994 "Tibetan nuns' Himalayan Odyssey". Excerpts of his interviewing the Buddhist nuns arrived from Tibet, *The Hindustan Times*, Vol. LXX, No. 47 February 16, 1994, P. 1 & 14.

Neville, Dyson Hudson.

1972 "The Study of nomads". *The Journal of Asian and African Studies,* Vol. 7, No. 1-2. pp. 2-29.

Nörman, E. Whitten Jr.

1969 "Strategies of Adaptive mobility". *American Anthropologist,* Vol. 71, No. 2. pp. 228-242.

Pardesi, Ghanshyam.

1975 "Some observations on the draft constitution of Tibet". *The Tibet Journal,* Vol. 1, No. 1, pp. 63-71. Dharmasala (H.P.) : Library of the Tibetan Works and Archieves.

Puntsok Wangyal.

1975 "The influence of religion on Tibetan politics". *The Tibet Journal,* Vol. 1, No. 1. pp. 78-86. Dharmasala: Library of the Tibetan Works and Archives.

Rahul, R.

1969 "The institution of Dalai Lama". *Journal of the Indian School of International Studies.* Vol. 10, No.4. Special Issue on Tibet. pp. 495-510. Bombay: Asia Publishing House

Ramu, G.N.

1971 "Migration, Acculturation and Social Mobility among the Untouchable: Gold Miners in South India: A case study. *Human Organization*, Vol. 30.No.2.pp. 170-178.

Singh, Bhagwan.

1933 "Disposal of the dead by mutilation in Spiti (Western Tibet)". *Man*, Vol. 33. pp. 141-143.

Singh, Payal

1993 "Tibet is not a part of China, Interview with the Dalai Lama. *The Illustrated weekly of India,* October 16,22, Vol. CXIII, No. 42 pp 8-9.

Wallace, Anthony F.C.

1972 "Paradigmatic processes in culture change". *American Anthropologist*, Vol. 74, No. 3. pp. 467-478.

Walter, Asboe.

1932 "Notes on Child Birth in Manchus (Western Tibet)". *Man*, Vol. 32. p. 139.

1936 "Sacrifices in Western Tibet". *Man*, Vol. 36.p. 75.

1936 "The Lahoulis of Western Tibet". *Man*, Vol. 36. p. 59.

1937 "Agricultural methods in Western Tibet". *Man*, Vol. 37. pp. 74-77.

Walter, Goldscmidt.

1965 "Theory and Strategy in the study of cultural adaptibility". *American Anthropologist*, Vol. 67, No.2. pp. 402-408.

Yishi Wangel.

1964 "International Status of Tibet". *National Integration*: Independence Number, Tibet Issue. New Delhi. pp. 59-61.

## Un published report:

Gurumurthy, K.G.

1979 Cultural Transplantation: A case study of Tibetan Refugees of Mundgod. UGC Sponsored Advanced Research Project Report.

# Appendix-A

## Clan Names Among the Tibetans

| Sr.No. | Clan Name | Meaning (Approx.) |
|---|---|---|
| 1 | 2 | 3 |
| 1. | Ba-bru | Name of a Monastery |
| 2. | Ba-ro | Wealthy one |
| 3. | Bu-r ghar | Name of a Monastery |
| 4. | Chaglā | Name of a peak |
| 5. | Tsa-wang Kar-ma | An Ancestor (male) |
| 6. | Cho-joan | Name of a temple |
| 7. | Cho-ngā Sā-wā | New shop |
| 8. | Cho-ngdo-t | a basal one |
| 9. | Chā-ng-ma | Beer selling one |
| 10. | Cho-sāār | New and rich house |
| 11. | Chu | Water |
| 12. | Chuk-po | A wealthy one |
| 13. | Chu-kya gha-ra | Blacksmith whose name is Chu-kya |
| 14. | Chumbia | Name of a Village |
| 15. | Chumzang | Name of a Village |
| 16. | Di-ckey Kang-sār | New House named after a girl |
| 17. | Dro-lā | Name of a Hill |
| 18. | Gāng-jen | Name of a Village |
| 19. | Gap-shi | A prosperous one |
| 20. | Gur-din | Old tented one |
| 21. | Ja-mu-ga-ng | Name of a hilly place |
| 22. | Ka-bar Ne-chun | Place where dark water is available |
| 23. | Kā-ng-mo-che | A hilly place where Kā-ng-mo-la, the princess of religion lives |
| 24. | Ka-ng-sur | Corner One |
| 25. | Ka-nji-shu-ndha | The younger brother's house |
| 26. | Kar-mo | Name of a star |

| 1 | 2 | 3 |
|---|---|---|
| 27. | Kar-wā Thun-gyā | A House with pillars |
| 28. | Kā-ya-kpā | A wealthy one |
| 29. | Ke-gu-n | The one who has no property |
| 30. | Khā-rwāo | The white one |
| 31. | Khim-tsu | The one of water |
| 32. | Kho-bā | The one inside the stomach |
| 33. | Ko-to-mb | Box made of leather |
| 34. | Ko-rpā | A servant of a monastry |
| 35. | Ko-ko Zong | Name of a district |
| 36. | Cha-thoa-n | Deep watered one |
| 37. | Lakh-ye-p | Behind the hill |
| 38. | Lha-mey Nor-bu | Name of a deity |
| 39. | Lha-ni-ngi | Ancient God |
| 40. | Lho-ma | Basket Maker |
| 41. | Li-mey | Name of a Village |
| 42. | Lun-gar Gom-pā | Name of a Monastery |
| 43. | Lung-ng-me | Name of an ancestor (female) |
| 44. | Mā-kh-pon | Name of an army officer |
| 45. | Mā-ru- Kho-ng | An ancestoral one |
| 46. | Mā-yā | Name of a Village |
| 47. | Nā-ng-lo | The one from the middle of the village |
| 48. | Nā-khpo-thin | Name of a village |
| 49. | Ngak-mbu-m | Repeating syllable for thousand times |
| 50. | No-rbu Kān-gsā | The one names the divine-Norbu |
| 51. | Nō-wu-o | Younger brother's one |
| 52. | Nye-pā Sur-wā | Private owner |
| 53. | Nyi-ru | The nearest one |
| 54. | Pa-lden-Sha | Goddess of wealth |
| 55. | Passong | Name of an ancestor |
| 56. | Pa-xi | Name of a village |
| 57. | Pema Tha-rgay | Name of an ancestor (male) |
| 58. | Phu-kh-pā | Name of a cave |

| 1 | 2 | 3 |
|---|---|---|
| 59. | Phu-tho-k | Above the prayer hall |
| 60. | Rā-mo-che | An oracle |
| 61. | Sa-mdu-ling | A place of happiness |
| 62. | Shā-bā | Name of a village |
| 63. | Shār-chok | A Southern one |
| 64. | Shung-ba-Trak-cha | A big rocky place |
| 65. | Su- rwā | A Private |
| 66. | Tam-din-Sha-lu | Name of an ancestor (male) |
| 67. | Tam-gyar | Name of an ancestor (Male) |
| 68. | Teng-zum | Name of an ancestor (female) |
| 69. | Te-ngo | One above the hill |
| 70. | Tha-kar-bā | Name of an ancestor(Male) |
| 71. | Thā-nak | Name of a Village |
| 72. | Thā-shi Kang-bā | The head of a Village |
| 73. | The-they | Name of a village |
| 74. | Thi-ngri (Kham-ba) | A village in Kham-ba province |
| 75. | Tho-ngi | The one inside the village |
| 76. | Tho-ng-me | Name of an ancestor |
| 77. | Tho-ng-tho | Name of an ancestor (lama) |
| 78. | Thong-tho | Name of a village. |
| 79. | Tok-thoyu | Name of a person |
| 80. | Tra-sāār | Name of a village |
| 81. | Tro-mey | Name of a village |
| 82. | Tro-ng | The one who killed the monk |
| 83. | Trong-theyw | Name of a village |
| 84. | Yon-gura | Name of a person |
| 85. | Ye-shoor | Name of a person |
| 86. | Yong-me | Name of a village |
| 87. | Yong-sār | Name of a village |

# Appendix- B

## Common Kinship Usages Among the Tibetans (Central Tibet)

| Sr.No. | Term | Term of reference | Term of Address |
|---|---|---|---|
| 1 | 2 | 3 | 4 |
| 1. | Fa | Pa-lā | Pa-Pā or Pā-lā |
| 2. | Fa-Fa | Po-lā | Po-lā |
| 3. | Fa-Fa-Fa | Immi-lā | Po-lā |
| 4. | Mo-Fa | Po-lā | Po-lā |
| 5. | Mo-Fa-Fa | Immi-lā | Immi-lā |
| 6. | Fa-Br (elder) | Pā-lā | Pā-lā |
| 7. | Fa-Br-(younger) | A-ghu | Aghu-lā |
| 8. | Mo-Br(elder) | A-shāng | A shāng-lā |
| 9. | Mo-Br (younger) | | |
| 10. | Mo | A-mā | A-mā |
| 11. | Mo-Mo | Mo-lā | Mo-lā |
| 12. | Mo-Fa-Mo | Mo-mmo-lā | Mo-mmo-lā |
| 13. | Fa-Mo | Mo-lā | Mo-lā |
| 14. | Fa-Mo-Mo | Mo-lā | Mo-lā |
| 15. | Fa-Si (elder) | A-ni | Ani-lā |
| 16. | Fa-Si (younger) | | |
| 17. | Mo-Si (elder) | Su-mo | So-mo-lā |
| 18. | Mo-Si (younger) | | |
| 19. | Br (elder) | Atcho | Cho-lā |
| 20. | Br (younger) | Noo | by name & -lā |
| 21. | Fa-Br-So (elder) | Agu-sā | Cho-lā |
| 22. | Fa-Br-So (younger) | Tsa-u | O-lā |
| 23. | Fa-Si-So (elder) | A-ni-Sā | Cho-lā |
| 24. | Fa-Si-So (younger) | A-ni-Sā | O-lā |
| 25. | Mo-Br-So (elder) | A-shang ki Sā | Cho-lā |
| 26. | Mo-Br-So (younger) | A-shang ki Sā | by name & -lā |
| 27. | Mo-Si-So ( elder) | Cho-lā | Cho-lā |
| 28. | Mo-Si-So (younger) | O-lā | by name & -lā |
| 29. | Si (elder) | A-tchā-lā | A-tchā-lā |
| 30. | Si (younger) | Sring-mō | by name & -lā |

| 1 | 2 | 3 | 4 |
|---|---|---|---|
| 31. | Fa-Br-Da (elder) | Tsā-mō | A-tchā-lā |
| 32. | Fa-Br-Da (younger) | Tsā-mo | by name & -lā |
| 33. | Fa-Si-Da (elder) | A-ni Sā-mo | A-tchā-lā |
| 34. | Fa-Si-Da (younger) | A-tchā-lā or O-lā | by name & -lā |
| 35. | Mo-Br-Da (elder) | A-shang ki Sā-mo | A-tchā-lā |
| 36. | Mo-Br-Da (younger) | A-shang ki Sā-mo | O-lā |
| 37. | Mo-Si-Da (elder) | So-mo-lā ki Sa-mo | A-tchā-lā |
| 38. | Mo-Si-Da (younger) | So-la-mo | O-lā or by name & -la |
| 39. | So | Pu or Sa | by name |
| 40. | Br-So | Tsu-u | by name |
| 41. | Elder-Br-So | Tsa-u | by name |
| 42. | Younger Si-so | | |
| 43. | Elder Si-So | Pu | by name |
| 44. | So-So | Pu-Pu | by name |
| 45. | So-So-So | Pu-Pu-Pu | by name |
| 46. | Da-So-So | Pu-Mo Pu-Pu | by name |
| 47. | Da | Pu-Mo | by name & -lā |
| 48. | Da-so | Pu-Mo Pu | by name |
| 49. | Br-Da | Tsā-mo | by name & -lā |
| 50. | Si-Da | Pu-Mo | by name & -lā |
| 51. | Da-Da | Pu-Mo Pu-Mo | by name |
| 52. | Da-Da-Da | Pu-mo Pu-mo Pu-mo | by name |
| 53. | So-Da | Pu -Pu-Mo | by name |
| 54. | So-So-Da | Pu -Pu Pu-Mo | by name |
| 55. | Wi | Na-mā San-da or Kun-dā | by name & -lā |
| 56. | Wi-Fa | Cham ki Yap | by name & -lā |
| 57. | Mo-Si-Hu | Su-mo-lā ki Kundā | by name & -lā |
| 58. | Mo-Br-Wi | A-shang-lā ki Cham | by name & -lā |
| 59. | Fa-Br-Wi | Agu-lā ki cham | by name & -lā |
| 60. | Wi-Mo | Cham ki Yum | by name & -lā |
| 61. | Hu Noble | Kungo or Kusho | by name & -lā |
| | Commoner | Khyoga or Kunda | |
| 62. | Wi-Br | Cham-ki Cho-la | by name & -l ā |
| 63. | El Si-Hu | A-tchā-lā ki kundā | by name or Cho-lā |
| 64. | Y Si-Hu | O-la ki Kundā | by name |
| 65. | Wi-el-Si-Hu | Cham ki A-tcha-lā ki Kunda | by name & -lā |

| 1 | 2 | 3 | 4 |
|---|---|---|---|
| 66. | Wi-y-Si-Hu | So-mo Sho-pā kun-Dā | by name & -lā |
| 67. | Da-Hu-Fa | Pu-mo Kun-dā Pa-lā | by name & -lā |
| 68. | Wi-Si (elder) | Cham-ki A-tchā-lā | by name & -lā |
| 69. | Wi-Si (younger) | | |
| 70 | Br-Wi (elder) | Cho-lā ki Chām | by name & -lā |
| 71. | Br-Wi (younger) | | |
| 72. | Da-Hu | Pu-mo Kun-dā | by name & -lā |
| 73. | S-wi | Pu Cham - Chum | by name & -lā |
| 74. | Wi-si-Da | Shon-pā Sa-mo | by name |

# Appendix - C

## Names of Family Gods and Goddesses

### Gods:

1. Ā-ju-chu-lā
2. Ā-pchi
3. Che-je-n
4. Chen-re-si
5. Chi-k-chā No -r-bu
6. Chi-u-ku-n
7. Dā-wā Thā-shi
8. Dhu-mma-r
9. Dhu-tche-n
10. Dō-la-k
11. Do-rje Bu-rwā
12. Dro-Kpo Po-ng-ro
13. Ga-l-jen
14. Gō-mbō
15. Gō-mbō Sha-ru-kpo
16. Gu-ru Chi-ngey
17. Gu-ru Ri-mpō-che
18. Gyā-lbā Kun-gā
19. Gya-lbo Pe-gā-r
20. Ha-chā Gō-bjum
21. I-shi Nō-rbu
22. Je-war Go-mbā
23. Jig-che
24. Ke-jen
25. Ku-ngā
26. Ku-ntso-k Lā-mā
27. Lā-ptchē-n
28. Mā-chāk
29. Mā-ka-ju-n Gyā-rmo
30. Me-yu-lu

31. Na-chu-rey Chō-gya-ny
32. Pē-wri
33. Pō-ngār
34. Rā-mā Tha-ksēy
35. Rō-wa Kyā-ptō
36. Sha-mbu-li-ng
37. Sha-ngri
38. Shā-ptā
39. Shā-rgyā
40. Shē-tup
41. Shi-thok
42. Shō-nge Chō-ndēn
43. Shu-ng-dēn
44. Ta-mji-n
45. Thā-k-lun
46. Thā-k-sey
47. Tha-m-chen
48. Thā-ng-lhā
49. Thā-r-gō
50. Thā-shu-mbā
51. Thō-pjen
52. To-m-bā
53. Tse-te-n
54. Yō-ng lā-mā

# Goddesses:

55. Bā-wā Be-ndun
56. Chā-lā Yō-ngdām
57. Che-jen Dro-lma
58. Che-my Lā-ptchēn
59. Chu-blen
60. Dō-la
61. Dō-rje Drō-lmā
62. Dra-blā
63. Dro-lgār
64. Jhā

65. Ko-nji thé-mo
66. Kum-wo
67. Ku-ndup Cha-ma-shin
68. Lē-bhe-ng Pe-mā
69. Me-ndu-llā
70. Nā-mjun
71. Nā-mkha pa-ng-shin
72. Pal-den Lhā-mō
73. Rō-lbā
74. Sā-lu-mā
75. Sā-rgyu
76. Thā-shi Lhā-mo
77. Trō-mō
78. Tse-mā-r
79. Tsō-mo Tse-ri-ng
80. Thu-mbā

# Appendix - D

**A Tibetan *Khã-tã* (*Khã-dãr*)**

A Tibetan *Khã-tã* (scarf) is a loosely woven white silk or cotton strip and varies in size, quality and colour. Higher the status of the person to be honoured the best type of Khã-tã is used.

*Khã-tã* is a common object used by Tibetans in expressing their gratitude, friendly and respectable feeling towards the honorary. Tibetans offer such *Khã-tã* even to friends who visit the family to express their warmth. When a letter is sent to a friend, relative or an officer a *Khã-tã* is also sent along with it, and without it the act is considered improper. On the other hand a letter accompanied by a *Khã-tã* is an indication of "submission with a god's robe" to support it. Now a days owing to the public postal facilities sending of the *Khã-tã* is discontinued.

There are mainly three modes of offering of the scarves. When a scarf is offered to a superior it should be raised to the level of his forehead and offered. When offered to an equal it is raised to shoulder level. It is spread on the nape when given to a person who is lower in status.

Now owing to poverty the different varieties have gone and only white, silken and the cotton *Khã-tãs* are found. Cotton *Khã-tãs* are even presented to seniormost lamas, which in the past was used only for the commoners.